A STUDY GUIDE TO CHEMICAL PRINCIPLES

Second Edition

WILBERT HUTTON *Iowa State University*

A STUDY GUIDE TO CHEMICAL PRINCIPLES

SECOND EDITION

W. A. BENJAMIN, INC.

Menlo Park, California • Reading, Massachusetts
London • Amsterdam • Don Mills, Ontario • Sydney

A STUDY GUIDE TO CHEMICAL PRINCIPLES
Second Edition

ISBN 0-8053-4732-1
ABCDEFGHIJ-DO-787654

PREFACE

College freshmen share a common problem: They find that college is considerably different from high school. The competition is greater, the pace and standards of education are higher, and the work is more challenging.

The organization of college courses is likely to force a student to make a major adjustment in his study habits. In high school the work is generally straightforward. Most of it is covered in classes. Homework assignments are relatively easy, and there may be fixed study periods in which to do assignments. To a large extent grades are based on tests and homework. In college, students spend only a few hours in class, aside from laboratories and quiz or recitation sessions. Thus, whether a student passes or fails depends primarily on how he performs in a few examinations. As a result, his success depends on how and what he studies.

This book has been written to assist the student in his study of general chemistry. In particular, it is a study guide to accompany the general chemistry textbook *Chemical Principles*, second edition, by Richard E. Dickerson, Harry B. Gray, and Gilbert P. Haight, Jr. This text, like all general chemistry textbooks, is written to teach the student the fundamental principles and concepts upon which chemistry is based and to help him to appreciate the importance of the science. Most general chemistry texts differ only in the order and methods used in presenting these fundamentals. For this reason, students who are taking their general chemistry from other textbooks can also be helped by this study guide.

This book follows the first seven chapters of the Dickerson, Gray, and Haight text on a section-by-section basis. It points out the most important topics in each chapter and assists the student in selecting areas in which he should concentrate. When necessary, additional background on a topic is provided; this brings the student to the level of presentation in the text. The more difficult concepts are explained in detail, often by an approach different from that of the text. Additional worked-out examples and problems are provided, and a brief self-evaluation test is given for each chapter.

Also included is an introduction that provides a review of relevant mathematics, tips on how to study and how to solve problems, a section on the use of the slide rule, and appendixes supplying additional help in mathematics.

In short, the study guide attempts to provide all of the information that the student needs for comprehending the principles of chemistry. If he should require additional help, he is urged to read *Programed Reviews of Chemical Principles* by Jean D. Lassila *et al.* This book and the study guide provide the kind of background that is essential for learning chemistry.

WILBERT HUTTON

CONTENTS

PART ONE | PRELUDE TO STUDYING CHEMICAL PRINCIPLES

HOW TO USE THIS STUDY GUIDE

This study guide has been written to accompany the textbook, *Chemical Principles*, by Richard E. Dickerson, Harry B. Gray, and Gilbert P. Haight, Jr. (W. A. Benjamin, Menlo Park, Calif., 1974, 2nd ed.). The purpose of the study guide is to assist the student using *Chemical Principles* in his study of general college chemistry. Since most of those who take general chemistry are freshmen, this book is addressed to them.

We realize that freshmen have different backgrounds in high school chemistry, physics, and mathematics. Some may not have studied chemistry at all in high school. Others may have had considerable experience in these sciences, and even may have completed high school courses that border on the college-level courses. This study guide has not been written to assist students in this last group. Although these students may find it helpful, it is quite likely that they will consider the text and lectures adequate to their needs, and some may regard the material in this guide too elementary and repetitious. Rather, *A Study Guide to Chemical Principles* has been written for students who can profit from a more detailed explanation of some of the more important topics than has been given to them in the text. No assumptions have been made as to the backgrounds of these students. We hope that even those who are being exposed to chemistry for the first time will find the material helpful.

This study guide is divided into two parts. The first part includes a series of expositions on those topics that may be of general use to the student in his study of chemistry. The second part is devoted to the specific subject matter of the course at the level and in the sequence given in *Chemical Principles*.

You should survey the material in the first part so you will become familiar with its content. Some of this information may be needed later in the course; and you should be aware of what is available in case you need it. All students are advised to read the chapter, "How to Study."

The format of the second part of the book follows the first seven chapters of *Chemical Principles*. With few exceptions, topics are presented section by section. If a concept that is the subject of a particular section in the text is not understood completely or requires elaboration, the student can find further information in the corresponding section of the study guide. We have attempted to identify topics or concepts in each section that are the most essential to understanding material to come later in the course. We have tried to present these topics in a way that will contribute to a student's understanding and help him to apply what he has learned. When we feel that the presentation in the text presumes prior knowledge beyond that of the average student, a rather detailed development of a concept or topic is presented, beginning at a more elementary level. When a topic appears in the text that we know from experience to be especially troublesome to beginning students, the same topic is presented in the study guide, but a different approach is taken in our presentation. Often a student can learn more from one approach than from another, or he can develop a more sound understanding by comparing two different approaches to the same topic.

A brief self-evaluation quiz for each chapter is given in Appendix 4. You should use these tests to determine whether you understand some of the more important concepts.

Occasionally, a section in the text will receive very little space (sometimes none) in the study guide. In these instances, we feel either that the presentation in the text should be adequate for the average student without further explanation, or that the subject discussed in the section is not of sufficient relevance to the basic aims of the general chemistry course to warrant further discussion.

In writing *Chemical Principles*, the authors have taken an historical approach to the subject matter. The evolution of a concept is presented from its inception to its present status. As to be expected, many of the original interpretations or theories used to explain chemical phenomena have been proved incorrect as more knowledge has been obtained. As a result, the definitions of many terms have been modified through the years until their present meaning bears little resemblance to their original meaning. This often can be a source of confusion to the student. In the study guide, the historical aspects of the presentation in the text are considered to be of importance only as background. Emphasis is placed on concepts and terms as they are used currently.

The student also should realize that the authors of *Chemical Principles* believe that a subject can be learned best if it is repeated at intervals during a course, rather than presented as a complete unit in one section or chapter of the text. Their approach is to introduce a subject early, expand on it in one or more subsequent chapters, and perhaps apply it rigorously still later in the text. As a result, a student may find himself spending an unwarranted amount of his study time attempting to understand a particular topic in depth at a time in the course when such a deep understanding is not expected and when he is not yet equipped to understand it adequately. In this study guide, an effort is made to indicate which topics will be presented later and to supply guidelines that the student can use to measure the depth of understanding he will need for a particular topic when it appears in the text.

Much of your learning in college is the product of how you apply yourself to your studies outside of the classroom. This study guide is just one part of a teaching system that has been provided by W. A. Benjamin, Inc., to accompany the textbook. The objective in supplying this system is to make available to the student all the resources he might need to enable him to gain as much as possible from his independent study. We recognize that some students will need more assistance in this effort than others.

Of course, the textbook is the core of the teaching system. As mentioned, *A Study Guide to Chemical Principles* complements the text with additional background material, more detailed explanations, and provides guidelines that the student can use to direct his studies. Most students taking a general chemistry course should be able to put the study guide to good use.

For those students whose high school chemistry background has been deficient in some areas that are important in the course, *Programed Reviews of Chemical Principles*, by Jean D. Lassila *et al.*, should be consulted. This book contains a series of self-instructional programs that begin with "first principles" and progress to the level of the text. The programs treat specific subjects and are keyed to the chapters in *Chemical Principles*. Those students who have average to below average backgrounds and ability in chemistry will find Dr. Lassila's programed reviews to be a valuable addition to their study resources.

Since problem-solving is of utmost importance in chemistry, a third part of the teaching system is the book *Relevant Problems for Chemical Principles*, by Ian S. Butler and Arthur E. Grosser. This book also is arranged according to the sequence of subject matter presented in *Chemical Principles*. The book contains a series of extremely interesting and relevant problems to supplement those given in the text. A unique feature of this book is that detailed solutions are provided for every problem. Mistakes that students are likely to make in solving the problems also are pointed out and analyzed. On the whole, the problems are a bit more demanding of the student than those in the textbook. Certainly, a student who incorporates the solution of these problems in his study program should be well equipped to handle any problems that occur on examinations. The student who already has had a rather extensive high school science background should find this book a stimulating and instructional teaching supplement.

HOW TO STUDY

Basic to your ability to learn is your ability to study effectively and efficiently. Since the objective of this study guide is to assist you with your studies in chemistry, it is appropriate to begin with a few comments on how to study.

Most freshmen have taken their ability to study for granted. Any difficulty they may have with their course work usually is attributed to difficult subject matter, poor background, poor teaching, crowded classroom facilities, noisy dormitory surroundings, and the like. These complaints may or may not be legitimate. Even if they do exist, they can be minimized and overcome by proper study habits. More often than not, these complaints arise because of a student's inability to study effectively.

It is not our purpose here to present a detailed and exhaustive analysis of techniques for effective study. Fortunately, there are a number of books available that treat this subject in considerable detail.[1] Unfortunately, few students consult such material unless it is presented as a required reading assignment or if in some other way they are coerced into giving this aspect of their training the attention that it deserves.

---

[1] See, for example, the short paperback, *How to Study*, by C. T. Morgan and J. Deese, McGraw-Hill, New York, 1969, 2nd ed.

We recommend that if you are having difficulty in any of your college work, direct your attention to your study habits. It is quite likely that your difficulties originate there, and with a little thoughtful planning you can minimize, if not completely remove, most of your troubles by changing the way you study.

There are certain basic skills all students are supposed to have mastered before they enter college. These are the ability to read at a reasonable rate and to comprehend what they read. Closely related to the ability to read with comprehension is the second skill, a substantial vocabulary. The third skill is a facility with elementary mathematics and the ability to translate simple problems into mathematical language. The latter trait is of primary importance in science courses and is generally the skill in which many students display the greatest deficiency. For this reason, a section of this study guide has been devoted to a review of relevant mathematics and a discussion of how to solve chemistry problems.

Let us assume that you have acquired these skills or are taking remedial steps to attain them. Then the remaining problem is principally one of budgeting your time efficiently. The demands on your time are great in college, and it is necessary that you make your study time count. You should prepare a schedule allowing sufficient time to study for each of your courses, as well as time for recreation and rest. Most textbooks on how to study give suggestions on preparing such schedules. The following paragraphs will consist of a few remarks on how to use your study time effectively.

Most chemistry courses are offered in three parts: lecture, recitation or quiz sections, and laboratory. In larger universities the lectures generally are presented to several hundred students at a time, and usually are given by the professor in charge of the course. The large class size does not allow the opportunity necessary for discussion or answering questions from the floor. The students are supposed to listen and take notes on what the lecturer says or presents in class as a demonstration. Generally the lecturer will tend to discuss those topics that he feels are the most important. Often he may add to the material given in the text, or present topics in a different way in hopes of strengthening your understanding of important concepts. You should take readable and comprehensive notes in the lectures because you will want to study them after class and before examinations. One word of caution: Some lecturers tend to follow the textbook very carefully; others tend to do just the opposite. It is necessary for you to determine the procedure your lecturer is following. If he is not following the text, it is important to determine where he will place the emphasis in his examinations. Often he will explain this during his introductory remarks on the first day of class. For this reason, it is important for you to attend the first lectures in the course. Until you are sure of the importance of the lectures relative to the examinations, it is wise to make a point of attending them regularly. In fact, it is recommended that freshmen attend all class meetings.

If you have a study period before a lecture, use it wisely to read the chapter assignment thoroughly. The lecturer expects you to do this, and his presentations will be made assuming that you have done so. The more you know about what the lecturer is saying, the more you will be able to learn from the lecture and will be able to take better and more meaningful notes. You also will be able to recognize any new technical terms he may use and be in a better position to identify what topics he feels are important.

If possible, arrange for a study period immediately after the lecture when the material is fresh in your mind. Review your notes during this study period. In fact, it is very helpful to reorganize your notes at this time. If you do this, it will help you to identify those areas in which your understanding is still uncertain, strengthen your understanding of the material in general, and provide a set of notes that will be more useful to you when you refer to them later in preparation for an examination.

The recitation or quiz sections are an opportunity for you to discuss the material, ask questions, and participate in drill. The recitation easily can be the most useful class meeting on your schedule. However, it is important that you understand its potential and its limitations and use it as effectively as possible. As a rule, most large universities are unable to provide enough members of the full-time teaching staff to supervise the recitation sections. Graduate students usually are employed as instructors in these sections and in the laboratory. These young men and women generally are quite knowledgeable in their subject matter, but few have had any experience as teachers. You should keep this in mind and realize that because of their limited experience they may have difficulty in identifying those areas in which a student is likely to experience trouble. Consequently, you should not hesitate to ask questions so your instructor becomes aware of your problems. Be as specific as you can in stating your difficulty. In all likelihood you will find that your instructor is far more successful in explaining specific points when he is asked than he is in anticipating your difficulty and preparing and presenting a general summary of the material in the text or homework.

Little new material is taught in the recitation sessions. As a result, the interest of students often slackens. To maintain interest and encourage students to study the material in the course on a day-to-day basis, short quizzes often are given as part of the recitation sessions. Consequently, the recitation often is referred to as a quiz section. Since these quizzes may count in your final grade, it may be necessary for you to attend the recitations in order to take them. If attendance is not necessary, you should evaluate the contribution made by the quiz section to your learning and understanding of the subject matter. If you are not receiving any value from the sessions, then you may be wise to spend the time studying on your own. No one rule can be given that applies to every situation. You must make this evaluation on your own, but do not act hastily. Remember that the success or failure of the recitation class to realize its potential value to you is determined largely by your ability to recognize the areas where you need assistance, ask the necessary questions, and participate in the discussion.

All sciences are directed basically at solving problems. Science begins with the collection of facts followed by an attempt to arrange the facts in an orderly way such that rules, principles, or laws can be formulated that will permit one to understand the facts and then to solve practical problems. Many of the problems in chemistry can be expressed in the language of mathematics; therefore, the homework in chemistry, like mathematics, is largely a process of gaining practice in solving problems. The key to successful study in chemistry is *understanding* rather than learning facts. If one understands, many of the facts can be predicted. As is pointed out in the next chapter, which is devoted to how to solve problems, the objective of a chemical problem is to develop and measure one's understanding of chemical principles. This understanding is communicated best by the correct formulation of the problem in mathematical language. The mathematics required to solve the problem once it has been set up generally is trivial.

Do all the homework problems even if the instructor never collects or grades them. You will be required to do problems on your examinations. The only way for you to prepare yourself so you will be able to solve these problems accurately in the time allowed is to do your daily assignments conscientiously. Include some problem-solving as part of your daily routine. When you complete a problem, check your work. At least consider your answer in terms of the known facts stated in the problem and confirm that it is reasonable.

Often in an examination a problem will be worded differently from similar problems given in homework assignments. To be prepared for this, we suggest that you make up problems by changing the wording in your homework problems. Time yourself when you do your homework. If you become accustomed to solving problems within a time limit, you will feel more at ease during an examination.

This brings us to the subject of taking an examination. When you receive the examination, try to decide how much time it will take to do each problem. Note also how many points are awarded to each of the problems if they do not all count equally toward the final score. Be prepared to spend more time on problems that will earn for you the most points. First do the easy problems, the ones for which you see an immediate method of solution.

Learn to use a slide rule at the first opportunity. Use it for all your calculations when doing homework so you will be able to use it rapidly and with confidence during examinations.

A few remaining points to be discussed are of special importance in studying chemistry. We wish to emphasize the value of a precise understanding of the vocabulary. There are many terms used in chemistry that will be new to you. These words generally have an exact meaning, and it is important that you understand fully the meaning of the word so you can use it and interpret it correctly when it is used by others. A second point to be emphasized is the importance of visualization in explaining chemical concepts. *Chemical Principles* contains a multitude of drawings, tables, and graphs. These are included in the text to clarify and illustrate important points. The written material accompanying these figures and tables should be read carefully. In some instances figure legends and tables are as important as the related sections of the text. You often can resort to these same visual techniques to answer an examination question or to illustrate the results of a laboratory experiment.

We will not discuss the laboratory phase of the course in this study guide. However, you should realize that the laboratory occupies a place in the chemical program that is equal in importance to that of the lecture and recitations. As with everything else, you must prepare yourself for the laboratory in advance if you are to realize the benefits of the few hours that you spend in the laboratory each week. Always study carefully the material pertaining to the day's experiment before going to the laboratory. If you do this, you will be prepared to perform the experiment in the allotted time, and you will be better able to recognize the significance of the observations that you make. Use care to record all the observations and numerical data that you obtain in the laboratory in a legible fashion so you will have all the information you need to write the laboratory report.

A REVIEW OF RELEVANT MATHEMATICS
AND HOW TO SOLVE PROBLEMS

The purpose of this chapter is to assist you with the numerical calculations that are part of introductory chemistry. With but a few exceptions, you will discover that you are quite familiar with what is discussed here. You should be, because contrary to what you might have heard in the dormitory, introductory chemistry is not a course in mathematics. In fact, the chief aim of solving chemistry problems is to master the chemical concepts and not to develop a deeper understanding of or to extend your proficiency in mathematics. In other words, our primary concern is *not* the answer but how it is obtained.

The mathematics needed to solve chemistry problems is of the most elementary variety. An understanding of basic arithmetic and a year of high school algebra should see you through 90% of the problems in the course. What about the remaining 10%?

Among the mathematical operations in this section are the use of significant figures, logarithms, and the solution of simultaneous equations and equations of higher orders by successive approximation. You may not be familiar with these procedures if your high school mathematics included only one year of algebra. The section on significant figures should be studied carefully. A knowledge of logarithms and their function will aid you in understanding the operation of the slide rule. Therefore, you should read this part early in the course. Problems requiring the solving of simultaneous equations or equations greater than second order will be encountered only occasionally. Generally, you will be able to identify approximations that can simplify the calculations and eliminate such complicated equations without significantly affecting the results. Should you need them, the procedures for solving these more complicated problems are included.

The following discussion necessarily must be rather brief: You should find most of this material of a review nature that is adequate for your needs. If, however, you feel more explanation is necessary, refer to your high school algebra textbook or the paperback, *Chemistry Problems*, by M. J. Sienko (W. A. Benjamin, Menlo Park, Calif., 1972, 2nd ed.). The first chapter of Professor Sienko's book includes an excellent review of mathematical procedures applied to working chemistry problems.

THE USE OF SIGNIFICANT FIGURES IN CHEMICAL CALCULATIONS

Calculations in chemistry (or any other science for that matter) involve numbers that owe their origin to an experimental measurement. For example, our problem may be to calculate the volume of a particular gas, given its weight, pressure, and temperature. The data are measured experimentally, and each measurement contains some error. Obviously, this error will be reflected in our calculated value for the volume of the gas. Students tend to carry out such a calculation to a greater number of decimal points than is justified by the experimental accuracy. Not only does the answer misrepresent the correct volume, but the student probably has expended much wasted effort in arriving at most of the digits. You certainly want to avoid doing this in your calculations. A scientist indicates how "good" a number is by including in it only those digits that are known with certainty *plus* one more. The known digits plus the doubtful one constitute *significant figures*. For example, recording the volume of a gas as 48.12 ml implies four significant figures, of which 4, 8, and 1 are known with certainty, but 2 is doubtful.

We should consider what factors determine the error in a measurement such as the volume of the gas referred to in the preceding paragraph. The error in the volume measured is a composite of the *accuracy* and the *precision* of the measurement. Accuracy concerns the absolute truth of a measurement, whereas precision involves the detail with which a measurement is made. For instance, suppose that the volume of the gas were measured in a 50-ml gas burette. The stated volume of 48.12 ml indicates that the chemist has made this measurement and that he can reproduce it in the same burette to within 0.01 ml (the last digit is doubtful).[1] His precision, implied in the number 48.12 ml, can be expressed as 48.12 $\pm$ 0.01 ml, or 48.12 $\pm$ 0.02% ml, because

$$\frac{0.01}{48.12} \times 100 = 0.02\%$$

However, the burette itself may be inaccurate; that is, its scale markings might be in error, temperature fluctuations in the room might alter the capacity of the burette from what it was when the markings were etched on the glass, or the volume-indicating liquid in the burette might not have drained completely when the measurement was made. In any of these events, the volume may be measured with great precision, but it would not be very accurate. Of course, all chemists hope that their instruments are calibrated accurately so that the validity of a measurement depends only on the precision with which the chemist is capable of making the measurement.

Although we may not be justified on some occasions, we will assume that all the instruments used for obtaining data have an accuracy comparable to the precision of the measurements. Therefore, so far as we are concerned, all numbers in problems contain significant figures; our objective is to make sure that when we manipulate these numbers we do not distort the information by throwing precision away or apparently adding to it. Some simple rules in this section will enable you to do this.

ADDITION AND SUBTRACTION

The reason for a rule in computations involving addition and subtraction can be understood from the following example. If an empty beaker weighs 64 g and you put a sample of NaCl weighing 0.176 g into the beaker, what is the total weight of the beaker and the salt?

Without thinking, you might follow the natural tendency simply to add the two numbers, 64 + 0.176, and report the final weight as 64.176 g. If you do this, you are wrong. Remember that we should write numbers with significant figures only. Stating that the combined weight of the beaker and NaCl is 64.176 g means that you are certain of the digits 6, 4, 1, and 7, and are doubtful of the last 6. You are, in fact, saying that the combined weight is known to $\pm$0.001 g, that is, to within plus or minus one part in 64,176—about one part in 64,000 or $\pm$0.0015%. Clearly this is nonsense. The weight of the empty beaker was stated as 64 g, which implies that its weight is known to be 64 $\pm$ 1 g. Not only are you in doubt as to the digit 4—it could be 3 or 5, for instance—you haven't been given the slightest indication as to what the values are of the digits to the right of the 4. Consequently, any digits to the right of the decimal point are uncertain, and you should

The Use of Significant Figures in Chemical Calculations

[1] A less experienced chemist may be capable of reproducing a reading on this burette to within $\pm$0.02 ml. In such a case, a notation such as 48.12 $\pm$ 0.02 ml should be used; otherwise, one will assume a precision of $\pm$1 unit in the doubtful significant figure.

not report them. To do so would be indicating that you have information that you really do not possess.

The correct answer can be computed easily by indicating the uncertain digits by question marks:

$$
\begin{array}{r}
64.??? \\
+\ \ 0.176 \\
\hline
64.???
\end{array}
$$

It is obvious that even though we know the digits 1, 7, and 6 in the second line, when they are added to the corresponding uncertain digits in the first line, the resulting values for the digits to the right of the decimal point also will be uncertain. Therefore, you should report 64 g as the correct weight of the beaker plus the salt.

The conclusions we reached in this example can be expressed as the following rule for addition and subtraction:

> Round off all the numbers in the group of numbers to be added or subtracted so each has the same number of digits to the right of the decimal point as that number in the series having the smallest number of digits to the right of the decimal point. Then add or subtract the resulting series of rounded off numbers.

For example, consider the addition of the numbers

    119.2
    204.12
      1.75
    260.3734

The number 119.2 has the smallest number of digits to the right of the decimal point: one. Therefore, round off all numbers in the series so each has one digit to the right of the decimal point, then add:

$$
\begin{array}{r}
119.2 \\
204.1 \\
1.8 \\
260.4 \\
\hline
585.5
\end{array}
$$

Two points need further discussion before proceeding.

(1) The convention for rounding off a number depends on the value of the digit to its right. If the digit to the right is greater than 5, the number is increased by one; thus, 260.3734 rounds off to 260.4. If the digit to the right is less than 5, the number is unchanged in rounding it off; thus, 204.12 rounds off to 204.1. If the number to the right is 5, the convention is to increase the value of the digit being rounded off by one if the digit is odd and to leave it unchanged if the digit is even; thus, 1.75 rounds off to 1.8, whereas 1.85 rounds off to 1.8. This latter convention, although somewhat arbitrary, can be justified by reasoning that the chance of there being an odd number to round off is as great as the chance of there being an even number. Therefore, by applying the convention stated here, on the average we will increase as many numbers in rounding off as we will leave unchanged. Any error introduced

in rounding off to a number that is too large eventually will be compensated by an error in rounding off a number to a value that is too small.

(2) We can alter the procedure stated in the rule and add or subtract the numbers as they are. Then we can round off the answer so it has the same number of digits to the right of the decimal point as does that number in the series with the smallest number of digits to the right of its decimal point. Occasionally, a slightly different answer will result, depending on which procedure you follow. Don't be concerned; remember that the last digit is doubtful anyway. Do the following exercises for practice, and express the answer to the correct number of significant figures.

EXERCISES.
(1) 4.72 + 203.6 + 121.780 + 55
(2) 3.1416 + 2.73 + 5.921 + 3.83
(3) 297.64 − 31.279
(4) 32.7945 + 121.5 − 326.73
(5) 49378.2 + 25.98 − 33

(*Answers:* (1) 385; (2) 15.62; (3) 266.36; (4) −172.4; (5) 49371.)

SOME ADDITIONAL REMARKS CONCERNING SIGNIFICANT FIGURES

Zeros further complicate the matter of significant figures because they serve two purposes in a number. A zero may indicate that a given decimal place has been measured to be zero; thus, it is significant. Second, a zero may be used to indicate the location of the decimal point, in which case it is not a significant figure. As examples, consider the following numbers: (a) 0.0123; (b) 2027.3; (c) 0.1072; (d) 0.200. (a) has three significant figures, the 1, the 2, and the 3. The zero between the decimal point and the 1 merely locates the decimal; that is, it indicates only that the number is 123 hundredths and not 123, 123 thousandths, and so forth. Thus, it is not counted as a significant figure. (b) has five significant figures. The zero here does not locate the decimal point; it is a necessary digit in the number. The same applys to the zero in (c), which has four significant figures. (d) represents an interesting case. The fact that the number two tenths can be expressed just as well either as 0.2 or 0.200 indicates that the two zeros to the right of 2 must be significant; otherwise, they would not be written as part of the number. Consequently, there are three significant figures in (d), and we can presume that the measurement was made with a device that is accurate to ±0.001.

One method often used to avoid the confusion presented by zeros is to write the number as a power of 10. In this form, the exponent locates the decimal point, and only significant figures are included in the base of the number. (If you cannot remember the meaning of exponents, refer to the next section.) The numbers in the preceding example are written as powers of 10 (often called scientific notation) in the following way:

(a) $0.0123 = 1.23 \times 10^{-2}$
(b) $2027.3 = 2.0273 \times 10^3$
(c) $0.1072 = 1.072 \times 10^{-1}$
(d) $0.200 = 2.00 \times 10^{-1}$

As a test of your understanding, indicate the number of significant figures in the following and express the numbers as powers of 10.

EXERCISES.

(1) 2305.0
(2) 0.00007062
(3) 21.070
(4) 0.02003
(5) 900.0
(6) 1000 apples when you are sure of the exact number of apples.
(7) 0.7020 ±0.001

(*Answers:* (1) five significant figures, 2.3050×10^3; (2) four significant figures, 7.062×10^{-5}; (3) five significant figures, 2.1070×10; (4) four significant figures, 2.003×10^{-2}; (5) four significant figures, 9.000×10^2; (6) four significant figures, 1.000×10^3; (7) three significant figures, 7.02×10^{-1}. The ±0.001 indicates the uncertainty is in the third decimal place; the digit 2 is uncertain.)

MULTIPLICATION AND DIVISION

The evaluation of the uncertainty in an answer acquired from a sequence of multiplication and division operations is more complicated than it is when the computations involve only addition and subtraction. A precise evaluation requires one to determine the uncertainty in each of the factors and then sum these together to find the uncertainty in the answer. The answer then is written in significant figures, in which the uncertainty appears in the last digit. This procedure is too time consuming to use in drill problems. A more rapid, if less precise, procedure is preferable. Such a procedure is stated in the following rule:

Express the answer to multiplication and/or division such that the answer has the same number of significant figures as does the factor having the smallest number of significant figures.

Note that the emphasis is on the number of *significant figures* in multiplication and division. It is not on the number of decimal places in the measurements, as was the case in addition and subtraction. The rule is based on the logical principle that the reliability of an answer determined from the combination of a sequence of numbers will not be any greater than the least reliable number in the sequence. Therefore, since the last digit in a number containing significant figures is doubtful, the uncertainty in the number can be approximated by the number of significant figures; that is, the more significant figures in a number, the more precisely is that number known. A number with four significant figures is known to at least one part in a thousand, three significant figures to at least one part in a hundred, and so on. We assume, of course, that the uncertainty in the doubtful digit is plus or minus one unit. This assumption will be considered valid for the data in problems.

Consider the following sequences of multiplications and divisions.

EXAMPLE.

$$2.760/5.46 = ?$$

SOLUTION.   The answer, carried to four decimal places, is 0.5055. To determine where the answer should be rounded off, we observe that there are four significant figures in the factor 2.760 (if the zero was not significant, it would not have been included as part of the number) and three significant figures in the factor 5.46. Consequently, the answer should be rounded off to three significant figures and written correctly as **0.506.**

EXAMPLE.

$$\frac{(2.56)(1.9)(3.725)}{(6.02 \times 10^{23})(0.0071)} = ?$$

SOLUTION.   The numbers of significant figures in the various factors are three in 2.56, two in 1.9, four in 3.725, three in 6.02×10^{23}, and two in 0.0071. The smallest number of significant figures in any of the factors is two, so the answer should be rounded off to two significant figures and is written correctly as **4.2×10^{-25}.**

Occasionally a complication occurs such as the following.

EXAMPLE.

$$\frac{(276)(9.9)}{2497.3} = ?$$

SOLUTION.   The answer to four decimals is 1.0941. Our rule dictates that we round off this number to two significant figures, that is, 1.1, since 9.9 is the factor known with the least precision (9.9 $\pm$ 0.1, or one part out of 99, or about 1%).

But something is not quite right in the preceding solution. The answer (1.1) indicates a precision of one part out of 11, or within about 10%. This is a precision less than that of the least precise factor. In a sense, we cheat ourselves a bit in expressing the answer this way because the most uncertain number that we have in the data is known with almost ten times the precision indicated by the answer, 1.1. On this basis, we are justified in adding an additional significant figure and expressing the answer as 1.09. This procedure would indicate that the answer is known to 1.09 ± 0.01 (i.e., within one part out of 109 or about 1%, which is a more honest estimate of what we know than is the 1.1 value.

Let us compute the volume of a sphere from the relationship $V = \frac{4}{3}\pi r^3$. The measured quantity is r, and the number of significant figures in the value for r will determine the correct answer. What about $\frac{4}{3}\pi$? Let us think about these numbers for a moment. π has an established value that can be determined to any desired number of significant figures, 3.141592653589793. We need only employ in our calculations a value having more significant figures than are known for r. The 4 and the 3 in the fraction $\frac{4}{3}$ each are exact numbers. Although by convention they are not written as such, they are known to an infinite number of significant figures (4.0000000 . . . , etc.). You will use many exact numbers in problems and should recognize that since these numbers are exact, they need not be considered in significant-figure decisions.

EXAMPLE. Suppose that we wish to calculate the volume of a sphere with a diameter, d, of 4.00 cm.

SOLUTION. Since $d = 2r$

$$r = \frac{d}{2} = \frac{4.00 \text{ cm}}{2} = 2.00 \text{ cm}$$

(2 is an exact number, so the number of significant figures in the radius is determined by the three digits in the value for the diameter. Therefore,

$$V = \frac{4}{3}\pi r^3 = \frac{4}{3}\pi(2.00 \text{ cm})^3$$

Because there are three significant figures in r, there will be three significant figures in the answer, provided that we use a value for π expressed to at least three significant figures. The correct answer is **33.5 cm³**.

To test your understanding, state the answers to the following exercises in the correct number of significant figures.

EXERCISES.

(1) $\dfrac{(2.75)(0.01267)}{(3.1416)} = 0.0110906$

(2) $(4.00 \times 10^2)^3 = 64000000$

(3) $\dfrac{(105.2)(3.21)}{(1.007)(3.1 \times 10^3)} = 108.176$

(4) $\dfrac{(55.2)(0.90)}{(0.4557)} = 109.01$

(5) Three samples of ore are weighed on different balances with the uncertainties indicated

$$376.6 \pm 0.5 \text{ g} \qquad 273.17 \pm 0.02 \text{ g} \qquad 0.1725 \pm 0.0001 \text{ g}$$

What is the average percent uncertainty in the measurements?

(*Answers:* (1) 0.0111; (2) 6.40×10^7; (3) 1.1×10^2; (4) 109; (5) The three percent uncertainties are 0.13%, 0.007%, and 0.058%; the average percent uncertainty is 0.06%.)

EXPONENTIAL NUMBERS

Not only does writing a number in exponential form enable us to express significant-figure information with minimal confusion, it avoids writing many zeros for either small or large numbers. On numerous occasions you will find it convenient to use this notation.

We use exponential numbers to express quantities as multiple powers of 10. An exponential number consists of two parts: a coefficient (chosen to be between 1 and 10) and a power of 10. For example, Avogadro's number is written 6.02×10^{23}; 6.02 is the coefficient and 23 is the power of 10.

A positive exponent, n, indicates that the coefficient should be multiplied by 10 n times; that is, the decimal should be moved n places to the right of its position in the coefficient. A negative exponent, $-m$, indicates that the coefficient should be divided by 10 m times; that is, the decimal should be moved m places to the left. For example,

$$0.0000000192 = 1.92 \times 10^{-8}$$
$$1 \text{ thousand} = 1 \times 10^3$$
$$96500 = 9.65 \times 10^4$$

To *add* or *subtract* exponential numbers, we must be certain that the powers of 10 are the same. Otherwise, the operation would be like adding different things: $2x + 2y = ?$, whereas $2x + 2x = 4x$. Put another way, 2 hundreds plus 2 thousands does not equal 4 hundreds or 4 thousands. But 2 hundreds plus 20 hundreds (2 thousands) equals 22 hundreds. Thus, before adding or subtracting quantities, the units (in this case, the relative position of the decimal point) must be the same. This requirement may force you to rewrite the exponential number. The revision is easy if you remember that each time the power of 10 becomes more positive by one unit it is the same as multiplying the number by 10, or moving the decimal in the coefficient one place to the right. Similarly, if the power of 10 is made more negative, the decimal in the coefficient must be moved to the left. For example,

$$6.022 \times 10^{23} + 7.65 \times 10^{21} = ?$$

Rewrite both numbers so they have the same power of 10; for example, 21. To write 6.022×10^{23} as a multiple of 10^{21} (the exponent has been decreased by two powers of 10) requires that the coefficient be *increased* by two powers of 10. Therefore, its decimal point should be moved two places to the right:

$$6.022 \times 10^{23} = 602.2 \times 10^{21}$$

Now the numbers can be added:

$$\begin{array}{r} 602.2 \ \times 10^{21} \\ +7.65 \times 10^{21} \\ \hline 609.8 \ \ \times 10^{21} \text{ or } \mathbf{6.098 \times 10^{23}} \end{array}$$

Do the following exercises to test your understanding.

EXERCISES.
(1) Add 2.46×10^{-9} cm to 2.46×10^{-8} cm.
(2) Subtract 1.625×10^{-1} cm from 2.234×10^{2} cm.
(3) Add 4.0075×10^{3} ml to 6.23×10^{2} ml.
(4) Subtract 1.725×10^{-1} g from 2.1623×10^{1} g.

(*Answers:* (1) 2.71×10^{-8} cm; (2) 2.236×10^{2} cm; (3) 4.630×10^{3} ml; (4) 2.1450×10 g.)

In *multiplication*, you need only multiply the coefficients together and then multiply the powers of 10 together (add their exponents) to obtain the coefficient and power of 10 for the answer. For example,

$$6.02 \times 10^{23} \times 1.76 \times 10^{-2} = ?$$

The product of the coefficients to the proper number of significant figures is $6.02 \times 1.76 = 10.6$. The product of the powers of 10 (exponentials) are $10^{23} \times 10^{-2} = 10^{[23+(-2)]} = 10^{21}$. The answer to the multiplication is 10.6×10^{21} or, writing the coefficient in the preferred way as a number between 1 and 10, $\mathbf{1.06 \times 10^{22}}$.

In *division*, the coefficients are divided separately and then the exponentials are divided. Recall that in division of exponential numbers, the exponent of the divisor (the denominator) is subtracted from the exponent of the dividend (the numerator). For example,

$$\frac{6.022 \times 10^{23}}{5.976 \times 10^{27}} = ?$$

Dividing 6.022 by 5.976 gives 1.008 to the correct number of significant figures. Dividing the exponentials gives $10^{23}/10^{27} = 10^{(23-27)} = 10^{-4}$. Therefore the answer is $\mathbf{1.008 \times 10^{-4}}$.

The same general procedure is followed when raising an exponential to a power. The coefficients are done first, the exponentials next, and the results of these computations combined for the answer. Thus,

$$(6 \times 10^{3})^{3} = 216 \times 10^{9} = \mathbf{2 \times 10^{11}} \quad \text{(if only one significant figure is justified)}$$

$$(5.1 \times 10^{-2})^{2} = 26 \times 10^{-4} = \mathbf{2.6 \times 10^{-3}}$$

To avoid fractional exponents when extracting a root, we must adjust the power of 10 so it becomes a whole number factor of 2 if a square root is to be extracted, a whole number factor of 3 if a cube root is to be extracted, and so forth. Therefore, to extract the cube root of Avogadro's number $(6.02 \times 10^{23})^{1/3}$ you first must rewrite the number so the power of 10 is a whole-number multiple of three. Since $3 \times 7 = 21$ and $3 \times 8 = 24$, either 10^{21} or 10^{24} are suitable exponentials. Let us rewrite the number as a coefficient times 10^{21} by moving the decimal in the coefficient two places to the right and decreasing the exponent of 10 by two units: $(602 \times 10^{21})^{1/3}$. The cube root of 602 is 8.45; the cube root of 10^{21} is 10^7. The answer is **8.45×10^7**.

As a self-test of your understanding, do the following exercises.

EXERCISES.

(1) $\dfrac{5.23 \times 10^{27}}{9.76 \times 10^3} =$

(2) $\dfrac{3.42 \times 10^{-29}}{6.704 \times 10^5} =$

(3) $\dfrac{(2.46 \times 10^3)(1.7 \times 10^{-5})}{3.25 \times 10^4} =$

(4) $(5.2 \times 10^{-3})^3 =$

(5) $(7.5 \times 10^{-5})^{1/2} =$

(*Answers:* (1) 5.36×10^{23}; (2) 5.10×10^{-35}; (3) 1.3×10^{-6}; (4) 1.4×10^{-7}; (5) 8.7×10^{-3}.)

ALGEBRAIC EQUATIONS

Some problems that you will be asked to solve in general chemistry will require the use of algebraic equations. When the problem involves one unknown, you need only one equation to solve for it; if there are two unknowns, such as x and y, then you need two independent equations (relationships) involving x and y before you can solve the problem; three unknowns, three equations are needed, and so on. Some equations will be first order (linear), others will be second order (quadratic), and a few will be of higher order. You probably will not have too much difficulty with the first two types. Fortunately, the higher-order equations occur infrequently, and when they do, you generally can solve them by a method of successive approximations. Let's review these types of equations.

FIRST-ORDER EQUATIONS

First-order equations contain only one unknown, appear only to the first power, and have only one root. They always can be written as

$$ax = b \tag{1}$$

in which a and b are numbers and x is the unknown. We find the answer to Equation 1 by dividing both sides of the equation by a:

$$\frac{ax}{a} = \frac{b}{a}$$

Since the a's in the numerator and denominator on the left cancel,

$$x = \frac{b}{a}$$

To rearrange the equations to a form resembling Equation 1, we collect the terms involving the unknown on one side and the known terms on the other side. By factoring or combining the terms we obtain the answer. The general principle for rearranging operations and for obtaining the final solution is that the equation should remain intact. That is, one side must equal the other, and it will, so long as we carry out the same operation on both sides of the equation.

EXAMPLE.
Solve the equation

$$(2 - x)(5) = (7)(3 - 2x)$$

SOLUTION. Multiplying the left and right sides as indicated gives

$$(10 - 5x) = (21 - 14x)$$

To collect the terms involving x on the left and the other terms on the right, we add $14x$ and subtract 10 from both sides of the equation:

$$14x - 10 + 10 - 5x = 21 - 14x + 14x - 10$$
$$9x = 11$$
$$x = 11/9 = \mathbf{1.2}$$

SECOND-ORDER EQUATIONS

Equations of the second order contain a single unknown that is raised to the second power. They have two roots. These equations always can be written as

$$ax^2 + bx + c = 0 \tag{2}$$

in which a, b, and c are numbers and x is the unknown. If $a = 0$, the equation is first order. It is also possible for b to be zero; thus, there would not be a term involving the unknown to the first power. Of course, c also may be zero.

Once the equation is in the form of Equation 2 it can be solved by substitution into the quadratic formula,

$$x = \frac{-b \pm \sqrt{b^2 - 4ac}}{2a} \tag{3}$$

The square root sign is equivalent to using the exponent $\frac{1}{2}$; thus, the term under the sign in Equation 3 can be written $(b^2 - 4ac)^{1/2}$.

In doing chemistry problems, only one of the two roots is an answer to the problem; the other is unrealistic. You generally can decide which of the two roots apply by considering the problem's physical circumstances. For instance, a common situation is when you use a quadratic equation to find the amount of a substance remaining after a chemical reaction. The solution of the equation will give two roots, each of which is a possible value for the amount of the remaining substance. If one of the roots gives a value larger than the amount of substance present when the reaction started, or if it gives a negative or imaginary number, it is obvious that this value does not apply. Hence, the other root must be the correct answer.

EXAMPLE. Consider the solution of the following equation in which x represents the amount (in moles per liter) of a substance B formed after a chemical reaction has reached equilibrium. Assume that we start with 1 mole per liter of a reacting substance and that 1 mole of it produces 1 mole of B.

$$\frac{(x)(x)}{(1 - x)} = 54$$

SOLUTION. Rearrange the equation to the form of Equation 2 by multiplying both sides by $(1 - x)$:

$$x^2 = (54)(1 - x)$$

Multiply the two quantities on the right, collect terms, and equate to zero:

$$x^2 + 54x - 54 = 0$$

Now substitute the corresponding quantities into the quadratic equation; $a = 1$, $b = 54$, and $c = -54$:

$$x = \frac{-54 \pm [54^2 - 4(1)(-54)]^{1/2}}{2(1)} = \frac{-54 \pm (2916 + 216)^{1/2}}{2}$$

$$x = \frac{-54 \pm (3132)^{1/2}}{2} = \frac{-54 \pm 55.9}{2}$$

$$x = \frac{-54 + 55.9}{2} = \frac{1.9}{2} = \mathbf{0.95}$$

and

$$x = \frac{-54 - 55.9}{2} = \frac{-109.9}{2} = -55.0$$

Logic indicates which of these two solutions is correct for the problem. Since the reaction began with 1 mole of the substance, the amount left after equilibrium is reached must be less than 1.0 mole. The first root, $x = 0.95$, satisfies this requirement. The second root, -55.0, cannot possibly be correct because the concept of a negative amount of material has no physical reality.

Quadratic equations and equations of higher order often are not necessary for solving problems in beginning chemistry. The reason is that frequently the conditions of the problem are such that one can foresee approximations that reduce the complexity of the calculations without introducing a significant error into the answer.

EXAMPLE. Let us look at a problem similar to the preceding one. Here, however, let us propose that the reaction reaches equilibrium when very little of the 1.0 mole per liter of starting material reacts. Thus, the amount of new substance formed, x, will be small, and the ratio of terms involving x will be smaller. The expression

$$\frac{(x)(x)}{(1-x)} = 1.2 \times 10^{-6}$$

fits these conditions and can illustrate our point.

SOLUTION. As before, to solve this expression by the quadratic formula, rearrange the equation so it is in the form

$$ax^2 + bx + c = 0$$

To do this, multiply both sides of the equation by $(1 - x)$:

$$x^2 = (1.2 \times 10^{-6})(1 - x)$$

Now multiply the two quantities on the right, collect terms, and equate to zero:

$$x^2 + 1.2 \times 10^{-6}x - 1.2 \times 10^{-6} = 0$$

Substitute the corresponding quantities into the quadratic equation; $a = 1.0$, $b = 1.2 \times 10^{-6}$, and $c = -1.2 \times 10^{-6}$:

$$
\begin{aligned}
x &= \frac{-b \pm (b^2 - 4ac)^{1/2}}{2a} \\
&= \frac{-1.2 \times 10^{-6} \pm [(1.2 \times 10^{-6})^2 - 4(1)(-1.2 \times 10^{-6})]^{1/2}}{2(1)} \\
&= \frac{-1.2 \times 10^{-6} \pm (1.44 \times 10^{-12} + 4.8 \times 10^{-6})^{1/2}}{2} \\
&= \frac{-1.2 \times 10^{-6} \pm (4.8 \times 10^{-6})^{1/2}}{2} \\
&= \frac{-1.2 \times 10^{-6} \pm 2.2 \times 10^{-3}}{2} \\
&= \mathbf{1.1 \times 10^{-3}} \text{ and } -1.1 \times 10^{-3}
\end{aligned}
$$

Since the concentration cannot be a negative number, the correct answer is $x = 1.1 \times 10^{-3}$ mole liter^{-1}. This is a small number; that is, only a small amount of product is formed by the time equilibrium is attained. We set up the problem to come out this way because many calculations in your course are similar.

Consider the denominator of the original expression $(1 - x)$. Since we have calculated the value for x, let us now evaluate its denominator:

$$(1.0 - x) = 1.0 - 1.1 \times 10^{-3} = 1.0 - 0.0011 = 1.0$$

Observe that if we follow the rules for subtracting significant figures, the result of subtracting the value of x from 1.0 is the same as if we had forgotten completely about the x. Its value is too small to be significant compared to 1.0.

What's the point of all this? Well, suppose you knew that the value for x was negligible compared to 1.0; thus, you omitted it from the $(1.0 - x)$ expression before you attempted to solve the problem. What a much simpler equation you would have obtained:

$$\frac{x^2}{1.0} = 1.2 \times 10^{-6}$$
$$x^2 = 1.2 \times 10^{-6}$$
$$x = (1.2 \times 10^{-6})^{1/2} = \mathbf{1.1 \times 10^{-3}}$$

And you would have calculated the same answer as you did from your laborious calculations with the quadratic formula.

The point now should be obvious. If you had a hint at the outset that the value of x might be negligible compared to 1.0, you could have omitted it from the denominator and saved yourself a lot of effort. Generally, enough information is given in the problem to indicate the possibility that such an omission is justified. When the opportunity presents itself, take advantage of it. Simplify the equation and solve for the answer. To ensure that your assumption was justified, place your value in the term or terms from which it was omitted. If it indeed yields the value for the term, unaltered within the precision governed by our rules for determining significant figures, you can feel confident that your answer is adequate. If this is not the case, then the alternative is to do the problem by the more tedious yet more exact method.

CUBIC AND HIGHER-ORDER EQUATIONS

Cubic equations and equations of higher order are rare in general chemistry problems. When they do occur, they are exceedingly tedious to solve; so you should look carefully for any assumptions that may simplify the equations.

Should you be faced with an equation of the third order or higher, a trial-and-error procedure or, described in more elegant terminology, the *method of successive approximations,* is available. Formulas similar to the quadratic formula are available for solving cubic equations; however, these formulas often prove as tedious to the beginner as the rather lengthy trial-and-error technique.

In this method, we assume that one or more terms can be neglected, so we have a simple *approximate* equation that gives a first *approximate* answer. Then this answer is substituted into the neglected terms, and the equation is solved for a second approximate answer. This second answer is presumed to be a better value for the answer than the first. The second approximation is substituted into the original equation, and a third, and hopefully better, answer is computed. This routine is repeated until two successive trials give the same self-consistent value for the answer.

Perhaps the best way to describe the method is to illustrate how it is used with a specific problem such as the cubic equation

$$4x^3 - 0.800x^2 + 0.0500x - 0.00060 = 0$$

The first step is to decide the magnitude of x. Generally, one can do this reasonably well in a problem in which x has some physical meaning. If you think that the value of x is less than one, then in the first approximation neglect the higher powers of x in the equation. If your hunch is that x is greater than one, then discard the lower powers of x in the equation. In this example, we will suppose that x is less than one. The solution of the problem proceeds as follows.

First approximation. Assume that $x = 0$ in the first two terms. The equation becomes $0.0500x - 0.00060 = 0$, for which the solution is $x = 0.012$.

Second approximation. Assume that $x = 0.012$ in the first two terms. The equation becomes $4(0.012)^3 - 0.800(0.012)^2 + 0.0500x - 0.00060 = 0$. This reduces to $0.0500x - 0.00070 = 0$, for which the solution is $x = 0.014$.

Third approximation. Assume that $x = 0.014$ in the first two terms. The equation becomes $4(0.014)^3 - 0.800(0.014)^2 + 0.0500x - 0.00060 = 0$, which reduces to $0.0500x - 0.00075 = 0$, for which the solution is $x = 0.015$.

Fourth approximation. Assume that $x = 0.015$ in the first two terms. The equation becomes $4(0.016)^3 - 0.800(0.016)^2 + 0.0500x - 0.00060 = 0$. This reduces to $0.0500x - 0.00077 = 0$, for which the solution is $x = 0.015$.

Since two successive trials lead to the same answer, $x = 0.015$, we assume that this is the answer. As an absolute check, you can substitute 0.015 for x in all three terms and see whether the left side of the equation equals zero.

Normally, if your first assumption was a reasonable one, you should find an answer after two or three approximations. However, it may take more. If your first assumption is a bad one, then, in general, the first few approximations will not converge to an answer. Thus, you should drop the calculations and begin again with a different initial assumption.

Some of your chemistry problems may have two unknowns; for instance, x and y. When this happens, you should look at the information in the problem and develop two different relationships involving the unknowns. Usually we can construct two linear equations that always can be rewritten as

$$y = ax + b$$
$$y = cx + d$$

in which a and b are numbers characteristic of one relationship and c and d are numbers characteristic of the other.

To solve such simultaneous equations, we eliminate one of the unknowns either by substituting into one of the equations (e.g., the first one) the expression for one of the unknowns (e.g., y) in terms of the other (e.g., $cx + d$), or by combining the equations in such a way that one of the unknowns disappears (e.g., subtracting one equation from the other).

EXAMPLE. Solve the simultaneous equations

$$x + y = 1.55 \tag{4}$$

and

$$\frac{x}{2.55} + \frac{y}{4} = 0.458 \tag{5}$$

SOLUTION 1. We shall use the first technique and solve by substituting into one of the equations an expression for one of the unknowns in terms of the other.

Solve Equation 5 for y in terms of x:

$$\frac{y}{4} = 0.458 - \frac{x}{2.55}$$
$$y = 1.832 - \frac{4x}{2.55}$$

Substitute this value for y into Equation 4:

$$x + 1.832 - \frac{4x}{2.55} = 1.55$$

Then we collect the terms in x on the left and the other terms on the right side of the equation:

$$x - \frac{4x}{2.55} = 1.55 - 1.832 = -0.28$$

Obtain a common denominator for the left term:

Algebraic Equations

$$\frac{2.55x - 4x}{2.55} = -0.28$$

Multiply both sides of the equation by 2.55:

$$1.45x = 0.28 \times 2.55$$

Solve for x:

$$x = \frac{0.28 \times 2.55}{1.45} = \mathbf{0.49}$$

Obtain y by substituting the value for x into Equation 4:

$$x + y = 1.55$$
$$0.49 + y = 1.55$$
$$y = 1.55 - 0.49 = \mathbf{1.06}$$

SOLUTION 2. Now we shall use the second technique and solve by combining the equations in such a way that one of the unknowns disappears.

Divide Equation 4 by four and obtain a new equation to solve with Equation 5:

$$\frac{x}{4} + \frac{y}{4} = 0.388 \qquad\qquad \text{(new Equation 4)}$$

$$\frac{x}{2.55} + \frac{y}{4} = 0.458 \qquad\qquad (5)$$

We see that subtracting Equation 5 from the new Equation 4 will eliminate y. The equation that results after the subtraction of Equation 5 from the new Equation 4 is

$$\frac{x}{4} - \frac{x}{2.55} = 0.388 - 0.458 = -0.070$$

Obtain a common denominator for the terms on the left:

$$\frac{2.55x - 4x}{(4)(2.55)} = -0.070$$

Multiply both sides of the equation by (4)(2.55) and subtract the terms in x:

$$-1.45x = (-0.070)(4)(2.55) = -0.71$$
$$x = (-0.71)/(-1.45) = \mathbf{0.49}$$

The value of y is obtained as before by substituting this value of x into Equation 4:

A Review of Relevant
Mathematics
and How to Solve
Problems

$$x + y = 1.55$$
$$0.49 + y = 1.55$$
$$y = 1.55 - 0.49 = \mathbf{1.06}$$

These procedures can be extended to more complicated problems

in which the number of unknowns and equations is greater than two.

The only condition necessary for solving a set of simultaneous equations is that we must have the same number of equations as there are unknowns.

LOGARITHMS

In the section on exponential numbers we discussed the advantages of expressing numbers in scientific notation, that is, as $a \times 10^x$, in which a, the coefficient, is a number between 1 and 10 and x is the exponent, or power, of 10. In the examples we considered, the exponent x was a positive or negative number (2, 3, -4, etc.). If x is zero, the entire exponential (10^0) equals 1 (any number raised to the zero power is unity) and is not written; for example, $2.54 \times 10^0 = 2.54 \times 1 = 2.54$. Also, if the coefficient a or the exponent x is unity, it generally is understood and not written as such; that is, 1×10^4 is written 10^4 and 4.2×10^1 is written 4.2×10.

Now if $10^0 = 1$ and $10^1 = 10$, it follows that any number between 1 and 10 can be expressed as a power of 10 with a coefficient of unity by using fractional exponents. Moreover, if negative powers are included, any number can be given in this way. This is the basis for expressing numbers as logarithms. The *logarithm* of a number is the exponent that must be put on 10 to give the number. For example, the number 2 can be expressed as $10^{0.301}$, in which case 0.301 is the logarithm (or "log") of 2. In Table 1 the powers of 10 needed to express the numbers 1 through 10 are listed. In other words, a table of the logarithms of the numbers 1 through 10 is given.

The exponent to which 10 must be raised to give the number is referred to as a logarithm to the *base* 10. These logarithms are the most convenient for general use since, for calculations, one can follow the simple rule that 1 is added to the logarithm of a number every time the number is multiplied by 10. However, numbers other than 10 can be used for the base. Logarithms to the base 2.718 . . . , so-called "Naperian base" or "natural base" logarithms are used frequently in science. This base, 2.718 . . . , is designated by the letter e. In terms of e, the number 2 can be expressed as $e^{0.693}$ (i.e., e to the 0.693 power), and we would say that the logarithm of 2 to the base e is 0.693. This last statement is written $\log_e 2 = 0.693$, or $\ln 2 = 0.693$, where the abbreviation "ln" refers to the natural or Naperian base logarithm. Logarithms to the base 10 generally are indicated by the word "log," and

Table 1

$1 = 10^0$, log 1 = 0	$6 = 10^{0.778}$, log 6 = 0.778
$2 = 10^{0.301}$, log 2 = 0.301	$7 = 10^{0.845}$, log 7 = 0.845
$3 = 10^{0.477}$, log 3 = 0.477	$8 = 10^{0.903}$, log 8 = 0.903
$4 = 10^{0.602}$, log 4 = 0.602	$9 = 10^{0.954}$, log 9 = 0.954
$5 = 10^{0.699}$, log 5 = 0.699	$10 = 10^1$, log 10 = 1.000

no base is specified (e.g., log 2 = 0.301). A simple relationship between base 10 and base e logs allows us to convert a logarithm from one base to the other. The relationship is $\log_e x = 2.303 \log x$.

Logarithms are useful because they make the multiplication of numbers a simple addition operation; division, a simple subtraction operation; and the computation of powers and roots, a simple multiplication or division process. Thus, much of the tedious digit-writing of arithmetic can be discarded, and operations can be performed faster and with less chance of error. The reason for this simplification is that when two powers of 10 are multiplied, their exponents are added, and when two powers of 10 are divided, their exponents are subtracted. These exponents are the logarithms. So, if we have tables that give the logarithms of numbers, we can take advantage of these simpler operations.

The logarithms of numbers expressed as powers of 10 with coefficients of unity are determined easily. They are simply the exponent. For example,

$$1 \times 10^5 = 10^0 \times 10^5 = 10^{(0+5)} = 10^5; \text{ the log } 10^5 = 5$$

Similarly,

$$\log (1 \times 10^6) = \log 10^6 = 6$$
$$\log (1 \times 10^{-7}) = \log 10^{-7} = -7$$

Now let us obtain the logarithms of some numbers that have been multiplied together. Recalling that multiplication of powers of 10 is carried out by adding exponents, we can see immediately that the log of a product 10^x times 10^y is simply $x + y$.

EXAMPLE. What is the log of $(1 \times 10^7)(1 \times 10^5)$?

SOLUTION.

$$(1 \times 10^7)(1 \times 10^5) = 1 \times 10^{12}$$
$$\log(1 \times 10^7)(1 \times 10^5) = \log(1 \times 10^{12}) = \mathbf{12}$$
or, if we omit the coefficients,
$$(10^7)(10^5) = 10^{12}$$
$$\log(10^7)(10^5) = \log 10^{12} = \mathbf{12}$$

An alternate solution is to add the logarithms:

$$\log(10^7)(10^5) = \log(10^7) + \log(10^5)$$
$$= \quad 7 \quad + \quad 5$$
$$= \mathbf{12}$$

EXAMPLE. What is the log of $(1 \times 10^9)(1 \times 10^{-7})$?

SOLUTION.

$$\log(10^9)(10^{-7}) = \log(10^9) + \log(10^{-7})$$
$$= \quad 9 \quad + \quad (-7)$$
$$= \mathbf{2}$$

Similarly, the logarithm of a quotient $10^x/10^y$ is $x - y$.

EXAMPLE.   What is the log of $(1 \times 10^9)/(1 \times 10^3)$?

SOLUTION.

$$\log\left(\frac{1 \times 10^9}{1 \times 10^3}\right) = \log 10^6 = 6$$

An alternate solution is to subtract the logarithms:

$$\log\left(\frac{1 \times 10^9}{1 \times 10^3}\right) = \log(1 \times 10^9) - \log(1 \times 10^3)$$
$$= \quad 9 \quad - \quad 3$$
$$= 6$$

EXAMPLE.   What is the log of $\dfrac{(1000)(10)}{(0.0001)}$?

SOLUTION.

$$\log\frac{(10^3)(10)}{(10^{-4})} = \log(10^3) + \log(10) - \log(10^{-4})$$
$$= \quad 3 \quad + \quad 1 \quad - \quad (-4)$$
$$= 8$$

In the preceding examples we have used only numbers that have coefficients of unity and whole-number powers of 10. In general, digits other than 1 will occur in the coefficients; in such cases we must look for these in a log table. Log tables should list the kind of information in Table 1, namely, the number and the exponent to which 10 must be taken to obtain the number—the number's logarithm. Appendix 1 contains a four-place table of logarithms. "Four-place" means that the logs are listed in the table to four decimal places and are given directly for all three-digit numbers from 1.00 to 9.99. By interpolation (i.e., by estimating values between the ones in Appendix 1) it is possible to find logs for all the four-digit numbers between 1.000 and 9.999. Since most of our computations rarely involve more than three significant figures, the four-place table will be sufficient. Five-, six-, and even ten-place tables are available for more precise calculations.

The table is set up as follows. The vertical column at the left of the table gives the first two figures of the number; the third digit of the number is read from the top line of the table. The four-digit numbers arranged in the 10 vertical columns within the table are the logarithms of the numbers. To obtain the log of the number 5.000, for example, you look up the digits 500 in the number column, the 50 in the left-hand vertical column, and the third digit—here a zero—in the top horizontal row. Hence, the log of 5.000 is located in the fifth row from the bottom of the table opposite the 50 and in the first column under the 0; it is 0.6990. Note that the value from the four-place log tables agrees with the one listed in Table 1.

Look up the logs of the other whole numbers from 0 to 10 in the four-place table. Check your answers by referring to Table 1.

Your next step should be to look up numbers expressed by coefficients larger than 1 and powers of 10 greater than zero. A few examples should illustrate how this is done.

EXAMPLE. What is the log of 2×10^3?

SOLUTION.

$$\log(2 \times 10^3) = \log(2) + \log(10^3)$$
$$= 0.301 + 3$$
$$= \mathbf{3.301}$$

The $\log(2)$ is found in the table; the $\log(10^3)$ is merely the exponent.

EXAMPLE. Now try a number with a negative exponent. Find the log of 7.52×10^{-4}.

SOLUTION.

$$\log(7.52 \times 10^{-4}) = \log(7.52) + \log(10^{-4})$$
$$= 0.8762 + -4$$
$$= \mathbf{-3.1238}$$

This last example illustrates three important points concerning logarithms. (1) No special operation is necessary to obtain logarithms for numbers with negative exponents. However, you always must write the number in preferred scientific notation; that is, the coefficient must be a number between 1 and 10. (2) The logarithm of a three-digit number is in the horizontal row opposite the first two digits (located in the vertical column) and in the column headed by the last digit in the number (in this example, 2). (3) To express the logarithm of 7.52×10^{-4} required five digits, whereas the number itself contained only three significant figures. The significant figure–logarithm relationship is discussed later in this section.

Now you should be ready to put all of these concepts into practice. To help you to begin, here is an example worked out in detail.

EXAMPLE. What is the logarithm of

$$\frac{(2.64 \times 10^{-3})(6.02 \times 10^{23})}{(5.0 \times 10^4)}$$

SOLUTION.

$$\log\left(\frac{(2.64 \times 10^{-3})(6.02 \times 10^{23})}{(5.0 \times 10^4)}\right) = [\log(2.64) + \log(10^{-3})]$$
$$+ [\log(6.02) + \log(10^{23})]$$
$$- [\log(5.0) + \log(10^4)]$$

A Review of Relevant Mathematics and How to Solve Problems

A Review of Relevant
Mathematics
and How to Solve
Problems

The imposing number of logarithms on the right of the equation may be a bit bewildering. Remember that the order in which a sequence of multiplications and divisions is carried out does not make any difference in the answer. You would obtain the same answer to the multiplication and division sequence if you divide the first factor in the numerator by the denominator and then multiply the result by the second factor in the numerator, as you would if you multiply both factors in the numerator and then divide their product by the denominator. The same is true if you do the multiplication and division with logarithms. In this problem, the two factors in the numerator have been multiplied first, and then their product is divided by the denominator by using logarithms. Now let us find the logarithms for the right side of the equation:

$$= [(0.4216) + (-3)]$$
$$+ [(0.7796) + (23)]$$
$$- [(0.6990) + (4)]$$
$$= 0.5022 + 16 = \mathbf{16.5022}$$

[*Note:* The number 16 in the preceding line derives from exact numbers (the exponents of 10) and is known to an infinite number of significant figures.]

Try these exercises to test your understanding.

EXERCISES.   (1) What is the log of

$$\frac{(4 \times 10^8)}{(2 \times 10^6)}$$

(2) What is the log of

$$\frac{(5 \times 10^{-6})(3 \times 10^{14})}{(2 \times 10^3)(1 \times 10^6)}$$

(3) What is the log of

$$\frac{(5.71 \times 10^{-5})(4.25 \times 10^8)}{(7.60 \times 10^2)(2.98 \times 10^2)}$$

(*Answers:* (1) 2.3011; (2) −0.1249; (3) −5.9700.)

So far, you might have formed the impression that we are putting undue emphasis on calculating logarithms of exponential numbers. But we have stressed this calculation because it is exactly what is necessary to find the pH of a solution when you study ionic equilibria. However, you also will need to perform the reverse procedure; that is, given the logarithm, express the number as an integral power of 10. To illustrate how to do this, we shall examine first some simple examples and then some more complicated ones.

EXAMPLE.   What is the number whose log is 3? [*Note:* The term "antilog" sometimes indicates "the number whose log is."]

SOLUTION.

$$\log x = 3$$
$$x = 10^3$$
$$x = 1 \times 10^3 = \mathbf{1000}$$

EXAMPLE. What is the number whose log is 3.301?

SOLUTION.

$$\log x = 3.301$$
$$x = 10^{3.301}$$
$$= 10^3 \times 10^{0.301}$$
$$= 10^3 \times 2 = \mathbf{2 \times 10^3}$$

The method here is to take the logarithm 3.301, extract the whole number (3) and use it to derive the power of 10 (10^3), and then use the decimal part (0.301) to derive the coefficient (2). This operation requires looking in a table of logarithms for the logarithm 0.301, and then noting what number corresponds to it.

Do the following exercise to test your understanding.

EXERCISE. What are the numbers whose logarithms are 6.9031, 4.7118, and 3.8102?

(*Answer:* 8.00×10^6; 5.15×10^4; 6.46×10^3.)

Finding the antilog of a negative logarithm is complicated because the table contains positive numbers only.

EXAMPLE. What is the number whose log is −4.272?

SOLUTION.

$$\log x = -4.272$$
$$x = 10^{-4.272}$$
$$= 10^{-4} \times 10^{-0.272}$$
$$= 10^{-4} \times \frac{1}{10^{0.272}}$$
$$= 10^{-4} \times \frac{1}{1.87}$$
$$= 10^{-4} \times 0.535$$
$$= \mathbf{5.35 \times 10^{-5}}$$

In the preceding solution, note that −4.272 is the sum of two negative numbers, −4 and −0.272. The number whose log is −4 is 10^{-4}, but the number whose log is −0.272 cannot be determined directly from the table because it lists only positive values. However, $10^{-0.272}$ is the same as $1/10^{0.272}$. The number whose log is +0.272 can be found in the table; it is 1.87. All that remains is to divide by 1.87 to obtain the coefficient in the answer. This division is a bit tedious. A much better method, which avoids this kind of division, can be used to solve this type of problem.

By this method, to find the number whose logarithm is -4.272, begin the same as before:

$$\log x = -4.272$$
$$x = 10^{-4.272}$$

Now note that -4.272 can be written as $-5 + 0.728$. Make this substitution and proceed as usual:

$$x = 10^{-4.272} = 10^{(-5+0.728)}$$
$$= (10^{-5})(10^{0.728})$$

In effect, we have transferred all of the minus signs to the whole-number exponent of 10 and have made the decimal exponent a positive number, the antilog of which can be found in the table. The antilog of 0.728 given in the table is 5.35; that is, $10^{0.728} = 5.35$. Therefore, $x = (10^{-5})$ $(10^{0.728}) = \mathbf{5.35 \times 10^{-5}}$.

As was mentioned previously, the number of significant figures change in a complex way when logarithms are involved. In the logarithm -4.272, for example, the digit before the decimal tells us only about the power of 10 and is not counted as a significant figure. The 2, 7, and 2 do count as significant figures. Accordingly, the answer to the preceding problem is expressed correctly to three significant figures.

EXTRACTING ROOTS AND RAISING NUMBERS TO POWERS

We can use logarithms to raise numbers to powers or to extract roots from numbers. For instance, the number a^x means that the number a is multiplied by itself x times. To do this with logarithms, we would write the log of a down x times and add; the sum would be the log a^x. That is, $\log a^x = x \log a$.

The xth root of a number a is expressed $a^{1/x}$. Reasoning similarly to the way that we did when raising numbers to powers, we find that $\log a^{1/x} = (1/x) \log a$.

EXAMPLE. What is the square of 298?

SOLUTION.

$$\begin{aligned} \log(298^2) &= 2[\log(298)] = 2[\log(2.98 \times 10^2)] \\ &= 2[\log(2.98) + \log(10^2)] \\ &= 2(0.4742 + 2) = 2(2.4742) \\ &= 4.9484 \end{aligned}$$

Therefore, 298^2 is the number whose log is 4.9484. The number whose log is 4 is 10^4, and the number whose log is 0.9484 is 8.88.

Therefore,
$$298^2 = \mathbf{8.88 \times 10^4}$$

EXAMPLE.   What is the cube root of 0.00752?

SOLUTION.

$$\log [(7.52 \times 10^{-3})^{1/3}] = \frac{1}{3} [(\log(7.52) + \log(10^{-3})]$$

$$= \frac{1}{3} [0.8762 + (-3)]$$

$$= \frac{1}{3} (-2.1238)$$

$$= -0.7079$$

Now we need to find the antilog of -0.7079; this will be the cube root of 0.00752.

$$10^{-0.7079} = 10^{(0.2921-1)}$$
$$= (10^{0.2921})(10^{-1})$$

We find the number equal to $10^{0.2921}$; it is the antilog of 0.2921 or 1.96. Therefore,

$$(0.00752)^{1/3} = \mathbf{1.96 \times 10^{-1}}$$

EXAMPLE.   Let us consider, as a final example, a problem that combines several operations. Evaluate $x = (2.94 \times 10^{-7})^{1/2}(3.72 \times 10^4)^2$.

SOLUTION.

$$\log x = \frac{1}{2} [\log(2.94 \times 10^{-7})] + 2[\log(3.72 \times 10^4)]$$

$$= \frac{1}{2} [\log(2.94) + \log(10^{-7})] + 2[\log(3.72) + \log(10^4)]$$

$$= \frac{1}{2} [0.4683 + (-7)] + 2[0.5705 + 4]$$

$$= \frac{1}{2} (-6.5317)' + 2(4.5705) = -3.2658 + 9.1410$$

$$= 5.8752$$

x is the number whose log is 5.8752.

$$x = 10^{5.8752} = 10^5 \times 10^{0.8752}$$

We find the number equal to $10^{0.8752}$; it is 7.50, the antilog of 0.8752. Therefore,

$$x = 10^5 \times 7.50 = \mathbf{7.50 \times 10^5}$$

INTERPOLATION OF TABLES OF LOGARITHMS

One last item remains in our discussion of logarithms: the interpolation of logarithms to extend the table. For example, suppose that you want to determine the log of the number 4.276 by using the four-place logarithm table in Appendix 1. From the table you find that the log 4.27 is 0.6304 and the log 4.28 is 0.6314. Since 4.276 is 0.6 of the way between 4.27 and 4.28, the log of 4.276 will be 0.6 of the distance between 0.6304 and 0.6314. The distance between 0.6304 and 0.6314 is 0.0010 (i.e., 0.6314 − 0.6304), and 0.6 of this distance is 0.0006 (i.e., 0.0010 × 0.6 = 0.0006). The log of 4.276 is determined by adding 0.0006 to 0.6304 to obtain 0.6310.

Antilogarithms are interpolated in a similar way. As an illustration, we compute the number whose logarithm is 9.8132. The number 9 indicates the power of 10, 10^9. The antilog of 0.8132 must be found from the table to complete the number. Although 0.8132 is not listed in the table, 0.8129 (its antilog is 6.50) and 0.8136 (its antilog is 6.51) are. We calculate that 0.8132 is 0.4 of the way between the two logarithms

$$\left(\frac{0.8132 - 0.8129}{0.8136 - 0.8129}\right) = \frac{0.0003}{0.0007} = \frac{3}{7} = 0.4$$

Therefore, the antilog will be 0.4 of the way between 6.50 and 6.51, that is, **6.504.**

Try the following exercises to test your ability to use logarithms.

EXERCISES.
(1) What is the log of 9.27×10^5?
(2) What is the log of 1.06×10^{-4}?
(3) What is the number that has as its logarithm 9.3421?
(4) What is the number that has as its logarithm −7.321?
(5) What is the fourth root of 2963?
(6) Evaluate $(2.34 \times 10^7)^5$ by logarithms.
(7) Evaluate the following expression by using logarithms:

$$\frac{(2.34 \times 10^5)(7.60 \times 10^2)^3}{(1.20 \times 10^3)}$$

(*Answers:* (1) 5.9671; (2) −3.9747; (3) 2.198×10^9; (4) 4.78×10^{-8}; (5) 7.376; (6) 7.015×10^{36}; (7) 8.56×10^{10}.)

HOW TO SOLVE PROBLEMS

Once the mathematical methods needed for the computation are familiar, the last hurdle in problem-solving is actually setting up the problem. This is the most important phase of problem-solving from your point of view because it is here that you demonstrate your understanding of chemical principles.

One of the two most frequently voiced laments among beginning students is, "I can do the math but I can't set up the problem." However, if the student really knows the math, he will know how to set up the problem. And once the problem is expressed in correct mathematical terms, it is essentially solved. The second lament is, "I understand the chemistry but I just can't do the problems." If the first part of this statement is accepted, then the latter difficulty is an echo of the former complaint. Here, too, the difficulty lies in applying the mathematical language, that is, setting up the problem.

Therefore, it would be good practice for you to concentrate your most intensive mental effort on "setting up the problem" rather than on the arithmetical computation that leads to the answer. Remember that the *concept* is the purpose of the problem, so postpone substituting into a formula until you have understood its underlying concept. For this reason, ratios should be avoided, especially when they are obtained by manipulating numbers from some set position on a page, such as above and below chemical formulas or from certain columns in tables.

Since you must apply your knowledge of chemical principles in solving the problem, your understanding of chemistry will be strengthened simultaneously. Your success at problem-solving will depend to a large extent on your experience. So get lots of practice. Work through the examples in the text and do the assigned homework problems. But also, at the very least, read every problem at the end of each chapter in the text and convince yourself that you know a method that will lead to a correct solution. If this does not give you sufficient practice, then consult supplementary problems books such as *Relevant Problems for Chemical Principles*, by Ian S. Butler and Arthur E. Grosser. This book contains more than 500 problems with detailed solutions so you can check your work. If you feel that your high school preparation in chemistry was insufficient to bring you up to the level of your college course, you may want to try some of the problems in *Programed Reviews of Chemical Principles*, by Jean D. Lassila *et al.*

The slide rule can be of great assistance to you. It provides a means of performing arithmetical computations such as multiplication and division with an accuracy sufficient for most problems. Furthermore, it substantially reduces the time necessary to do calculations. Once you have the problem set up, finding the answer with a slide rule consumes such little time that this step becomes almost trivial. For this reason, you are encouraged to purchase a 10-inch slide rule (the most inexpensive variety is adequate) and use it to do all your problems. Initially it will be a slow process, but your proficiency will improve markedly each time you use your slide rule. You will discover that the effort you spend developing this proficiency will be rewarded many times over. (Instructions for using the slide rule are in the next chapter.)

Two general techniques commonly are used to emphasize the concept-learning aspects of problem-solving. One is called the *factor-label method* (often referred to as *dimensional analysis*), and the other, the *stepwise-logical approach*. Of course, the first method also is logical.

To gain a better appreciation of the two methods, a sample problem will be solved by these two procedures.

EXERCISE. A bin in a sporting goods store contains an assortment of baseballs, tennis balls, and golf balls. There is a total of 700 balls. The entire assortment weighs 56.0 kilograms (kg). Half of this total weight is due to the baseballs. Knowing that the weights of an individual baseball, tennis ball, and golf ball are 140 g, 70 g, and 45 g, respectively, how many of each kind of ball are contained in the bin?

SOLUTION A (STEPWISE-LOGICAL METHOD).
What is the weight of each ball?
  A baseball weighs 140 g.
  A tennis ball weighs 70 g.
  A golf ball weighs 45 g.
How much does each type of ball contribute to the total weight?
  The problem states that half of the total weight is due to base-balls; therefore, the baseballs weigh $\frac{1}{2}$(56.0 kg) = 28.0 kg or 2.80×10^4 g. The remaining 28.0 kg or 2.80×10^4 g must be comprised of tennis balls and golf balls.
How many of each kind of ball are there?
  Since each baseball weighs 140 g and there are 2.80×10^4 g of baseballs in the bin, there must be

$$\frac{2.80 \times 10^4}{1.40 \times 10^2} = 2.00 \times 10^2 = \textbf{200 baseballs}$$

Of the total of 700 balls, $700 - 200 = 500$ of them must be tennis balls and golf balls. Let the number of tennis balls equal x. The number of golf balls will equal $500 - x$. Since each tennis ball weighs 70 g and each golf ball weighs 45 g, the weight of the x tennis balls equals $70x$ g, the weight of the $(500 - x)$ golf balls equals $45(500 - x)$ g, and the combined weight of the tennis and golf balls is $70x$ g $+ 45(500 - x)$ g $= 2.80 \times 10^4$ g. Solving for x, we obtain

$$25x = 2.80 \times 10^4 - 2.25 \times 10^4$$
$$25x = 0.55 \times 10^4$$
$$x = \textbf{220 tennis balls}$$

There must be $500 - x = 500 - 220 = \textbf{280 golf balls.}$

SOLUTION B (THE FACTOR-LABEL METHOD—DIMENSIONAL ANALYSIS).
What is the weight of each ball?

$$\frac{\text{grams}}{\text{baseball}} = 140$$

$$\frac{\text{grams}}{\text{tennis ball}} = 70$$

$$\frac{\text{grams}}{\text{golf ball}} = 45$$

How much does each type of ball contribute to the total weight?

$$\text{g baseballs} = \frac{1 \text{ kg baseballs}}{2 \text{ kg all kinds of balls}} \times 56.0 \text{ kg all kinds of balls}$$
$$= 28.0 \text{ kg baseballs}$$

g tennis and golf balls = 56.0×10^4 g all kinds of balls − 28.0
$$\times 10^4 \text{ g baseballs}$$
$$= 28.0 \times 10^4$$

How many of each kind of ball are there?

$$\frac{2.80 \times 10^4 \,\cancel{g}}{140 \,\cancel{g}/\text{baseball}} = 2.00 \times 10^2 = \textbf{200 baseballs}$$

(700 balls − 200 baseballs) = 500 tennis and golf balls.
Let the number of tennis balls equal x.

number of golf balls = tennis and golf balls
    − tennis balls = $500 - x$

$$(\cancel{x \text{ tennis balls}}) \left(70 \, \frac{g}{\cancel{\text{tennis ball}}}\right)$$
$$+ [(500 - x) \, \cancel{\text{golf balls}}] \left(45 \, \frac{g}{\cancel{\text{golf ball}}}\right) = 2.80 \times 10^4 \text{ g}$$

Solving this equation for x gives

x = the number of tennis balls = **220**
500 golf and tennis balls − 220 tennis balls = **280 golf balls**

UNIT CONVERSIONS

The conversion of units is of paramount importance in chemistry problems. Your calculations generally will involve units in the metric system; on occasion it will be necessary to convert numbers expressed in English units to the metric system or vice versa.

Dimensional analysis is an ideal method to follow for unit conversions. Tables of conversion factors enable you to transform almost any number from one set of units to another in one or two simple multiplication or division steps. Such tables are not always available, however, and it will be useful if you know a unit of length, mass, and volume in the metric system and its English equivalent. Although familiarity with a single unit may require a rather lengthy conversion, this is not a prohibitive factor, especially if you are using a slide rule. All the examples discussed here assume a knowledge of the prefixes for the metric numbers and English–metric equivalents to three significant figures.

Metric Prefixes

deci (d)	= tenth (10^{-1})	deka (dk)	= ten (10)
centi (c)	= hundredth (10^{-2})	hecto (h)	= hundred (10^2)
milli (m)	= thousandth (10^{-3})	kilo (k)	= thousand (10^3)
micro (μ)	= millionth (10^{-6})	mega (M)	= million (10^6)
nano (n)	= thousandth	giga (G)	= billion (10^9)
	millionth (10^{-9})	terra (T)	= million million
pico (p)	= millionth millionth		(10^{12})
	(10^{-12})		

Length	1 inch (in.)	= 2.54 centimeters (cm)
Mass	1 pound (lb)	= 454 grams (g)
Volume	1 quart (qt)	= 0.946 liter

EXAMPLE.   How many centimeters are there in 1.00 mile?

SOLUTION.

$$1.00 \text{ mile} \times 5.28 \times 10^3 \text{ ft/mile} \times 12 \text{ in./ft} \times 2.54 \text{ cm/in.}$$
$$= \mathbf{1.61 \times 10^5 \text{ cm}}$$

EXAMPLE.   A rock weighing 2.05 lb is submerged in water, and 1.20 qt of the water are displaced. The volume of the rock is the same as the volume of displaced water. Calculate the density of the rock in g cm^{-3}.

SOLUTION.

$$D = \frac{\text{mass}}{\text{volume}} = \frac{2.05 \; \cancel{\text{lb}} \times 454 \frac{\text{g}}{\cancel{\text{lb}}}}{1.20 \; \cancel{\text{qt}} \times 0.946 \frac{\cancel{\text{liter}}}{\cancel{\text{qt}}} \times 1000 \frac{\text{cm}^3}{\cancel{\text{liter}}}}$$
$$= \mathbf{0.819 \text{ g cm}^{-3}}$$

Do the following exercises to test yourself in converting units by dimensional analysis.

EXERCISES.

(1) On a certain day, more than 2 megashares of stock are traded on the New York Stock Exchange. How many shares is this?

(2) Calculate the wavelength in nanometers of the sodium light appearing at 5889 Å (1 Å = 1 angstrom unit = 1×10^{-8} cm).

(3) Mount Everest is about 8890 meters high. What is its altitude in feet?

(4) Work, W, is done when a force, F, pushes an object through a distance, d. The relationship is given by

$W = Fd$

The fundamental unit of work is the *erg*, defined as the work done when a force of 1 dyne moves an object through a distance of 1 cm.

$W = 1 \text{ erg} = 1 \text{ dyne} \times 1 \text{ cm}$

Force can be thought of as the push or pull on an object that tends to change its motion. This is given by

$F = ma$

in which m is the mass of the object and a is its acceleration. The *dyne*, a unit of force, is defined as the force needed to give an object having a mass of 1 g an acceleration of 1 cm sec^{-2}. Show that work has the dimensions of g cm^2 sec^{-2}.

(Answers: (1) 2,000,000; (2) 588.9 nm; (3) 29,200 ft; (4) By defini-

How to
Solve
Problems

43

tion, $F = ma$, so 1 dyne = 1 g $\times$ 1 cm sec^{-2}; therefore, the units of force are dyne = g cm sec^{-2}.)

[*Note:* 1 cm per second per second = 1 cm (1/sec) (1/sec) = 1 cm/(sec $\times$ sec) = 1 cm sec^{-2}.] Substituting these units for F in the expression for work gives $W = Fd =$ (g cm sec^{-2}) (cm) = **g cm^2 sec^{-2}.**]

This problem illustrates another point concerning units. You will encounter many new terms in your study of chemistry. Some of these will involve numerical relationships, and they will be applied in numerical calculations. The units of such terms are generally implicit in their definitions. For example, when the term "mole" is used to mean the weight in grams of a substance equal to its molecular weight, the units of mole are g/g mol wt. The point is that you should pay close attention to the definitions of new terms because you may need to assign units to them when they are used in a problem.

HOW TO USE THE SLIDE RULE

A slide rule can be of great assistance to you in your work in chemistry and physics and any other course in which numerical calculations are required. It provides a rapid way of performing arithmetical operations such as multiplication, division, raising numbers to powers, and extracting roots. The time it can save you in doing problems in your homework, quizzes, and examinations will compensate for the time you spend learning how to use the slide rule and obtaining the practice necessary to gain proficiency.

Many slide rules have been designed for specific types of applications in addition to the mathematical operations mentioned in the preceding paragraph. These slide rules differ in the number and kind of scales imprinted on them and the types of operations for which they may be used. The most widely used slide rule is the one developed in 1859 by Amede Mannheim, a French artillery officer. Most of the nine scales on this rule are included on all slide rules. The Mannheim rule often is referred to as the standard slide rule. We shall confine ourselves to a discussion of seven of the nine Mannheim scales, the A, B, C, D, C1, K, and L scales. These scales permit us to multiply, divide, extract square roots and cube roots, and obtain base-ten logarithms. The remaining two scales, S and T, are used to obtain trigonometric functions of angles.

THE PARTS OF A SLIDE RULE

The slide rule consists of a stationary part, called the *body*, and a movable central part called the *slide*. One scale, lettered C, is inscribed on the slide so it can be moved to be in coincidence with an identical scale, lettered D, that is imprinted on the body. The number 1 appears at both the left and right ends of the C scale; this point is referred to as the *index*. The remaining part of the rule is a transparent glass or plastic window called the *cursor*, or *indicator*, which can be moved along the body of the rule. A thin hairline engraved on the cursor can be positioned over the graduations on the various scales. (See Figure 1.)

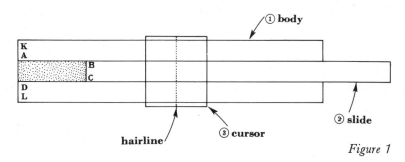

Figure 1

The above description pertains to the more common straight slide rule. A circular version is also available. The alterations in technique required to operate a circular rule can be deduced readily from the procedures used with the straight variety. We will present this discussion assuming that a straight rule is to be used.

THE BASIS OF THE SLIDE RULE

The operation of the slide rule is based on the properties of logarithms. Recall that when using logarithms, the mathematical operations of multiplication and division are reduced to addition and subtraction, and the operations of raising a number to a power or extracting a root are reduced to simple multiplication and division.

Look closely at the identical C and D scales on your slide rule. Observe that the large graduations on these scales are numbered 1, 2, 3, 4, 5, 6, 7, 8, 9, and 1 (the right-hand index is labeled 1 instead of 10 for a reason which will be obvious later). These graduations are different from those we are accustomed to seeing on thermometers, burettes, meter sticks, rulers, and other measuring devices. The spacing between the consecutive graduations decreases as you read the scale from left to right. That is, the space between the 1 and 2 graduations is much larger than the spacing between the 2 and 3 graduations; in turn, this spacing is larger than that between 3 and 4.

Now, refer to the table of logarithms in Appendix 1. Observe that the relative change in the value of the logarithms is less for the larger numbers than it is for the smaller ones. Like the graduations on the

C and D scales on the slide rule, the relationship between the numbers and their logarithms is not linear. For example, the difference between the logs of 2.0 and 3.0 is 0.1761 logarithm units (0.4771 − 0.3010), whereas the difference between the logarithms of 8.0 and 9.0 is 0.0511 logarithm units (0.9542 − 0.9031). Although 2.0 and 3.0, and 8.0 and 9.0, differ only by one numerical unit, their logarithms differ by a factor of about 3. The difference between the logarithms of two intermediate numbers separated by one unit, for example 4 and 5, is intermediate: 0.6990 − 0.6021 = 0.0869. Like the C and D scales, the differences between the logarithms of the numbers decrease continuously from 1 to 10.

The graduations corresponding to the numbers on the C and D scales are separated by distances that are proportional to the logarithms of these numbers. For example, if you measure the distance between 2 and 3 on the C scale of your slide rule and compare it to the distance between 8 and 9 you will find that the ratio (2 to 3)/(8 to 9) is 3.44, the same as the ratio of the differences between the logarithms of these numbers (0.1761/0.0511 = 3.44).

READING THE SCALES

The scales are read in the same way as the scales on a thermometer or a graduated cylinder. For example, consider the graduations between the numbers 1 and 2 on the C or D scale. The distance is divided into ten increments, indicated by the large graduations. Each graduation represents a digit in the decimal fraction indicated on the scale. Thus, the positions between the numbers 1 and 2 on the scale represent all numbers that have 1 as the first digit. The second digit in the number is given by the first largest subdivision; the third digit, by the next largest subdivision; and so forth. The spacings at the left end of the rule are of sufficient size that the graduation corresponding to the second digit is numbered, and there is a ruling for every tenth part of the second digit. There is insufficient space to number the intermediate graduations for numbers beginning with digits 2 or larger. Thus, the space between the 2 and 3 is graduated into ten equal (but unnumbered) divisions that give the second digit in the number. The distance between these graduations is subdivided in two-tenths increments that indicate the third digit. To understand this arrangement, refer to Figure 2, which shows the portion of the C or D scale between the major

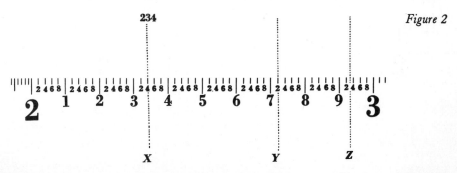

234   *Figure 2*

graduations 2 and 3. In the figure, the divisions are numbered; on your slide rule, only 2 and 3, the principal divisions, are numbered. This portion of the scale is used to represent all numbers, the first digit of which is 2. The number 234 is located by reading the 2 from the numbered major division, the 3 from the second subdivision (not numbered on your rule), and the 4 from the smallest subdivision.

EXAMPLE. Locate the number 272 on the scale in Figure 2.

SOLUTION. The dotted line Y in Figure 2 is positioned at 272.

A fourth significant figure can be measured for numbers beginning with the digit 2 by estimating between the ruled graduations.

EXAMPLE. Locate the number 293 on the scale in Figure 2.

SOLUTION. The location of 293 on the slide rule is indicated by the line Z in Figure 2. Note that the last digit, 3, must be estimated by the position one half the way between the graduation that corresponds to 292 and the graduation that corresponds to 294.

The slide rule measures only the digits in a number; therefore, the position Y in Figure 2 is not only the position for the number 272, but it is also the position for 0.0272, 27.2, 272,000, and so forth. Any number having as significant figures the digits 272 is located at position Y on the slide rule.

Figure 3 is another reproduction of the section on the C or D scale between the principal graduations 2 and 3. The graduations are those that actually appear on your slide rule. The numbers on the smaller subdivisions do not appear on your rule. You would obtain these numbers on your rule by counting the large subdivisions: The first division is 1; the second, 2; the third, 3; and so forth. The third digit is estimated by the position between the subdivisions. To aid you in this estimation, a small graduation is included at the point halfway between the subdivisions.

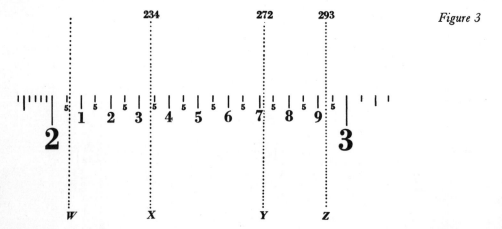

Figure 3

Since the third digit must be estimated when a number is read from the slide rule, only three significant figures can be obtained. One exception is for numbers that have the number 1 as the first digit. For such numbers, graduations appear up to the third digit, and a fourth significant figure can be obtained by estimating the distance between the two smallest divisions. Since the scale on the slide rule becomes more compressed as the numbers increase, the precision of the third significant figure becomes more and more uncertain. For this reason, it is necessary for you to practice reading the slide rule and positioning the scales and hairline until you can locate and read numbers precisely. In other words, any calculation on a slide rule is made with a certain amount of "experimental error" due to uncertainties in the operator's ability to read and position the slide rule.

EXAMPLE. Locate the numbers 234, 272, and 293 under the hairline on your slide rule.

SOLUTION. The positions for these numbers are shown in Figure 3.

EXAMPLE. What is the value for the number located at position W in Figure 3?

SOLUTION. The principal graduation 2 indicates the three significant figures 200. If the dotted line were positioned over the first subdivision, indicated by the first large graduation (numbered 1 in Figure 3), the number would be 210, to three significant figures. The number W lies between 200 and 210, and, more precisely, we see that it lies six tenths of the way between 200 and 210. Therefore, W corresponds to the number 206.

MULTIPLICATION WITH THE SLIDE RULE

To illustrate the procedure for multiplication, carry out the following operations on your slide rule. Move the slide so the index on the C scale (the number 1 on the left-hand end of the C scale) is positioned directly above the number 2 on the D scale. Now slide the cursor so the number 3 on the C scale lies directly below the hairline. Look on the D scale under the hairline. You should see the number 6, the product of 2×3. The reason for this should be obvious when you consider that the C and D scales are graduated in proportion to logarithms of the numbers. What you did was to measure a length on the C scale that is proportional to the log of 3 and add it on the D scale to a length that is proportional to the log of 2. The sum of these two lengths, read on the D scale, is proportional to the logarithm of the sum of the two logarithms. We have, in effect, added log 2 to log 3 and obtained an answer that is the log 6. Therefore, 6 is the product of 2×3.

We can summarize the operations for multiplication as follows: To multiply, set the index on the C scale over one of the numbers on the D scale. Position the hairline over the other number on the C scale. The answer is read under the hairline on the D scale.

> EXAMPLE. Multiply the following on your slide rule:
> $$234 \times 272 = ?$$

> SOLUTION. Refer to Figure 4. Position the left-hand index on the C scale over the number 234 on the D scale. Then slide the hairline so it lies over 272 on the C scale. Now read the digits in the number under the hairline on the D scale; the number is 636.

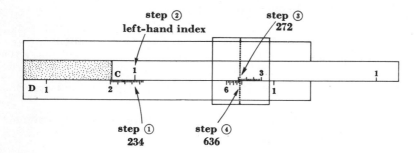

Figure 4

The slide rule determines only the digits in the answer. The location of the decimal point is determined by making an estimate of the product. To do this estimate, scientific notation is most helpful. For example, we observe that 234 is about 200 and that 272 is about 250; therefore, the product is about $(2 \times 10^2) \times (2.5 \times 10^2)$, or 5×10^4. The answer to the product of 234×272 is about 5×10^4; that is, $234 \times 272 = \mathbf{6.36 \times 10^4}$.

> EXAMPLE. Multiply the following:
> (1) 0.00265×3267
> (2) 259.4×698
> (3) $524 \times 6.02 \times 10^{23}$
> (4) 107.2×22.4

> (*Answers:* (1) **8.66**; (2) $\mathbf{1.81 \times 10^5}$; When the left-hand index on the C scale is placed over 259 on the D scale, the second number, 698, lies on that portion of the C scale that extends outside the rule. Therefore, we position the right-hand index on the C scale over 259 on the D scale and proceed as before. The hairline is moved over 698 on the C scale and the answer, 1.81×10^5, is read under the hairline on the D scale; (3) $\mathbf{3.15 \times 10^{26}}$; (4) $\mathbf{2.40 \times 10^3}$.)

A sequence of multiplications can be performed by multiplying the answer to the multiplication of two numbers by the next number in the sequence.

EXAMPLE.   Multiply 298 × 0.297 × 103.2.

SOLUTION.   Set the left-hand index on the C scale over 298 on the D scale. Position the hairline over 297 on the C scale. The product of these two numbers lies under the hairline on the D scale (885), but we need not record this answer. Instead, we will multiply this number by 103.2. To do this (using care not to move the hairline), slide the C scale so the left-hand index is under the hairline, that is, over the product of the first two numbers. Now, slide the hairline over the third number, 1032, on the C scale. The answer to the multiplication of all three numbers lies under the hairline on the D scale. It is 913. (The decimal is obtained by the following estimate: $298 \times 0.297 \times 103.2 \simeq (3 \times 10^2) \times (3 \times 10^{-1}) \times 10^2 \simeq 9 \times 10^3 = \mathbf{9.13 \times 10^3}$.)

EXERCISES.   Try these exercises for practice.
(1) $529 \times 1.07 \times 10^{-6} \times 0.0739 = ?$
(2) $(4.69)(7.34 \times 10^6)(3.02 \times 10^2)(5280) = ?$
(3) $(1.098)(208)(0.0760) = ?$

(*Answers:* (1) $\mathbf{4.2 \times 10^{-5}}$ (It is necessary to use the right-hand index on the C scale to multiply the product of the first two numbers by 0.0739.); (2) $\mathbf{5.49 \times 10^{13}}$; (3) $\mathbf{17.36}$ or $\mathbf{17.4}$ to three significant figures.)

DIVISION WITH THE SLIDE RULE

The operations for division are simply the opposite to those of multiplication. Recall that to divide two numbers, we subtract the log of the divisor (denominator) from the log of the dividend (numerator) to obtain the log of the quotient. Using the slide rule, we subtract from a length equal to the log of the numerator a length equal to the log of the denominator. The difference in these lengths equals the log of the quotient. Slide rule division is summarized: To divide, position the hairline over the numerator on the D scale. Slide the C scale so the denominator on the C scale also lies directly under the hairline. The quotient appears on the D scale at the index.

EXAMPLE.   Divide 0.321 by 6.02×10^{23}.

Division with the
Slide Rule

SOLUTION.   Set the hairline over 321 on the D scale. Then slide the C scale so 602 lies under the hairline. Use care not to change the position of the cursor when moving the slide. The digits in the answer lie under the index on the D scale; read 533. (See Figure 5.)

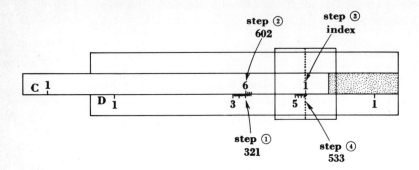

Figure 5

To locate the decimal point, we estimate $(0.321)/(6.02 \times 10^{23}) \simeq (3 \times 10^{-1})/(6 \times 10^{23}) \simeq 0.5 \times 10^{-24}$ or 5×10^{-25}. The answer is $\mathbf{5.33 \times 10^{-25}}$.

Note that when division is expressed as a fraction, the fraction is inverted when set on the slide rule; the numerator of the fraction is set on the D scale below the denominator, which is set above on the C scale.

EXERCISES. Do these exercises for practice:
(1) $102.7/359 = ?$
(2) $427/22.4 = ?$
(3) $0.0762/298.3 = ?$

(*Answers:* (1) **0.286**; (2) **19.06** or **19.1** to three significant figures; (3) $\mathbf{2.554 \times 10^{-4}}$ or $\mathbf{2.55 \times 10^{-4}}$ to three significant figures.)

A series of multiplications and divisions can be performed conveniently on a slide rule. The procedure is much like the one used to multiply a series of fractions, except that it is generally more convenient to alternate divisions and multiplications. To illustrate this, consider the problem

$$\frac{(232)(598)}{(6.21)} = ?$$

First we shall divide 232 by 6.21 and then multiply the result by 598. Set the hairline over 232 on the D scale. Slide the C scale so the number 6.21 lies directly under the hairline. The digits in the answer to this division (373) lie on the D scale at the index. We wish to multiply this result by 598. Note that the index is already positioned over this result, so we need only move the cursor along the C scale until the hairline is over the 598. The digits in the answer, 223, lie under the hairline on the C scale.

The factor by which we wish to multiply often will lie on the C scale at a position off the slide rule. In such cases, the other index must be used. To change to the other index, slide the cursor to locate the number to be multiplied under the hairline. Then move the slide to position the other index under the hairline. The following problem will illustrate this operation:

$$\frac{(198)(233)}{(784)} = ?$$

Place 198 under the hairline on the D scale. Slide the C scale so 784 appears under the hairline also. The answer (2528) is under the right index. To multiply this answer by 233, we slide the hairline over 233 on the C scale; however, 233 lies outside the slide rule to the left. We must change to the left index. Slide the cursor so the hairline lies over the index and the answer to the division. Without moving the cursor, move the slide until the left index lies under the hairline and over the division. Now we are ready to multiply by 233. Move the cursor so the hairline lies over the 233 on the C scale. The digits in the answer (588) lie under the hairline on the D scale. We estimate that the answer is $(4 \times 10^4)/(8 \times 10^2)$, or about 0.5×10^2; the answer is **58.8**.

SQUARING A NUMBER WITH THE SLIDE RULE

The A scale is used in conjunction with the D scale in squaring a number. If you look at the A scale, you will observe that it consists of two logarithmic scales, but each is half as long as the D scale. That is, the A scale is compressed twice as much as the D scale. When a number is squared, one multiplies its logarithm by 2. This is, in effect, what is accomplished by compressing two D scales into the single A scale. In summary, to square a number, move the cursor so the hairline is positioned over the number to be squared on the D scale. Read the square of the number on the A scale under the hairline.

EXAMPLE.   What is the square of 234?

SOLUTION.   See Figure 6. Set the hairline over 234 on the D scale. Read 548 on the A scale under the hairline. To establish the decimal point, we estimate as we did in multiplication and division. Thus, $234^2 \simeq (2 \times 10^2)^2 \simeq 4 \times 10^4$; therefore, $234^2 = \mathbf{5.48 \times 10^4}$.

step ② 548   *Figure 6*

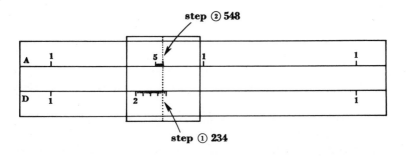

step ① 234

EXTRACTING THE SQUARE ROOT OF A NUMBER

The A and D scales are used for extracting the square root of a number but in reverse order of the procedure used to square a number. The number is set on the A scale, and its square root is read on the D scale. One complication arises, however. The A scale is divided into two sections, and it is necessary to determine which section to use for obtaining the square root of a given number. To determine this we write the number in scientific notation and make certain that the power of 10 is an even number. Thus, we can obtain an integral power of 10 when we extract the square root. For example, suppose that we wish to extract the square root of 698. We write this in exponential notation and obtain 6.98×10^2. To find the square root, we take the square root of the coefficient (6.98) and multiply it by the square root of the exponential (10^2). Hence, $(6.98 \times 10^2)^{1/2} = (6.98)^{1/2} \times 10^1$. However, should we wish to extract the square root of 6980, it is necessary to express the coefficient as a number greater than 10 (in this case 69.8) to obtain an exponential power of 10 that is not a fraction. Thus, $(69.8 \times 10^2)^{1/2} = (69.8)^{1/2} \times 10^1$. What we have demonstrated here is a general rule. To write a number as an exponential to an even power of 10, the coefficient will lie between 1 and 10 or between 10 and 100. The left half of the A scale is used to obtain the square roots of numbers with coefficients between 1 and 10, and the right half of the A scale is used to find the square roots of numbers with coefficients between 10 and 100.

EXAMPLE. What is the square root of 234?

SOLUTION. Write 234 in scientific notation as an even power of 10. Thus, $234 = 2.34 \times 10^2$. The square root of 10^2 is obtained by dividing the exponent by 2. The square root of 2.34 is obtained from the slide rule. Since 2.34 lies between 1 and 10, the left half of the A scale is used. Place the cursor so the hairline lies over 234 on the left half of the A scale. Read the square root of 2.34 on the D scale under the hairline; the number is 1.53. (See Figure 7.) Therefore, $(234)^{1/2} = 1.53 \times 10 = \mathbf{15.3}$.

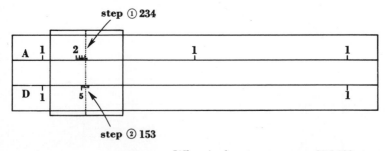

step ① 234

step ② 153

Figure 7

EXAMPLE. What is the square root of 2340?

SOLUTION. Writing this number in scientific notation as an even power of 10 gives 23.4 × 10². Since 23.4 lies between 10 and 100, set the hairline over 234 on the right half of the A scale. The number 4.84 lies under the hairline on the D scale. (See Figure 8.) So $(2340)^{1/2} = 4.84 \times 10 = 48.4$.

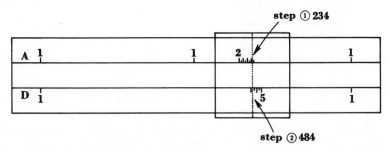

Figure 8

CUBING A NUMBER

To obtain cubes of numbers, we multiply the logarithm of the number by 3. The K scale is used in conjunction with the D scale to cube a number. Note that the K scale consists of three compressed log scales, each one third as long as the D scale. The procedure for cubing a number is analogous to that followed in squaring a number. The number is set under the hairline on the D scale, and its cube is read on the K scale under the hairline. The decimal is located by estimation. Figure 9 shows the positions for finding the cube of 4, which is 64.

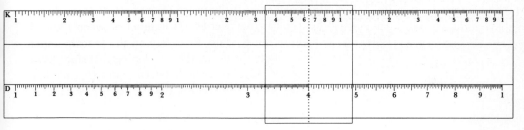

Figure 9

EXAMPLE. Cube 6.02 × 10²³.

SOLUTION. Move the cursor to position the hairline over 602 on the D scale. Read the digits (218) in the answer under the hairline on the K scale. To locate the decimal, estimate that 6^3 is about 200 (actually 216), so the answer is about 216 × 10⁶⁹. The correct answer obtained from the slide rule is 218 × 10⁶⁹ = **2.18 × 10⁷¹**.

EXTRACTING THE CUBE ROOT OF A NUMBER

To obtain the cube root of a number, we use a procedure analogous to that used in extracting the square root of a number. If the number is less than 1 or greater than 1000, it is written as an exponential, with a coefficient having one, two, or three digits to the left of the decimal, and

10 raised to a power divisible by 3. This requires that the coefficient of the number be between 1 and 1000. For example, the following numbers are rewritten in a form suitable for extracting their cube roots by using the slide rule:

$$6072 = 6.072 \times 10^3$$
$$60720 = 60.72 \times 10^3$$
$$6.072 \times 10^5 = 607.2 \times 10^3$$
$$0.0607 = 60.7 \times 10^{-3}$$
$$1000 = 1 \times 10^3$$

The numbers 6.072, 60.72, and 607.2 need not be rewritten in exponential form because they already are between 1 and 1000.

To extract the cube root of a number, the procedure used to cube the number is performed in reverse order. The hairline is positioned over the number on the K scale, and the cube root of the number is read under the hairline on the D scale. If the number has a coefficient between 1 and 10, the hairline is set on the left third of the K scale. If the number has a coefficient between 10 and 100, the middle segment is used. The right third of the K scale is used for locating coefficients of 100 to 1000.

EXAMPLE.　What is the cube root of 5.43×10^{-7}?

SOLUTION.　Rewriting the number so the exponent of 10 is divisible by 3 and the coefficient is between 1 and 1000, we obtain 543×10^{-9}. Set the hairline over 543 (a number between 100 and 1000) on the right of the K scale. Read 816 on the D scale under the hairline. We estimate the decimal by reasoning that since $5^3 = 125$ and $10^3 = 1000$, $(543)^{1/3}$ must be between 5 and 10, and 8.16 must be the correct answer. Therefore, $(543 \times 10^{-9})^{1/3} = \mathbf{8.16 \times 10^{-3}}$.

EXERCISES.　Confirm these settings on your slide rule.

Answers:
$(6072)^{1/3} = (6.072 \times 10^3)^{1/3} = 1.82 \times 10 = \mathbf{18.2}$
$(60720)^{1/3} = (60.72 \times 10^3)^{1/3} = 3.93 \times 10 = \mathbf{39.3}$
$(6.072 \times 10^5)^{1/3} = (607.2 \times 10^3)^{1/3} = 8.47 \times 10 = \mathbf{84.7}$
$(0.0607)^{1/3}) = (60.7 \times 10^{-3})^{1/3} = 3.93 \times 10^{-1} = \mathbf{0.393}$
$(1000)^{1/3} = \mathbf{10}$

THE RECIPROCAL OF A NUMBER

We can use the D and C scales to obtain the reciprocal of a number by dividing the number by 1. Set the hairline over 1 on the D scale and position the number on the C scale under the hairline. The C and C1 scales are reciprocals of each other. The reciprocal of a number on the C scale lies directly above it on the C1 scale. Note that the C1 scale reads from right to left. It is, in fact, a duplicate of the C scale, printed in the reverse direction.

EXAMPLE. Obtain the reciprocal of 273 by using the C and C1 scales.

SOLUTION. Position the hairline over the number 273 on the C scale. Read the reciprocal, 366, on the C1 scale under the hairline. Read from right to left on the C1 scale. As $\frac{1}{273} \simeq \frac{1}{300}$ or 0.03, we estimate the decimal point and write the solution: $(273)^{-1} =$ **0.0366**.

OBTAINING A BASE 10 LOGARITHM ON THE SLIDE RULE

The L scale, a linear scale, is used to obtain the logarithm of any number on the D scale. The L scale is used in the same way as a table of logarithms.

EXAMPLE. Find the log of 298.6.

SOLUTION. Write the number in scientific notation:

$$\log 298.6 = \log(2.986 \times 10^2) = \log 2.98 + \log 10^2$$
$$= \log 2.98 + 2.00$$

Set the hairline over 298 on the D scale. Read 0.474, the log of 2.98, on the L scale under the hairline. Therefore, log 298.6 = 0.474 + 2.000 = **2.474**.

PART TWO   CHEMICAL PRINCIPLES

CHAPTER 1 ATOMS, MOLECULES, AND MOLES

This chapter presents an historical survey of work that led to the concept of the atom and the molecule. It discusses how properties such as atomic and molecular weights and the atomic composition of matter were determined. To draw a coherent picture, the authors introduce a large number of specialized terms and computations. Because of their utility in chemistry, many of these terms and computations will be treated in considerable detail later in the text. The authors present much of this material in the first chapter to provide the student with a perspective of chemistry. Not much more than a casual acquaintance with some of these concepts is needed, at this point.

The student who already has taken a course in chemistry probably will find this chapter quite readable and interesting. However, the beginner may feel overwhelmed by a large number of puzzling concepts, many of which lack detailed explanation. One of the objectives in reviewing this chapter in the study guide is to emphasize material that requires immediate study. We will minimize any exposition on concepts that will be treated in detail later. Because some of the topics in *Chemical Principles* are not dealt with in the study guide, the section numbers are not consecutive. Material in the study guide that corresponds to topics in *Chemical Principles* will be identified by the corresponding text section number and title. You can satisfy the objectives of Chapter 1 of the text without developing expertise in some of the topics covered. Nevertheless, any extra effort that you devote to strengthening your understanding certainly will be of help when more detailed study becomes necessary.

1–1 THE STRUCTURE OF ATOMS AND THE CONCEPT OF MOLES

The structure of atoms and the concept of moles is basic to your understanding of chemistry. Therefore, we will elaborate on these topics as presented in *Chemical Principles*.

ATOMIC STRUCTURE

The three major particles that comprise the atom are described in Table 1–1. An atom can be thought of as a sphere with a radius of about 10^{-8} cm. (The angstrom unit, Å, measures distances of atomic dimensions, 1 Å $= 10^{-8}$ cm.) The protons and neutrons are packed together in an extremely tiny nucleus (10^{-13} cm, or 10^{-5} Å, in diameter) at the center of the sphere. The nucleus has a positive charge equal to the number of protons, that is, its *atomic number*. In a neutral atom, the remainder of the volume is occupied by an equal number of electrons.

ATOMIC MASS

Atomic mass is measured in atomic mass units, amu. One amu is defined as exactly $\frac{1}{12}$ the mass of the atom of carbon that contains six protons and six neutrons.

To the thousandths of an atomic mass unit, the masses of the proton, neutron, and electron are 1, 1, and 0 amu, respectively. Therefore, we would expect the atomic mass of most atoms to be an integral number of amu equal to the sum of the number of protons plus the number of neutrons in the nucleus. A table of atomic weights shows that many elements have atomic weights differing from integral values by more than 0.1 amu. There are three reasons why there are so many of these nonintegral atomic weights (or atomic masses):

(1) The masses of the electrons have not been considered. However,

Table 1–1

Particle	Units of electrical charge	Mass in amu
Proton	$+1$	1.007
Electron	-1	1/1823
Neutron	0	1.009

they contribute very little to the atomic weight. For example, 104 electrons would contribute only 104 electrons $\times$ 0.000549 amu/electron = 0.05 amu to the atomic weight.

(2) Einstein has indicated that mass can be converted to energy, E, according to the relationship $E = mc^2$, in which c is the velocity of light (2.9980 $\times$ 10^{10} cm sec^{-1}), m is the mass in grams, and E is its energy equivalent in ergs. When the protons and neutrons pack together to form a nucleus, some mass is lost as energy. This energy (the nuclear binding energy) holds the protons and neutrons together. The amount of mass lost by conversion of matter to energy is very small. It varies with the numbers of neutrons and protons involved in forming the nucleus. For this reason, the atomic masses of the neutron and proton themselves are not exact integers.

(3) Almost all elements have isotopes. These are atoms that have the same number of protons but different numbers of neutrons. Therefore, isotopes of the same element have different atomic weights. Most elements in nature consist of a mixture of isotopes. The resulting atomic weight of a naturally occurring element, the value listed in the atomic weight tables, is an average weight determined by the relative abundances of these isotopes.

Neglecting the electron masses and the loss in mass caused by conversion to nuclear binding energy, we can compute an approximate atomic mass merely by summing the number of protons and neutrons in the nucleus. This value sometimes is referred to as the atomic mass number. For example, all atoms of chlorine have 17 protons in their nuclei (atomic number of chlorine = 17). The atomic mass number of the isotope containing 18 neutrons is 17 + 18 = 35 amu. The atomic mass number of the isotope of chlorine that contains 20 neutrons is 17 + 20 = 37 amu. The first isotope is symbolized ^{35}Cl and the second, ^{37}Cl. The actual atomic masses of these two isotopes are 34.97 and 36.97 because of the loss in mass by conversion to nuclear binding energy. [*Note:* The atomic masses agree closely (in the preceding example, they agree within 0.03 amu) with the integral atomic mass numbers.]

In naturally occurring chlorine, 75.5% of the atoms are the ^{37}Cl isotope; the remaining 24.5% are the ^{37}Cl isotope. The atomic weight recorded in tables is the average isotopic composition. It is calculated in the following way.

Assume that we have 1000 atoms of naturally occurring chlorine. The average atomic weight (in amu/atom) would equal the total weight of all the atoms divided by 1000.

no. of ^{35}Cl isotopes = 75.5% of 1000 = (0.7550 $\times$ 1000)

no. of ^{37}Cl isotopes = 24.50% of 1000 = (0.2450 $\times$ 1000)

$$\text{wt of } ^{35}\text{Cl isotopes} = (0.7550 \times 1000) \text{ isotopes} \times 34.97 \frac{\text{amu}}{\text{isotope}}$$

$$\text{wt of } ^{37}\text{Cl isotopes} = (0.2450 \times 1000) \text{ isotopes} \times 36.97 \frac{\text{amu}}{\text{isotope}}$$

$$\text{average at. wt Cl} = \frac{\text{total wt of all atoms}}{\text{no. of atoms}}$$

$$= \frac{(0.7550)(1000)(34.97) + (0.2450)(1000)(36.97)}{1000}$$

$$= (0.7550)(34.97) + (0.2450)(36.97)$$

$$= \textbf{35.46 amu atom}^{-1}$$

This is the result recorded in the atomic weight table in the inside back cover. It varies considerably from an integral value principally because of the natural abundance of its isotopes. Also notice that the number of atoms cancel from each term in the expression for the average atomic weight. Consequently, to obtain the atomic weight in the table, we need only express the percentage abundances as decimal fractions and take that fraction of each of the corresponding isotope's atomic mass. Summing the results gives the average atomic weight. This is the procedure followed in arriving at the expression in Section 1–1 of the text.

EXAMPLE. Calculate the atomic weight of silicon if the isotopic composition of natural silicon is 92.28% ^{28}Si (atomic mass 27.98 amu), 4.67% ^{29}Si (atomic mass 28.98 amu), and 3.05% ^{30}Si (atomic mass 29.97 amu).

SOLUTION.

$(0.9228)(27.98) + (0.0467)(28.98) + (0.0305)(29.97)$
$= \textbf{28.09 amu}$

UNITS FOR MEASURING ATOMS AND MOLECULES

The atomic weights of H, O, and S are 1.0, 16, and 32, respectively (to two significant figures). This means that a single S atom weighs twice as much as an O atom, and 32 times as much as a H atom. The ratio of the weights of each atom, H/O/S, is 1/16/32.

To gain some quantitative understanding of what occurs in chemistry, we must be able to weigh and count atoms. In one respect, the problem is similar to the one confronting a wholesale egg dealer. Eggs are small, and when business is good the dealer is concerned with marketing thousands of eggs. It is not practical to count and sell individual eggs; rather, he markets 144 eggs at a time and deals with this larger unit, the gross. His bookkeeping is considerably simplified: An entry of 10 gross at $4.80 per gross = $48.00 is much simpler to compute than 1440 eggs at $3\frac{1}{3}$¢ per egg = $48.00.

The chemist's bookkeeping and business transactions involve large numbers of atoms and molecules. For the same reason that the egg dealer resorts to a unit consisting of several eggs, the chemist deals with a unit consisting of several atoms or molecules. The egg dealer is concerned with thousands of eggs, whereas the chemist usually is concerned with billions of billions of atoms. Consequently, the unit chosen by the chemist is larger than a gross, namely, 6.022×10^{23} or Avogadro's number. He refers to this many atoms as a gram-atom (abbreviated g-atom).

Atoms,
Molecules,
and Moles

64

The tabulation that follows illustrates the similarity between how the egg dealer counts eggs and how the chemist counts atoms.

Eggs	Atoms

$144 \text{ eggs} = 1 \text{ gross eggs}$

$432 \text{ eggs} = \dfrac{432 \text{ eggs}}{144 \text{ eggs gross}^{-1}} = 3 \text{ gross}$

$36 \text{ eggs} = \dfrac{36 \text{ eggs}}{144 \text{ eggs gross}^{-1}} = 0.25 \text{ gross}$

$6.022 \times 10^{23} \text{ atoms} = 1 \text{ g-atom}$

$1.807 \times 10^{24} \text{ atoms} = \dfrac{1.807 \times 10^{24} \text{ atoms}}{6.022 \times 10^{23} \text{ atoms g-atoms}^{-1}}$
$= 3000 \text{ g-atoms}$

$1.505 \times 10^{23} \text{ atoms} = \dfrac{1.505 \times 10^{23} \text{ atoms}}{6.022 \times 10^{23} \text{ atoms g-atoms}^{-1}}$
$= 0.25 \text{ g-atom}$

The egg dealer can see to count his eggs: The chemist cannot see to count atoms. Fortunately, nature provides a way out for the chemist. The isotopic composition of a particular element is quite constant in nature. Consequently, 6.022×10^{23} atoms of a particular element will have a constant weight; 6.022×10^{23} hydrogen atoms weigh 1.008 g, which is the atomic weight of hydrogen expressed in grams. It follows that the same number of atoms of any other element also will be the atomic weight of that element in grams. This is true because the atomic weights express the relative weights of the individual atoms. A sample calculation with oxygen will demonstrate our explanation. (Note the cancellation of units.)

$$\frac{\text{wt of } 6.02 \times 10^{23} \text{ atoms H}}{\text{wt of } 6.02 \times 10^{23} \text{ atoms O}} = \frac{(6.02 \times 10^{23})(\text{wt of one H atom})}{(6.02 \times 10^{23})(\text{wt of one O atom})}$$
$$= \frac{\text{wt of one H atom}}{\text{wt of one O atom}} = \frac{1.008}{16.00}$$

Since the weight of 6.02×10^{23} atoms of H equals 1.008 g, the weight of 6.02×10^{23} atoms of O must equal 16.00 g. This is a unique feature of the gram-atom as compared to the egg dealer's gross. One gross of eggs from different farmers' hen houses (or hens, for that matter) probably will not weigh the same.

In summary,

$$1 \text{ g-atom} = 6.022 \times 10^{23} \text{ atoms} = 1 \text{ at. wt expressed in g}$$
$$\text{no. of g-atoms} = \frac{\text{no. of atoms}}{6.022 \times 10^{23} \text{ atoms g-atom}^{-1}}$$
$$= \frac{\text{wt of the element in g}}{\text{wt in g g-atom}^{-1}}$$

The term "the atomic weight in grams" sometimes is referred to as "the gram atomic weight."

UNITS FOR MEASURING MOLECULES

The same reasoning used to develop units for counting atoms is applied to molecules. The unit chosen is 6.022×10^{23} molecules. This unit is referred to as a gram-molecule, by convention shortened to gram-mole or simply *mole*. Since each time an atom occurs in a molecule it contributes its gram atomic weight to the weight of 6.022×10^{23} of those molecules, the weight of a mole will be the sum of the atomic weights of the atoms in the molecule in grams. To illustrate this statement, follow the reasoning below for the CCl_4 molecule.

$$6.022 \times 10^{23} \text{ molecules of } CCl_4 = 1 \text{ mole}$$

therefore, the wt of

$$1 \text{ mole of } CCl_4 = 6.022 \times 10^{23} \text{ (wt of one molecule of } CCl_4)$$
$$\text{wt of 1 mole } CCl_4 = (\text{wt of } 6.022 \times 10^{23} \text{ C atoms}) + [\text{wt of}$$
$$4(6.022 \times 10^{23}) \text{ Cl atoms}]$$
$$= \text{g at. wt of C} + 4 \times \text{g at. wt of Cl}$$
$$= 12.01 \text{ g g-atom}^{-1} \text{ C} + 4(35.45 \text{ g g-atom}^{-1} \text{ Cl})$$
$$= 153.81 \text{ g mole}^{-1} CCl_4$$

The weight of 1 mole was determined in the next to the last step by taking the sum of the atomic weights in the molecule: $CCl_4 = 1$ carbon $+ 4$ chlorines $= 1(12.01) + 4(35.45) = 153.81 \text{ g} = 1 \text{ mole } CCl_4$. In summary,

$$1 \text{ mole} = 6.022 \times 10^{23} \text{ molecules} = 1 \text{ g molecular wt}$$

$$\text{no. of moles} = \frac{\text{no. of molecules}}{6.022 \times 10^{23} \text{ molecules mole}^{-1}}$$

$$= \frac{\text{wt in g}}{\text{molecular wt in g mole}^{-1}}$$

SYMBOLS AND FORMULAS

Each of the 104 elements is represented by a one- or two-letter symbol generally taken from the first letters of the element's accepted name. A left-hand superscript indicates the atomic mass number when referring to a particular isotope of the element. On occasion, the atomic number is written as a left-hand subscript. Examples: ^4_2He or ^4He, $^{35}_{17}Cl$, $^{16}_8O$ or ^{18}O, and so forth.

Compounds are symbolized by formulas in which the conventional symbols for the elements indicate the kinds of atoms present, and right-hand subscripts indicate the atomic composition of the compound. An empirical formula is written with right-hand subscripts that give the simplest ratio of the atoms present in the compound. The molecular formula shows the exact number of each kind of atom in a molecule of the compound. (A detailed discussion of formulas is included in Section 4–1 of *Chemical Principles*.)

Molecular weights are calculated by taking the sum of the atomic weights of the atoms as they appear in the molecular formula. For example, the molecular formula for glycerin is $C_3H_5(OH)_3$. The atomic weights are C = 12, H = 1, and O = 16. The gram molecular weight of $C_3H_5(OH)_3$ is

3 C atoms = 3(12) = 36
8 H atoms (includes 3 H atoms in the 3 OH groups) = 8(1) = 8
3 O atoms (contained in the 3 OH groups) = 3(16) = 48
gram molecular weight of glycerin = 36 + 8 + 48 = 92 g mole^{-1}

As you will read in Chapter 4, some compounds cannot be thought of as molecules. However, formulas for such compounds can be written. The sum of the gram atomic weights of the atoms in the formula is called a *gram formula weight*. One gram formula weight contains 6.022×10^{23} atoms for each of the elements' symbols in the formula and is referred to as 1 mole.

EXAMPLE. How many atoms of phosphorus are in 3.10 g $Ca_3(PO_4)_2$?

SOLUTION.

1 g formula wt $Ca_3(PO_4)_2 = 3(Ca) + 2(P) + 8(O)$

where the parentheses indicate g atomic wt of the atoms enclosed.

1 g formula wt $Ca_3(PO_4)_2 = 3(40) + 2(31) + 8(16)$
= 310 g mole^{-1}

$$\frac{3.10 \text{ g } Ca_3(PO_4)_2}{310 \text{ g mole}^{-1} Ca_3(PO_4)_2} = 0.010 \text{ mole } Ca_3(PO_4)_2$$

One mole of $Ca_3(PO_4)_2$ contains 2 g-atoms P; therefore, 0.010 mole of $Ca_3(PO_4)_2$ contains

$$\frac{2 \text{ g-atoms P}}{\text{mole } Ca_3(PO_4)_2} \times 0.010 \text{ mole } Ca_3(PO_4)_2 = 0.020 \text{ g-atom P}$$
no. of atoms of P = 0.020 g-atom P $\times 6.022 \times 10^{23}$ atoms g-atom^{-1} = **1.2 × 10²² atoms P**

In large industrial operations, units such as pound-atoms, ton-atoms, pound-moles, or ton-moles are used. One ton-atom of an element is its atomic weight in tons; that is, 1 ton-atom of iron (at. wt = 55.85) is 55.85 tons of iron. Of course, a ton-atom of any element will contain the same number of atoms as a ton-atom of any other element, but that number will be much larger than Avogadro's number. We can calculate the number of atoms in a ton-atom; we shall use hydrogen as an example.

$$\frac{(1.00 \text{ ton H ton-atom}^{-1} \text{ H})(2000 \text{ lb-ton}^{-1})(454 \text{ g lb}^{-1})}{1.00 \text{ g g-atom}^{-1} \text{ H}}$$

$$\times 6.02 \times 10^{23} \frac{\text{atoms}}{\text{g-atom H}} = \textbf{5.47} \times \textbf{10}^{\textbf{29}} \textbf{ atoms ton-atom}^{\textbf{-1}} \textbf{ H}$$

If you are having difficulty in understanding these concepts and working this type of problem, you probably will find programed instruction useful. Review 1 of *Programed Reviews of Chemical Principles* by J. D. Lassila *et al.*, treats this subject in detail.

ACIDS, BASES, AND SALTS

Acids and bases are treated more thoroughly in later sections of *Chemical Principles*. For now, it is helpful to know that common acids used in the laboratory are aqueous solutions of substances such as HCl (hydrochloric acid), HNO_3 (nitric acid), H_2SO_4 (sulfuric acid), and $HC_2H_3O_2$, often written CH_3COOH (acetic acid). Aqueous solutions of metal hydroxides are among the more common bases: KOH (potassium hydroxide) and $NaOH$ (sodium hydroxide) are examples. These substances are formed when metal oxides react with water; for example, $Na_2O + H_2O \rightarrow 2\ NaOH$. Salts are compounds that are formed by the reaction of an acid with a base. Salts consist of a metal that originates from a base and a nonmetal or complex grouping of atoms that comes from an acid; for example, $NaCl$ (from HCl and $NaOH$) and $CaSO_4$ [from $Ca(OH)_2$ and H_2SO_4].

1-4 DOES A COMPOUND HAVE A FIXED COMPOSITION?

One of the major sources of confusion in the early studies that eventually led to the laws of composition was the inability to differentiate between pure compounds and solutions. Solutions are homogeneous mixtures of compounds or elements. Like pure compounds, they have a uniform composition throughout. Unlike pure compounds, their composition is variable. Alloys are solutions of metals in one another. A type of brass, for example, consists of different amounts of tin dissolved in copper. The proportion of tin can be varied within rather narrow limits without any noticeable change in the appearance of the brass. Nonstoichiometric compounds, such as the compound of iron and sulfur mentioned in Section 1-4 of *Chemical Principles*, are examples of solution phenomena. Within the composition range of 1.1 to 0.91 g-atoms Fe to 1 g-atom S, the iron sulfide compound is a solution containing various amounts of Fe or S dissolved in the compound FeS. The basic terminology used in describing solutions is given in Section 4-4 of *Chemical Principles*.

The laws of constant composition, equivalent proportions, and multiple proportions support Dalton's atomic theory. For atoms of a particular element to be indivisible units of matter and have a fixed weight requires that only 1, 2, 3, and so forth (i.e., whole units of atoms) combine to form molecules.

Atoms,
Molecules,
and Moles

THE ATOMIC THEORY IS SUPPORTED
BY THE LAW OF DEFINITE COMPOSITION

Each molecule of a particular compound contains a certain number and kind of atoms. Therefore, the weight composition for this substance must be constant. For example, the carbon dioxide in the air in Paris is identical to the carbon dioxide in the air in your room, or the carbon dioxide that we might prepare by heating limestone ($CaCO_3$). All carbon dioxide (CO_2) contains one carbon and two oxygen atoms that are chemically combined. As each C and O atom has a fixed average weight, and their relative weights are given by their atomic weights, it follows that the composition by weight will be the one given by the atomic and molecular weights. The composition of carbon dioxide can be calculated as follows:

$$\% \ C = \frac{(wt \ carbon)}{(wt \ CO_2)} \times 100 \ and \ \% \ O = \frac{(wt \ oxygen)}{(wt \ CO_2)} \times 100$$

$$\frac{12 \ amu \ C}{[12 + 2(16)] \ amu \ CO_2} \times 100 = \textbf{27.2\% carbon}$$

$$\frac{2(16) \ amu \ O}{44 \ amu \ CO_2} \times 100 = \textbf{72.8\% oxygen}$$

It is worthwhile to think that, had experimental techniques been more precise, the law of definite composition and Dalton's atomic theory would have experienced more difficulty in gaining acceptance. Most of the variances in composition among nonstoichiometric compounds are so small that they were classed as experimental errors and discounted. The isotopic composition of an element can vary, depending on the source of the element. A constant composition depends on constant atomic weights, and these, in turn, depend on the isotopic composition. The variances in natural isotopic composition associated with most elements are very small; hence, they were not detectable by techniques available to early investigators. Even today, these differences are not considered except when one is concerned with the most precise measurements.

THE ATOMIC THEORY IS SUPPORTED
BY THE LAW OF EQUIVALENT PROPORTIONS

From his analytical data, Richter found that when two elements which combine with one another also combine with a third, the ratio of the weights of the two elements combined with a fixed weight of the third are the same as when they combine with each other. The data from two experiments are given in Section 1–4 in *Chemical Principles*. In one experiment oxygen and carbon form compounds with hydrogen (water and methane) as well as with each other (carbon dioxide). The experiment shows that 16 g of O combine with 2 g of H in water, and 24 g of C combine with 8 g of H in methane. Computing the weight of O and C combined with the same weight of H (here taken as 1 g)[1] in the two compounds gives

---

[1] The weight of an element combined with 1.008 g of H or 8.00 g of O in a compound is called its combining weight.

In water: $$\frac{16\ \text{g O}}{2\ \text{g H}} = 8\ \frac{\text{g O}}{\text{g H}}$$

In methane: $$\frac{24\ \text{g C}}{8\ \text{g H}} = 3\ \frac{\text{g C}}{\text{g H}}$$

Richter's law of equivalent proportions predicts that the ratio of O to C in carbon dioxide is the same, 8/3. This prediction is confirmed by an analysis of carbon dioxide. We find that 24 g of carbon combine with 64 g of O in this compound. The weight ratio of O to C is indeed

$$\frac{64\ \text{g O}}{24\ \text{g C}} = \frac{8\ \text{g O}}{3\ \text{g C}}$$

A similar experiment with compounds of chlorine and arsenic with hydrogen (hydrogen chloride and arsine) indicates that, in hydrogen chloride, the weight of chlorine combined with 1 g of H is 35.5 g Cl/g H, and in arsine there are 25 g As/g H. The ratio of As to Cl combined with 1 g H is

$$\frac{25\ \text{g As}}{35.5\ \text{g Cl}} = \frac{5\ \text{g As}}{7.1\ \text{g Cl}}$$

In arsenic chloride, the As/Cl ratio is

$$\frac{75\ \text{g As}}{106\ \text{g Cl}} = \frac{5\ \text{g As}}{7.1\ \text{g Cl}}$$

We know now the formulas of the compounds involved in these experiments. If atoms are indivisible and characterized by a fixed weight (their atomic weights), we can confirm the above weight ratios.

Water, H_2O: $$\frac{\text{g O}}{\text{g H}} = \frac{1(16)}{2(1)} = \frac{16}{2} = \frac{8\ \text{g O}}{1\ \text{g H}}$$

Methane, CH_4: $$\frac{\text{g C}}{\text{g H}} = \frac{1(12)}{4(1)} = \frac{3\ \text{g C}}{1\ \text{g H}}$$

The ratio of O/C combined with 1 g H in the two compounds is

$$\frac{8\ \text{g O/g H}}{3\ \text{g C/g H}} = \frac{8\ \text{g O}}{3\ \text{g C}}$$

The data from compounds of Cl and As are given as a second example in the text. That they conform with the known formulas can be seen in the following:

Hydrogen chloride (HCl): $$\frac{\text{g Cl}}{\text{g H}} = \frac{1(35.5)}{1(1)} = 35.5\ \frac{\text{g Cl}}{\text{g H}}$$

Arsine (AsH_3): $$\frac{\text{g As}}{\text{g H}} = \frac{1(75)}{3(1.0)} = \frac{75\ \text{g As}}{3\ \text{g H}}$$

The As/Cl ratio in the two compounds is

$$\frac{75\ \text{g As}/3\ \text{g H}}{35.5\ \text{g Cl}/\text{g H}} = \frac{75}{3(35.5)} = \frac{5}{7.1}\ \frac{\text{g As}}{\text{g Cl}}$$

In arsenic trichloride ($AsCl_3$)

$$\frac{\text{g As}}{\text{g Cl}} = \frac{1(75)}{3(35.5)} = \frac{5 \text{ g As}}{7.1 \text{ g Cl}}$$

THE LAW OF MULTIPLE PROPORTIONS AS EXPLAINED BY THE ATOMIC THEORY

The same two elements can form more than one compound. For example, in addition to carbon dioxide, carbon and oxygen form another compound, carbon monoxide. Arsenic trichloride and arsenic pentachloride are two different arsenic–chlorine compounds. In these compounds, the ratios are not as the law of equivalent proportions predicts. The C/O ratio in carbon monoxide is 3/4 and not 8/3, and the As/Cl ratio in arsenic pentachloride is 3/7.1, not 5/7.1. For this reason, Richter's work never received much support.

The atomic theory allows for such compounds by stating that different numbers of atoms of the same element can form different compounds (one C and two O atoms in carbon dioxide or one C atom and one O atom in carbon monoxide, and the two arsenic–chlorine compounds; $AsCl_3$ and $AsCl_5$). The experimentally confirmed law of multiple proportions is a natural consequence of the fact that any combination of indivisible atoms must involve whole numbers of atoms. This law is, in reality, an extension of Richter's law of equivalent proportions to include situations in which more than one compound is formed by the same elements. The law of multiple proportions states that if two elements are capable of forming more than one compound, the weights of one of the elements that combine with a fixed weight of the other in each of the compounds are small whole number ratios of each other.

Using the original experimental data of Davy for some oxides of nitrogen given in Section 1–5 in *Chemical Principles* and repeated in Table 1–2, we can illustrate the law of multiple proportions. To do this, we calculate the weight of nitrogen combined with a fixed weight of oxygen in each of the compounds. We shall set this weight at 1 g. Then we compare the ratios of the resulting weights. The data give the percentages of N and O in three oxides, A, B, and C. We choose 100 g as a total weight of oxide. The corresponding percentages of 100 g will be the weight in grams of the N and O in the compounds. The results are summarized in Table 1–2.

Allowing for some error, we could conclude that the ratios of the grams of N combined with 1 g of O in the compounds A, B, and C are $1/1.6/4$, $1/\frac{5}{3}/4$, or $3/5/12$, which are ratios of small whole numbers.

Davy's results were considerably in error as the three compounds he studied were (A) NO_2, (B) NO, and (C) N_2O. Had he analyzed them correctly, his compositions would have been

Does a Compound Have a Fixed Composition?

(A) NO_2: $\dfrac{1(14) \text{ g N}}{(14) + 2(16) \text{ g } NO_2} = \dfrac{14}{46} = 0.30$ or 30% N

(B) NO: $\dfrac{1(14) \text{ g N}}{1(14) + 1(16) \text{ g NO}} = \dfrac{14}{30} = 0.47$ or 47% N

(C) N_2O: $\dfrac{2(14) \text{ g N}}{2(14) + 1(16) \text{ g NO}} = \dfrac{28}{44} = 0.64$ or 64% N

If we use these corrected values in the calculations, we obtain the final nitrogen ratios of 1/2/4 in the three compounds.

1-5 JOHN DALTON AND THE THEORY OF ATOMS

With but few modifications, we now view atoms as did Dalton. We know that although atoms remain indivisible during normal chemical reactions, they can be divided or "split" if extremely high energies are available. Of course, the existence of isotopes requires a modification in his original postulate that all atoms of the same element have the same weight. The common factor among atoms of the same element is that they have the same number of protons (the atomic number) and the same number of electrons.

Much of Dalton's work involved the calculation of combining weights and atomic weights. More is to be said about combining weights in Sections 1–7 and 1–8, but the basic idea should be understood here.

Suppose that we accept the atomic theory and assume that we are able to isolate and determine the composition of a compound, each molecule of which contains one atom of hydrogen and one atom of some other element X. Such a molecule would be formulated HX. By analysis, we could obtain the weight of H and X in a sample of the compound and calculate the weight of the element X (call it x g) combined with 1 g of H. By definition, the combining weight of hydrogen is 1 g. Define the combining weight of any other element as that weight of the element which combines with 1 g of hydrogen. In our example, the combining weight of the element X is x g. Now, if we follow Dalton and define the gram atomic weight of hydrogen as 1.00 g, then the combining weight of X is the weight of the same number of atoms of X as

Table 1–2

Oxide	% N and % O	g N and g O	g N combined with 1 g O
A	29.50% N 70.50% O	29.50 g N 70.50 g O	$\dfrac{29.50 \text{ g N}}{70.50 \text{ g O}} = 0.4184 \dfrac{\text{g N}}{\text{g O}}$
B	44.05% N 55.95% O	44.05 g N 55.95 g O	$\dfrac{44.05 \text{ g N}}{55.95 \text{ g O}} = 0.7873 \dfrac{\text{g N}}{\text{g O}}$
C	63.30% N 36.70% O	63.30 g N 36.70 g O	$\dfrac{63.30 \text{ g N}}{36.70 \text{ g O}} = 1.725 \dfrac{\text{g N}}{\text{g O}}$

Dividing each final weight by the smallest, 0.4184, gives

A: $\dfrac{0.4184}{0.4184} = 1.00$ B: $\dfrac{0.7873}{0.4184} = 1.64$ C: $\dfrac{1.725}{0.4184} = 4.12$

there are atoms in 1.00 g of H. Therefore, the X atom has a weight that is x times greater than a H atom. If we arbitrarily assign 1 atomic mass unit to the H atom, then x will be the atomic weight of the X atom in atomic mass units.

The work of Gay-Lussac and Avogadro enabled Cannizzaro to obtain accurate atomic weights.

The combining weight concept is quite useful for finding the formulas for compounds. We shall accept as combining weights for H and O the Dalton values of 1.00 g and 8.00 g, respectively. And we shall define the combining weight of any element as that weight which combines with 1.00 g H, 8.00 g O, or the combining weight of any other element.

EXAMPLE. In aluminum oxide, 54 g of aluminum are combined with 48 g of oxygen. What is the combining weight of aluminum?

SOLUTION.

$$\frac{54 \text{ g Al}}{48 \text{ g O}} = 1.13 \text{ g Al/g O}$$

By definition, the combining weight of Al is that weight of Al combined with 8.00 g of oxygen, or

$$1.13 \frac{\text{g Al}}{\text{g O}} \times 8 \text{ g O} = \textbf{9.04 g Al}$$

EXAMPLE. An amount of 1.500 g aluminum reacts with 5.90 g of chlorine to make aluminum chloride. What is the combining weight of chlorine?

SOLUTION. Since we just calculated the combining weight of aluminum as 9.04 g, the combining weight of Cl is the weight combined with 9.04 g Al.

$$\frac{5.90 \text{ g Cl}}{1.50 \text{ g Al}} \times (9.04 \text{ g Al}) = \textbf{35.5 g Cl}$$

The relationship between the combining weight and the formula of a compound can be seen by calculating the combining weights of nitrogen in a series of nitrogen-containing compounds: NH_3, NO_2, NO, and N_2O.

Ammonia (NH_3): $\dfrac{14 \text{ g N}}{3(1) \text{ g H}} = 4.67 \dfrac{\text{g N}}{\text{g H}} = \textbf{4.67}$

Nitrogen dioxide (NO_2): $\dfrac{1(14) \text{ g N}}{2(16) \text{ g O}} = \dfrac{14}{32} = 0.44 \dfrac{\text{g N}}{\text{g O}}$

$$0.44 \frac{\text{g N}}{\text{g O}} \times (8.00 \text{ g O}) = \textbf{3.5 g}$$

$$\text{Nitric oxide (NO)}: \frac{1(14) \text{ g N}}{1(16) \text{ g O}} = \frac{14}{16} = 0.88 \frac{\text{g N}}{\text{g O}}$$

$$0.88 \frac{\text{g N}}{\text{g O}} \times (8.0 \text{ g O}) = \mathbf{7.0 \text{ g}}$$

$$\text{Nitrous oxide (N}_2\text{O)}: \frac{2(14) \text{ g N}}{1(16) \text{ g O}} = \frac{28}{16} = 1.8 \frac{\text{g N}}{\text{g O}}$$

$$1.8 \frac{\text{g N}}{\text{g O}} \times (8.0 \text{ g O}) = \mathbf{14 \text{ g}}$$

The ratios of the combining weights relative to the combining weight in N_2O are

$$\frac{4.67 \text{ in NH}_3}{14 \text{ g in N}_2\text{O}} = \frac{1}{3} \qquad \frac{3.5 \text{ g in NO}_2}{14 \text{ g in N}_2\text{O}} = \frac{1}{4} \qquad \frac{7.0 \text{ g in NO}}{14 \text{ g in N}_2\text{O}} = \frac{1}{2}$$

We will see when we discuss the concept of combining capacity and the chemical bond that the denominators in these ratios equal the combining capacity of nitrogen in the three compounds. Its combining capacity in N_2O is one.

1–6 EQUAL NUMBERS IN EQUAL VOLUMES: GAY-LUSSAC AND AVOGADRO

Avogadro's law (equal volumes of all gases at the same temperature and pressure contain the same number of molecules) explains Gay-Lussac's law of combining volumes (when gases combine and form gaseous products they do so in simple whole-number ratios by volume at the same temperature and pressure).

Certain elements are diatomic in the gas state at normal temperatures: H_2, N_2, O_2, Cl_2, F_2, Br_2, and I_2. Some other elements are molecules of higher order, for example, P_4 and S_8. This concept is important, so study carefully Figure 1–1. Test your understanding by showing that nitrogen is formulated correctly as N_2 if we assume that H_2 is the correct formula for hydrogen. You are given the information that in the formation of ammonia gas (NH_3), 2 liters of nitrogen and 3 liters of hydrogen produce 2 liters of ammonia.

1–7 CANNIZZARO AND A RATIONAL METHOD OF CALCULATING ATOMIC WEIGHTS

The density of a gas is the weight of 1 liter of the gas at some specified temperature and pressure. If the temperature and pressure are 0°C and 760 torr, the density is referred to as the density at standard conditions. We know from Avogadro's law that if we have 1 liter each of two different gases at the same temperature and pressure, they will contain the same number of molecules. The weight of the same number of molecules is proportional to the molecular weight. Consequently, the weight of a liter of any gas (its gas density is D) varies directly with the molecular weight, M. Expressing this mathematically, we obtain Equation 1–1 in *Chemical Principles*.

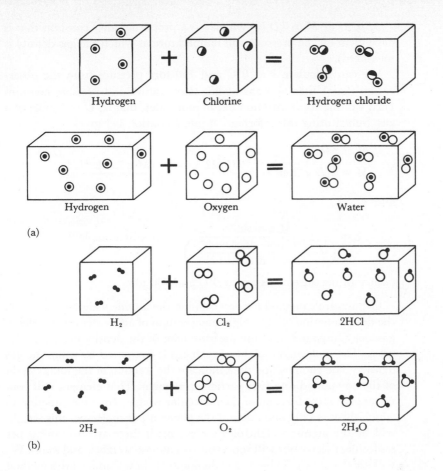

Hydrogen   Chlorine   Hydrogen chloride

Hydrogen   Oxygen   Water

(a)

H_2 Cl_2 $2HCl$

$2H_2$ O_2 $2H_2O$

(b)

Figure 1–1. Gay-Lussac's results on the combining volumes of gases and the explanations by (a) Dalton and (b) Avogadro. Gay-Lussac found that one volume of hydrogen and one of chlorine produce two volumes of HCl gas, and that two volumes of hydrogen react with one of oxygen to produce two volumes of steam. (a) Dalton argued that, if the volume of HCl is twice the volume of either hydrogen or chlorine, then there must be half as many molecules per volume unit in the HCl. Similarly, if there are N molecules of hydrogen per volume unit, and if each of these produces a water molecule in the same total volume, there also will be N molecules per volume unit in water. But only half the volume of oxygen is required, so the density of oxygen must be 2N molecules per volume unit. Thus, in hydrogen chloride, hydrogen, and oxygen, the numbers of molecules per volume unit are N/2, N, and 2N. (b) Avogadro proposed that each molecule of hydrogen, chlorine, and oxygen contained two atoms. With this assumption, all of the participants in the HCl reaction have the same number of molecules per volume unit of gas. Applying this same assumption to the water reaction leads to a new formula for water, H_2O, and ultimately to a complete revision of Dalton's atomic weight scale.

$M \propto D$ or $M = kD$ (in which k is a proportionality constant that is dependent on the pressure and temperature at which the gas density is measured).

We can calculate k at 0°C and 760 torr pressure from the observation that 1 liter of a gas at this temperature and pressure contains 1/22.4 of the Avogadro number of molecules, that is, 1/22.4 mole of a gas. Substituting this information into Equation 1–1 gives

$$M = kD$$

$$M = k(D \text{ g liter}^{-1}) = \frac{k(1/22.4 \text{ mole}) (M \text{ g mole}^{-1})}{1 \text{ liter}}$$

and

$$k = \frac{M \text{ g mole}^{-1}}{\left(\frac{1/22.4 \text{ mole } M \text{ g mole}^{-1}}{1 \text{ liter}}\right)} = 22.4 \text{ liters mole}^{-1}$$

(when all measurements are at 0°C and 760 torr).

Cannizzaro's method for determining the atomic weight depends on the determination of the weight composition of an element in a series of gaseous compounds and the measurement of the density of each of the gases. The molecular weight of each gas is computed by using the gas density. The composition data indicate the fraction of the total weight of the compound due to a particular element. That element will contribute the same fraction of the molecular weight. In any compound in which there is only one atom of the element per molecule, this weight will be the atomic weight of the element; if there are two atoms per molecule, this weight will represent two atomic weights, and so on. We will use the data in Table 1–3 to demonstrate how Cannizzaro's method works in determining the atomic weight of carbon.

Table 1–3. Data for Determining Molecular Weights, Atomic Weights, and Formulas by Cannizzaro's Method

	Density, D (g liter^{-1})	Molecular weight: $M = kD$	Elemental composition, percent by weight			Weight per molecular unit			Probable formula
			C	H	Cl	C^a	H	Cl	
Methane	0.715	16.0	74.8	25.0	—	12.0	4.03	—	CH_4
Ethane	1.340	29.9	79.8	20.2	—	23.9	6.04	—	C_2H_6
Benzene	3.48	77.8	92.3	7.7	—	71.8	6.00	—	C_6H_6
Chloroform	5.34	119.1	10.05	0.844	89.10	12.0	1.01	106.2	$CHCl_3$
Ethyl chloride	2.88	64.3	37.2	7.8	55.0	23.9	5.02	35.4	C_2H_5Cl
Carbon tetrachloride	6.83	152.6	7.8	—	92.2	11.9	—	141.0	CCl_4
			Greatest common factor =			12.0	1.0	35.3	

^{a} Carbon occurs only in multiples of 12.0 (slide rule accuracy), so 12 is an acceptable atomic weight. But so are 6, 4, or any other common factor. Cannizzaro's atomic weights will be either the correct values or, at worst, integral multiples of them.

The density of methane at standard conditions is 0.715 g liter^{-1}. The molecular weight is

$$M = kD = \left(22.4 \frac{\text{liters}}{\text{mole}}\right) D$$

$$= \left(22.4 \frac{\text{liters}}{\text{mole}}\right)\left(0.715 \frac{\text{g}}{\text{liter}}\right)$$

$$= 16.0 \text{ g mole}^{-1}$$

By experiment, we determine that when 0.784 g of carbon is converted to methane, 1.000 g of methane is formed. The weight composition of methane is

$$\frac{0.750 \text{ g C}}{1.000 \text{ g methane}} \times 100 = 75.0\% \text{ C}$$

wt of hydrogen = 1.000 g methane − 0.750 g C = 0.250 g

$$\frac{0.250 \text{ g H}}{1.000 \text{ g methane}} \times 100 = 25.0\% \text{ hydrogen}$$

The atomic weight of each element is calculated by taking the percentages of the molecular weight;

at. wt carbon: $(16.0 \text{ g mole}^{-1})(0.750) = 12.0 \text{ g mole}^{-1} \text{ C}$

Identical calculations with the data for the other gases listed in Table 1–3 give the following weights of carbon per mole: 23.9, 71.8, 12.0, 23.9, 11.9; that is, 24, 72, 12, 24, and 12 to the nearest whole number. Since the number 12 is obtained for two compounds and all other values are multiples of 12, the assumption is that the atomic weight of carbon is 12.0. Methane, chloroform, and carbon tetrachloride have one carbon atom in each molecule. Ethane must have $24/12 = 2$, benzene has $72/12 = 6$, and ethyl chloride has $24/12 = 2$ carbon atoms per molecule.

The formulas of the various gases can be derived, and a more accurate atomic weight[2] obtained in the following way.

From measurements of the H/O ratio in water, a precise value for the atomic weight of hydrogen (1.008) can be obtained relative to the atomic weight of oxygen (15.999+) as a standard. From the percentages of H in the first five compounds in the table and the measurements of the gas density molecular weights, we can determine how many H atoms are in each of the molecules. We illustrate this by using the methane data.

$$0.250 \times 16.0 \text{ g mole}^{-1} = 4.00 \text{ g H mole}^{-1}$$

$$\frac{4.00 \text{ g H}}{1.008 \frac{\text{g}}{\text{g-atom H}}} = \textbf{4.00 g-atoms H mole}^{-1}$$

We already have determined that there is but one C atom in a methane molecule; therefore, the formula for methane is CH_4.

---

[2] We shall see in Chapter 2 that gas density measurements generally allow calculation of only approximate atomic weights.

Once the molecular formulas are established, accurate combining weight data can be found and a correspondingly accurate atomic weight for the carbon atom computed.

EXAMPLE. The C_6H_6 formula for benzene has been established. Careful combining weight experiments show that the composition of benzene is 92.264% C and 7.736% H. Calculate a precise value for the atomic weight of carbon.

SOLUTION. If we assume 100 g of benzene, the combining weight of C is

$$\frac{92.264 \text{ g C}}{7.736 \text{ g H}} = 11.93 \text{ g C/g H}$$

In C_6H_6, there is one atom of C with each atom of H, so the weight of carbon combined with 1 gram atomic weight of hydrogen (1.008 g) will be the gram atomic weight of carbon.

$$11.93 \frac{\text{g C}}{\text{g H}} \times 1.008 \frac{\text{g H}}{\text{g-atom}} = \textbf{12.02 g C g-atom}^{-1}$$

A SUMMARY OF THE PROCEDURE FOR DETERMINING PRECISE MOLECULAR WEIGHTS FROM GAS DENSITY MEASUREMENTS: THE CANNIZZARO METHOD

(1) Obtain the approximate gram molecular weight by multiplying the gas density at standard conditions by 22.4 liters mole^{-1}.

(2) Determine the elemental composition in percent by weight from the combining weight data.

(3) Determine the approximate weight of the element per mole by taking its percentage of the approximate gram molecular weight determined in step (2).

(4) The three preceding steps are repeated for several compounds that contain the atom in question. The smallest weight, of which the others are whole-number multiples, is the approximate atomic weight.

(5) To refine the value, use known atomic weights and the composition data to ascertain the formula of the compound.

(6) From the precise atomic composition, calculate the combining weights of the element, and from this and the formula, determine the precise atomic weight.

You will return to a more detailed study of the determination of formulas in Chapter 4 of *Chemical Principles*. As the examples in Sections 1–7, 1–8, and 1–9 show, the data available for an atomic weight determination can be used to discover the empirical or simplest formula of a substance. For this reason, the determination of formulas is introduced in these sections of the text. We have included additional examples here. You will find it profitable to return to this material when reading Chapter 4.

EXAMPLE. A sample of a compound contains 0.545 g carbon, 0.092 g hydrogen, and 0.363 g oxygen. Calculate the formula for the compound.

SOLUTION. The coefficients in a formula indicate the number of atoms in a molecule, that is, the number of gram-atoms of each element in a mole of the compound. We calculate the number of gram-atoms of each element.

$$\text{g-atoms C} = \frac{0.545 \text{ g C}}{12.0 \text{ g g-atom}^{-1} \text{ C}} = 0.0454$$

$$\text{g-atoms H} = \frac{0.092 \text{ g H}}{1.01 \text{ g g-atom}^{-1} \text{ H}} = 0.0911$$

$$\text{g-atoms O} = \frac{0.363 \text{ g O}}{16.0 \text{ g g-atom}^{-1} \text{ O}} = 0.0227$$

Find the whole-number ratio between these atoms by dividing each number by the smallest (0.0227).

$$\frac{0.0454}{0.0227} = 2.00 = 2 \text{ C} \qquad \frac{0.0911}{0.0227} = 4.01 = 4 \text{ H}$$

$$\frac{0.0227}{0.0227} = 1.00 = 1 \text{ O}$$

The formula C_2H_4O is the empirical formula because it expresses the smallest whole-number ratio of atoms in the molecule. The same results would have been obtained if the formula of this compound were $C_4H_8O_2$, $C_6H_{12}O_3$, and so forth (i.e., any whole-number multiple of C_2H_4O). To obtain the molecular formula, an approximate molecular weight is needed.

Suppose that the vapor density of the compound in the preceding paragraph is 4.0 g liter^{-1} at standard conditions. What is the molecular formula for this compound?

$$M = kD = (22.4 \text{ liters mole}^{-1})(4.0 \text{ g liter}^{-1})$$
$$= 89.6 \text{ g mole}^{-1}$$

The molecular formula will be an integral multiple of the empirical formula. Therefore,

$$\frac{\text{actual gram molecular weight}}{\text{empirical gram formula weight}} = \text{an integer}$$

$$\frac{89.6}{2(12) + 4(1) + 1(16)} = \frac{89.6}{44} = 2.04$$

or 2 to the nearest whole number. The molecular formula is $2(C_2H_4O) = C_4H_8O_2$.

1–8 ATOMIC WEIGHTS FOR THE HEAVY ELEMENTS: DULONG AND PETIT

The law of Dulong and Petit can be stated by summarizing the data in Table 1–5 in *Chemical Principles*:

$$\text{(specific heat in cal g}^{-1}\text{ deg}^{-1})\text{(atomic weight)} \simeq 6$$

in which 6 is the average molar heat capacity in units of cal deg^{-1} mole^{-1}.

In the footnote to Table 1–5 in *Chemical Principles* the question was asked: Do modern atomic weights make the molar heat capacities determined by Dulong and Petit more similar? The average value for molar heat capacities is 6, the constant that we have employed in stating the law of Dulong and Petit.

the molar heat capacities obtained in the original work with those calculated by using modern atomic weights. To do this, we calculate the average value of the molar heat capacities; then we determine the deviation of each value from this average. Finally, we determine the average of these deviations. This is done in Table 1–4 of this study guide. Dulong and Petit's original data are taken from Table 1–5 of *Chemical Principles*. The molar heat capacities are calculated by multiplying the specific heat (in cal deg^{-1} g^{-1}) by the gram atomic weight.

Table 1–4. Comparison of the Molar Heat Capacities Calculated by Dulong and Petit with Those Calculated by Using Modern Atomic Weights

Element	Dulong & Petit's specific heat (cal deg^{-1} g^{-1})	Modern atomic weight	Molar heat capacities, C_p, in cal deg^{-1} mole^{-1}		Deviations in C_p $\|C_p - \text{average } C_p\|$	
			Dulong & Petit's value	Calculated from modern at. wt	Dulong & Petit's value	Calculated from modern at. wt
Bi	0.0288	208.98	6.13	6.02	0.13	0.05
Au	0.298	196.97	5.93	5.87	0.07	0.20
Pt	0.0314	195.09	5.98	6.13	0.02	0.06
Sn	0.0514	118.69	6.05	6.10	0.05	0.03
Zn	0.0927	65.37	5.98	6.06	0.02	0.01
Ga	0.0912	69.72	5.88	6.36	0.12	0.29
Cu	0.0949	63.54	6.01	6.03	0.01	0.04
Ni	0.1035	58.71	6.11	6.076	0.11	0.01
Fe	0.1100	55.847	5.97	6.144	0.03	0.07
Ca	0.1498	40.08	5.90	6.004	0.10	0.07
S	0.1880	32.064	6.05	6.027	0.05	0.04
		Totals	65.99	67.08	0.71	0.87
		Average values	$\dfrac{65.99}{11}$ $= 6.00$	$\dfrac{67.08}{11}$ $= 6.07$	$\dfrac{0.71}{11}$ $= 0.0645$	$\dfrac{0.87}{11}$ $= 0.079$

Average deviation of original Dulong and Petit values

$$\frac{0.0645}{6.00} \times 100 = \mathbf{1.1\%}$$

Average deviation using modern atomic weights

$$\frac{0.079}{6.07} \times 100 = \mathbf{1.3\%}$$

As shown in Table 1–4, a slightly larger deviation (1.3%) is observed when the more modern atomic weights are used to determine the molar heat capacities. The average molar heat capacity for the elements in the table is 6.07 ± 1.3%, or 6.07 ± 0.08 cal mole^{-1} deg^{-1}. The deviation becomes even more uncertain when the data for other elements are considered. For this reason, we have used only one significant figure, 6, in expressing the law. The molar heat capacities for the heavier solid elements are about 6 cal deg^{-1} mole^{-1}.

Accurate combining weight data for solid compounds can be used with the law of Dulong and Petit to determine accurate atomic weights.

Almost all elements react with oxygen, so the combining weights of oxides commonly are employed for atomic weight determinations by this method. However, chlorides (the combining weight of chlorine equals its atomic weight) and other compounds also are used.

We reason as follows: If a metal oxide has the formula M_2O, there will be 2 g-atoms of the metal M combined with 1 g-atom of oxygen (16.0 g O) or 1 g-atom M combined with 0.5 g-atom oxygen (8.00 g O). Therefore, the combining weight of M in this compound will be the atom's atomic weight. [*Recall:* A combining weight is the weight combined with 8.00 g oxygen.] If the formula is MO, the combining weight of M is twice its atomic weight; if MO_2, the combining weight is one fourth the atomic weight, and so on.

The procedure we follow in this method for determining atomic weights is the following.

(1) The relative weights of M and O in the oxide are determined precisely by experiment.

(2) The combining weight of M is calculated from the data. (Such a computation was described in Section 1–5 of this book.)

(3) The combining weight will be some whole-number fraction of the atomic weight ($\frac{1}{1}, \frac{1}{2}, \frac{1}{3}$, etc.), depending on its formula. To determine what this fraction is, the approximate atomic weight is computed by using the specific heat of the metal and the law of Dulong and Petit:

$$\text{approximate atomic weight} = \frac{6}{\text{specific heat}}$$

(4) The approximate atomic weight is divided by the combining weight, and the answer is expressed to the nearest whole number or whole-number fraction (1, $\frac{1}{2}, \frac{1}{3}, \frac{2}{3}$, etc.).

(5) The accurate atomic weight is the product of this fraction times the combining weight.

To illustrate how these operations are carried out, we elaborate on some of the examples given in the text in Section 1–8.

EXAMPLE.   An amount of 0.8662 g of lead combines with 0.1338 g of oxygen in forming a lead oxide. What is the atomic weight of lead? The specific heat of lead is 0.0308 cal g^{-1} deg^{-1}.

SOLUTION.

(1) Calculate the combining weight of lead.

$$\frac{0.8662 \text{ g Pb}}{0.1338 \text{ g O}} \times 8.000 \text{ g O} = 51.79 \text{ g Pb}$$

(2) Compute the approximate atomic weight of lead.

$$\text{approx. at. wt} = \frac{6 \text{ cal mole}^{-1} \text{ deg}^{-1}}{0.0308 \text{ cal g}^{-1} \text{ deg}^{-1}} = 200 \text{ g g-atom}^{-1} \text{ Pb}$$

(If you are concerned about the units in this calculation, read "A Revised Definition of a Mole" in Chapter 4.)

(3) Find what fraction the atomic weight is of the combining weight.

$$\frac{200}{51.79} \simeq 4$$

(4) The accurate atomic weight = 4 × (combining weight)

at. wt = 4(51.79) = **207.2 g g-atom^{-1} Pb**

We also can write the empirical formula for this oxide. We know that one fourth of an atomic weight is the combining weight. This means that one fourth of a gram-atom of Pb is combined with one half of a gram-atom of oxygen (one combining weight of oxygen = 8.00 g O = $\frac{1}{2}$ g-atom O). The formula must be $Pb_{1/4}O_{1/2} = Pb_{1/2}O = PbO_2$.

In the text, you were asked to show that if the formula for lead oxide is Pb_xO_y, the atomic weight of lead is (103.6) × (y/x). Dividing the coefficients by y gives the ratio of gram-atoms Pb to 1 g-atom O:

$$Pb_xO_y = Pb_{x/y}O$$

The combining weight of Pb is the weight that is combined with 8 g of O, that is, $\frac{1}{2}$ g-atom O. Therefore, if there are x/y g-atoms of Pb with 1 g-atom O, there will be $\frac{1}{2}(x/y)$ g-atom Pb with $\frac{1}{2}$ g-atom O. The combining weight of Pb = $\frac{1}{2}(x/y)$ (at. wt Pb).

In the preceding example, we found the combining weight of Pb to be 51.79. Therefore,

at. wt Pb = (51.79) (2) (x/y)
at. wt Pb = **(103.6) (x/y)**

EXAMPLE.   Silver oxide is 93.05% silver by weight. What is the atomic weight of silver? The specific heat of silver is 0.0557 cal g^{-1} deg^{-1}.

SOLUTION.   If we assume 100 g of oxide, 93.05 g Ag will be combined with 6.95 g oxygen (100 g oxide − 93.05 g Ag = 6.95 g O).

(1) Combining wt of Ag = $\dfrac{93.05 \text{ g Ag}}{6.95 \text{ g O}} \times (8.00 \text{ g O}) = 107 \text{ g}$

$$\text{(2) Approx. at. wt Ag} = \frac{6 \text{ cal mole}^{-1} \text{deg}^{-1}}{0.0557 \text{ cal g}^{-1} \text{deg}^{-1}} = 100 \text{ g mole}^{-1}$$

$$\text{(3)} \quad \frac{\text{approx. at. wt}}{\text{combining wt}} = \frac{100}{107} \simeq 1$$

$$\text{Accurate at. wt} = 1(107) = \textbf{107 g g-atom}^{-1} \textbf{ Ag}$$

The formula for the oxide must be Ag_2O because 1 g-atom Ag combined with 8 g O or $\frac{1}{2}$ g-atom O, that is, $AgO_{1/2} = Ag_2O$.

1–9 COMBINING CAPACITIES AND EMPIRICAL FORMULAS

This section answers, in part, the question of why only certain numbers of atoms combine to form molecules. That is, there are compounds PbO_2 and PbO, but why not PbO_3, Pb_2O_5, and so forth?

The simplest explanation by the early chemists was that a particular atom has only certain combining capacities. If an element has a combining capacity of one, it can combine only with one other atom with a combining capacity of one. An atom with a combining capacity of two can combine either with one atom having a combining capacity of two or else with two atoms, each of which has a combining capacity of one, and so on.

An early interpretation of the differences in the ability of an atom to combine was to picture each atom as having hooks. According to this picture, an atom A that has one hook can join its hook to only a single hook on another atom. Therefore, the combining capacity of this atom is one. If the atom has two hooks, its combining capacity is two, and so forth. When an atom combines (joins hooks) with another atom it is said to form a bond. Long ago, the concept of hooks was proven incorrect. Much of the early nomenclature is still used; however, it has been modified to fit the modern concepts of molecular structure.

As we shall see later, there are forces of interaction that hold atoms together in molecules. These forces are called *chemical bonds*. The number of bonds that an atom forms is called its *valence*. The terms *covalence* and *electrovalence* are used to distinguish between two types of chemical bonding forces. "Electrovalence" refers to the bonding in compounds made of atoms that are not neutral but carry electrical charges of opposite sign. Atoms that have electrical charges are called ions; therefore, electrovalent bonding sometimes is referred to as ionic bonding. When an atom's electrovalence is stated, the number and sign of the electrical charge is indicated. The electrovalent bond is treated in detail in Chapter 3 in *Chemical Principles*.

The combining capacity of hydrogen, the simplest atom, is one. In water (H_2O) it is obvious that the combining capacity of oxygen is two since it can bond to two hydrogen atoms. These two atoms have this combining capacity in all their compounds. Many elements display more than one combining capacity.

The assignment of a combining weight of 8.00 g to oxygen was based on the weight of oxygen equivalent in its combining capacity to 1.008 g of hydrogen. With these assignments, the combining capacity of any element will be the ratio between the atomic weight and the combining weight:

$$\text{combining capacity} = \frac{\text{atomic weight}}{\text{combining weight}}$$

EXAMPLE. Calculate the combining capacities of nitrogen and carbon in the following compounds: NH_3, NO_2, NO, N_2O, CH_4, CO_2, C_2H_6, C_2H_4, and C_2H_2. Use the combining weights in Table 1–2 from *Chemical Principles*. The atomic weights in these calculations are $H = 1$, $N = 14$, and $C = 12$.

SOLUTION.

$$NH_3: \frac{14}{4\frac{2}{3}} = \frac{14}{\frac{14}{3}} = 3$$

$$NO_2: \frac{14}{3\frac{1}{2}} = \frac{14}{\frac{7}{2}} = \frac{28}{7} = 4$$

$$NO: \frac{14}{7} = 2$$

$$N_2O: \frac{14}{14} = 1$$

$$CH_4 \text{ and } CO_2: \frac{12}{3} = 4$$

$$C_2H_6: \frac{12}{4} = 3$$

$$C_2H_4 \text{ and } CO: \frac{12}{6} = 2$$

$$C_2H_2: \frac{12}{12} = 1$$

Let us return to the early concept of atoms being held together by hooks. Each atom was thought to have at least one hook. When two atoms formed a molecule, they did so by joining hooks. The combining capacity of an atom was thought to indicate the number of hooks. The H atom had one hook, O had two hooks, and so forth. This concept applies quite well to the N—O compounds in the preceding example. If we represent the combining capacity as the number of hooks on each atom, H equals one hook, O equals two hooks, and N equals three, four, two, and one hook, as calculated.

There is a difference between the number of hooks as measured by the combining capacity and what we now call the *valence*, the number of bonds formed by an atom. This can be seen by looking at one of the carbon compounds, C_2H_4. The C in this compound has a combining capacity of two, that is, two hooks. Overall this appears to be reasonable: Two carbons, each with two hooks, have a total bonding capacity of four, which is what is required to satisfy the four H atoms' each having one hook. But two hooks on each carbon are not enough. One hook on each C must be used to hold the two C atoms together. This leaves only two hooks available to the four H atoms.

We know now that there are four hooks (chemical bonds) on each carbon atom in all the compounds in the example except CO; C in CO has three bonds. In C_2H_4, two bonds bind the two H atoms and two bind the two C atoms together. The term "valence" has since been applied to these forces and is defined as the number of bonds formed by an atom. Thus, the carbon atoms in the example are quadrivalent. With this distinction, valence and combining capacity are not necessarily the same.

This section in the text ends with examples of how empirical formulas can be calculated. We have discussed this as part of atomic weight determination in Section 1–8. It will be discussed again in more detail in Chapter 4.

CHAPTER 2 THE GAS LAWS AND THE ATOMIC THEORY

An understanding of the principles discussed in this chapter is essential to further study of chemistry. Knowledge of the relationships between the amount of a gas and its pressure, volume, and temperature is essential when observing chemical phenomena in the gas phase in the laboratory. Gas measurements also afford a means of obtaining valuable molecular weight information. The kinetic molecular theory explains the behavior of gases in considerable detail. We will see that, with appropriate modifications, this theory can explain the behavior of matter in the liquid and solid state as well. The understanding of the factors that determine the rates of chemical reactions (chemical kinetics) has its foundation in the kinetic molecular theory.

2-1 AVOGADRO'S LAW

Avogadro's law usually is stated in one of three ways. (1) At a given temperature and pressure, equal volumes of all gases contain the same number of molecules. (2) At the same temperature and pressure, equal volumes of all gases contain the same number of moles of gas. (3) The volume occupied by a gas at a fixed pressure and temperature is proportional to the number of moles of the gas present;

that is, $n = kV$, when P and T are constant; k is a proportionality constant, n the number of moles of gas, and V its volume.

2-2 THE PRESSURE OF A GAS

The force per unit area exerted by a gas is called the gas pressure, P. Although force is measured in units of dynes or g cm sec^{-2}, gas pressure commonly is measured by the length of a column of mercury that the gas is capable of supporting against the action of the forces of gravity. Air pressure at sea level is sufficient to support a column of mercury 760 mm high. This pressure (referred to as standard pressure) is equal to 1 atmosphere (atm) or 760 torr, where 1 torr = 1 mm of mercury pressure.

Let us calculate the force exerted by a gas at standard pressure. If we do this, we will be able to show that the length of the mercury column is adequate for measuring pressure since the length is directly proportional to the force.

$$\text{force} = \text{mass } (m) \times \text{acceleration } (a)$$

(See Problem 4 in the section on unit conversions in Part 1.)

At 1 atm, m is the mass of mercury in the column, and a is the acceleration attributed to gravity, 980.7 cm sec^{-2}. Since the force is distributed uniformly over the surface of the mercury, let us calculate the force over 1 cm^2. The mass of mercury will be that of a column of mercury exactly 1 cm^2 in cross section and 760 mm high.

$$m = (\text{density of Hg}) \times (\text{height}) \times (\text{area})$$
$$\text{force} = ma = (\text{density of Hg}) \times (\text{height}) \times (\text{area}) \times (\text{acceleration})$$
$$= (13.60 \text{ g cm}^{-3})(76.00 \text{ cm})(1.0000 \text{ cm}^2)(980.7 \text{ cm sec}^{-2})$$
$$= 1.013 \times 10^6 \text{ g cm sec}^{-2} \text{ or } 1.013 \times 10^6 \text{ dynes}$$
$$(1 \text{ g cm sec}^{-2} = 1 \text{ dyne})$$

This force, 1.013×10^6 dynes, is the force per unit area (1 cm^2) that corresponds to 1 atm. Therefore,

$$1 \text{ atm} = 1.013 \times 10^6 \text{ dynes cm}^{-2}$$

The density of Hg, the area (1 cm^2), and the acceleration of gravity all are fixed quantities; their product is a constant. Since the force = (a constant)(the height of the Hg column), we can express the pressure in terms of only the height of the mercury column.

Another way to express the pressure is in terms of the amount of matter that the gas supports when its pressure is exerted on a square centimeter of the mercury in a manometer. One atmosphere (atm) amounts to a pressure sufficient to support a 760 mm, or 76.0 cm, column of mercury.

$$1 \text{ atm} = (76.00 \text{ cm})(13.60 \text{ g cm}^{-3}) = 1033.6 \text{ g cm}^{-2}$$

That is, 1 atm pressure results from 1033.6 g Hg covering a 1-cm² area. In pounds per square inch,

$$1 \text{ atm} = (1033.6 \ \cancel{\text{g}} \ \cancel{\text{cm}^{-2}}) \left(\frac{1}{454} \text{ lb } \cancel{\text{g}^{-1}} \right) (2.54^2 \ \cancel{\text{cm}^2} \text{ in.}^{-2})$$

$$= 14.7 \text{ lb in.}^{-2}$$

2-3 BOYLE'S LAW RELATING PRESSURE AND VOLUME

For a given number of moles of gas at a constant temperature, the volume varies inversely as the pressure; that is,

$$PV = k$$

in which k is a constant. (This is not the same k as the one in Section 2–1.) If the pressure on a confined quantity of gas is doubled while the temperature is maintained constant, the volume is reduced by one half. Or, if the volume of a gas is doubled, the pressure decreases by one half, and so forth.

The text discusses the development of Boyle's law by a graphical interpretation of the experimental data. This interpretation is discussed in more detail in Appendix 2 of this study guide.

Suppose that you have a certain quantity of a gas at a particular temperature. The pressure–volume relationship of this gas must satisfy Boyle's law,

$$P_1 V_1 = k_1$$

Now suppose that the pressure on this gas is altered to a new value, P_2, while keeping the quantity of gas and the temperature the same. The volume of the gas must change to V_2; then

$$P_2 V_2 = k_2$$

Because the amount of gas and the temperature remain the same during the change, $k_1 = k_2$. Therefore,

$$P_1 V_1 = P_2 V_2$$

or

$$\frac{P_1}{P_2} = \frac{V_2}{V_1}$$

and

$$V_2 = V_1 \left(\frac{P_1}{P_2} \right) \quad \text{and} \quad P_2 = P_1 \left(\frac{V_1}{V_2} \right)$$

With these expressions we can calculate the PV relationships of a confined amount of a gas at constant temperature. However, there is no need to concern yourself with memorizing these formulas and running the risk of confusing the "sub one's" and "sub two's" in the notation.

EXAMPLE. A box contains 6.0 liters of a gas at 300 torr. What will be its volume at standard pressure? Temperature, T, and n, the number of moles of the gas, are maintained constant.

SOLUTION. We know from Boyle's law that the new volume V = (the old volume) × (a factor containing the two pressures). The question is what is the nature of this pressure factor? Is it

$$\frac{300 \text{ torr}}{760 \text{ torr}}$$

or is it

$$\frac{760 \text{ torr}}{300 \text{ torr}}$$

where 760 torr is standard pressure?

In changing the pressure from 300 torr to 760 torr, we increase the pressure; the volume should decrease according to the pressure ratio. Multiplication of the 6.0 liters by

$$\frac{760 \text{ torr}}{300 \text{ torr}}$$

will give a volume larger than 6 liters, which is obviously incorrect. The only other choice,

$$\frac{300 \text{ torr}}{760 \text{ torr}}$$

must be the correct one. We write

$$V = (6.0 \text{ liters}) \left(\frac{300 \text{ torr}}{760 \text{ torr}} \right) = ?$$

The problem is set up for easy solution with a slide rule.

$$V = \textbf{2.4 liters}$$

Let's try another.

EXAMPLE. Calculate the pressure in mm Hg exerted by a gas in a 1.00-liter container at 1.00 atm when the gas is allowed to expand into a 1.50-liter container at the same temperature.

SOLUTION. At constant temperature, an increase in volume results in a decrease in pressure; thus, we multiply the original pressure by the ratio of the two volumes that is less than one:

$$P = 1.00 \text{ atm (volume ratio)} = (1.00 \text{ atm}) \left(\frac{1.00 \text{ liter}}{1.50 \text{ liters}} \right)$$

$$= (0.666 \text{ atm}) = (0.666 \text{ atm}) \left(760 \frac{\text{mm Hg}}{\text{atm}} \right) = \textbf{506 mm Hg}$$

At a constant pressure, the volume of a given number of moles (n) of gas is directly proportional to the absolute temperature (T). Therefore,

$$V = kT$$

when n and P are constant and T is in degrees Kelvin; k is a different proportionality constant from the preceding ones.

For a fixed amount of gas at a constant pressure

$$V_1 = k_1 T_1 \quad \text{and} \quad k_1 = \frac{V_1}{T_1}$$

If the temperature is altered to a different value, T_2, and the pressure and amount of gas are kept constant, the volume will change to a new value, V_2, and

$$V_2 = k_2 T_2 \quad \text{and} \quad k_2 = \frac{V_2}{T_2}$$

For the same gas, by keeping n and P constant, $k_1 = k_2$, or

$$\frac{V_1}{T_1} = \frac{V_2}{T_2}$$

or

$$V_2 = V_1 \left(\frac{T_2}{T_1}\right) \quad \text{and} \quad T_2 = T_1 \left(\frac{V_2}{V_1}\right)$$

That is, $V_2 = V_1 \times$ (temperature factor) and $T_2 = T_1 \times$ (volume factor).

As before, the nature of the temperature or volume ratios can be determined as a logical consequence of Charles' law.

EXAMPLE. A 20.0-ml sample of a gas at 27°C is heated to 100°C at constant pressure. What is the resulting volume?

SOLUTION. The temperature must be expressed in degrees Kelvin:

$$T_1(°K) = t(°C) + 273 = 27 + 273 = 300°K$$
$$T_2(°K) = 100 + 273 = 373°K$$

The resulting volume, V_2, will be equal to the initial volume, V_1, times a factor expressed as a ratio of the absolute temperatures. In going from 300°K to 373°K, the temperature is increased; therefore, the volume must also increase. Of the two possible temperature ratios,

$$\left(\frac{373}{300}\right) \quad \text{and} \quad \left(\frac{300}{373}\right)$$

only multiplication by the first ratio will give a larger volume; therefore,

$$V_2 = 20.0 \text{ ml}\left(\frac{373°\text{K}}{300°\text{K}}\right) = 24.9 \text{ ml}$$

EXAMPLE.   What is the resulting gas temperature if 5.00×10^2 ml of a gas at 27°C is allowed to expand into a volume of 10.0×10^3 ml at constant pressure?

SOLUTION.   Charles' law indicates that the increase in volume at constant pressure must be accompanied by an increase in temperature. Therefore, to effect the expansion, the gas must be heated.

$$T_2 = T_1 \text{ (volume factor)} = (273 + 27)°\text{K} \times \left(\frac{10.0 \times 10^3 \text{ ml}}{5.00 \times 10^2 \text{ ml}}\right)$$
$$= (3.00 \times 10^2)(20.0) = 6.00 \times 10^3°\text{K}$$
$$= 6000 - 273 = 5727°\text{C}$$

GAS THERMOMETERS

It is appropriate here to expand the text's reference to the greater accuracy available from gas thermometers. From Charles' law, $V = kT$. The volume of a gas is directly proportional to the absolute temperature. Hence, the volume of a gas can be used as an indication of temperature. One advantage in using the volume of a gas to measure temperature is that the proportionality constant for the volume expansion for all gases is practically the same. This is not true for liquids. The volume change that mercury undergoes when subjected to a 1-degree temperature change is different from the change in volume that alcohol experiences for the same change in temperature. If a thermometer scale is defined by having a liquid thermometer as a reference, the liquid must be specified. This is not necessary for a gas except at abnormally low temperatures.

Another disadvantage complicates the use of liquid thermometers for precise temperature measurements. The volume of a liquid does not vary linearly with temperature. The volume change experienced by mercury when its temperature is increased from 25°C to 26°C is not the same as its volume change when its temperature is increased from 90°C to 91°C. In calibrating a mercury thermometer, for example, it is usually placed in an ice–water bath and the 0°C position located. Then it is placed in boiling water and the 100°C position noted. The distance between the 0° and 100° marks is divided into 100 equal units. However, the temperature required to advance the mercury column one of these graduations at the low end of the scale is different from the temperature required at the high end of the scale. As a consequence, any temperature reading between 0°C and 100°C is in error. (For most experiments, the errors are not large enough to affect the validity of temperature measurement with liquid thermometers.) The change in volume of a gas, however, is a linear function of the temperature.

The equation for the combined gas law is

$$PV = nRT$$

in which R is the gas constant. You will find many occasions to use this expression, so it will be convenient for you to know a value for R. Solving the ideal gas law for R gives

$$R = \frac{PV}{nT}$$

If we know the P, V, and T values for a particular amount of gas, we can calculate R from this expression. You may recall this information: At standard conditions, 1 mole of any gas occupies 22.4 liters. Substituting these values into the ideal gas law and solving for R yields

$$R = \frac{(1.00 \text{ atm})(22.4 \text{ liters})}{(1.00 \text{ mole})(273°K)} = 0.0820 \text{ liter atm mole}^{-1} \text{ deg}^{-1}$$

The units of R are important. We could have evaluated R as follows and obtained a different numerical value.

$$R = \frac{(760 \text{ torr})(22.4 \times 10^3 \text{ ml})}{(1.00 \text{ mole})(273°K)} = 6.23 \times 10^4 \text{ torr ml mole}^{-1} \text{ deg}^{-1}$$

You should memorize a value for R and its units so you can use the ideal gas law. We will use $R = 0.0820$ liter atm mole^{-1} deg^{-1} in the examples in this study guide.

EXAMPLE. What will be the volume occupied by 0.276 g of Cl_2 at 640 torr and 25°C? Use $PV = nRT$ to solve this problem.

SOLUTION. If we use $R = 0.0820$ liter atm mole^{-1} deg^{-1}, the volume must be expressed in liters, the pressure in atmospheres, the amount of gas in moles, and the temperature in degrees Kelvin. Substitute the data into the ideal gas law and solve for V.

$$PV = nRT$$

$$\left(\frac{640 \text{ torr}}{760 \text{ torr atm}^{-1}}\right) \times (V \text{ liters}) = \left(\frac{0.276 \text{ g } Cl_2}{71.0 \text{ g mole}^{-1}}\right)$$

$$\times \left(0.0820 \frac{\text{liter atm}}{\text{mole °K}}\right) \times ((273 + 25)°K)$$

$$V = \frac{\left(\frac{0.276}{71.0} \text{ mole } Cl_2\right) \times \left(0.0820 \frac{\text{liter atm}}{\text{mole °K}}\right) \times (298°K)}{\left(\frac{640}{760} \text{ atm}\right)}$$

$$= \frac{(0.276)(0.0820)(298)(760)}{(71.0)(640)} = \textbf{0.113 liter}$$

[*Note:* When doing this problem, we have carried the numbers to the end and arranged them in one single equation for the solution. This expression is in a form that is solved readily on a slide rule.]

If we used 6.23×10^4 torr ml mole^{-1} deg^{-1} to represent R, the calculation would have been somewhat easier.

$$V = \frac{nRT}{P} = \frac{\left(\dfrac{0.276 \, \cancel{g}}{71.0 \, \cancel{g \, mole^{-1}}}\right)\left(6.23 \times 10^4 \, \dfrac{\cancel{torr} \, ml}{\cancel{mole} \, °K}\right)(298 \, °K)}{640 \, \cancel{torr}}$$

$$= \frac{(0.276)(6.23 \times 10^4)(298)}{(71.0)(640)} = 113 \text{ ml or } 0.113 \text{ liter}$$

Often we want to determine either the volume, pressure, or temperature of a fixed amount of gas after P, V, or T changes have occurred. Initially,

$$P_1V_1 = nRT_1 \quad \text{or} \quad \frac{P_1V_1}{T_1} = nR$$

After the PVT values change to State 2,

$$P_2V_2 = nRT_2 \quad \text{or} \quad \frac{P_2V_2}{T_2} = nR$$

Since R and the number of moles, n, are constant,

$$\frac{P_1V_1}{T_1} = \frac{P_2V_2}{T_2}$$

which gives the following expressions relating P, V, and T:

$$P_2 = P_1\left(\frac{V_1}{V_2}\right)\left(\frac{T_2}{T_1}\right) \quad V_2 = V_1\left(\frac{P_1}{P_2}\right)\left(\frac{T_2}{T_1}\right) \quad T_2 = T_1\left(\frac{P_2}{P_1}\right)\left(\frac{V_2}{V_1}\right)$$

Again, rather than contend with the formulas, it is preferable to apply the simple laws of Boyle and Charles to problems of this type.

EXAMPLE. A 200-ml (V_1) sample of a gas measured at 273°C and 5.00 atm is placed in a container that is maintained at a temperature of 150°C and a pressure of 2.00 atm. What is the volume of the container?

SOLUTION. Since the gas will fill the container, the volume of the gas (V_2) is equal to the volume of the container (V).

$$V = V_2 = V_1 \times (\text{pressure factor}) \times (\text{temperature factor})$$

We can consider the pressure and temperature effects separately when evaluating the two factors. The pressure is decreased from 5.00 atm to 2.00 atm. Therefore, the volume should increase by the factor

$$\left(\frac{5.00 \text{ atm}}{2.00 \text{ atm}}\right); \text{ that is, } \frac{P_1}{P_2}$$

The temperature has been lowered from 273°C (546°K) to 150°C (423°K), so the volume will be decreased by the factor

$$\left(\frac{423°K}{546°K}\right); \text{ that is, } \frac{T_2}{T_1}$$

Therefore,

$$V = (200 \text{ ml}) \left(\frac{5.00 \text{ atm}}{2.00 \text{ atm}}\right) \left(\frac{423°K}{546°K}\right) = \textbf{388 ml}$$

which gives the same result as if we had substituted into the equation $V_2 = V_1(P_1/P_2)(T_2/T_1)$.

MOLECULAR WEIGHT DETERMINATIONS

We illustrated how molecular weights might be determined by gas density measurements in Section 1–7. In those examples, the density of the gas at 0°C and 1 atm was used in the $M = kD$ expression. In practice, the gas density seldom is measured at STP. Not only is it too difficult to maintain these conditions during the experiment, but many substances that are gases at higher temperatures or lower pressures will condense to liquids at standard conditions. The following example illustrates how gas density molecular weights are calculated from practical laboratory measurements.

EXAMPLE. A glass bulb having a volume of 250.0 ml weighs 25.2341 g when it is empty. When filled with a vapor at 100°C and 624 torr, it weighs 26.2761 g. What is the molecular weight of the vapor?

SOLUTION.

$$PV = nRT$$

$$n = \frac{PV}{RT} = \frac{\left(\frac{624 \text{ torr}}{760 \text{ torr atm}^{-1}}\right)\left(\frac{250.0 \text{ ml}}{1000 \text{ ml liter}^{-1}}\right)}{(0.0820 \text{ liter atm mole}^{-1}°K^{-1})(273 + 100)°K}$$

$$= \frac{(624)(0.2500)}{(760)(0.0820)(373)} = 6.71 \times 10^{-3} \text{ mole}$$

The weight of the vapor equal to the weight of the filled bulb minus the weight of the empty bulb is $26.2761 - 25.2341 = 1.0420$ g

$$\text{mol wt of the gas} = \frac{1.0420 \text{ g}}{6.71 \times 10^{-3} \text{ mole}} = \textbf{155 g mole}^{-1}$$

Or, if we wished to do the entire calculation in one step on the slide rule, the setup would be as follows. (The units have not been included. For practice, why don't you confirm the consistency of the units in the expression?)

Recall that the number of moles

$$n = \frac{\text{wt in g}}{\text{g mol wt in g mole}^{-1}} = \frac{W}{M}$$

$$PV = nRT = \left(\frac{W}{M}\right) RT$$

$$M = \frac{WRT}{PV} = \frac{(1.0420)(0.0820)(373)(760)}{(624)(0.2500)} = \textbf{155 g mole}^{-1}$$

2–6 KINETIC MOLECULAR THEORY OF GASES

This theory pictures a gas as consisting of molecules in continuous motion. The molecules move in a straight line until they undergo a collision with each other or with the walls of the container. These collisions are perfectly elastic; that is, there is no loss of energy upon collision although there is a transfer of momentum. The transfer of a portion of a molecule's momentum to the walls of the container is responsible for the pressure displayed by a gas. The gas molecules travel at all velocities. However, there is a distribution of the velocities such that many more molecules are traveling with a velocity near the average rather than at the extremes. The theory predicts (see the derivation in Section 2–6 of *Chemical Principles* and the discussion of this derivation in this section of the study guide) that the absolute temperature of a gas is proportional to the average kinetic energy, $\frac{1}{2} m\overline{v^2}$, of the gas molecules. (The bar over v^2 indicates an average.) Increasing the temperature raises the average velocity of a gas by increasing the proportion of the molecules that have the higher velocities.

The derivation presented in Section 2–6 of the text is one example of how kinetic molecular theory supports the observed behavior of gases. The significance of the constant in Boyle's law is shown. The relationship between the temperature and the kinetic energy of the gas molecules also is derived. These are extremely important relationships.

Some elementary physics and vector algebra has been applied in the derivation. You probably will find your mathematics background sufficient to follow the derivation satisfactorily. However, if you find it unusually difficult to follow some steps, don't despair. Appendix 3 describes the resolution of three component vectors, which, together with Figure 2–9 in *Chemical Principles*, can clarify the vector algebra employed by the authors. You do not need a complete understanding of each step in the derivation to realize the significance of the result. You can deduce the significance from Equation 2–20 in *Chemical Principles*. From this equation,

$$PV = \tfrac{1}{3}Nm\overline{v^2} = \tfrac{2}{3}N \times \tfrac{1}{2}m\overline{v^2}$$

it can be shown that the PV product of a gas is proportional to the average kinetic energy per mole of the gas molecules, $Nm\overline{v^2}/2$. Since we know from experiment that for 1 mole of a gas $PV = RT$, it follows that

$$RT = \tfrac{2}{3}N \times \tfrac{1}{2}m\overline{v^2} \quad \text{or} \quad RT = \tfrac{2}{3}E_k$$

in which E_k represents the average kinetic energy of a mole of the gas and R is the gas constant. The conclusion is that the absolute temperature of a gas is solely dependent on and directly proportional to the average kinetic energy of the gas molecules.

UNITS OF THE GAS CONSTANT, R

If $R = \frac{2}{3}(E_k/T)$, then R should have units of energy deg^{-1} mole^{-1}. Ergs, calories, or joules are units that one generally associates with energy. You may not have recognized that "liter atmosphere" is actually a measure of energy. We shall show here that "liter atmosphere" is a measure of energy and find its equivalent in some of the more familiar energy units.

$$\text{pressure} \times \text{volume} = (\text{force}/\text{area})(\text{area} \times \text{length})$$
$$= \text{force} \times \text{length}$$

Work or energy is defined as the product of force and distance. Therefore, we see that PV does have the units of energy. To express R in ergs, joules, and calories, we use the following relationships:

1 erg = 1 dyne cm
1 joule = 10^7 ergs
1 erg = 2.39×10^{-8} cal

In Section 2–2, we showed that 1 atm = 1.013×10^6 dynes cm^{-2}. Of course, 1 liter is 10^3 cm^3.

$$1 \text{ liter atm} = (10^3 \text{ cm}^3)(1.013 \times 10^6 \text{ dynes cm}^{-2})$$
$$= 1.013 \times 10^9 \text{ dynes cm}$$
$$= 1.013 \times 10^9 \text{ dynes cm} \left(1 \frac{\text{erg}}{\text{dyne cm}}\right)$$
$$= 1.013 \times 10^9 \text{ ergs}$$
$$R = \left(0.08205 \frac{\text{liter atm}}{\text{mole deg}}\right) \times \left(\frac{1.013 \times 10^9 \text{ ergs}}{\text{liter atm}}\right)$$
$$= 8.312 \times 10^7 \text{ ergs mole}^{-1} \text{ deg}^{-1}$$
$$R = \left(8.312 \times 10^7 \frac{\text{ergs}}{\text{mole deg}}\right) \times \left(\frac{1 \text{ joule}}{10^7 \text{ ergs}}\right)$$
$$= 8.312 \text{ joules mole}^{-1} \text{ deg}^{-1}$$
$$R = \left(8.312 \times 10^7 \frac{\text{ergs}}{\text{mole deg}}\right) \times \left(2.39 \times 10^{-8} \frac{\text{cal}}{\text{erg}}\right)$$
$$= 1.987 \text{ cal mole}^{-1} \text{ deg}^{-1}$$

2–7 PREDICTIONS OF THE KINETIC MOLECULAR THEORY

We can use the kinetic molecular theory to predict the size and speeds of gas molecules.

MOLECULAR SIZE

Kinetic theory treats gas molecules as if they were points. Although molecules are not points, they are indeed small relative to the space that they occupy. For example, the volume occupied by a CO_2 molecule in solid carbon dioxide is 47.0 Å^3. In the gas state, the volume occupied by a CO_2 molecule is 36,800 Å^3. Let us assume that the volume occupied by a CO_2 molecule in solid carbon dioxide is representative of the volume of a single CO_2 molecule. The space occupied by a CO_2 molecule in the gaseous state is only

$$\left(\frac{47.0 \text{ Å}^3}{36,800 \text{ Å}^3}\right) = \frac{1}{800}$$

of the volume available.

MOLECULAR SPEEDS

Not all molecules of a gas move at the same velocity at a particular temperature. Figure 2–1 shows a typical distribution of the velocities at various temperatures. An important thing to notice in looking at these

Figure 2–1.   The distribution of speeds among molecules in nitrogen gas at three different temperatures.

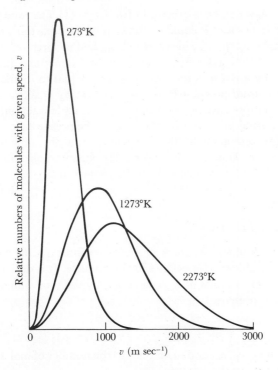

curves is that, at any given temperature, there is a large fraction of the molecules with velocities corresponding to the maximum in the curve. This velocity, since more molecules have it than any other, is called the *most probable velocity*. The most probable velocity, the arithmetical average velocity, and the root-mean-square average velocity are not the same, but they generally do not vary much from one another. As the temperature is increased, the distribution of velocities changes. The most probable velocity increases, and the fraction of molecules with higher velocities increases at the expense of molecules with lower velocities. For example, compare the relative fraction of molecules having a velocity of 500 m sec^{-1} at 273°K with the ones having this velocity in a gas at 1273°K (Figure 2–1).

Equation 2–21 in *Chemical Principles* shows that the average kinetic energy is proportional to the square of the average velocity of the molecules:

$$E_k = \tfrac{1}{2} N m \overline{v^2}$$

As Figure 2–1 illustrates, when the temperature is increased, the proportion of the molecules with higher kinetic energies is increased. We will have more to say about this relationship between the temperature and the distribution of molecular velocities when we discuss vapor pressures of liquids and solids and the rates of chemical reactions.

DALTON'S LAW OF PARTIAL PRESSURES

Dalton's law can be expressed in two ways. (1) The total pressure P_T of a mixture of gases is equal to the sum of their partial pressures: $P_T = p_A + p_B + p_C + \dots$, in which p_A, p_B, and so forth refer to the partial pressures of the gases A, B, and so on, in the mixture. (2) The pressure exerted by a gas in a mixture of gases is equal to its mole fraction X_A times the total pressure P_T of the mixture: $p_A = X_A P_T$, in which p_A is the partial pressure of gas A and X_A is its mole fraction.

The partial pressure of a gas refers to the pressure that the gas would exert if it were alone in the same container at the same temperature as the mixture. Dalton's law reflects the kinetic molecular theory in its assumption that molecules in a gas behave independently of one another.

THE MOLE FRACTION

The mole fraction, X_A, of A in a mixture indicates the fraction of A in the total number of molecules in the mixture. It is derived by dividing the number of moles of A present, n_A, by the total number of moles of molecules present.

$$X_A = \frac{n_A}{n_A + n_B + n_C + \dots}$$

in which n_A, n_B, n_C, and so on refer to the number of moles of each of the components in the mixture.

EXAMPLE. A solution consists of a mixture of 4.00 g H_2O, 2.30 g ethyl alcohol (C_2H_5OH), and 0.117 g NaCl. What is the mole fraction of NaCl present?

SOLUTION.

$$X_{NaCl} = \frac{n_{NaCl}}{n_{H_2O} + n_{C_2H_5OH} + n_{NaCl}}$$

$$n_{NaCl} = \frac{0.117 \text{ g NaCl}}{58.5 \text{ g mole}^{-1}} = 0.00200 \text{ mole of NaCl}$$

$$n_{H_2O} = \frac{4.00 \text{ g } H_2O}{18.0 \text{ g mole}^{-1}} = 0.222 \text{ mole } H_2O$$

$$n_{C_2H_5OH} = \frac{2.30 \text{ g } C_2H_5OH}{46.0 \text{ g mole}^{-1}} = 0.0500 \text{ mole } C_2H_5OH$$

$$X_{NaCl} = \frac{2.00 \times 10^{-3}}{0.222 + 0.0500 + 0.00200} = \frac{2.00 \times 10^{-3}}{2.74 \times 10^{-1}}$$

$$= 7.30 \times 10^{-3}$$

VAPOR PRESSURE

As we shall see later, whenever a liquid is placed in a container, some of the molecules will leave the liquid and occupy the container as gas molecules. This process is called *vaporization* or *evaporation*. The extent to which vaporization progresses is determined by the temperature. Since the vaporized liquid is a gas, it will exert a pressure. This pressure, called the vapor pressure of the liquid, is dependent on the temperature and the nature of the liquid. When liquid and vapor are in equilibrium at 25°C, the vapor pressure of water is 23.76 mm and the vapor pressure of mercury is 0.002 mm.

In the laboratory, gases often are collected by displacing a liquid such as water or mercury from a container. Under such conditions, the collected gas will include vapors of the liquid at the liquid's equilibrium vapor pressure. At normal temperatures, the vapor pressure of mercury is so small that its presence usually is neglected. Corrections for the presence of water vapor are generally necessary in such measurements.

EXAMPLE. When 2.000 g of solid are heated, the solid liberates an unknown gas and 1.806 g of solid residue remains. This gas is collected over water in an apparatus similar to the one in Figure 2–13 of *Chemical Principles*. The volume of gas in the container at 640 torr and 23°C is 200 ml. What is the molecular weight of the unknown gas liberated from the solid? The equilibrium vapor pressure of water at 23°C is 19.8 torr.

Predictions of the
Kinetic Molecular
Theory

SOLUTION. The weight of the gas collected is 2.000 g − 1.806 g = 0.194 g. From Dalton's law, $P_T = p_{gas} + p_{H_2O}$.

pressure of unknown gas = $p_{gas} = P_T - p_{H_2O} = 640 - 19.8$

$$= 620 \text{ torr}$$

$$PV = nRT$$

$$\left(\frac{620 \text{ torr}}{760 \text{ torr atm}^{-1}}\right)\left(\frac{200 \text{ ml}}{1000 \text{ ml liter}^{-1}}\right)$$

$$= \left(\frac{0.194 \text{ g}}{M \text{ g mole}^{-1}}\right)\left(0.0820 \frac{\text{liter atm}}{\text{mole deg}}\right)((273 + 23) \text{ deg})$$

$$M = \text{molecular weight} = \frac{(0.194)(0.0820)(296)(760)}{(620)(0.200)}$$

$$= 28.9 \text{ g mole}^{-1}$$

EXAMPLE. One liter of a gas sample contains a mixture of xenon and water vapor. The temperature and the pressure of the mixture are 20°C and 200 torr. The gas mixture is passed through a drying agent that removes all the water vapor. The xenon remaining in the flask exerts a pressure of 107.5 torr at 20°C. How many grams of H_2O and how many grams of Xe were in the mixture?

SOLUTION.

$$PV = n_t RT$$

in which $n_t = $ moles Xe + moles $H_2O(g)$

$$n_t = \frac{PV}{RT}$$

$$= \frac{(200 \text{ torr})(1.00 \text{ liter})}{(760 \text{ torr atm}^{-1})(0.0820 \text{ liter atm mole}^{-1} \,^\circ K^{-1}(293 \,^\circ K)}$$
$$= 0.0110 \text{ mole of Xe and } H_2O$$

From Dalton's law,

$$p_{Xe} = X_{Xe} P_T$$

in which $P_T = $ the total pressure of the mixture

$$X_{Xe} = \frac{p_{Xe}}{P_T}$$

$$= \frac{107.5}{200.0} = 0.538$$

Since the fraction of the total number of moles is the mole fraction X,

$$n_{Xe} = X_{Xe} n_t$$
$$= 0.538(0.0110)$$
$$= 0.00592 \text{ mole Xe}$$

$$n_{H_2O} = n_t - n_{Xe} = 0.0110 - 0.00592 = 0.0051 \text{ mole } H_2O$$

wt Xe $= (5.92 \times 10^{-3} \text{ mole Xe})(131 \text{ g mole}^{-1}) = \textbf{0.776 g}$

wt $H_2O = (5.1 \times 10^{-3} \text{ mole } H_2O)(18.0 \text{ g mole}^{-1}) = \textbf{0.092 g}$

As part of the discussion of Dalton's law of partial pressures in Section 2-7 in *Chemical Principles*, an example problem was presented. This problem concerned a gas mixture consisting of 50% He and 50% Xe by weight at a total pressure of 600 torr at 100°C. The calculations showed that the partial pressures of the two gases were $p_{He} = 582$ torr and $p_{Xe} = 18$ torr.

There was no need to specify the volume in this problem for two reasons: (1) The molecules in the gas are distributed uniformly; as a result, the mole fractions of Xe and He are the same throughout; (2) The pressure, which measures the force per unit area exerted by a gas, is the same throughout the gas; that is, a 500-ml sample of the gas will have the same pressure as a 2-liter portion of the same gas at the same temperature. Consequently, any arbitrary sample of the gas has the same P_T, p_{Xe}, and p_{He}.

If the mixture of Xe and He is heated, it will expand. If the same total pressure is maintained during the expansion, the partial pressures exerted by the two gases will be the same at the high temperature as at the low temperature. The total number of gas molecules in a unit volume is less at the high temperature, but the proportion of Xe and He (their mole fractions) will remain constant. Should the expansion be prevented by confining the mixture of gases to a fixed volume, the pressure will increase as the temperature is increased. In this instance, the partial pressures of the gases will be increased proportionally.

EXAMPLE. A second example problem in Section 2–7 in *Chemical Principles* involves a calculation of the number of moles of oxygen gas collected at 25°C by displacing water from a gas-collecting bottle. The 1750 ml of oxygen and water vapor contained in the bottle exerted a total pressure equal to that of the external atmosphere, 760 torr or 1 atm. The partial pressure of O_2 (736.2 torr) was determined from Dalton's law, $P_T = 760$ torr $= p_{O_2} - p_{H_2O}$, where $p_{H_2O} = 23.8$ torr at 25°C. The number of moles of O_2 in the bottle was calculated, with the ideal gas law, to be 0.0694.

The question then was asked: "What would the answer have been had the pressure of water vapor been neglected?"

SOLUTION. To answer this, assume 1 atm to be the pressure of oxygen instead of being the total pressure of the O_2 and the H_2O vapor.

$$n = \frac{PV}{RT} = \frac{(1\,\cancel{atm})\ \dfrac{1750\,\cancel{ml}}{1000\,\cancel{ml\,liter^{-1}}}}{(0.0820\,\cancel{liter\,atm}\,mole^{-1}\,°K^{-1})(298°K)}$$

$$= \frac{(1.00)(1.750)}{(1000)(0.0820)(298)} = \mathbf{0.0716\ mole}$$

Note: The error introduced by neglecting the presence of water vapor in the gas mixture is

$$\frac{0.0716 - 0.0694}{0.0694} \times 100 = \frac{0.0022}{0.0694} \times 100 = 3.2\%$$

Graham's law involves the rate of diffusion of two gases. The rate is tested experimentally by measuring the time it takes for a given amount of gas to diffuse through a small orifice. If conditions are such that the gas molecules pass through the hole as they move randomly through the gas, we can state that, at the same temperature and pressure, the average kinetic energies of two gases, A and B, are given by Equation 2–25 in *Chemical Principles.*

$$\text{For gas A: } T_A = \frac{M_A \overline{v_A^2}}{3R}$$

$$\text{For gas B: } T_B = \frac{M_B \overline{v_B^2}}{3R}$$

in which M equals the molecular weight of the gas and $\overline{v^2}$ equals the square of the average velocity of the gas molecules.

In the Graham's law experiment, the same apparatus is used to compare the rates of diffusion of each gas at the same temperature; that is, $T_A = T_B$. Therefore,

$$\frac{M_A \overline{v_A^2}}{3R} = \frac{M_B \overline{v_B^2}}{3R}$$

$$\frac{\overline{v_A}}{\overline{v_B}} = \left(\frac{M_B}{M_A}\right)^{1/2}$$

Since the rate of diffusion will depend directly on the molecules' velocity,

$$\frac{\text{the rate of diffusion of A}}{\text{the rate of diffusion of B}} = \left(\frac{M_B}{M_A}\right)^{1/2}$$

Graham observed such diffusion behavior and stated his law: At the same temperature, the rates of diffusion of two gases vary inversely as the square roots of their densities or molecular weights. Gas diffusion measurements can be used to determine molecular weights.

EXAMPLE. In a Graham's law experiment performed at 50°C, it takes 7.56 sec for 1 liter of a gas to diffuse through the orifice of the apparatus. In the same apparatus, at the same pressure and temperature it takes 10.0 sec for 1 liter of N_2 gas to diffuse through the orifice. What is the molecular weight of gas A?

SOLUTION. The rates of diffusion of the two gases are

$$\text{rate}_A = \frac{1 \text{ liter}}{7.56 \text{ sec}} \qquad \text{rate}_{N_2} = \frac{1 \text{ liter}}{10.0 \text{ sec}}$$

Substitute in the Graham's law expression:

$$\frac{\text{rate}_A}{\text{rate}_B} = \left(\frac{M_B}{M_A}\right)^{1/2}$$

$$\frac{1 \text{ liter}/7.56 \text{ sec}}{1 \text{ liter}/10.0 \text{ sec}} = \left(\frac{28.0 \frac{\text{g}}{\text{mole}^{-1}\text{N}_2}}{M_\text{A}}\right)^{1/2}$$

$$\frac{10.0}{7.56} = \left(\frac{28.0}{M_\text{A}}\right)^{1/2}$$

$$1.32 = \left(\frac{28.0}{M_\text{A}}\right)^{1/2}$$

$$M_\text{A} = \left(\frac{28.0}{(1.32)^2}\right) = \textbf{16.1 g mole}^{-1}$$

2–8 REAL GASES DEVIATE FROM THE IDEAL GAS LAW

The ideal gas law states that $PV/RT = n$. For 1 mole of an ideal gas, $PV/RT = 1$. A plot of the term PV/RT (the compressibility coefficient, Z) against P for 1 mole of a gas should give a straight line at $Z = 1$ that is parallel to the P axis. As Figures 2–2 and 2–3 show, both negative and positive deviations from this behavior are observed. In deriving the ideal gas law, we make two basic assumptions: (1) The actual volume of a gas molecule is so small that it can be treated as a point; (2) the gas molecules are inert bodies that do not attract one another. These properties are not characteristic of all gases under all conditions; the result is the observed deviation from the ideal gas law.

Real gas molecules have forces of attraction for one another. This characteristic causes the molecules to come closer together and to reduce the volume more than is predicted for an ideal gas. The volume

Figure 2–2. Deviations from the ideal gas law for several gases at 273°K in terms of the compressibility factor $Z = PV/RT$ and gas pressure.

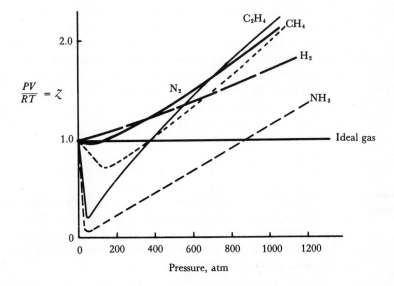

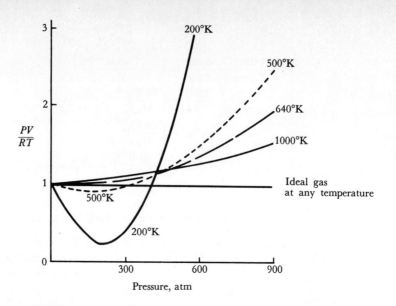

Figure 2–3. PV/RT plotted against P for 1 mole *of methane gas at several temperatures.*

contraction is responsible for the low PV/RT values and makes the compressibility curves drop below $Z = 1$. As the pressure is increased, molecules are brought closer together. This increases the forces of attraction. These forces are principally electrostatic in nature; they tend to become stronger as the distance between the molecules decreases. The molecules eventually will come close enough to touch one another. No longer is there any free space into which the molecules can move; hence, a minimum in the compressibility curve is reached. The volume remains essentially constant after this point. As the pressure is increased, the PV/RT value steadily increases in a manner that is essentially linear, as shown in Figure 2–3.

The minimum in the compressibility curve can be reduced or removed completely by increasing the temperature. This procedure increases the velocity of the gas molecules and reduces the effect of the attractive forces. There is a temperature, called the Boyle temperature, for a gas. At or above this temperature, the compressibility factors for a gas are all equal to or greater than one. As shown in Figure 2–3, the Boyle temperature for methane is 640°C.

Several other important principles relating to real gas behavior are illustrated in Figures 2–2 and 2–3. Note the magnitude of the pressure scale. On this scale, 1 atm is nearly coincident with the Z axis. The curves of all the gases appear to meet at this point. In the range of 1 to 2 atm, the compressibility curves deviate only slightly from the $Z = 1$ line, which is characteristic of ideal gas behavior. We can conclude that at this pressure and at temperatures of 25°C or more, gases follow a behavior similar to the one outlined by the ideal gas law. However, we must qualify this statement.

Observe the abrupt drop in the curve for NH_3 and the small minima in the curves for H_2 and CH_4. There is obviously a good chance that NH_3 will vary appreciably from ideal behavior even at 1 or 2 atm. Certainly NH_3 will not follow the ideal gas law as well as CH_4 and H_2. We can make an obvious generalization from Figure 2–2. Since the depression in the compressibility curve is due to the existence of attractive forces between molecules, in some gases (such as H_2 and, to a lesser extent, CH_4) these forces are very small. In other gases, like NH_3, these forces may be quite strong. The ideal gas law is reasonably accurate in calculations involving many gases at 1 to 2 torr, at room temperature or higher. However, there are some gases in which the intramolecular attractions are so great that the ideal gas law is likely to produce erroneous results.

Equations of state for real gases have been developed. Usually these are modifications of the ideal gas law. One such equation of state is van der Waals'

$$\left(P + \frac{na}{V^2}\right)\left(V - nb\right) = nRT$$

or, for 1 mole of a gas,

$$\left(P + \frac{a}{V^2}\right)\left(V - b\right) = RT$$

The a/V^2 term is added to the observed pressure. It compensates for the attractive forces between the molecules being less than the observed pressure given by the ideal gas. The b term is related to the volume occupied by the molecules of the gas. Because other molecules cannot occupy this "excluded" volume, the b term is subtracted from the observed volume of the gas. The result should be the volume in which the molecules are free to move (the free volume). We can compute b, the excluded volume. Figure 2–4 illustrates how the presence of one molecule

Figure 2–4. A sketch showing how the center of one molecule of radius r and diameter d cannot come any closer to the center of another molecule than its molecular diameter d, where d = 2r. The volume around each molecule from which other molecules are excluded is then $\frac{4}{3} \pi d^3$.

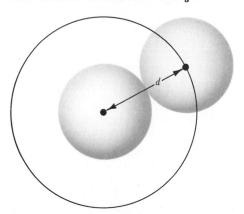

with a radius r excludes from any other molecule a volume equal to a sphere with a radius of $2r$. Twice the radius of the molecule, $2r$, is equal to its diameter, d. For a collection of molecules, half of them will exclude this volume from the other half, so the total excluded volume in a mole of gas is

$$\frac{N}{2}\left(\tfrac{4}{3}\pi d^3\right) = \tfrac{2}{3}N\pi d^3 = b$$

One application of van der Waals' equation is to measure the PVT for a given gas. Values for a and b (which fit the data) are determined empirically (from equations or graphs). The value for b is used to compute the radius of the gas molecule. The radii of atoms that have been determined in this way are referred to as van der Waals' gas radii.

CHAPTER 3 MATTER WITH A CHARGE

A major portion of Chapter 3 in *Chemical Principles* is devoted to the evidence from which Arrhenius and other chemists proved the existence of ions. To derive a thorough understanding of this chapter, first you should read it through once to develop an historical perspective of the subject. Then reread the chapter more slowly. Concentrate on those principles that have further application in your studies. In this chapter, we apply ionic theory to chemistry in an effort to emphasize the principles in the text. We will not be concerned with confirmation of the theory of ionization; rather, we will accept as fact that ions exist. We will recognize that some solids are comprised of ions that dissociate when the solid dissolves in a solvent such as water. There are also some compounds that do not exist as ions in the pure state; but when they dissolve, they react with the solvent to produce ions in the solution. The so-called mineral acids, HNO_3, HCl, H_3PO_4, and H_2SO_4, are examples of this type of substance.

3-1 ELECTROLYSIS

Electrolysis is carried out in an electrolysis cell. A schematic drawing of such a cell is shown in Figure 3–1. Two inert metal

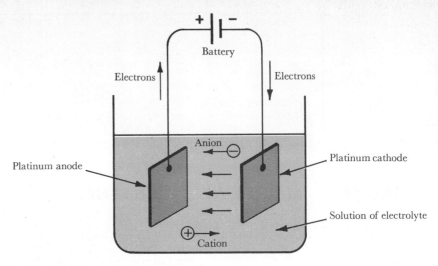

Figure 3–1. An electrolysis cell.

(platinum in this case) or graphite electrodes are connected to a storage battery or other source of direct current. The electrodes are immersed in a solution of an electrolyte or a molten ionic salt. Electricity will flow from the negative pole of the battery through the wire to one electrode (platinum at the right in Figure 3–1.) The current passes through the solution (or melt) in the electrolysis cell to the other electrode. Then it goes through the wire and returns to the battery at the positive pole.

An *electric current* is the passage of electric charge from one point to another through a conductor. This is brought about by a flow of electrons through the conductor. Each electron possesses an electric charge. A given quantity of electricity corresponds to a given number of electrons. The unit for measuring the quantity of electricity is the coulomb.

The electric current, or the rate of movement of electric charge, is measured in amperes (amp). One ampere corresponds to the passage of 1 coulomb of electricity through a conductor in 1 sec:

1 amp = 1 coulomb sec^{-1}

Ammeters are essentially flow meters that measure the rate of flow of electricity. By placing an ammeter in an electric circuit and measuring the current and the length of time that the current flows, we can determine the quantity of electricity passed:

coulombs passed = current (amps) $\times$ time (sec)

The electron flow between the two electrodes in the electrolysis cell proceeds by a mechanism that is quite different from the one in the metal wires connecting the cell to the battery. As described in Section 3–7 of *Chemical Principles*, the electrons in metals are extremely mobile and move easily throughout the metal's structure. The battery can be considered to function as a pump for electrons. The electrons are pumped out of the battery at the negative pole. They flow through the metal comprising the wire and the electrodes much like water is pumped through a pipe. They return to the battery at the positive pole.

Electrons do not pass through the solution or melt between the two electrodes in the electrolysis cell. Instead, positive ions (cations) move toward the negatively charged electrode (the cathode), and negative ions (anions) move toward the positively charged electrode (the anode). When the ions reach the electrodes, there is a chemical reaction that results in the deposition of electrons on the anode and the removal of a like number of electrons at the cathode.

The reaction that occurs at the cathode is called reduction. *Reduction* is a reaction in which a substance gains electrons. These electrons generally are gained by a positive ion that migrates through the solution in the electrolysis cell to the cathode where the electrons being pumped out of the battery have accumulated. The accumulation of electrons on the cathode gives it a negative charge that attracts positive ions. When positive ions reach the cathode, they absorb the electrons and are reduced. An equation representing the reduction reaction at the cathode is

$$M^{n+} + ne^- \rightarrow M(s)$$

The negative ions migrate to the anode, the electrode at which oxidation occurs. In *oxidation*, electrons are lost:

$$X^{n-} \rightarrow X + ne^-$$

These electrons are absorbed by the anode and move through the wire back to the battery. For each electron removed from the cathode during a reduction, an electron is deposited on the anode in the oxidation. In this way, electric current flows from the negative pole of the battery, through the electrolysis cell, and back to the battery at the positive pole.

The oxidation and reduction reactions are referred to as half-cell reactions or *half-reactions*. Their sum gives the overall reaction that occurs during electrolysis. The procedure for carrying out oxidation and reduction reactions by passing an electric current through the reactants is called *electrolysis*.

Suppose that Avogadro's number (N) of electrons are used in the reduction of positive ions at the cathode in an electrolysis. If the cations being reduced have single positive charges,

$$M^+ + 1e^- \rightarrow M$$

we see that N electrons are sufficient to reduce N M^+ ions to N M atoms, or 1 g-atom of M.

If each cation carries two positive charges, two electrons are required to reduce one cation to the neutral atom:

$$M^{2+} + 2e^- \rightarrow M$$

Therefore, N electrons will reduce $N/2$ M^{2+} ions to $N/2$ M atoms or $\frac{1}{2}$ g-atom of M.

Similarly, the passage of N electrons will result in the production of $\frac{1}{3}$ g-atom of M by the reduction of a tripositive M ion:

$$M^{3+} + 3e^- \rightarrow M$$

[*Note:* It is possible to reduce cations to other cations instead of to the metal. An example is Fe^{3+} to Fe^{2+}.]

We see from the oxide formulas for these compounds that the weight of M produced by the passage of N electrons is always the same as the combining weight of the element M. For M^+, the oxide is M_2O, and the combining weight of M is 1 g-atom of M:

$$\frac{2 \text{ atoms of M}}{1 \text{ atom of O}} = \frac{2 \text{ g-atoms M}}{16 \text{ g O}} = \frac{1 \text{ g-atom M}}{8 \text{ g O}}$$

For M^{2+}, the oxide is MO, and the combining weight of M is 0.5 g-atom of M:

$$\frac{1 \text{ atom M}}{1 \text{ atom O}} = \frac{1 \text{ g-atom M}}{16 \text{ g O}} = \frac{0.5 \text{ g-atom M}}{8 \text{ g O}}$$

For M^{3+}, the oxide is M_2O_3, and the combining weight of M is $\frac{1}{3}$ g-atom of M:

$$\frac{2 \text{ atoms M}}{3 \text{ atoms O}} = \frac{2 \text{ g-atoms M}}{3(16 \text{ g O})} = \frac{1 \text{ g-atom M}}{24 \text{ g O}} = \frac{\frac{1}{3} \text{ g-atom M}}{8 \text{ g O}}$$

Similarly, N electrons will result in the oxidation of one combining weight of anions. [*Note:* It is also possible to oxidize cations; for example, Fe^{2+} can be oxidized to Fe^{3+}.]

This description of what takes place during electrolysis has used two pieces of information that were unknown to Faraday. (1) Ions are present in solutions of electrolytes and ionic melts (Arrhenius' theory of ionization). (2) There are 6.022×10^{23} atoms in 1 gram atomic weight of an element (Avogadro's number). The historical sequence of events were such that Faraday's laws were used as support of Arrhenius' theory and as a means of calculating the Avogadro number.

FARADAY'S LAWS OF ELECTROLYSIS

Faraday's observations were expressed in his two laws. (1) During an electrolysis, the weight of a substance deposited at the electrodes is proportional to the amount of current passed. (2) The weights of different substances deposited during electrolysis with a given quantity of electricity is proportional to their combining weights.

Accordingly, a certain quantity of electricity is sufficient to deposit one combining weight of a substance. Faraday determined this quantity as 96,500 coulombs, 1 faraday ($\mathscr{F}$). From our discussion of the mole and gram-atom relationships, we see that there are 6.022×10^{23} electrons

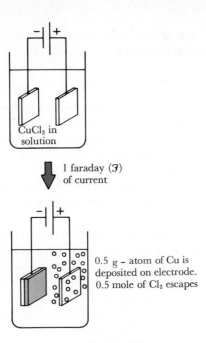

Figure 3–2.   The electrolysis of a $CuCl_2$ solution.

in 96,500 coulombs or 1 ℱ of electricity. This is the basis of the determination of Avogadro's number in Section 3–6 of *Chemical Principles*.

The salt $CuCl_2$ is an electrolyte. In aqueous solution it dissociates into Cu^{2+} and Cl^- ions:

$$CuCl_2(s) \rightarrow Cu^{2+}(aq) + 2Cl^-(aq)$$

Let us place this solution in the electrolysis cell depicted in Figure 3–2 and pass 1 ℱ of electricity through the solution. On the basis of what we have said, we can offer the following explanation of what takes place: When 1 ℱ of electricity passes through the solution, 6.022×10^{23} electrons have entered the solution at the cathode and exited at the anode. The presence of the electrons on the cathode will give it a negative charge corresponding to the polarity of the battery. The positive Cu^{2+} ions move to the negative cathode where reduction occurs. Electrons are taken from the cathode by the Cu^{2+} ions, and metallic copper deposits (plates) on the cathode:

$$Cu^{2+} + 2e^- \rightarrow Cu(s) \tag{3-1}$$

At the same time, the negatively charged Cl^- ions will travel toward the positive anode. Here oxidation will occur. Electrons from the Cl^- ions will be lost to the anode, and neutral atoms of chlorine will form. At room temperature, Cl atoms immediately combine to form gaseous Cl_2 molecules. The anode half-reaction is

$$2Cl^- \rightarrow Cl_2(g) + 2e^- \tag{3-2}$$

The total reaction that occurs in the cell, the electrolysis reaction, is the sum of Half-reactions 3–1 and 3–2:

$$Cu^{2+} + 2Cl^- \rightarrow Cu(s) + Cl_2(g) \tag{3-3}$$

From Equation 3–1, we see that twice Avogadro's number of electrons, 2 $\mathfrak{F}$, are required to produce 1 g-atom of Cu. Therefore, 1 $\mathfrak{F}$ will produce $\frac{1}{2}$ g-atom of $Cu(s)$, or one combining weight of Cu. From Equation 3–2, we can conclude that two times Avogadro's number of electrons, 2 $\mathfrak{F}$, are released with the production of 1 mole of $Cl_2(g)$. Therefore, $\frac{1}{2}$ mole of Cl_2 will be released by 1 $\mathfrak{F}$ of electricity; $\frac{1}{2}$ mole $\times$ 71.0 g mole^{-1} Cl_2 = 35.5 g, or one combining weight of chlorine, is produced as Cl_2 gas.

In Chapter 7, a gram equivalent weight of a substance involved in an oxidation-reduction reaction is defined as the weight that receives or donates Avogadro's number of electrons. On this basis, Faraday's law states that 1 $\mathfrak{F}$ is the amount of electricity sufficient to deposit 1 gram equivalent weight of a substance at an electrode during electrolysis. In fact, one combining weight of a substance, as we have defined it, represents 1 gram equivalent weight. The combining weight, or equivalent weight, can be calculated easily by dividing the formula weight of the substance as it appears in the half-reaction by the number of electrons indicated in the half-reaction. Thus, the combining weights (or equivalent weights) of the following substances are obtained by dividing the indicated formula weights as shown.

$$Ag^+ + 1e^- \rightarrow Ag(s) \qquad \text{comb. wt or equiv wt} = Ag/1$$
$$= 108/1 = 108$$
$$Cr^{3+} + 3e^- \rightarrow Cr(s) \qquad \text{comb. wt or equiv wt} = Cr/3$$
$$= 52/3 = 17.3$$
$$2I^- \rightarrow I_2(s) + 2e^- \qquad \text{comb. wt or equiv wt} = I_2/2$$
$$= \cancel{2}(127)/\cancel{2} = 127$$

Sometimes the reaction taking place at an electrode during electrolysis is a bit difficult to predict. For example, when aqueous $CuSO_4$ is electrolyzed, $Cu(s)$ plates at the cathode, but oxygen is released at the anode. Studies have shown that this oxygen does not come from the SO_4^{2-} ions present in the solution but from the water present. The following half-reactions occur.

At the cathode: $Cu^{2+} + 2e^- \rightarrow Cu(s)$
At the anode: $2H_2O \rightarrow O_2(g) + 4H^+ + 4e^-$

The weights of Cu^{2+}, $Cu(s)$, $O_2(g)$, H_2O, and H^+ participating in the reaction when 1 $\mathfrak{F}$ of electricity is passed (their combining weights or gram equivalent weights) are computed by dividing the gram formula weights by n, where n is the number of electrons in the half-reaction involving the substance.

$$\frac{Cu^{2+}}{2} \quad \frac{Cu(s)}{2} \quad \frac{O_2(g)}{4} \quad \frac{2H_2O}{4} = \frac{H_2O}{2} \quad \frac{4H^+}{4} = \frac{H^+}{1}$$

In the electrolysis of molten NaCl, $Cl_2(g)$ is evolved at the anode and $Na(s)$ is deposited at the cathode, as we would predict:

$$Na^+ + 1e^- \rightarrow Na(s) \quad \text{and} \quad 2Cl^- \rightarrow Cl_2(g) + 2e^-$$

However, when an aqueous solution of NaCl is electrolyzed, $Cl_2(g)$ (and O_2, depending on the NaCl concentration) is produced at the anode, but $H_2(g)$ is released at the cathode.

At the cathode: $2H_2O + 2e^- \rightarrow H_2(g) + 2OH^-$
At the anode: $2Cl^- \rightarrow Cl_2(g) + 2e^-$

When $K_2Cr_2O_7$ solution is electrolyzed, chromium metal can be deposited at the cathode. The half-reaction is

$$Cr_2O_7{}^{2-} + 14H^+ + 12e^- \rightarrow 2Cr(s) + 7H_2O$$

These more complicated electrolysis reactions will be discussed in more detail in Section 17–4 of *Chemical Principles*. For the present, we will concern ourselves with reactions involving simple cations and anions.

In summary, to solve electrolysis problems involving Faraday's laws, the following relationships may be needed:

quantity of electricity (coulombs) = current (amp) × time (sec)
96,500 coulombs = 1 faraday ($\mathscr{F}$)

$$1 \text{ combining weight} = 1 \text{ equivalent weight} = \frac{\text{formula weight}}{n}$$

in which n is the number of electrons that appear with one formula unit of the substance in the half-reaction.

A coulometer measures the amount of electricity passed through a circuit. There are no meters with a scale and pointer for this measurement. Instead, one common coulometer consists of a platinum electrode serving as a cathode in a small electrolysis cell containing an aqueous solution of $AgNO_3$. This device is placed in the electrical circuit. The weight of $Ag(s)$ deposited on the Pt electrode is used as a measure of the amount of electricity that flows through the circuit. The cathode reaction in the coulometer is

$$Ag^+ + 1e^- \rightarrow Ag(s) \tag{3-4}$$

As stated in Section 3–1 of *Chemical Principles*, the international definition of the coulomb is that amount of electricity which will deposit 0.0011180 g of Ag in such a coulometer.

A more precise value for the faraday can be calculated from this standard. One faraday is the amount of electricity necessary to deposit one combining weight of silver. According to Equation 3–4, the combining weight of silver is

$$\text{comb. wt Ag} = \frac{\text{g-atomic wt Ag}}{1} = \frac{107.870}{1} = 107.870 \text{ g}$$

Therefore, 107.870 g Ag are deposited per faraday. The number of coulombs in 1 $\mathscr{F}$ is

$$\frac{107.870 \text{ g Ag } \mathscr{F}^{-1}}{0.0011180 \text{ g Ag coulomb}^{-1}} = \textbf{96,485 coulombs } \mathscr{F}^{-1}$$

EXAMPLE. A source of electricity is connected in series to a silver coulometer and an electrolysis cell containing a solution of $AuCl_3$. After some time, the current is shut off and the silver deposited on the cathode in the coulometer is weighed; 2.70 g of silver have deposited. (1) How many faradays of electricity passed through the solution? How many coulombs? (2) How many grams of Au are deposited on the cathode in the electrolysis cell? (3) How many liters of Cl_2, measured at STP, were evolved at the anode?

SOLUTION. The reaction that occurs at the cathode in the coulometer is $Ag^+ + 1e^- \rightarrow Ag(s)$. The combining weight (equivalent weight) of Ag is 108/1. Therefore, 108 g Ag will be deposited per faraday of electricity passed.

(1)   no. of faradays passed $= \dfrac{2.70 \text{ g Ag}}{108 \text{ g Ag } \mathscr{F}^{-1}} = \textbf{0.0250 } \mathscr{F}$

no. of coulombs passed $= 0.0250 \mathscr{F} \times 96,500 \text{ coulombs } \mathscr{F}^{-1}$
$= \textbf{2410 coulombs}$

(2) The reaction at the cathode in the electrolysis cell is

$$Au^{3+} + 3e^- \rightarrow Au(s)$$

The weight of gold deposited by 1 $\mathscr{F}$ of electricity (its combining weight or gram equivalent weight) is $\frac{1}{3}$ g-atom; that is, Au/3 = 197/3 = 65.6 g $\mathscr{F}^{-1}$.

wt of Au deposited $= 65.6 \text{ g } \mathscr{F}^{-1} \times 0.0250 \mathscr{F}$
$= \textbf{1.64 g Au}$

(3) The anode reaction in the electrolysis cell is

$$2Cl^- \rightarrow Cl_2(g) + 2e^-$$

$Cl_2/2$; that is, $\frac{1}{2}$ mole $Cl_2(g)$ is released per faraday of current passed.

0.5 mole Cl_2 $\mathscr{F}^{-1} \times 0.0250 \mathscr{F} = 0.0125$ mole Cl_2 produced

As the volume of 1 mole of a gas at STP is 22.4 liters, the Cl_2 produced will occupy 22.4 liters mole^{-1} $Cl_2 \times 0.0125$ mole $Cl_2 =$ **0.280 liter.**

Had the problem asked for the volume of Cl_2 produced at some pressure and temperature other than STP, we would have used the ideal gas law, $PV = nRT$ (with $n = 0.0125$) and solved for V.

EXAMPLE. An automobile bumper is attached to the cathode of an electrolysis cell containing a solution of $CrCl_3$. If the solution is electrolyzed at a current of 20 ± 1 ampere for 5.0 hours, how much chromium can be plated on the bumper.

SOLUTION.   Coulombs = amperes × time (sec)
$$= 20 \text{ amp} \times 5.0\cancel{\text{ hr}} \times 60 \cancel{\text{ min}}\cancel{\text{ hr}}^{-1}$$
$$\times 60 \text{ sec}\cancel{\text{ min}}^{-1}$$
$$= 3.6 \times 10^5 \text{ coulombs}$$
$$\text{faradays passed} = \frac{3.6 \times 10^5 \cancel{\text{coulombs}}}{9.65 \times 10^4 \cancel{\text{coulombs}}\cancel{\mathcal{F}}^{-1}} = 3.73 \ \mathcal{F}$$

The cathode reaction is $Cr^{3+} + 3e^- \rightarrow Cr(s)$. One faraday will deposit $Cr/3 = 53.0/3 = 17.3$ g Cr. The amount of Cr plated on the bumper will be 17.3 g Cr $\mathcal{F}^{-1} \times 3.73 \ \mathcal{F} = $ **64.5 g Cr.**

EXAMPLE.   We want to prepare 50.0 g of metallic sodium by electrolyzing molten NaCl. If a current of 100 ± 1 amp is available for the electrolysis, how long must the melt be electrolyzed?

SOLUTION.   The cathode reaction is $Na^+ + 1e^- \rightarrow Na(s)$. One faraday of electricity will deposit $Na/1 = 23.0/1 = 23.0$ g Na.

$$\frac{50.0 \ \cancel{\text{g}} \text{ Na}}{23.0 \ \cancel{\text{g}} \ \mathcal{F}^{-1}} = 2.17 \ \mathcal{F}$$

An amount of 2.17 $\mathcal{F} \times 96{,}500$ coulombs $\mathcal{F}^{-1} = 2.09 \times 10^4$ coulombs is required.

$$\text{coulombs} = \text{current (amps)} \times \text{time (sec)}$$
$$\text{time} = \frac{2.09 \times 10^4 \text{ coulombs}}{1.00 \times 10^2 \text{ amps}} = 209 \text{ sec}$$
$$= \frac{209 \text{ sec}}{60 \text{ sec min}^{-1}} = \textbf{3.48 min}$$

3–2 ARRHENIUS' THEORY OF IONIZATION

Some of the material presented in this section of *Chemical Principles* has been incorporated in the preceding section of the study guide.

THE CHARGE ON AN ION

Table 3–3 in *Chemical Principles* lists the charge on many common ions. It isn't necessary to take the time to commit the chart to memory. You will learn many of these ions as you become familiar with the chemistry of the different elements. Sometimes you will be able to recall the formula of a substance. Since the positive charge contributed by the cations equals the total negative charge contributed by the anions, you can determine the charge on one ion in the compound if you know the charge on the other.

The periodic table is available for ready reference. In Chapter 6, you will be introduced to this valuable method for classifying chemical information. We can make a few generalizations here about the charges on ions and the position of the elements in the periodic table. Refer to your periodic table as you read the rest of this section.

The vertical columns in the table are called *groups*. The groups are of two types: A groups and B groups. The A groups are the long groups and are numbered from I through VII from left to right across the table. If you compare the ions in Table 3–3 in *Chemical Principles* with the position of the atoms in the periodic table, you can make a few, easily remembered generalizations.

Elements in Group IA (Li, Na, K, Rb, Cs, and Fr) all form ions with $+1$ charges. Those in Group IIA (Mg, Ca, Sr, Ba, and Ra) have $+2$ charges. Among the negative ions containing a single atom, those in Group VIIA (F, Cl, Br, I, and At) have -1 charges. Those in Group VIA (O, S, Se, Te, and Po) have -2 charges.

Also in Table 3–3 are the common oxidation numbers of many elements. The oxidation number of a simple ion is the same as the charge on the ion. Oxidation numbers can be assigned to any element in any compound, even if there are not any ions present. In these cases, oxidation numbers do not represent a real charge but are merely positive and negative values; they can be fractional and zero values as well as integral. The elements Be, B, and, generally, Al, for example, do not form compounds in which they have lost electrons and exist as Be^{2+}, B^{3+}, and Al^{3+} ions. However, in most of their compounds, these elements commonly exhibit oxidation states of $+2$, $+3$, and $+3$, respectively. More is discussed about oxidation numbers and how to determine them in Section 7–2 of *Chemical Principles* and in Section 7–2 of this book.

Ions containing more than one atom exist. Among the more familiar of these complex ions are SO_4^{2-}, NO_3^-, PO_4^{3-}, and NH_4^+.

3–4 CHEMICAL EVIDENCE FOR IONIZATION

Section 3–4 of *Chemical Principles* summarizes some of the chemical evidence in support of the existence of ions. Aqueous solutions of certain compounds that have elements in common react to form the same product. The interpretation is that the common elements in these solutions exist as ions. The ions react with each other to make characteristic products when the solutions containing these ions are mixed. These products form regardless of the presence of other ions. Thus, the aqueous solutions of HCl, H_2SO_4, HNO_3, and H_3PO_4 contain H_3O^+ (hydronium ions). All these solutions are colorless. Each has a sour taste and affects certain indicator dyes in a way that shows acid behavior. We conclude that one colorless ion, H_3O^+, is responsible for these acid properties.

Solutions of metal hydroxides such as KOH, NaOH, LiOH, and $Ca(OH)_2$ have a bitter taste, soapy feel, and affect indicator dyes in a manner different from the one shown by acids. The OH^- ion, the ion common to all these substances, is believed to be responsible for these "basic" characteristics.

When any of the acid solutions cited are mixed with any of these metal hydroxides, the same reaction always occurs. The H_3O^+ ions react with the OH^- ions to form water:

$$H_3O^+ + OH^- \rightarrow 2H_2O + 13{,}600 \text{ cal per} \atop \text{mole of } H_2O \text{ formed} \qquad (3\text{-}5)$$

The other cations and anions present do not react but remain in the solution as so-called *spectator ions*.

Equation 3–5 expresses the one and only reaction occurring in all the mixtures of the type just mentioned. This is substantiated by the fact that the same amount of heat is released per mole of water formed regardless of which acid or base is used. Had there been any difference in the reactions, a different energy change would be expected, and a different quantity of heat released.

Certain combinations of ions result in insoluble precipitates. For example, when a solution of any soluble silver salt is mixed with a solution of any soluble chloride salt, a white precipitate of AgCl forms. The solutions contain Ag^+ ions and Cl^- ions. The balanced equation for the reaction that occurs (which is always independent of the other spectator ions present) is

$$Ag^+ + Cl^- \rightarrow AgCl(s)$$

3-5 PHYSICAL EVIDENCE FOR IONS

According to Arrhenius' theory of ionization, compounds can be classified into three categories.

(1) *Strong electrolytes.* These are compounds that are completely dissociated into ions when placed in solution: NaCl, KCl, $CaCl_2$, HCl, H_2SO_4, HNO_3, NaOH, and Na_2SO_4 are of this type.

(2) *Weak electrolytes.* These are compounds that only partially ionize when placed in solution. Such solutions contain ions as well as molecules of the undissociated solute. The concentrations of ions and undissociated molecules depend on the degree of dissociation of the solute. Solutions of weak electrolytes have a moderate to weak electrical conductance. Weak (slightly dissociated) acids such as acetic acid (CH_3COOH), hydrocyanic acid (HCN), nitrous acid (HNO_2), and weak bases such as ammonium hydroxide (NH_4OH), and slightly soluble salts are examples of weak electrolytes.

(3) *Nonelectrolytes.* These compounds do not form ions in aqueous solution. Urea [$(CH_2NH_2)_2CO$] and sugars such as sucrose ($C_{12}H_{22}O_{11}$) and glucose ($C_6H_{12}O_6$) are examples of nonelectrolytes that are soluble in water. Gasoline, benzene and other hydrocarbons, CCl_4, fats, and oils are examples of nonelectrolytes that are insoluble in water.

The freezing point of a solution containing a nonvolatile solute is always lower than that of the pure solvent. The theory that explains this effect is discussed in Section 3–5 of the text. At present, we need only concern ourselves with the fact that this is an observed property of all solutions. The number of degrees by which the freezing point of a solvent is lowered below that of the pure solvent, ΔT_f, is directly proportional to the relative number of particles (moles) of solute and solvent. This relationship generally is expressed by the equation

$$\Delta T_f = -k_f m$$

in which m is the molal concentration and k_f is a constant called the molal freezing point depression constant. The molal concentration expresses the ratio of the number of moles of solute per kilogram of solvent. One kilogram of solvent represents a particular number of moles of solvent:

$$\frac{1 \text{ kg} \times 1000 \text{ g kg}^{-1} \text{ H}_2\text{O}}{18 \text{ g mole}^{-1}} = 55.6 \text{ moles H}_2\text{O}$$

For our purposes here, a 1-molal aqueous solution of a nonvolatile nonelectrolyte has a freezing point, T_f, of $-1.86\,°C$. The freezing point of pure water, T_f^0, is $0°C$. Therefore, the freezing point depression, ΔT_f, for such solution is

$$\Delta T_f = T_f^0 - T_f = 0°C - (-1.86°C) = 1.86°C$$

This information permits the evaluation of the molal freezing point depression constant for water.

$$\Delta T_f = k_f m$$
$$1.86 = k_f (1.00)$$
$$k_f = \frac{1.86}{1.00} = 1.86°C\ m^{-1}$$

Strong and weak electrolytes depress the freezing point of water to a greater extent than is given by the preceding equation. Arrhenius interpreted this to mean that electrolytes dissociate into ions in aqueous solution. The ions act the same as molecules in depressing the freezing point. If 1 mole of NaCl dissociates completely in a kilogram of water, 1 mole of Na^+ ions and 1 mole of Cl^- ions will be formed, that is, 2 moles of solute particles. Consequently, the freezing point depression should be twice that observed for a solution containing 1 mole of a nonelectrolyte solute per kilogram of solvent.

A method of referring to electrolytes is to classify them according to the ionic charge on the cation and anion. Thus, NaCl, KCl, KOH, and so forth are referred to as 1–1 electrolytes because the cation is charged $+1$ and the anion is -1. $CaCl_2$, $Ba(NO_3)_2$, and so on, are 2–1 electrolytes, and Na_2SO_4, K_2SO_4, and so on, are 1–2 electrolytes. $Al(NO_3)_3$ is a 3–1 electrolyte. $Al_2(SO_4)_3$ is a 3–2 electrolyte.

With the Arrhenius theory of ionization, we could predict that a solution of a 2–1 electrolyte such as $CaCl_2$ would show a freezing point depression three times as large as the one for a nonelectrolytic solution at the same concentration. For example, the freezing point depression of a 0.010-molal aqueous solution of a nonelectrolyte should be

$$\Delta T_f = k_f m$$
$$= (1.86)(0.010) = 0.0186°C$$

$CaCl_2$ dissociates to produce three ions per formula unit:

$$CaCl_2(s) \rightarrow Ca^{2+} + 2Cl^-$$

Since there are three times as many solute particles present in the solution than in a solution of a nonelectrolyte at the same concentration, the freezing point depression of a 0.010-molal $CaCl_2$ solution is expected to be $3 \times 0.0186 = 0.0558°C$. The solution should freeze at

$$\Delta T_f = T_f^0 - T_f = 0.0558$$
$$T_f = -\Delta T_f + T_f^0 = -0.0558 + 0.00 = -0.0558°C$$

The mole number or van't Hoff factor, i, is defined as

$$i = \frac{\Delta T_f(\text{observed for a solution})}{\Delta T_f(\text{calculated for a solution}} = \frac{\Delta T_f(\text{obs})}{\Delta T_f(\text{calc})}$$
$$\text{of a nonelectrolyte}$$
$$\text{at the same concentration})$$

We would expect i to equal the number of ions formed per formula unit of the solute. In the preceding example, if a 0.010-molal solution of $CaCl_2$ freezes at $-0.0558°C$ as we predicted, then

$$i = \frac{\Delta T_f(\text{obs})}{\Delta T_f(\text{calc})} = \frac{(T_f^0 - T_f)}{(1.86)(0.010)} = \frac{[0.000 - (-0.0558)]}{0.0186} = 3$$

Table 3–1 gives the observed results of freezing point depression measurements and the mole numbers for some aqueous solutions. The observed freezing point of 0.010-molal $CaCl_2$ is $-0.0511°C$.

$$\Delta T_f = T_f^0 - T_f = 0.00000 - T_f = 0.0511°C$$

Table 3–1. Freezing Point Data on Electrolytes[a]

Solute	Molality	$\Delta T_f(°C)$	Mole number, i	Number and kind of ions formed
HCl	0.0100	−0.0360	1.93	2 (H^+, Cl^-)
HNO_3	0.0100	−0.0364	1.95	2 (H^+, NO_3^-)
NaOH	0.010	−0.0355	1.90	2 (Na^+, OH^-)
K_2SO_4	0.010	−0.0501	2.70	3 ($2K^+$, SO_4^{2-})
$CaCl_2$	0.010	−0.0511	2.75	3 (Ca^{2+}, $2Cl^-$)
$K_4Fe(CN)_6$	0.0075	−0.0690	4.93	5 [$4K^+$, $Fe(CN)_6^{4-}$]
$Co(NH_3)_5Cl_3$	0.020	−0.1088	2.93	3 [$Co(NH_3)_5Cl^{2+}$, $2Cl^-$]
$Co(NH_3)_6Cl_3$	0.010	−0.0643	3.46	4 [$Co(NH_3)_6^{3+}$, $3Cl^-$]
$MgSO_4$	0.010	−0.0308	1.62	2 (Mg^{2+}, SO_4^{2-})
NH_4Cl	0.010	−0.0358	1.92	2 (NH_4^+, Cl^-)
CH_3COOH	0.010	−0.0193	1.04	2 (H^+, CH_3COO^-)[b]

[a] Some complex electrolytes, such as $Co(NH_3)_6Cl_3$, are included here to show how the concept of mole numbers can be used to obtain information about the structure of complicated materials.

[b] Only 4% ions, the rest being CH_3COOH molecules of acetic acid.

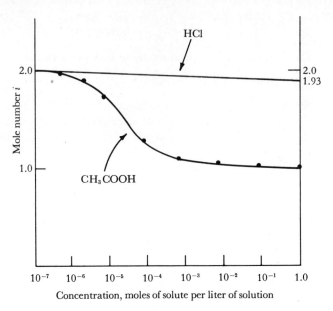

Figure 3–3. Mole number versus concentration for a strong electrolyte (HCl) *and a weak electrolyte, acetic acid* (CH₃COOH).

From this we calculate $T_f = -0.0511°C$. The mole number $i = 0.0511/0.0186 = 2.75$. The freezing point is higher than the $-0.0558°C$ we predicted, and the i value is less than the three expected for a 2–1 electrolyte. A quick survey of the table shows that all of the i values are less than the whole number of ions produced per formula unit of solute, but they do approximate this number.

Figure 3–3 is a graph showing the values for the mole number obtained from measurements of the freezing points of HCl solutions at different concentrations. As the concentration of HCl is decreased, the value of two (the predicted mole number for 1–1 electrolyte) is approached. At 10^{-7} molal, i indeed equals two. Similarly, the value for i for the other salts in the table approaches the predicted value as the concentration of the solution is decreased.

The dilution necessary to obtain the predicted value for i ($i = 2$ for 1–1, 2–2, and 3–3 electrolytes; $i = 3$ for 1–2 or 2–1 electrolytes, etc.) is greater for ions of higher charge than it is for ions of lower charge. This is illustrated in Table 3–1 by the data for 0.010-molal solutions of MgSO₄ ($i = 1.62$) and NH₄Cl ($i = 1.92$). The i value obtained for the NH₄Cl solution (a 1–1 electrolyte) is much closer to the predicted value of two than is the i value obtained for the 2–2 electrolyte, MgSO₄, at the same concentration. Both solutes should produce the same number of ions per mole.

Arrhenius tried to explain these deviations in terms of mole number by assuming that the salts were incompletely ionized. We know now that this is not a valid explanation. The acids HCl and HNO₃ react completely with water to form ions, and all the rest of the compounds in Table 3–1, with the exception of acetic acid, are completely ionized in the solid state. When the solid dissolves, the ions must be set free in the solution.

Low mole numbers are explained by the interionic attraction theory of Debye and Hückel. The free ions that are in solutions of electrolytes cannot be independent of one another. Any positive ions in the solution will exert an attraction for any negative ions around it. This attraction prevents the cation from behaving as a fully free particle. If the attractive forces become strong enough, two oppositely charged ions can become so closely associated that they will act as a single molecule in their effect on the freezing point. Such a unit consisting of a positive and negative ion is called an *ion pair*. Ion triplets and higher association products have been identified in solutions of electrolytes. A 1-molal solution of a 2–1 electrolyte such as $CaCl_2$ indeed contains 3 moles of ions; however, some of the ions are so influenced by the interionic attractions in the solution that they form ion pairs or other associated ionic species. The result is that an amount less than 3 moles of solute particles are in the solution. The freezing point depression is less than would be given by 3 moles of independent particles, and the mole number observed for the solution is less than three.

The interionic attraction theory explains the experimental observation that ionic association will increase as the concentration of ions increases. At higher concentrations, the ions are forced closer together and can interact more strongly. As we have demonstrated, it is only in dilute solutions (in which ions are far apart) that we obtain the mole numbers predicted by assuming free ions.

The higher the charge on an ion, the more it can interact with ions of opposite charge. Therefore, the Debye–Hückel theory accounts for the larger deviations observed for 2–2, 3–3, and other highly charged salts relative to the i values obtained for 1–1 electrolytes at the same concentration.

DEGREE OF IONIZATION

All compounds mentioned in Table 3–1 are strong electrolytes except for acetic acid, CH_3COOH. Acetic acid is only partially ionized unless it is in extremely dilute solutions. Figure 3–3 shows the variation of the i number with concentration for acetic acid. At a concentration of 1 mole liter^{-1} of solution, the mole number is one; that is, acetic acid appears to be only slightly ionized, or not at all. At 10^{-7} mole liter^{-1}, the mole number would be two. This would indicate that all the acetic acid in the solution is in the form of ions. The degree of ionization of a weak electrolyte can be calculated from the freezing point depression of the solution and the mole number i.

In Section 3–5 in *Chemical Principles*, the relationship for calculating the percent ionization,

$$\text{Percent ionization} = 100\,(i - 1)$$

applies only to 1–1, 2–2, and 3–3, and similar electrolytes. We will derive the expression for a more general case.

Consider a solution of a weak electrolyte M_pA_q at a concentration of m molal. The compound will dissociate as follows:

$$M_pA_q \longrightarrow pM^{c+} + qA^{a-}$$

Since M_pA_q is a weak electrolyte, there will be M^{c+} and A^{a-} ions and un-ionized M_pA_q molecules in the solution. The freezing point depression will depend on the molal concentration of these three kinds of solute particles. Let α equal the fraction of the solute that is dissociated into ions (i.e., the degree of ionization). From the balanced equation, we see that for every mole of M_pA_q that dissociates, p moles of M^{c+} ions and q moles of A^{a-} ions are formed. The concentration m is the number of moles of M_pA_q dissolved in 1 kg of solvent. If α is the fraction of the M_pA_q that dissociates, αm must equal the number of moles of M_pA_q that ionizes in a kilogram of solvent. Neglecting any ion association of the Debye–Hückel type, we can state the following: As we obtain p moles of M^{c+} ions and q moles of A^{a-} ions for every mole of M_pA_q that dissociates

(1) the molal concentration of $M^{c+} = p\alpha m$
(2) the molal concentration of $A^{a-} = q\alpha m$
(3) the molal concentration of un-ionized $M_pA_q = (1 - \alpha)m$

To calculate i, we can write

$$\begin{aligned}
\text{total moles of solute particles per kg of solvent} &= p\alpha m + q\alpha m + (1 - \alpha)m \\
&= p\alpha m + q\alpha m + m - \alpha m \\
&= m(p\alpha + q\alpha + 1 - \alpha)
\end{aligned}$$

$$i = \frac{\Delta T_f(\text{obs})}{\Delta T_f(\text{calc})} = \frac{k_f m(p\alpha + q\alpha + 1 - \alpha)}{k_f m}$$

$$i = p\alpha + q\alpha + 1 - \alpha$$

Then we rearrange the equation and solve for α, the degree of dissociation:

$$p\alpha + q\alpha - \alpha = i - 1$$
$$\alpha(p + q - 1) = i - 1$$
$$\alpha = \frac{i - 1}{p + q - 1}$$

The percent dissociation is given by

$$\text{Percent dissociation} = 100\,\alpha = 100 \times \frac{i - 1}{p + q - 1}$$

For electrolytes of the type 1–1, 2–2, 3–3, and so on

$$\text{Percent ionization} = \frac{100(i-1)}{1+1-1} = 100(i-1)$$

This is the relationship given in *Chemical Principles*. For 1–2 or 2–1 electrolytes

$$\text{Percent ionization} = \frac{100(i-1)}{1+2-1} = \frac{100(i-1)}{2}$$

For 1–3 or 3–1 electrolytes

$$\text{Percent ionization} = \frac{100(i-1)}{1+3-1} \quad \frac{100(i-1)}{3}$$

EXAMPLE. Calculate the percent ionization of acetic acid in a 0.010-molal aqueous solution if such a solution freezes at $-0.0193°C$. Treat acetic acid as a 1–1 electrolyte; it dissociates partially: $CH_3COOH + H_2O \rightarrow H_3O^+ + CH_3COO^-$.

SOLUTION.

$$\Delta T_f = 0.0000 - (-0.0193) = 0.0193°C$$
$$i = \frac{\Delta T_f(\text{obs})}{\Delta T_f(\text{calc})} = \frac{0.0193}{1.86(0.010)} = \frac{0.0193}{0.0186} = 1.04$$
$$\text{percent dissociation} = 100(i-1) = 100(1.04-1) = 4\%$$

[*Note:* If a 0.010-molal solution is 4% dissociated into ions, then in such a solution there will be $0.04 \times 0.010 = 0.0004$ molal H_3O^+ ions, $0.04 \times 0.010 = 0.0004$-molal CH_3COO^- ions, and $0.96 \times 0.010 = 0.0096$-molal un-ionized CH_3COOH molecules.]

3-7 IONS IN SOLIDS

Ions exist in two types of solids: metals and ionic or electrovalent compounds. Metals consist of positive ions surrounded by rather loosely held electrons. Ionic or electrovalent compounds consist of positive and negative ions occupying fixed sites in a crystal lattice. Salts and metal oxides are ionic compounds. Since ions exert their charge uniformly in all directions, they are pictured as charged spheres.

The structure of a crystalline solid is dictated by several factors; the major one is the energy involved in packing the charged spheres. Ionic compounds require that the total positive charge in the crystal equal the total negative charge in the crystal. There is also a relative size factor that must be considered when constructing an ionic crystal lattice since the ions frequently have different radii.

To understand the structures of ionic compounds, we first consider metals. Here the problem can be reduced to the factors governing the packing of spheres with the same diameters.

Figure 3–4.   Two layers of closest packed spheres.

CLOSE PACKING OF SPHERES AND THE STRUCTURES OF METALS

If we take a collection of spheres that have the same radius and place them on a table such that they are as close together as possible, we will have the arrangement shown by the dark circles in Figure 3–4. In this arrangement, each sphere is touching six other spheres that are in contact. Lines connecting the centers of each of these six spheres form a hexagon. This arrangement of spheres is called a *hexagonal* arrangement.

To continue packing the spheres in three dimensions, we stack layers of hexagonally arranged spheres on top of each other. A second layer of spheres can be placed on the first so the spheres in the second layer nestle in the depressions between the spheres in the first layer. In placing the third layer on the array, two possibilities exist.

Refer again to Figure 3–4. The light circles outline the spheres in the second layer. If you look closely at the holes between the spheres in this layer you will see that they are of two types. The holes marked with the number 3 lie directly above holes between the spheres in the bottom layer. The unmarked holes in the second layer lie directly above the centers of spheres in the bottom layer.

In placing the third layer of spheres, we can nestle the spheres in the depressions over the unmarked holes. This will position the center of a sphere in the third layer directly above the unmarked hole in the second layer. In this arrangement, we see that, proceeding upward from the center of a sphere in the first layer, there is a center of a sphere, a hole, and again a center of a sphere. The spheres in alternate layers lie directly above each other. This type of sequence for packing spheres is referred to as a -1-2-1-2-1-2-, or -ababab-, sequence. The resulting structure is *hexagonal close packed*.

The second choice for positioning the third layer is to nestle the spheres in the depressions over the holes marked with the number 3. Thus, the sequence is a center of a sphere, a hole, a hole, a center of a sphere, and so forth. This sequence is referred to as a -1-2-3-1-2-3-, or -abcabcabc-, sequence. The resulting structure is referred to as a *cubic close packed* arrangement.

To understand the naming of the various types of packing, we need to look at the pattern of the spheres. To observe the symmetry of an array of spheres such as we have discussed here, it is more convenient to locate the centers of the spheres with points. The arrangement of points that locate the position of atoms or ions (spheres) in a crystal is called a *crystal lattice*. Figure 3–13 in *Chemical Principles* is an illustration of a crystal lattice for NaCl.

Careful examination of a crystal lattice indicates that there is a certain collection of points repeated throughout the entire lattice. A small group of points that illustrates the essential arrangement of the atoms or ions in a crystal is called the *unit cell*. When the points that define a unit cell are moved in any direction through a distance equal to the dimension of the unit cell in that direction, they will coincide with other points that locate the same kind of ion or atom in the crystal lattice. That is, we could completely reproduce the entire crystal lattice by moving the unit cell up and down and back and forth in steps equal to its own dimensions.

Four common unit cells are the simple cubic (sc), the face-centered cubic (fcc), the body-centered cubic (bcc), and the hexagonal close packed (hcp). A simple cubic unit cell has atoms located at the corners

Figure 3–5. (a) *A face-centered cubic unit cell of spheres.*

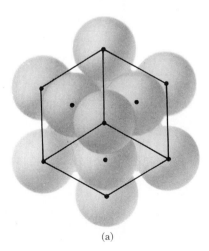

(a)

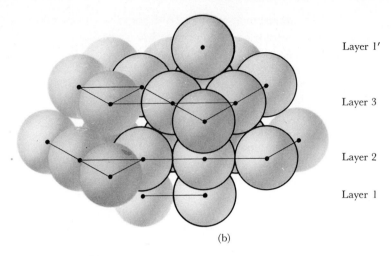

Layer 1'

Layer 3

Layer 2

Layer 1

(b)

Figure 3–5. (b)*Spheres in a cubic close packed array. Note that the spheres in* (a) *are those shown shaded in* (b).

of a cube. Figures 3–5(a) and 3–8 show spheres arranged in a face-centered cubic unit cell. Note the points locating the centers of the spheres. These points constitute a unit cell for the lattice. Observe that the points in the unit cell lie at the corners of a cube and in the center of each of the cube faces. As shown in Figure 3–5(b), this arrangement of spheres is the one in the cubic close packed (ccp) arrangement. Figure 3–6 illustrates a bcc unit cell, an arrangement with atoms at the corners of a cube and one atom in the center. The hcp unit cell is illustrated in Figure 3–7.

Both the hcp and the ccp are called closest packed structures because the packing of the spheres in these arrangements makes the best use of the available space. All but 26% of the available space is filled in both these structures.

Figure 3–6.   A body-centered cubic unit cell.

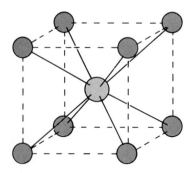

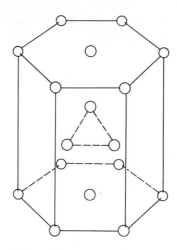

Figure 3–7. A hexagonal close packed unit cell. Note the -ababab- arrangement of the atoms.

EXAMPLE. Calculate what percent of the total volume is occupied by spheres in a cubic close packed arrangement of atoms. See Figure 3–8.

SOLUTION. We can base our calculation on the unit cell, which is face-centered cubic. In the figure, the unit cell is the solid bounded by the planes connecting the points that locate the centers of the atoms. Note that only one eighth of each atom located at the corners of the unit cell is contained within the unit cell. Also observe that only one half of each face-centered atom lies within the unit cell. Therefore, the total number of atoms within the unit cell is as follows:

$\frac{1}{8}$ of an atom at each of the 8 corners $= 8 \times \frac{1}{8} = 1$ atom
$\frac{1}{2}$ of an atom in each of the 6 faces $\quad = 6 \times \frac{1}{2} = 3$ atoms
Total number of atoms in the unit cell $\quad = 4$ atoms

Figure 3–8. Cubic close packed arrangement of atoms: the face-centered cubic unit cell.

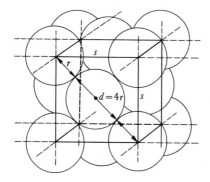

Let r equal the radius of the atoms. The volume of each atom is $\frac{4}{3}\pi r^3$. The volume within the unit cell occupied by atoms is $4(\frac{4}{3}\pi r^3) = \frac{16}{3}\pi r^3$. Note that the corner atoms and the face-centered atoms are in contact. Therefore, the diagonal, d, across the face of the unit cell is $4r$. Let s equal the side of the cube. From the Pythagorean theorem we know that

$$s^2 + s^2 = d^2 = (4r)^2$$
$$2s^2 = 16r^2$$
$$s^2 = \frac{16}{2}r^2 = 8r^2$$
$$s = (2\sqrt{2})r$$

The volume of the unit cell is

$$s \times s \times s = s^3 = (2\sqrt{2}r)^3 = 16\sqrt{2}r^3$$

The fraction of the unit cell volume occupied by atoms is

$$\frac{\text{volume of atoms in the unit cell}}{\text{total volume of the unit cell}} = \frac{\frac{16}{3}\pi r^3}{16\sqrt{2}r^3} = \frac{\pi}{3\sqrt{2}} = 0.74$$
$$= \textbf{74\% of the volume available}$$

We have calculated that 74% of the volume available in the unit cell is occupied by atoms. Since the entire crystal is represented by a repetition of the unit cell, this is also the percent of the space occupied in the crystal.

Most of the metals and alloys crystallize in either the hcp or ccp structure. A few crystallize in the bcc arrangement, that is, a structure for which a body-centered cube is the unit cell. The packing in this structure is less efficient than in the hcp and ccp structures. Only 68% of the total volume is occupied in the bcc structure.

EXAMPLE. Show that 68% of the volume available in the bcc structure of metallic sodium is occupied by sodium ions.

SOLUTION. Rather than carry out the solution to this problem in detail, some hints will be given as to how it can be solved. You should complete the calculations yourself. The procedure is analogous to the one used in the preceding example.

(1) Carry out your calculations on a single unit cell. The fraction of the volume occupied in a unit cell will be the same as for the entire crystal.

(2) Determine the number of Na^+ ions in one unit cell. (Did you find two?)

(3) Let r equal the radius of a Na^+ ion, and calculate the volume occupied.

(4) Let s equal the side of a unit cell; then s^3 equals the volume available.

(5) Calculate s^3 in terms of r. To do this, observe that the Na^+ ions on the *opposite corners* of the cube touch the body-centered atom. The *diagonal of the cube* will equal $4r$. This cube diagonal is the hypotenuse of a right triangle that has, as its other two sides, an edge (s) of the cube and the diagonal of one of the cube faces (d). Use the Pythagorean theorem to evaluate d^2 in terms of the edge s. Again apply the theorem to the right triangle that has the *cube diagonal* $4r$ as the hypotenuse. Solve the final relation for s in terms of r.

(6) Percent volume occupied equals

$$100 \times \frac{\text{volume occupied by } Na^+ \text{ ions in terms of } r}{\text{volume of unit cell in terms of } r}$$

Octahedral and tetrahedral holes or interstitial sites exist in the close packed structures. The holes are defined by the number and relative position of atoms or ions that form the holes. Figures 3–11 and 3–12 in *Chemical Principles* illustrate the octahedral hole and the tetrahedral hole, respectively. There are twice as many tetrahedral holes as there are atoms or ions in a close packed lattice. This is because in any close packed lattice each sphere is in contact with three spheres above it and three spheres below it. In each instance, two tetrahedral holes will be formed. The number of octahedral holes is the same as the number of atoms or ions in the lattice.

CRYSTALLINE SALTS

When oppositely charged ions come together, the resulting structure that they assume in the crystal depends on a balance between two tendencies: (1) the tendency for an ion of one charge to surround itself with as many ions of opposite charge as possible; (2) the tendency for ions of the same charge to avoid each other as much as possible. These tendencies operate in opposition. For example, consider a cation trying to attract anions around itself to form a crystal lattice. As the anions approach the cation, the anions also approach each other. The final position that the ions assume is a compromise between the cation–anion attractions and the anion–anion repulsions. If we think of the ions as being hard spheres with radii corresponding to the ionic radii measured in crystals, simple geometrical considerations can account for most of the observed structures. We can regard the larger ions as being in a close packed arrangement in which the smaller ions fill the octahedral or tetrahedral holes.

The charge balance required for an ionic crystal must be satisfied. Recall that there are twice as many tetrahedral holes in a close packed structure as there are atoms; the number of octahedral holes is equal to the number of atoms. Therefore, a salt having the composition AB_2 could be formed by the B ions occupying all the tetrahedral holes in a closest packed arrangement of A atoms. Many ionic compounds of the

2–1 charge type crystallize in this arrangement; CaF_2, as found in the mineral fluorite, is typical of these compounds. This arrangement of ions is called the fluorite or CaF_2 structure. The Ca^{2+} ions are in a ccp arrangement. The F^- ions occupy all the tetrahedral holes.

The structure of NaCl can be thought of as a ccp arrangement of Cl^- ions with Na^+ ions in all the octahedral holes. This arrangement is the one shown not only by NaCl, but also by many 1–1 electrolytes and some 2–2 oxides and sulfides. These compounds have the NaCl or rock salt structure.

The mineral zinc blende, an allotropic form of ZnS, has the 1–1 ratio of atoms exhibited by NaCl. However, this substance, as well as CuCl, CuBr, CuI, AgI, and BeS, have a structure that differs from that of rock salt. Obviously, the requirement that the total ionic charges balance is not the only factor to be considered when predicting structures. The zinc blende structure can be considered to be an expanded cubic close packing of the anions with the cations in every other tetrahedral hole.

The relative size of the cation and anion can be a major factor in determining the structure of a crystal. The hole in the closest packed arrangement must be large enough to accommodate the ion that will occupy it. Ideally, the ion should fit exactly in the hole to maintain contact with all the ions of opposite charge that are around it. In practice, a smaller ion or an ion slightly larger than the ordinary hole formed by closest packed ions can enter the site. For example, in NaCl the Cl^- ions are in fcc arrangement, but they do not touch one another. They have been forced apart to accommodate the Na^+ ions that are otherwise unable to fit in the octahedral hole formed when the Cl^- ions are in contact in a ccp arrangement.

The minimum size of the hole will depend on the size of the close packed ions making it. We can calculate the radius ratio between the ions in a close packed arrangement and the ion that will occupy a given hole in the structure.

EXAMPLE. Calculate the minimum cation-to-anion radius ratio that will permit a cation of a radius c to fit in the octahedral hole formed by six anions having a radius a. Refer to Figure 3–9(c). This figure shows four of the anions in contact with the cation. The other two anions will be above and below the cation. All seven ions will touch each other if the cation and the four anions are in contact.

SOLUTION. Construct a right triangle by connecting the centers of two anions with each other and with the center of the cation. The sides of this right triangle will be of length $c + a$, and the hypotenuse will be of length $2a$. Apply the Pythagorean theorem:

$$(a + c)^2 + (a + c)^2 = (2a)^2$$
$$2(a + c)^2 = 4a^2$$

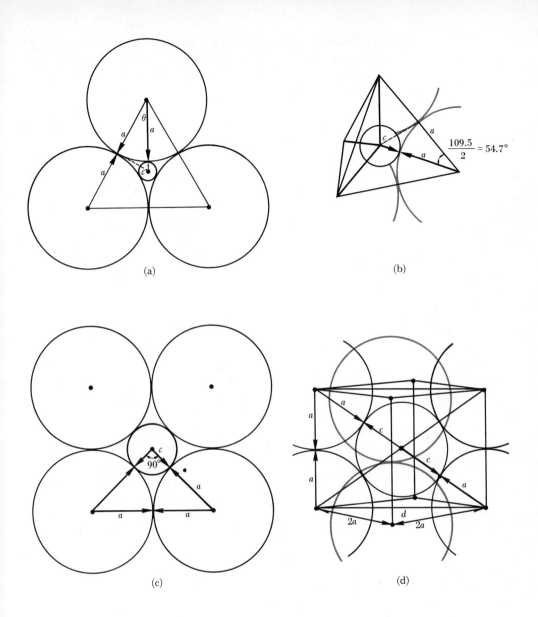

Figure 3–9

$$(a + c)^2 = \frac{4a^2}{2} = 2a^2$$
$$(a + c) = \sqrt{2a^2} = \sqrt{2}a$$
$$c = \sqrt{2}a - a = a(\sqrt{2} - 1) = a(0.414)$$
$$\frac{c}{a} = 0.414$$

EXAMPLE. Calculate the minimum cation-to-anion radius ratio that will permit a cation of radius c to fit in the cubical hole made by eight tangent spheres of radius a located such that their centers lie at the corners of a simple cube. The cation in the body-centered position will be in contact with all eight anions, but the anions will not be in contact with each other. See Figure 3–9(d).

SOLUTION. Calculate the diagonal, d, of the cube base by using the Pythagorean theorem:

$$d^2 = (2a)^2 + (2a)^2 = 8a^2$$

This is one side of the right triangle that has $2a$ for the other side and the diagonal of the cube, $2a + 2c$, for the hypotenuse. Again, apply the Pythagorean theorem:

$$d^2 + (2a)^2 = (8a^2) + (2a)^2 = (2a + 2c)^2$$
$$8a^2 + 4a^2 = (2a + 2c)^2$$
$$12a^2 = (2a + 2c)^2$$
$$2\sqrt{3}\, a = 2a + 2c$$
$$a(2\sqrt{3} - 2) = 2c$$
$$\frac{c}{a} = \frac{2\sqrt{3} - 2}{2} = \sqrt{3} - 1 = 0.732$$

The radius ratios for the other arrangements shown in Figure 3–9 can be calculated by using simple trigonometry.

EXAMPLE. Calculate the minimum cation-to-anion radius ratio that will permit a cation of radius c to fit in the triangular hole formed by three anions having radius a. See Figure 3–9(a).

SOLUTION. The lines connecting the centers of the anions form an equilateral triangle. Therefore, the angle θ equals 30°. The triangle formed by drawing a line (dashed in the figure) from the center of the cation to the point of tangency of the two anions is a right triangle. Then

$$\text{cosine } 30° = \frac{\text{adjacent side}}{\text{hypotenuse}} = \frac{a}{a + c} = 0.8660$$

$$a = 0.8660a + 0.8660c$$
$$a(1 - 0.8660) = 0.8660c$$
$$\frac{c}{a} = \frac{(1 - 0.8660)}{0.8660} = \frac{0.134}{0.8660} = 0.155$$

EXAMPLE. Calculate the minimum cation-to-anion radius ratio that will permit a cation of radius c to fit in the tetrahedral hole formed by the cubic close packing of four anions with radius a. See Figure 3–9(b).

SOLUTION. Draw a line (dashed in the figure) from the center of the cation to the point of tangency of two anions. This will form a right triangle that has $a + c$ as the hypotenuse and a as one side. The tetrahedral angle, 109.5°, is bisected by this line. Then

$$\text{cosine } \frac{109.5°}{2} = \frac{a}{a+c} = \text{cosine } 54.7° = 0.816$$

$$a = 0.816a + 0.816c$$

$$(1 - 0.816)a = 0.816c$$

$$\frac{c}{a} = \frac{1 - 0.816}{0.816} = 1.225 - 1 = \mathbf{0.225}$$

Figure 3–10 summarizes our calculations for the arrangements of large negative ions around small positive ions. Note that the cation-to-anion radius ratios given in the figure cover a range. They begin with our calculated values and extend to the value obtained for the arrange-

Figure 3–10. Arrangements for large negative ions packing around small positive ions.

Number of (−) ions touching each (+) ion	Arrangement		Radius ratio	Examples
2	Linear		0.15 or less	F^- H^+ F^-
3	Triangular	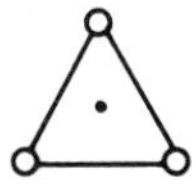	0.15 to 0.22	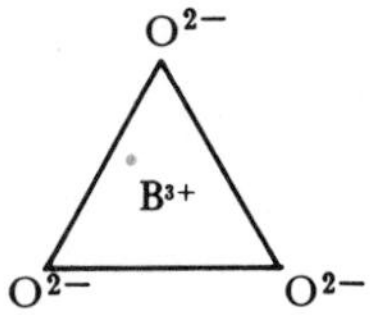
4	Tetrahedral		0.22 to 0.41	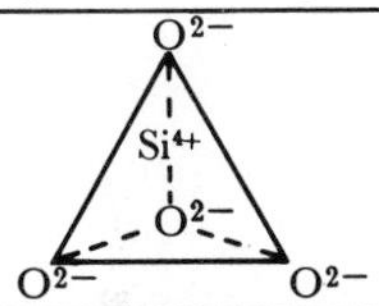
6	Octahedral	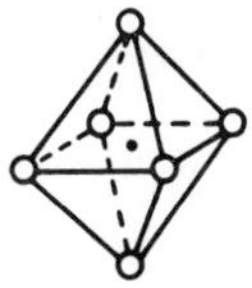	0.41 to 0.73	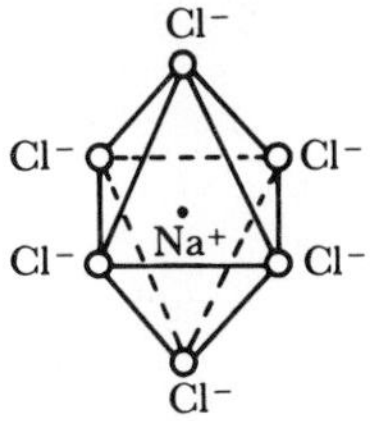
8	Cubic	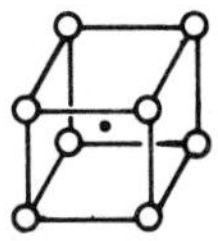	0.73 and up	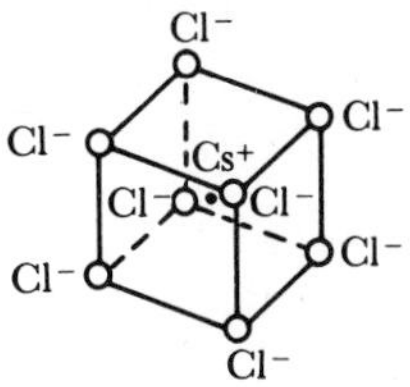
12			Does not occur since spheres would have to be identical, not allowing for positive and negative ions in the same crystal	

ment that gives the cation its next highest coordination number. Recall that we mentioned that if a hole is undersized, the lattice of close packed atoms or ions can be expanded a bit. For example, a cation can be accommodated in a tetrahedral hole formed by the cubic close packing of anions if the cation-to-anion radius ratio is 0.22 or less. With this radius ratio, the four anions are touching each other as well as the cation that occupies the tetrahedral hole formed by the anions. To fit a larger cation into the hole, it is necessary to spread the anions apart. If this happens, the four anions still will be in a tetrahedral arrangement around the cation, and they still will touch the cation; however, they no longer will be in contact with each other. The table indicates that this arrangement is favored until the radius ratio becomes as large as 0.41. At this radius ratio, the cation can occupy an octahedral hole with the anions in contact in a close packed arrangement. The tendency is for the crystal to favor this close packed structure.

Table 3–8 in *Chemical Principles* lists the ionic radii for some common ions. You can use these radii and the radius ratios in Figure 3–10 to determine if the structures of the compounds correspond to what one would predict from their radius ratios.

CHAPTER 4 QUANTITIES IN CHEMICAL CHANGE: STOICHIOMETRY

Stoichiometry is concerned with the quantities of matter that participate in a chemical reaction. As mentioned in Section 1–3, accurate quantitative measurements are essential to science. Accordingly, the principles discussed in this chapter are of prime importance. In your study of chemistry, you often will apply the concepts developed here.

The units with which the chemist measures quantities of matter, the gram-atom and the mole, were defined and developed in Section 1–1. The definitions of these units in Chapter 1 of *Chemical Principles* were the ones proposed before we established an accurate value for Avogadro's number. They also preceded our discussion of ionic compounds, such as solid NaCl, that cannot exist as molecules, Since there are no NaCl molecules in solid sodium chloride, many chemists consider it incorrect nomenclature to refer to 58.5 g of NaCl as 1 gram molecular weight or as 1 mole of NaCl. One partial solution to this problem is to refer to 58.5 g as 1 gram formula weight. Many chemists were disturbed at applying the term "mole" to such compounds because, as it was defined originally, the mole referred to molecules. The word "*form*" was even proposed as a synonym for a gram formula weight but was not widely adopted.

A REVISED DEFINITION OF A MOLE

In an effort to minimize the confusion in the nomenclature for measuring the amounts of substances at the atomic level, the International Union of Pure and Applied Physics proposed that the term "mole" be redefined as the amount of substance containing the same number of molecules (or atoms, or radicals, or ions, or electrons, as the case may be) as there are atoms in 12 g of ^{12}C. This number is Avogadro's number.

This definition was communicated to the International Union of Pure and Applied Chemistry, was included in the *Report of the Ninth General Assembly of IUPAC* (1960), and was adopted officially in 1971.[1]

Thus, a mole of molecules, a mole of atoms, a mole of formula units, or a mole of anything is in agreement with this definition. Then 6.022×10^{23} atoms of Ni (58.71 g) can be referred to as 1 mole of Ni atoms as well as 1 g-atom of Ni. A mole of hydrogen molecules (2.016 g) is 6.022×10^{23} H_2 molecules. A mole of NaCl formula units specifies 6.022×10^{23} NaCl's, or 6.022×10^{23} Na^+ ions, and a like number of Cl^- ions, or $23.0 + 35.5 = 58.5$ g of NaCl. With this expression we must specify to what the mole refers. For example, 1 mole of nitrogen molecules, written as 1 mole N_2, refers to Avogadro's number of N_2 molecules; whereas 1 mole of nitrogen atoms, written as 1 mole N, refers to Avogadro's number of N atoms. It is ambiguous to say "1 mole of nitrogen." The official definition is used throughout the remaining chapters of *Chemical Principles* and in this study guide.

4–1 FORMULAS AND MOLES

These topics have been discussed in Section 1–1 of *Chemical Principles* and the study guide. We have given examples of how combining weights can be used in conjunction with approximate atomic and molecular weights to determine empirical and molecular formulas (Sections 1–7 and 1–8 in *Chemical Principles* and in the study guide). A substance's composition by weight can be used with the known atomic weights to determine empirical formulas. If this information is supplemented by an approximate molecular weight of the substance, the molecular formula can be computed.

---

[1] If you are interested in the history associated with this phase of scientific nomenclature, we recommend four articles from the *Journal of Chemical Education*, Volume 38, 1961: "The Mole and Related Quantities," by E. A. Guggenheim, pages 86–87; "A Redefinition of Mole," by Shiu. Lee, pages 549–551; "The Mole in Quantitative Chemistry," by G. N. Copley, pages 551–553; and "Moles and Equivalents: Quantities of Matter," by I. Cohen, pages 555–556.

EXAMPLE. Analysis of 1.0000 g of a compound shows that it contains 0.7686 g carbon, 0.1290 g hydrogen, and 0.1024 g oxygen. What is the empirical formula for this compound?

SOLUTION. Calculate the number of gram-atoms (moles of atoms) of each element in the compound.

$$\frac{0.7686 \text{ g C}}{12.01 \text{ g mole}^{-1}} = 0.06400 \text{ mole C}$$

$$\frac{0.1290 \text{ g H}}{1.008 \text{ g mole}^{-1}} = 0.1280 \text{ mole H}$$

$$\frac{0.1024 \text{ g O}}{16.00 \text{ g mole}^{-1}} = 0.006400 \text{ mole O}$$

Establish the simplest whole number ratio between the number of moles of atoms in the compound. Divide all three answers by the smallest value, 0.006400.

$$C: \frac{0.06400}{0.006400} = 10 \quad H: \frac{0.1280}{0.006400} = 20 \quad O: \frac{0.006400}{0.006400} = 1$$

The empirical formula is $C_{10}H_{20}O$.

EXAMPLE. In a separate experiment, an approximate molecular weight of 300 g mole^{-1} is obtained from a freezing point depression measurement. What is the molecular formula for this compound?

SOLUTION. The basis for this type of molecular weight determination is introduced in Section 3–5 of *Chemical Principles*. It is discussed in more detail in Chapter 15. The empirical formula weight is

$$C_{10}H_{20}O = 10(12) + 20(1) + 1(16) = 156 \text{ g mole}^{-1}$$

The molecular formula is

$$\frac{300}{156} \simeq 2; \ 2(C_{10}H_{20}O) = C_{20}H_{40}O_2$$

EXAMPLE. A sample of a highly volatile compound contains 0.5214 g carbon, 0.1313 g hydrogen, and 0.3473 g oxygen. Calculate the empirical formula for the compound.

SOLUTION. Calculate the number of moles of each element in the compound.

$$\frac{0.5214 \text{ g C}}{12.01 \text{ g mole}^{-1}} = 0.04341 \text{ mole C}$$

$$\frac{0.1313 \text{ g H}}{1.008 \text{ g mole}^{-1}} = 0.1303 \text{ mole H}$$

$$\frac{0.3473 \text{ g O}}{16.00 \text{ g mole}^{-1}} = 0.02171 \text{ mole O}$$

Establish the simplest whole-number ratio between the moles of atoms in the compound. To do this, first divide all the answers by the smallest value, 0.02171.

$$C: \frac{0.04341}{0.02171} = 2 \qquad H: \frac{0.1303}{0.02171} = 6 \qquad O: \frac{0.02171}{0.02171} = 1$$

The empirical formula is **C_2H_6O**.

EXAMPLE. In a separate experiment, 1.150 g of the compound in the preceding example are vaporized in a 1.50-liter container at 97°C and 0.500 atm. What is the molecular formula of the compound?

SOLUTION. Calculate the molecular weight of the compound by using the ideal gas law.

$$PV = nRT = \frac{W}{\text{mol wt}} RT$$

$$\begin{aligned}
\text{mol wt} &= \frac{WRT}{PV} \\
&= \frac{(1.150 \text{ g})(0.0820 \text{ liter atm mole}^{-1} °K^{-1})(370°K)}{(0.500 \text{ atm})(1.50 \text{ liters})} \\
&= 46.5 \text{ g mole}^{-1}
\end{aligned}$$

In the preceding example the empirical formula weight is $2(12.0) + 6(1.00) + 1(16.0) = 46.0$. Since this agrees with the molecular weight obtained from the gas-density measurement, the molecular formula must be the same as the empirical formula, that is, **C_2H_6O**.

EXAMPLE. In the example in Section 1-1 of *Chemical Principles*, the empirical formula of gas B is CH_2, and the empirical formula of another gas, C, is CH_3. The results of gas-density measurements show that the molecular weights of both these gases are in the range 22.4 to 31.2 g mole^{-1}, that is, 26.8 ± 4.4 g mole^{-1}. What are the molecular weights?

SOLUTION. The empirical formula weight for gas B is $CH_2 = 1(12) + 2(1) = 14$.

$$\frac{26.8 \pm 4.4}{14} = 1.9 \pm 0.3 = 2$$

The molecular formula for gas B is $2(CH_2) = $ **C_2H_4**. The empirical formula weight for gas C $= CH_3 = 1(12) + 3(1) = 15$.

$$\frac{26.8 \pm 4.4}{15} = 1.8 \pm 0.3 = 2$$

The molecular formula for gas C is $2(CH_3) = $ **C_2H_6**.

Review the preceding examples and those in *Chemical Principles* (Sections 1–7 and 1–8). Also, review the examples in Sections 1–7 and 1–8 of the study guide. If you still are having difficulty in calculating formulas from composition data, consult Section 1–3 of *Programed Reviews of Chemical Principles*.

4-2 EQUATIONS

The chemical equation is the language for expressing the stoichiometry of a chemical reaction. It is important to realize that the products of a reaction must be determined experimentally before the chemical equation for the reaction can be written. The balancing of reactants and products must satisfy certain requisites, primarily the conservation of mass. The coefficients in the balanced equation give the ratios between the moles of reactants and products. In stoichiometry calculations, you generally are concerned with the quantity of a reactant needed or the amount of a product.

The procedure for making such calculations can be generalized as follows.

(1) Convert all quantities to moles.

(2) Use the balanced equation to establish the mole ratios for substances with which you are concerned. (Any confusion you might encounter in setting up the mole ratios can be eliminated if you carry through the units in your calculation.)

(3) Using this mole ratio, give the answer in terms of moles.

(4) Finally, convert the moles to weight or volume, if desired.

The best way to understand these calculations is to look at some examples. We will do a few examples here to illustrate some typical calculations.

EXAMPLE. How many grams of Al_2O_3 can be prepared from 25 g of aluminum. The balanced chemical equation for the reaction is

$$4Al(s) + 3O_2(g) \rightarrow 2Al_2O_3(s) \qquad \Delta H = -798.2 \text{ kcal}$$

SOLUTION.

(1) First we convert the weight to moles.

$$\frac{25 \text{ g Al}}{27 \text{ g mole}^{-1}} = 0.93 \text{ mole Al}$$

(2) Develop the ratio of moles of Al_2O_3 to moles of Al from the equation:

4 moles Al give 2 moles Al_2O_3

or

$$\frac{2 \text{ moles } Al_2O_3}{4 \text{ moles Al}}$$

(3) Answer the question, "How many moles of Al_2O_3 can be prepared?"

$$\text{moles of } Al_2O_3 \text{ produced} = 0.93 \text{ mole Al} \left(\frac{2 \text{ moles } Al_2O_3}{4 \text{ moles Al}}\right)$$

$$= 0.46$$

(4) Convert moles of Al_2O_3 to grams of Al_2O_3.

$$\text{grams } Al_2O_3 \text{ produced} = (0.46 \text{ mole } Al_2O_3)$$
$$\times (102 \text{ g mole}^{-1} Al_2O_3)$$
$$= 46.9 = \textbf{47 g}$$

EXAMPLE. How many liters of oxygen measured at STP will be required to burn 25 g of aluminum. The reaction is the same as in the preceding problem.

SOLUTION. Again change the quantities to moles.

$$\frac{25 \text{ g Al}}{27 \text{ g mole}^{-1}} = 0.93 \text{ mole Al}$$

Develop the mole ratio and obtain the answer to the question in moles.

$$\left(\frac{3 \text{ moles } O_2}{4 \text{ moles Al}}\right) (0.93 \text{ mole Al}) = 0.69 \text{ mole } O_2$$

At STP, 1 mole of any gas occupies 22.4 liters; therefore, 0.70 mole of O_2 will occupy

$$(0.69 \text{ mole } O_2) \times \left(22.4 \frac{\text{liters } O_2}{\text{mole}}\right) = \textbf{16 liters of } O_2 \textbf{ at STP}$$

The following procedure would have been used if we had asked, "How many liters of oxygen measured at 100°C and 0.50 atm are required to burn completely 25 g aluminum?"

As before, we would have found the number of moles of O_2 needed.

$$\left(\frac{25 \text{ g Al}}{27 \text{ g mole}^{-1}}\right) \times \left(\frac{3 \text{ moles } O_2}{4 \text{ moles Al}}\right) = 0.69 \text{ mole } O_2$$

Then we would have used the ideal gas law to compute the volume of O_2 needed.

$$PV = nRT$$

$$V = \frac{nRT}{P} = \frac{(0.69 \text{ mole})(0.082 \text{ liter atm mole}^{-1} \text{ deg}^{-1})(373°K)}{(0.50 \text{ atm})}$$

$$= \textbf{42 liters of } O_2$$

In practice, one usually adds an excess of one reactant when carrying out a chemical reaction. In such cases some of the excess reagent remains after the reaction has been completed. The amount of the product depends on the reactant that is not in excess, the so-called *limiting reagent.* We must base the stoichiometry on this limiting reagent. It can be identified by comparing the number of moles of each reactant with the mole ratios required by the reaction. In Chapter 4 of *Chemical Principles*, this comparison is referred to as the *stoichiometric unit.*

EXAMPLE. When 20.0 g of aluminum and 80.0 g of oxygen gas are heated, Al_2O_3 is formed according to the equation in the preceding two examples. Calculate the amount of aluminum oxide produced.

SOLUTION. Convert all the weights to moles.

$$\frac{20.0 \text{ g Al}}{27.0 \text{ g mole}^{-1}} = 0.741 \text{ mole Al}$$

$$\frac{80.0 \text{ g } O_2}{32.0 \text{ g mole}^{-1}} = 2.5 \text{ moles } O_2$$

From the equation, establish the Al to O_2 mole ratio.

$$\frac{4 \text{ moles Al}}{3 \text{ moles } O_2}$$

Determine the moles of O_2 required to react with the 0.741 mole of Al. This determination will indicate whether there is sufficient Al present to use all the O_2.

$$(0.741 \text{ mole Al}) \times \left(\frac{3 \text{ moles } O_2}{4 \text{ moles Al}}\right) = 0.556 \text{ mole } O_2$$

Since 2.5 moles of O_2 are in the mixture, the O_2 is in excess and the Al is the limiting reagent. We base the remaining calculations on the reaction of the Al.

$$(0.741 \text{ mole Al}) \times \left(\frac{2 \text{ moles } Al_2O_3}{4 \text{ moles Al}}\right) = 0.370 \text{ mole } Al_2O_3$$

Convert the moles produced to weight in grams.

$$Al_2O_3 \text{ produced} = (0.370 \text{ mole } Al_2O_3)(102 \text{ g mole}^{-1} Al_2O_3)$$
$$= \textbf{37.7 g}$$

MOLECULAR, IONIC, AND NET IONIC EQUATIONS

The balanced chemical equation for the reaction that occurs when potassium permanganate is added to an aqueous sulfuric acid solution containing hydrogen peroxide is

$$2KMnO_4(aq) + 5H_2O_2(aq) + 3H_2SO_4(aq) \rightarrow 2MnSO_4(aq)$$
$$+ 5O_2(g) + 8H_2O + K_2SO_4(aq)$$

This equation is called a *molecular equation* because the molecular formula for every substance is indicated. It is not a completely accurate description of the products and reactants. The compounds $KMnO_4$,

H_2SO_4, $MnSO_4$, and K_2SO_4 are strong electrolytes, and they exist in aqueous solution as ions. However, H_2O_2 is only slightly ionized and will be present principally as H_2O_2 molecules. An equation that shows ions as substances which are strongly ionized under the conditions of the reaction is an *ionic equation*. The ionic equation for the preceding reaction is

$$2K^+ + 2MnO_4^- + 5H_2O_2(aq) + 6H^+ + 3SO_4^{2-} \rightarrow 2Mn^{2+}$$
$$+ 3SO_4^{2-} + 5O_2(g) + 8H_2O + 2K^+$$

By far the most common reactions involving ions are carried out in aqueous solution. Unless otherwise indicated, any ions written in chemical equations in this text are considered to be in aqueous solution, and the symbol *(aq)* is not necessary.

If you study the preceding ionic equation, you will notice that some of the ions written as reactants on the left-hand side appear on the right-hand side as products. We can conclude that these ions have not undergone any overall chemical change during the reaction. An ionic equation that includes only those substances which react is called a *net ionic equation*. The balanced net ionic equation for this reaction is

$$2MnO_4^- + 5H_2O_2(aq) + 6H^+ \rightarrow 2Mn^{2+} + 5O_2(g) + 8H_2O$$

The ions that do not change in the overall reaction are omitted from the net ionic equation. Such ions are called *spectator ions*.

EXAMPLE. In Section 4–2 of *Chemical Principles*, you are asked to calculate the quantities of each substance remaining if 2.00 liters of HI gas at STP are added to 5.73 g $K_2Cr_2O_7$ in 0.250 liter of a solution of $HClO_4$ that contains 1.00 mole of $HClO_4$ per liter. That 4.38 g of $K_2Cr_2O_7$ are consumed and 1.35 g remain was computed in the text. Let us obtain the complete solution to this problem. The equation is

$$K_2Cr_2O_7 + 8HClO_4 + 6HI \rightarrow 2KClO_4 + 2Cr(ClO_4)_3$$
$$+ 3I_2 + 7H_2O$$

SOLUTION. First, change all quantities to moles. In the initial reaction mixture, we have

$$\frac{5.73 \text{ g } K_2Cr_2O_7}{294 \text{ g mole}^{-1}} = 0.0195 \text{ mole } K_2Cr_2O_7$$

$$0.250 \text{ liter } HClO_4 \times 1.00 \text{ mole } HClO_4 \text{ liter}^{-1}$$
$$= 0.250 \text{ mole } HClO_4$$

$$\frac{2.00 \text{ liters HI}}{22.4 \text{ liters mole}^{-1}} = 0.0893 \text{ mole HI}$$

Next, determine the limiting reagents. From the equation, we see that the mole ratios $K_2Cr_2O_7/HClO_4/HI$ required for the reaction are 1/8/6. Since the amount of HI required is intermediate between the other two reactants, see if there is sufficient $K_2Cr_2O_7$ and $HClO_4$ to use all the HI present.

$$0.893 \ \cancel{\text{mole}} \ \text{HI} \times \frac{1 \text{ mole } K_2Cr_2O_7}{6 \ \cancel{\text{moles}} \ \text{HI}}$$

$$= 0.0149 \text{ mole } K_2Cr_2O_7 \text{ is needed}$$

0.0195 mole $K_2Cr_2O_7$ is present; there is more than enough

$$0.0893 \ \cancel{\text{mole}} \ \text{HI} \times \frac{8 \text{ moles } HClO_4}{6 \ \cancel{\text{moles}} \ \text{HI}}$$

$$= 0.119 \text{ mole } HClO_4 \text{ is needed}$$

0.250 mole $HClO_4$ is present; there is more than enough

Therefore, all of the 0.0893 mole of the HI should react; thus, HI is the limiting reagent. When HI does react, as we have shown, 0.0149 mole $K_2Cr_2O_7$ and 0.119 mole $HClO_4$ will be consumed. After the reaction, $(0.0195 - 0.0149) = 0.0046$ mole $K_2Cr_2O_7$ and $(0.250 - 0.119) = 0.131$ mole $HClO_4$ will remain.

0.0149 mole $K_2Cr_2O_7 \times 294$ g $K_2Cr_2O_7$ mole^{-1} = 4.38 g $K_2Cr_2O_7$ will react, and

$5.73 - 4.38 = $ **1.35 g $K_2Cr_2O_7$ will remain**

0.119 mole $HClO_4 \times 100.5$ g $HClO_4$ mole^{-1} = 12.0 g $HClO_4$ will be consumed, and

0.131 mole $HClO_4 \times 100.5$ g $HClO_4$ mole^{-1} = **13.2 g $HClO_4$ will remain**

ACID–BASE REACTIONS

According to the Brønsted definition, an acid is any substance that donates a proton (H^+); a base is any substance that accepts a proton. Therefore, to function as an acid, a substance, HA, must react with a base, B, to form a new substance, HB. An equation symbolizing this process is

$$HA + B \rightarrow HB + A$$

The substance, A, in the acid, HA, must have accepted a proton from some other substance in the initial formation of HA. Therefore, A must be a base. We will find (except for gaseous reactions involving free H^+ ions) that all acids are compounds in which protons have combined with bases. HB is also a potential acid. The base that combines with the proton to produce the acid is called the *conjugate base* of that acid. Our example, $HA + B \rightarrow HB + A$, also might be described as the reaction of the acid, HA, with the base, B, to form a new acid, HB, and the conjugate base, A, of the acid, HA.

In the reaction of HCl with water,

$$HCl + H_2O \rightarrow H_3O^+ + Cl^-$$

acid₁ base₁ acid₂ base₂

the acid HCl donates a proton to the base H_2O to form a new acid, hydronium ion (H_3O^+), and Cl^-, the conjugate base of HCl. The hydronium ion is capable of acting as an acid; this can be seen by considering the reverse of this reaction:

$$H_3O^+ + Cl^- \rightarrow HCl + H_2O$$

acid₁   base₁   acid₂   base₂

Here, the H_3O^+ acts as an acid by donating a proton to the base Cl^-, releasing its conjugate base H_2O, and forming a different acid, HCl.

HCl is a strong acid. This means that the tendency for the proton in HCl to be donated to H_2O is much greater than the tendency for a H_3O^+ ion to donate a proton to Cl^-. Expressing this differently, we state that HCl is a strong acid in water because Cl^- is a weak base compared to H_2O. When HCl is added to water, there is a competition between Cl^- ions and H_2O molecules. Both can accept the proton, but water is a much stronger base (proton acceptor) than Cl^-. Practically all the protons are accepted by the H_2O molecules and converted to H_3O^+ ions.

Other examples of conjugate acid–base pairs are indicated in the following equations. In this notation, the conjugate of a substance marked with the subscript 1 is the substance marked with the subscript 2 on the opposite side of the equation.

$$HClO_4 + H_2O \rightarrow H_3O^+ + ClO_4^- \tag{1}$$

acid₁   base₁   acid₂   base₂

$$OH^- + H_3O^+ \rightarrow H_2O + H_2O \tag{2}$$

base₁   acid₁   base₂   acid₂

$$NH_3 + H_2O \rightarrow NH_4^+ + OH^- \tag{3}$$

base₁   acid₁   acid₂   base₂

$$NH_4^+ + NH_2^- \rightarrow NH_3 + NH_3 \tag{4}$$

acid₁   base₁   acid₂   base₂

In Equation 1, $HClO_4$, an acid, produces its conjugate base, ClO_4^-. The conjugate base of H_3O^+ is H_2O; and H_2O, a base, produces its conjugate acid, H_3O^+.

In Equation 3, NH_3 acts as a base by accepting a proton from water. Water acts as an acid. The conjugate acid of NH_3 is NH_4^+; the conjugate base of H_2O is OH^-. [*Note:* In Equation 1 water acts as a base; in Equation 3 it acts as an acid. A substance that exhibits both acidic and basic properties is *amphoteric*.]

In Equations 2 and 4, only one product is formed. In Equation 2, H_2O is the conjugate acid of OH^- as well as the conjugate base of H_3O^+. In Equation 4, NH_3 is the conjugate acid of NH_2^- (amide ion) and also the conjugate base of NH_4^+. This is another example of amphoterism.

When Reaction 2 occurs in aqueous solution, the process is called *neutralization*. The acid and base have reacted to form the solvent (H_2O). When the neutralization is complete, the solution will contain the cation and the anion that accompanied the acid and base. The compound obtained upon evaporation of the solvent is called a *salt*. Reaction 4 is an example of neutralization in a solution in which liquid ammonia is the solvent.

4–4 SOLUTIONS AS CHEMICAL REAGENTS

In general, it is more convenient to measure chemical reactants and to perform chemical reactions when the reagents are dissolved in a solvent. The amount of solute in the solution is referred to as its concentration. Basically, there are two ways of expressing the concentration; the choice depends on how the solution is to be used.

(1) CONCENTRATION UNITS THAT SPECIFY THE RELATIVE AMOUNT OF SOLUTE AND SOLVENT

Mole fraction. This concentration unit was discussed in Section 1–7 in this book and in Section 2–7 of *Chemical Principles*. It relates the moles of solute to the moles of solution (solvent plus solute).

$$X_A = \frac{n_A}{\sum_i n_i}$$

In this expression, X is the mole fraction of component A, n_A is the number of moles of component A, and $\sum_i n_i = n_A + n_B + n_C + \ldots$, the sum of the number of moles of each of the i components in the solution.

Molality. The molal unit (m) expresses the amount of solute with a fixed weight (1000 g) of solvent. The molality states the concentration in terms of the number of moles of solute per kilogram of solvent. A simple formula used in calculations involving concentration units can be expressed by the units in the definition. For example, molality (m) is defined as the number of moles of solute per kilogram of solvent; therefore,

$$m = \frac{\text{moles of solute}}{\text{kg of solvent}}$$

(2) CONCENTRATION UNITS THAT SPECIFY THE AMOUNT OF SOLUTE PER UNIT VOLUME OF SOLUTION

Molarity. The number of moles of solute per liter of solution is called the molar concentration, M. Again, a simple formula for calculation purposes can be written by simply expressing the units mathematically:

$$M = \frac{\text{moles of solute}}{\text{liters of solution}}$$

Normality. The normality, N, of a solution is the number of gram equivalent weights (equivalents) of solute per liter of solution.

$$N = \frac{\text{no. equivalents of solute}}{\text{liters of solution}}$$

The equivalent weight concept will be discussed later. *Note:* Simple rearrangement of the expressions for molarity and normality give two extremely important relationships that are used frequently in stoichiometry:

no. of moles of solute = (M) × (liters of solution)
no. of equivalents of solute = (N) × (liters of solution)

Students often confuse molal (m), molar (M), and normal (N) units of concentration. Be certain that you have the definitions firmly in mind.

In the following examples, notice how you must return to the definition of the concentration units to work the problem. These examples involve molarity and molality only. Examples of mole fraction calculations are in Section 2–7 of this book. We shall discuss normality later in this section in connection with chemical equivalents in acid–base reactions.

EXAMPLE. A solution is made by dissolving 25.0 g of sucrose $(C_{12}H_{22}O_{11})$ in 50.0 g of water. What is the molal concentration?

SOLUTION. The molecular weight of sucrose $(C_{12}H_{22}O_{11})$ is 342.

$$m = \frac{\text{moles solute}}{\text{kg solvent}}$$

$$\text{moles solute} = \frac{25.0 \text{ g sucrose}}{342 \text{ g mole}^{-1}} = 0.0731 \text{ mole sucrose}$$

$$\text{kg solvent} = (50.0 \text{ g } H_2O) \frac{1 \text{ kg}}{1000 \text{ g}} = 0.0500 \text{ kg } H_2O$$

$$m = \frac{\text{moles solute}}{\text{kg solvent}}$$

$$m = \frac{0.0731 \text{ mole}}{0.0500 \text{ kg}} = \mathbf{1.46}\boldsymbol{m}$$

Of course, the entire problem can be set up easily in a single expression.

$$m = \frac{\text{moles solute}}{\text{kg solvent}} = \frac{\text{g solute/mol wt}}{\text{kg solvent}}$$
$$= \frac{25.0 \text{ g sucrose}/342 \text{ g mole}^{-1}}{50.0 \text{ g}/1000 \text{ g kg}^{-1}}$$
$$= \frac{(25.0)(1000) \text{ moles sucrose}}{(342)(50) \text{ kg } H_2O} = \mathbf{1.46}\boldsymbol{m}$$

[*Note:* The density of water is 1.00 g ml^{-1}; therefore, the volume of 250 g H_2O is 250 ml. Upon the addition of the 50.0 g of sucrose, the resulting solution probably will not be exactly 250 ml. It will be generally larger because the dissolved solute adds its volume to that of the solvent. However, sometimes the volume of a liquid will diminish when a solute is added to it. Only when the amount of solute added is small can we feel confident that there is no significant change in volume of the solution upon mixing.]

EXAMPLE. What is the molarity of a solution made by dissolving 20.0 g of KNO_3 in enough water to make 500 ml of solution?

SOLUTION. The molecular weight of KNO_3 is 101.

$$\text{moles of solute} = \frac{20.0 \text{ g } KNO_3}{101 \text{ g mole}^{-1}} = \frac{20.0}{101} \text{ mole } KNO_3$$

$$\text{liters of solution} = (500 \text{ ml}) \times \left(\frac{1 \text{ liter}}{1000 \text{ ml}}\right) = \frac{500}{1000} \text{ liters}$$

$$M = \frac{\text{moles of solute}}{\text{liters of solution}} = \frac{20.0/101 \text{ moles}}{500/1000 \text{ liters}} = \frac{(20.0)(1000)}{(101)(500)}$$
$$= 0.396M$$

EXAMPLE. The label on a bottle of concentrated nitric acid specifies that the acid has a density of 1.41 g ml^{-1} and is 69% HNO_3 by weight. Compute the molality and molarity of the concentrated acid.

SOLUTION. To determine the molal concentration, we need the weight of solvent (H_2O) and the weight of solute (HNO_3). Since the solution is 69% HNO_3 by weight, 69% of 1.41 g will be the weight of HNO_3 in 1 ml of the solution.

$$(0.69)(1.41 \text{ g } HNO_3 \text{ ml}^{-1}) = 0.97 \text{ g } HNO_3 \text{ ml}^{-1}$$
$$\text{g } H_2O \text{ in 1 ml of the solution} = 1.41 - 0.97 = 0.44 \text{ g}$$

$$m = \frac{\text{moles of } HNO_3}{\text{kg of } H_2O} = \frac{0.97 \text{ g } HNO_3/63 \text{ g mole}^{-1}}{0.44 \text{ g } H_2O/10^3 \text{ g kg}^{-1}}$$
$$= \frac{(0.97)(10^3) \text{ moles } HNO_3}{(63)(0.44) \text{ kg } H_2O} = 35m$$

To determine the molarity, we need the weight of solute in a given volume of solution. The weight of HNO_3 in 1 ml of the solution was just calculated: 69% of 1.41 g ml^{-1} = 0.97 g HNO_3 ml^{-1}.

$$M = \frac{\text{moles of } HNO_3}{\text{liters of solution}} = \frac{0.97 \text{ g } HNO_3/63 \text{ g mole}^{-1}}{1 \text{ ml}/1000 \text{ ml liter}^{-1}}$$
$$= \frac{(0.97) \text{ mole } HNO_3}{(63)(0.0010) \text{ liters}} = 15M$$

EXAMPLE. In an example in *Chemical Principles* (Section 4–4) you are asked to calculate the volume of water needed along with 264.30 g of $(NH_4)_2SO_4$ to make 1 liter of a 2-molar solution. This example shows that a large quantity of solid solute will contribute appreciably to the volume of the solution. We estimate the volume of the solution after mixing by assuming that the volume of solute added to the solution is the same as the volume of the solid solute. The volume of the solid is calculated from its density; for $(NH_4)_2SO_4$, the density is 1.769 g cm^{-3}. In most of our problems, unless it is stated to the contrary, you should assume that the volume of solvent does not change when a solid solute is added. However, this assumption is valid only for dilute solutions (about $10^{-3}M$).

SOLUTION. Convert the weight of solute to moles:

$$\frac{264.30 \text{ g } (NH_4)_2SO_4}{132.15 \text{ g mole}^{-1}} = 2.0000 \text{ moles } (NH_4)_2SO_4$$

When this amount of solute is diluted with water to give 1 liter of solution, the solution will be 2 molar.

The volume of the $(NH_4)_2SO_4$ is calculated from its density

$$(264.30 \text{ g}) \left(\frac{1.0000 \text{ cm}^3}{1.769 \text{ g}}\right) = 149.4 \text{ cm}^3 = 149.4 \text{ ml}$$

Therefore, the volume of water needed will be approximately 1000 ml $-$ 149 ml $=$ **851 ml.**

DILUTION PROBLEMS

You frequently will find it necessary to use a solution of a reagent at one concentration to prepare a more dilute solution of this same reagent.

EXAMPLE. An amount of 25.0 ml of 6.00-molar HCl is added to 20.0 ml of water. Assume that the volumes of the solutions are additive when mixed. Calculate the molarity of the resulting solution.

SOLUTION.

$$M = \frac{\text{moles of solute}}{\text{liters of solution}}$$

The solute is the HCl, and it is in a solution. Note from our definition of molarity that

$$\text{moles of solute} = M \times V$$

in which V is the volume of the solution in liters. Therefore,

$$\text{moles of HCl} = (6.00 \text{ moles of HCl liter}^{-1})(0.0200 \text{ liter})$$
$$= 6.00 \times 0.0200 = 0.120 \text{ mole HCl}$$

Calculate the molarity of the solution. After mixing, the volume will be 45.0 ml, 25.0 ml HCl $+$ 20.0 ml H_2O = 45.0 ml solution.

$$M = \frac{\text{moles of HCl}}{\text{liters of solution}} = \frac{0.120 \text{ mole}}{45.0 \text{ ml}/1000 \text{ ml liter}^{-1}} = \textbf{2.67} \textbf{\textit{M}}$$

Again, this entire calculation (a type that you will encounter frequently) is easily set up in one step. [*Note:* Milliliters can be converted to liters by dividing by 1000, i.e., by moving the decimal point three places to the left.]

$$M = \frac{\text{moles of HCl}}{\text{liters of solution}} = \frac{(6.00 \text{ moles HCl liter}^{-1})(0.020 \text{ liter})}{(0.0450 \text{ liter})}$$
$$= 2.67 \, M$$

EXAMPLE. How many milliliters of a 0.107-molar solution of NaCl will contain 0.0240 mole of Na^+ ion.

SOLUTION. Since 1 mole of Na^+ ions will be in the solution for every mole of NaCl dissolved $[NaCl(s) \rightarrow Na^+(soln) + Cl^-(soln)]$, the molarity of the NaCl solution will be the same as the moles of the Na^+ ion.

$$M = \frac{\text{moles of NaCl}}{\text{liters of solution}} \quad \text{and}$$
$$\text{liters of solution} = \frac{\text{moles of NaCl}}{M}$$
$$\text{liters of solution} = \frac{0.0240 \text{ mole NaCl}}{0.107 \text{ mole NaCl liter}^{-1}}$$
$$= 0.224 \text{ liter} = 224 \text{ ml}$$

EXAMPLE. How many ml of 3.0*M* $CaCl_2$ and how many ml of water must be mixed to prepare 50.0 ml of a 1.50*M* $CaCl_2$ solution? Assume no volume change on mixing.

SOLUTION. The number of moles of solute in the resulting solution will be that contained in 50.0 ml of a 1.50*M* solution.

$$M \times \text{liters of solution} = \text{moles of solute}$$
$$1.50 \text{ moles liter}^{-1} \times 0.0500 \text{ liter} = 0.0750 \text{ mole } CaCl_2$$

Sufficient 3*M* $CaCl_2$ solution must be used to contain this amount of $CaCl_2$.

$$M = \frac{\text{moles of solute}}{\text{liters of solution}} \quad \text{and}$$
$$\text{liters of solution} = \frac{\text{moles of solute}}{M}$$
$$\text{liters of solution} = \frac{0.0750 \text{ mole } CaCl_2}{3.0 \text{ moles liter}^{-1}}$$
$$= 0.025 \text{ liter or } 25 \text{ ml}$$

An amount of 25 ml of 3.0*M* $CaCl_2$ solution plus (50.0 ml − 25 ml) 25 ml of water must be mixed to give 50 ml of a 1.50*M* $CaCl_2$ solution.

A more direct approach to this problem is to observe that we wish to reduce the concentration of the 3.0M $CaCl_2$ by (1.50M/3.00M) or $\frac{1}{2}$. One half the volume of the solution should be 3.0M $CaCl_2$; the other half should be water. To prepare 50 ml of the solution, 25 ml of 3.0M $CaCl_2$ and 25 ml of H_2O are required.

EXAMPLE.   In the last example of a dilution problem presented in Section 4–4 of *Chemical Principles*, you are asked to determine the molarity after 175 ml of a 2.00M solution is diluted to 1 liter.

SOLUTION.   The final solution will contain 2.00 moles liter^{-1} × 0.175 liter = 0.350 mole solute in 1 liter of the diluted solution. The molarity will be

$$M = \frac{0.350 \text{ mole of solute}}{1 \text{ liter of solution}} = 0.350M$$

CHEMICAL EQUIVALENTS IN ACID–BASE REACTIONS

The gram equivalent weight of an acid is the weight, in grams, of the acid that donates 1 mole of protons to a base. Similarly, the gram equivalent weight of a base is the weight, in grams, of the base that accepts 1 mole of protons from an acid. The single word "equivalent" (abbreviated "equiv") is used often as a synonym for "gram equivalent weight." Thus, 1 gram equivalent weight of a substance is 1 equiv of that substance, and 0.5 gram equivalent weight is 0.5 equiv.

Table 4–1.   Equivalent Weights of Some Acids and Bases

	Molecular weights		Equivalent weights (g equiv^{-1})	
Reaction	Acid	Base	Acid	Base
1	HCl, 36.5	NaOH, 40.0	$\dfrac{HCl}{1} = \dfrac{36.5}{1} = 36.5$	$\dfrac{NaOH}{1} = \dfrac{40.0}{1} = 40.0$
2	H_2SO_4, 98	NaOH, 40.0	$\dfrac{H_2SO_4}{2} = \dfrac{98}{2} = 49$	$\dfrac{NaOH}{1} = \dfrac{40.0}{1} = 40.0$
3	H_2SO_4, 98	KOH, 56	$\dfrac{H_2SO_4}{1} = \dfrac{98}{1} = 98$	$\dfrac{KOH}{1} = \dfrac{56}{1} = 56$
4	H_3PO_4, 98	$Ca(OH)_2$, 73	$\dfrac{H_3PO_4}{2} = \dfrac{98}{2} = 49$	$\dfrac{Ca(OH)_2}{2} = \dfrac{73}{2} = 36.5$
5	H_3PO_4, 98	$Ca(OH)_2$, 73	$\dfrac{H_3PO_4}{3} = \dfrac{98}{3} = 33$	$\dfrac{Ca(OH)_2}{2} = \dfrac{73}{2} = 36.5$

The equivalent weights in Table 4–1 are based on the following reactions.

$$\text{(1) } HCl + NaOH \rightarrow NaCl + H_2O$$
$$\text{(2) } H_2SO_4 + 2NaOH \rightarrow Na_2SO_4 + 2H_2O$$
$$\text{(3) } H_2SO_4 + KOH \rightarrow KHSO_4 + H_2O$$

(4) $H_3PO_4 + Ca(OH)_2 \rightarrow CaHPO_4 + 2H_2O$

(5) $2H_3PO_4 + 3Ca(OH)_2 \rightarrow Ca_3(PO_4)_2 + 6H_2O$

The equivalent weight of H_2SO_4 is different in Reactions 2 and 3 in Table 4–1. In Reaction 2, both protons in the H_2SO_4 are transferred; so 1 mole of H_2SO_4 transfers 2 moles of protons, and $\frac{1}{2}$ mole of H_2SO_4 transfers 1 mole of protons. Therefore, the gram equivalent weight is the weight of $\frac{1}{2}$ mole of H_2SO_4, $98/2 = 49$ g equiv^{-1}. In Reaction 3, only 1 mole of protons is transferred per mole of H_2SO_4 (the second hydrogen ion is not transferred but remains with the SO_4^{2-} as HSO_4^-). Thus, the equivalent weight of sulfuric acid in Reaction 3 is the same as the weight of 1 mole, 98 g. All three protons are lost by H_3PO_4 in Reaction 5; its equivalent weight is $H_3PO_4/3 = 32.7$ g equiv^{-1}. However, in Reaction 4 only two protons per mole of phosphoric acid are donated to the base; so the equivalent weight of the acid is $H_3PO_4/2 = 49.0$ g equiv^{-1}.

We can summarize our observations in the following statement: To define the equivalent weight of an acid (or base) we need to know the number of protons lost (or gained) by each formula unit of acid (or base).

The unit that expresses the concentration of a solution in terms of the number of gram equivalent weights of solute per liter of solution is the normality. The normality of a solution is defined in Section 4–4 as

$$N = \frac{\text{no. equiv solute}}{\text{liters of solution}}$$

EXAMPLE. Calculate the normality of a solution prepared by dissolving 10.00 g of sulfuric acid (H_2SO_4) in enough water to make 750 ml of solution. Assume complete neutralization of the acid. (Complete neutralization means that all the acidic protons are donated to a base.)

SOLUTION.

$$H_2SO_4 \rightarrow SO_4^{2-} + 2H^+ \text{ donated to a base}$$

$$\text{no. equiv } H_2SO_4 = \frac{\text{g of } H_2SO_4}{\text{equiv wt } H_2SO_4} = \frac{10.00 \text{ g } H_2SO_4}{\dfrac{98.08}{2} \text{ g equiv}^{-1}}$$

$$= \frac{(20.00)}{(98.08)} = 0.2039 \text{ equiv}$$

$$N = \frac{\text{no. equiv } H_2SO_4}{\text{liters of solution}} = \frac{0.2039 \text{ equiv}}{0.750 \text{ liter}} = \mathbf{0.272}N$$

The equivalent weight concept can simplify stoichiometry calculations. The number of equivalents of an acid and a base that participate in a reaction always will be identical. For example, if there is 1 equivalent of an acid present, there is sufficient acid to donate 1 mole of protons to a base. Therefore, the amount of base required to react with the acid must be sufficient to accept 1 mole of protons, which, by definition, is 1 equivalent of the base. Similarly, 0.5 equivalent of acid will react with 0.5 equivalent of base. Regardless of the coefficients in the balanced chemical equation for an acid–base reaction, the equivalents of acid that react always will be equal to the equivalents of base present. Consequently, the balanced chemical equation is not needed to perform a stoichiometric calculation with the equivalent weight concept. All we need to know about the chemistry of the reaction are the formulas of the pertinent conjugate acid–base pairs. One basic relationship that applies to all reactions is the starting point in the calculations: The number of equivalents of acid equals the number of equivalents of base. To determine the number of equivalents of any substance, we use the defining equations mentioned previously. From the definition of the normality of a solution,

$$N = \frac{\text{no. equiv of solute}}{\text{liters of solution}}$$

$$\text{no. equiv of solute} = N \times V$$

in which V is the volume of the solution in liters. Also, by definition, the units for the gram equivalent weight are grams per equivalent. Therefore,

$$\text{g equiv wt} = \frac{\text{wt in g}}{\text{no. of equiv}}$$

and

$$\text{no. equiv} = \frac{\text{wt in g}}{\text{g equiv wt}}$$

TITRATIONS

Titration is a technique that is used widely in chemical analysis. To analyze a substance A the following conditions must be met.

(1) An accurate amount (weight or volume) of the sample being analyzed must be measured.

(2) A reagent B must be available to react completely with A. Also, B must not react with any other substances in the sample.

(3) A solution containing a known concentration of B must be prepared. Such a solution is called a *standard solution*.

(4) In the titration, enough standard solution of B must be added to the sample to react with all of the A. The volume of the standard solution required to reach this stage in the titration, *the equivalence point*, generally is measured with a burette. (See Figure 4–1 in *Chemical Principles*.)

(5) We require a method of identifying the equivalence point. A common procedure is to add indicators to the solution being titrated. These indicators change color at the equivalence point in the titration.

The instant that the color change is observed is referred to as the *end point* in the titration.

Calculations involving titration data can be in terms of either moles or equivalent weights. If equivalent weights are used, the balanced chemical equation need not be written. With the mole method, the concentrations should be expressed in moles per liter. The method of equivalent weights requires normality units. Therefore, you may wish to change from one concentration unit to another when doing a problem. The conversion factor required to do this is derived readily.

Consider a solution containing W grams of a solute that has a molecular weight A. The molarity of this solution is

$$M = \frac{W/A}{V} \quad \text{and} \quad (M)(A) = \frac{W}{V}$$

in which V is the volume of the solution in liters. The normality of this same solution is

$$N = \frac{W/(A/x)}{V} \quad \text{and} \quad \frac{(N)(A)}{x} = \frac{W}{V}$$

Here x is the number of moles of protons donated (or moles of protons accepted if the solute is a base) per mole of solute.

The weight per unit volume of solution is a constant. Equating the two expressions for W/V gives

$$\frac{NA}{x} = MA$$

or

$$N = xM \quad \text{and} \quad M = N/x$$

That is, to convert a concentration in molarity units to normality, we need only multiply by x [where x is the number of moles of protons donated (or accepted) per mole of acid (or base)]. To convert normality units to molarity, we divide by x. Since x can equal 1, it will help to remember that the normality of a solution will have a numerical value that is either the same or larger than the molarity.

Convert the following concentration units from M to N or from N to M. The conjugate acid–base pair required to make the conversion is shown.

Acid or base	Conjugate pair		Equiv wt (formula wt/x)	Conversion	
$1M$ HNO_3	HNO_3	NO_3^-	$HNO_3/1$	$(1M)\ 1$	$= 1N$
$2M$ H_2SO_4	H_2SO_4	SO_4^{2-}	$H_2SO_4/2$	$(2M)\ 2$	$= 4N$
$3N$ H_3PO_4	H_3PO_4	PO_4^{3-}	$H_3PO_4/3$	$(3N)/3$	$= 1M$
$3N$ H_3PO_4	H_3PO_4	HPO_4^{2-}	$H_3PO_4/2$	$(3N)/2$	$= 1.5M$
$3N$ H_3PO_4	H_3PO_4	$H_2PO_4^-$	$H_3PO_4/1$	$(3N)/1$	$= 3M$
$0.1M$ $Ca(OH)_2$	$Ca(OH)_2$	Ca^{2+}	$Ca(OH)_2/2$	$(0.1M)\ 2$	$= 0.2N$
$0.1M$ $Fe(OH)_3$	$Fe(OH)_3$	$Fe(OH)^{2+}$	$Fe(OH)_3/2$	$(0.1M)\ 2$	$= 0.2N$

EXAMPLE. An amount of 50.00 ml of a $Ca(OH)_2$ solution is titrated with sulfuric acid. An amount of 25.00 ml of $0.0200M$ H_2SO_4 is required to reach the end point. What is the molar concentration of the $Ca(OH)_2$ solution?

SOLUTION. We will work the problem first by using moles.

(1) Balance the equation for the reaction:

$$Ca(OH)_2 + H_2SO_4 \rightarrow CaSO_4 + 2H_2O$$

(2) Convert to moles:

$M \times V$ = number of moles, where V is in liters
$(0.0200 \text{ mole liter}^{-1})(0.0250 \text{ liter}) = 5.00 \times 10^{-4} \text{ mole } H_2SO_4$

(3) Determine the moles of base by using the mole ratios from the equation:

$$(5.00 \times 10^{-4} \text{ mole } H_2SO_4) \times \frac{1 \text{ mole } Ca(OH)_2}{1 \text{ mole } H_2SO_4}$$
$$= 5.00 \times 10^{-4} \text{ mole } Ca(OH)_2$$

(4) Calculate the molarity:

$$M = \frac{\text{moles of } Ca(OH)_2}{\text{liters of solution}} = \frac{5.00 \times 10^{-4} \text{ mole } Ca(OH)_2}{5.000 \times 10^{-2} \text{ liter}}$$
$$= 1.00 \times 10^{-2} = \mathbf{0.0100\,M}$$

Now we work the same problem by using equivalents.

(1) Change concentrations to normality units. We need only know that $H_2SO_4 \rightarrow SO_4^{2-}$; that is, two protons are lost per molecule of H_2SO_4 or 2 moles of protons per mole H_2SO_4. Therefore,

$$N_{H_2SO_4} = 2 \times M_{H_2SO_4} = 2(0.0200) = 0.0400N$$

(2) Number of equiv H_2SO_4 = number of equiv of $Ca(OH)_2$

$N_{H_2SO_4} \times V_{H_2SO_4} = N_{Ca(OH)_2} \times V_{Ca(OH)_2}$
$(0.02500 \text{ liter } H_2SO_4)(0.0400 \text{ equiv } H_2SO_4 \text{ liter}^{-1})$
$$= [N_{Ca(OH)_2}][0.0500 \text{ liter } Ca(OH)_2]$$

$$N_{Ca(OH)_2} = \frac{(0.02500)(0.0400)}{(0.0500)} = 0.0200N$$

and since $Ca(OH)_2$ accepts 2 moles of protons per mole,

$$M_{Ca(OH)_2} = \frac{N}{2} = \frac{0.0200N}{2} = \mathbf{0.0100M}$$

EXAMPLE. A 5.00-g sample of a substance is analyzed for H_3PO_4. The sample is dissolved in water and titrated with $0.500M$ NaOH until all the H_3PO_4 in the sample is converted to HPO_4^{2-} ions; 25.00 ml of the NaOH is required. What is the percent by weight of H_3PO_4 in the sample?

SOLUTION. Solve the problem by using equivalents.

(1) Obtain the concentration in normality units. For NaOH, one proton is accepted per formula unit. Therefore,

$$N = 1 \times M = 1(0.500) = 0.500N$$

(2) Determine the equivalent weight of H_3PO_4. In this reaction, $H_3PO_4 \rightarrow HPO_4^{2-}$, two protons are lost per molecule of H_3PO_4. The equivalent weight of H_3PO_4 equals (formula wt H_3PO_4)/2 = 98.00/2 = 49.00.

(3) The number of equivalents of NaOH equals the number of equivalents of H_3PO_4.

$$(V_{NaOH}) \times (N_{NaOH}) = \frac{g\ H_3PO_4}{g\ equiv\ wt\ H_3PO_4}$$

in which V is in liters.

$$(0.02500\ \text{liter NaOH})(0.500\ \text{equiv NaOH liter}^{-1})$$
$$= \frac{X\ g\ H_3PO_4}{49.00\ g\ H_3PO_4\ equiv^{-1}}$$

$$X = (0.02500)(0.500)(49.00) = 0.613\ g\ H_3PO_4$$

$$\%\ H_3PO_4\ \text{in the sample} = \frac{0.613\ g\ H_3PO_4}{5.00\ g\ \text{sample}} \times 100 = \textbf{12.3\%}$$

Now solve the problem by using the mole concept.

(1) Write the balanced equation for the reaction:

$$2NaOH + H_3PO_4 \rightarrow Na_2HPO_4 + 2H_2O$$

(2) Change to moles:

$$\text{no. of moles} = M \times V$$

in which V is in liters.

$$(0.500\ \text{mole NaOH liter}^{-1})(0.02500\ \text{liter})$$
$$= 0.0125\ \text{mole NaOH}$$

(3) Determine the moles of H_3PO_4 from the mole ratio:

$$(0.0125\ \text{mole NaOH}) \times \left(\frac{1\ \text{mole } H_3PO_4}{2\ \text{moles NaOH}}\right)$$
$$= 0.00625\ \text{mole } H_3PO_4$$

(4) Change to weight in grams:

$$(0.00625\ \text{mole } H_3PO_4)(98.00\ g\ H_3PO_4\ \text{mole}^{-1})$$
$$= 0.613\ g\ H_3PO_4$$

(5) Calculate the percent H_3PO_4 in the sample:

$$\frac{0.613\ g\ H_3PO_4}{5.00\ g\ \text{sample}} \times 100 = \textbf{12.3\%}$$

EXAMPLE.   A 0.712-g sample of an unknown acid is titrated with 30.27 ml of a 0.01230N standard NaOH solution. What is the equivalent weight of the acid?

SOLUTION.   This problem requires equivalents.

$$\text{equiv NaOH} = \text{equiv acid}$$

$$N_{\text{NaOH}} \times V_{\text{NaOH}} = \frac{\text{g acid}}{\text{g equiv wt acid}}$$

$$(0.01230 \text{ equiv NaOH liter}^{-1})(0.03027 \text{ liter NaOH})$$
$$= \frac{0.712 \text{ g acid}}{\text{g equiv wt acid}}$$

$$\text{g equiv wt acid} = \frac{(0.712)}{(0.01230)(0.03027)} = \textbf{1910 g equiv}^{-1}$$

4–5   QUANTITIES OF ENERGY IN CHEMICAL CHANGES

A more thorough description of enthalpy and the other energy relations involved in chemical change must await the discussion of thermodynamics in Chapter 15 of *Chemical Principles*. For now, you may reach a better understanding of this section by knowing that all substances possess a certain heat content, or enthalpy H.

Consider a collection of molecules that is going to participate in a chemical reaction. The total enthalpy represented by these reactants will equal the sum of the enthalpies of all the molecules present. When all the reactant molecules have reacted, the total enthalpy of the products of the reaction will equal the sum of the enthalpies of all the product molecules. The product molecules may have a total enthalpy that is less than the total enthalpy of the reactants. If so, when the reaction takes place, the difference in enthalpy, ΔH, between the products and the reactants will appear as heat energy. Since this heat appears as the reaction proceeds, the reaction is exothermic. We can calculate any difference in enthalpy during the reaction by taking the difference between the total heat content of the products and that of the reactants.

$$\Delta H = \text{total enthalpy of products} - \text{total enthalpy of reactants}$$
$$\Delta H = \sum H_{\text{products}} - \sum H_{\text{reactants}} \tag{4–1}$$

As we have indicated, in an exothermic process the total enthalpy of the reactants is greater than that of the products; so ΔH, as we have obtained it, will have a negative sign. Similarly, ΔH will be positive in an endothermic reaction, $\sum H_{\text{products}} > \sum H_{\text{reactants}}$.

We could evaluate ΔH for a reaction if we could measure the enthalpies for each of the reactant and product substances. Such enthalpies are called *absolute enthalpies*. This measurement cannot be made, however. All we can measure is the heat evolved or absorbed when changes in enthalpy occur, that is, ΔH values. The heat produced by a reaction in a calorimeter at constant pressure is the ΔH of that reaction.

In trying to assign absolute enthalpies to substances, we are faced with a situation similar to the one confronting chemists who attempted to measure atomic weights before the value of Avogadro's number was known. Relative weights of the numbers of atoms were available, so an arbitrary standard was set as a unit of atomic weight; Dalton assigned to the hydrogen atom the weight of 1 atomic weight unit. With this basis, each atom could be assigned a weight in atomic weight units.

To assign enthalpies to substances, a reference enthalpy is arbitrarily established as a standard. The enthalpies of all other substances are expressed relative to this standard. The chosen standard is the assignment of an enthalpy $H = 0$ for all elements in their standard states. These standard states are strictly defined conditions. For solids and liquids, the standard state is the most stable state of the substance at 25°C and 1 atm external pressure. For gases, the standard state is the gas at 1 atm pressure and 25°C.

HESS' LAW

This law states that whenever a series of chemical reactions can be combined algebraically to yield a net reaction, the values of ΔH can be combined in exactly the same way to give the ΔH for the net reaction. This law is valuable because it permits us to determine enthalpies of some reactions without making the calorimetric measurement and without knowledge of the absolute enthalpies of substances.

A particularly useful way to catalog enthalpy information is as enthalpies of formation ΔH_f. These are the enthalpy changes that occur when a compound is formed from its elements in their standard states. Extensive tables of ΔH values for a multitude of compounds are available. These tables generally give values for the formation of the substance at 25°C. This is indicated by the symbol $\Delta H_f{}^0$, and the values are referred to as standard enthalpies of formation.

What makes enthalpies of formation so useful is that they represent the enthalpy H for the product molecule relative to the $H = 0$ for elements in their standard states. This can be shown by analyzing a typical reaction for the formation of a substance from the elements in their standard states. Consider the reaction

$$C(\text{graphite}) + \tfrac{1}{2}O_2(g) \rightarrow CO(g)$$

The enthalpy change, ΔH^0, for this reaction at 25°C is found experimentally to be -67.6 kcal mole^{-1}. The ΔH^0 for this reaction is, by definition, the enthalpy of formation for $CO(g)$, $\Delta H_f{}^0$. Now recall that $\Delta H_{\text{reaction}} = \sum H_{\text{products}} - \sum H_{\text{reactants}}$. For this reaction at 25°C,

$$\Delta H^0{}_{\text{reaction}} = H_{CO(g)} - [H(\text{graphite}) + \tfrac{1}{2}H_{O_2}(g)] = -67.6 \text{ kcal}$$

By assignment, the enthalpies for elements in their standard states are zero; that is, $H_C(\text{graphite})$ and $H_{O_2(g)} = 0$. Therefore,

$$\Delta H^0_{\text{reaction}} = \Delta H_{CO(g)} - 0 - 0 = -67.6 \text{ kcal}$$

However, as we have pointed out, ΔH^0 for this reaction is the heat of formation of $CO(g)$ at 25°C. Thus,

$$\Delta H_f^0 = \Delta H_{CO(g)} = -67.6 \text{ kcal}$$

We can rewrite Equation 4–1 in terms of the heats of formation instead of the absolute enthalpies.

$$\Delta H^0_{\text{reaction}} = \sum \Delta H_f^0_{\text{products}} - \sum \Delta H_f^0_{\text{reactants}} \qquad (4\text{--}2)$$

If a compound such as $CO(g)$ is formed at 25°C and then heated to a higher temperature, the added heat will be absorbed by the CO and become part of its heat content or enthalpy. As a result, the H_{CO} will be larger than it was at 25°C, and ΔH_f at the higher temperature will be more positive. We can correct ΔH values for temperature change in a rather straightforward way by using the specific heats or heat capacities of the substances. For the moment, we will make all our calculations at 25°C.

EXAMPLE.   Calculate the enthalpy change associated with the combustion of acetic acid.

$$HC_2H_3O_2(l) + 2O_2(g) \rightarrow 2CO_2(g) + 2H_2O(g)$$

SOLUTION.   Although we can calculate this directly from Equation 4–2,

$$\Delta H^0 \text{ reaction} = 2\,\Delta H_f^0(CO_2, g) + 2\,\Delta H_f^0(H_2O, g)$$
$$- [\Delta H_f^0(HC_2H_3O_2, l) + 2\,\Delta H_f^0(O_2, g)]$$

we give the equations and heat summations to demonstrate how such calculations follow Hess' law.

All the reactions that we use are for the formation of the compounds at 25°C from the elements in their standard states. Therefore, the enthalpy changes will be ΔH_f^0 values. (We can find standard heats of formations listed in Appendix 2 of *Chemical Principles*.)

$$C(\text{graphite}) + O_2(g) \rightarrow CO_2(g) \qquad \Delta H_f^0 = -94.05 \text{ kcal}$$
$$(4\text{--}3)$$

$$H_2(g) + \tfrac{1}{2}O_2(g) \rightarrow H_2O(g) \qquad \Delta H_f^0 = -57.79 \text{ kcal}$$
$$(4\text{--}4)$$

$$2H_2(g) + 2C(\text{graphite}) + O_2(g) \rightarrow HC_2H_3O_2(l)$$
$$\Delta H_f^0 = -116.4 \text{ kcal} \qquad (4\text{--}5)$$

To combine these equations and obtain the reaction, we need to reverse Equation 4–5 and double Equations 4–3 and 4–4. We must treat the enthalpy changes in the same manner.

$$2C(\text{graphite}) + 2O_2(g) \rightarrow 2CO_2(g)$$
$$\Delta H^0 = 2\Delta H_f^0 = 2(-94.05) = -188.10 \text{ kcal} \quad (4\text{--}6)$$
$$2H_2(g) + O_2(g) \rightarrow 2H_2O(g)$$
$$\Delta H_f^0 = 2\Delta H_f^0 = 2(-57.79) = -115.58 \text{ kcal} \quad (4\text{--}7)$$
$$HC_2H_3O_2(l) \rightarrow 2H_2(g) + 2C(\text{graphite}) + O_2(g)$$
$$\Delta H^0 = -\Delta H_f^0 = -(-116.4) = +116.4 \text{ kcal} \quad (4\text{--}8)$$

Adding the three preceding equations and canceling like terms from each side gives

$$2\cancel{C(\text{graphite})} + 2O_2(g) + 2\cancel{H_2(g)} + \cancel{O_2(g)} + HC_2H_3O_2(l)$$
$$\rightarrow 2CO_2(g) + 2H_2O(g) + 2\cancel{H_2(g)} + 2\cancel{C(\text{graphite})} + \cancel{O_2(g)}$$
$$\Delta H_{\text{reax}} = -188.10 - 115.58 + 116.4 \text{ kcal}$$
$$HC_2H_3O_2(l) + 2O_2(g) \rightarrow 2CO_2(g) + 2H_2O(g)$$
$$\Delta H^0{}_{\text{reax}} = -187.3 \text{ kcal}$$

Before we leave this problem, let us look again at the final combination of enthalpies given by applying Hess' law to this problem

$$\Delta H_{\text{reax}} = \quad 2(-94.05) \quad + \quad 2(-57.79) \quad - \quad (-116.4)$$
$$\downarrow \qquad\qquad \downarrow \qquad\qquad \downarrow$$
$$2\Delta H_f^0(CO, g) \quad 2\Delta H_f^0(H_2O, g) \quad \Delta H_f^0(HC_2H_3O_2, l)$$

That is,

$$\Delta H^0{}_{\text{reax}} = \sum \Delta H_f^0{}_{\text{products}} - \sum \Delta H_f^0{}_{\text{reactants}}$$

This is Equation 4–2. If you accept the validity of this equation, you can rapidly calculate the problems involving enthalpies of reaction by using ΔH_f^0 values. You need not write the chemical equations.

EXAMPLE. One of the reactions that occurs in a blast furnace during the manufacture of iron is

$$Fe_2O_3(s) + 3CO(g) \rightarrow 2Fe(s) + 3CO_2(g)$$

Calculate the enthalpy change for this reaction at 25°C.

SOLUTION. The following ΔH_f^0 values are available in tables in kcal mole^{-1}: $Fe_2O_3(s)$, -196.5; $CO(g)$, -26.41; $CO_2(g)$, -94.05.

$$\Delta H^0{}_{\text{reax}} = \sum \Delta H_f^0{}_{\text{products}} - \sum \Delta H_f^0{}_{\text{reactants}}$$
$$= [2\Delta H_f^0(Fe, s) + 3\Delta H_f^0(CO_2, g)]$$
$$\quad - [\Delta H_f^0(Fe_2O_3, s) + 3\Delta H_f^0(CO, g)]$$
$$= [2(0) + 3(-94.05)] - [-196.5 + 3(-26.41)]$$
$$= -282.15 - (-196.5 - 79.23)$$
$$= -282.15 + 275.7 = -6.5 \text{ kcal}$$

We have worked this problem without writing the equations. Why don't you combine the equations and see if we have, indeed, calculated ΔH^0 for the reaction?

CHAPTER 5 WILL IT REACT?
AN INTRODUCTION
TO CHEMICAL EQUILIBRIUM

Up to this chapter in *Chemical Principles*
we have been concerned with the nature
of matter in its various physical states and
the relationships between quantities of
matter that interact and those formed
during a chemical reaction. The key to
the latter is the use of the mole as a means
of expressing the number and amount of
atoms and molecules involved in a reaction
and the shorthand notation used to
describe the reaction—the balanced
chemical equation. These same concepts are
fundamental to understanding the material
in Chapter 5, which deals with the extent
to which reactions proceed. You should be
prepared to think in terms of moles and
balanced equations as you work the problems
included in this chapter.

5–1 SPONTANEOUS REACTIONS

The major point of this section involves the
distinction between the rate at which a
reaction occurs and whether it will occur at
all. The factors that determine whether a
reaction will occur are developed in detail
in Chapters 15 and 16. The point to be
made now is that reactions occur with a
variety of rates, from extremely rapid
(virtually instantaneous) to rates so slow
that in any reasonable time it is almost
impossible to detect any reaction. To
illustrate these extremes, consider the

decomposition of the compound 1,2,3,-trinitropropane, commonly called nitroglycerine, or glycerol trinitrate. The reaction is represented by the chemical equation

$$4C_3H_5(ONO_2)_3(l) \rightarrow 6N_2(g) + 12CO_2(g) + 10H_2O(g) + O_2(g)$$

Note that 4 moles of liquid nitroglycerine (density $= 1.60$ g cm^{-3}) produces 29 moles of products, all of which are gases. From the reaction temperature and molar volume we can calculate that 908 g (about 0.568 liter) of nitroglycerine produces about 650 liters (at STP) of gaseous products in an instant. The tremendous detonation wave produced from this change in volume is propagated through space at a rate of about 7700 miles per second. Nitroglycerine is one of the most powerful explosives known.

Contrast this very rapid reaction with the combustion of wood. Wood is essentially cellulose, and the products of its complete combustion are carbon dioxide and water. The equation for this reaction is

$$C_6H_{10}O_5(s) + 6O_2(g) \rightarrow 6CO_2(g) + 5H_2O(g)$$

That this reaction proceeds rather rapidly at elevated temperatures is illustrated by the burning of a stick of wood. But at room temperature the combustion rate is extremely slow. You do not expect an article of wooden furniture to disappear as it combines with the oxygen in the air in your lifetime or, for that matter, in the lifetime of future generations of people who may cherish that article of furniture as an antique. However, the presence of stone axes and other ancient implements in the burial sites of very early man testify that this reaction does take place, but at a very, very slow rate, because the handles of the axes, presumably made of wood, have long been returned to the atmosphere as carbon dioxide and water—a natural recycling process.

Spontaneous reactions are of interest to chemists because they generally can find ways of controlling the reaction rate. Increasing the temperature always will increase the rate of a spontaneous reaction. The addition of a catalyst, which provides a means by which the reaction can take place by a different and more efficient pathway, increasing the pressure, if gaseous reactants are involved, grinding or powdering solid reactants or dissolving them in solution so that there is a larger surface area available for interaction, all are methods that are used to increase the rate of a spontaneous reaction. Similar techniques, in particular lowering the temperature and using appropriate catalysts, can be used to slow down reactions that proceed too rapidly, thereby avoiding explosions.

5-2 EQUILIBRIUM AND THE EQUILIBRIUM CONSTANT

To understand better the principles in this section let's look at the relationship between the concentration of the reacting molecules and the reaction rate. We assume that for two molecules or atoms (call them A and B) to react, they must come in contact. Since molecules are in motion, A and B can collide with one another as they move through space. It follows that the greater the number of A and B molecules moving in a given volume, the greater will be the collision frequency of A and B molecules. And the more collisions that take place in a given time, the faster will be the rate of the reaction between A and B to produce products. We express the number of molecules (atoms or ions) in a unit volume as the molar concentration, that is, the number of moles of molecules, atoms, or ions per liter. The standard notation of a bracket enclosing the formula of a substance represents the concentration of that substance in moles per liter. To describe the relationship between concentration and reaction rate, we use a mathematical expression, called a rate law or rate equation.

The rate laws for the reaction, $N_2 + O_2 \rightarrow 2NO$, and the reverse reaction, $2NO \rightarrow N_2 + O_2$, are developed in the text.

It is very important that one have a sound understanding of why the rate equation for a given reaction is formulated as it is, if one is to appreciate fully the nature of chemical equilibrium and the origin of the equilibrium-constant expression. For this reason, a more detailed development of the rate equations of two general types of reactions will be presented in this study guide. The development will follow a different approach than that taken in the textbook, but will be based on the same principle mentioned earlier, that is, for two or more species to react, they must collide. The species produced as a result of this collision will be referred to as the products. Both reactant and product species can be atoms, molecules, ions, or radicals. The exact nature of the species is irrelevant to our discussion, so for the purpose of simplicity we shall refer to them as molecules and symbolize them by letters. The two types of reactions to be considered are one in which two different molecules collide to give the products of the reaction:

$A + B \rightarrow$ products

and a reaction in which two molecules of the same kind collide to give products:

$2A \rightarrow$ products

It is important to emphasize that in the reactions we will be considering, it is assumed that the products are formed directly upon their collision. Such reactions are called primary processes. In fact, few reactions occur by a single primary process. Rather, most reactions occur by a series of stepwise reactions, each involving the collision of two or more molecules, that produce product molecules, radicals, or ions. These products may, in turn, react by a simple collision process to form other products, and so on. This sequence of reactions, each representing a simple collision between two or more molecules, is referred to as the mechanism of the reaction. One seldom detects the products formed in these simple primary reaction processes because

Will It React?
An Introduction
to Chemical
Equilibrium

162

they are used as reactant molecules in subsequent reaction steps in the mechanism. What is observed are the molecules left at the end of the reaction sequence. These are termed the products of the overall reaction. They are the products indicated on the right side of the conventional chemical equation, which describes the reaction stoichiometry in terms of the relative amounts of substances one puts into the reaction and the relative amounts of the substances one eventually gets out.

Another important fact that should be pointed out is that, although a collision between the reacting molecules is absolutely necessary for a primary reaction process to take place, not every collision will lead to the production of new products. A detailed discussion of this is treated in Chapter 18 in *Chemical Principles*, which is devoted to the kinetics and mechanisms of reactions.

THE FORMULATION OF THE RATE EQUATION FOR A REACTION OF TYPE A + B PRODUCTS

Let us consider a case in which four A molecules and four B molecules are confined in a container of fixed volume. We can count the number of collisions that the A particles can have with the B molecules in this container, using a diagram such as shown in Figure 5–1. One sees that

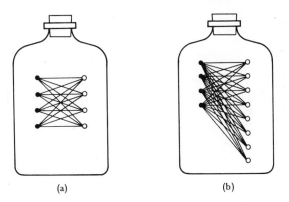

(a)   (b)

Figure 5–1.   The number of collisions between molecules is equal to the product of the number of molecules. (a) Four A molecules (solid dots) and four B molecules (open circles). Total number of collisions = 4 + 4 + 4 + 4 = 16 or 4 × 4 = 16. (b) Four A molecules and eight B molecules. Total number of collisions = 8 + 8 + 8 + 8 = 32 or 4 × 8 = 32. Since the number of molecules in a container is measured by molar concentration, the number of collisions is proportional to the molar concentrations of the reacting molecules (A and B); that is, the number of collisions is proportional to [A][B].

the first A molecule may collide with any of the four B molecules; this amounts to four collisions. The second A molecule can collide with any of the four B molecules; this gives another four collisions. Continuing this counting procedure it should be apparent that each A molecule has the opportunity for collision with each of the four B molecules. This gives a total of $4 \times 4 = 16$ possible collisions.

To see the effect of changing the number of one or the other of the reactant molecules, let us add an additional four particles of B to the container, that is, let us double the number of B molecules. As illustrated in Figure 5–1(b), each A atom now has eight chances to collide with a B atom. The total number of opportunities for collision has been increased to $4 \times 8 = 32$. Our conclusion is that doubling the number of molecules of one of the reactants results in doubling the number of opportunities for collision.

Instead of counting the individual molecules, we could have expressed the numbers in terms of the number of moles of molecules. Since the volume of the container was kept constant during our hypothetical reaction, the changes in the concentration of the particles, expressed in moles per liter, would display the same effect on the relative number of collisions as we observed for the individual molecules. Namely, the opportunity for collisions between A and B will be equal to the product of the molar concentrations of A and B. The greater the opportunity for collision, the larger should be the number of collisions that take place in a unit of time in the container, therefore, the faster will be the rate of the reaction.

In summary, the rate of the reaction in which two different molecules, A and B, collide to produce products will be directly proportional to their molar concentrations:

$$\text{Rate of reaction} \propto [A][B]$$

or

$$\text{Rate of reaction} = k_1[A][B]$$

The proportionality constant k_1 is called the specific rate constant for this reaction.

As we learned in the study of the kinetic molecular theory of matter, when one increases the temperature of a system of molecules, their average kinetic energy increases; on the average, the molecules will move faster. If the velocity of the A and B molecules in our closed container increases, then one can expect that the number of collisions the molecules will make in a unit of time will increase, and this should result in an increase in the rate of the reaction. If the concentrations of A and B are kept the same, the rate law indicates that an increase in rate must be reflected in a larger value for k_1. Therefore, we can expect that the specific rate constant for a given reaction will vary with the temperature, and that it will increase as the temperature is increased.

Will It React?
An Introduction
to Chemical
Equilibrium

164

THE FORMULATION OF THE RATE EQUATION
FOR A REACTION OF THE TYPE 2A → PRODUCTS

The reaction to be considered is one in which two molecules of the same kind collide to produce the products of a reaction. Following the same

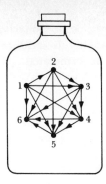

Figure 5–2. The total number of collisions between 6 A molecules (solid dots) = 5 + 4 + 3 + 2 + 1 = 15. If the number of A molecules were doubled, the number of collisions would be: 11 + 10 + 9 + 8 + 7 + 6 + 5 + 4 + 3 + 2 + 1 = 66. The number of collisions is equal to the sum of the series $(n - 1) + (n - 2) + (n - 3) \cdots (n - n)$, in which n is the number of molecules.

procedure used before, let us consider six A molecules in a closed container and count the number of chances for collision. Using Figure 5–2, in which the A molecules are represented by circles numbered for identification purposes, we see that the A particle numbered 1 may collide with A particles numbered 2, 3, 4, 5, and 6, a total of 5 chances for collision. The A molecule numbered 2 will have only 4 chances for collision (collisions with molecules 3, 4, 5, and 6) since the collision with the A molecule numbered 2 was counted in the first series. Similarly, molecule 3 will have 3 chances for collision; 4 will have 2 chances; only one opportunity remains for collisions involving particles 5 and 6 that have not already been considered and counted. Summing these gives a total of $5 + 4 + 3 + 2 + 1 = 15$ possible collisions. If we double the number of A molecules by placing 12 A molecules in the container, the total number of collisions will be $11 + 10 + 9 + 8 + 7 + 6 + 5 + 4 + 3 + 2 + 1 = 66$. To generalize, for N particles, the total number of collisions will be $(N - 1) + (N - 2) + (N - 3) + \cdots + 1$. The mathematical formula for determining the sum of such a series of numbers is $(N - 1)N/2$. Therefore, we can state that the number of collisions when two A molecules collide to produce products is proportional to $(N - 1)N$, in which $N =$ the number of A particles in the container. In chemical reactions, the number N of atoms, molecules, radicals, or ions which participate is extremely large and the subtraction of 1 from such a large number will have no significant effect[1]. That is to say, $(N - 1)N$ is essentially equal to N^2, and we

[1] As an example, consider the reaction of one hundred millionth of a mole of Na atoms, *i.e.*, $23/10^8 = 2.3 \times 10^{-7}$ g of Na, an almost immeasurable amount. There will be $(6.02 \times 10^{23})/10^8 = 6.02 \times 10^{15}$ Na atoms present. $6.02 \times 10^{15} - 1 = 6.02 \times 10^{15}$. To as many as 14 significant figures, the 1 is completely negligible; we only know the value of Avogadro's number to six significant figures.

can conclude that the rate is directly proportional to N^2. Since the number of A molecules in the container is measured by its molar concentration $[A]$, the rate law can be formulated

Rate of the reaction $\propto [A]^2$

or

Rate of the reaction $= k_2[A]^2$

THE RELATIONSHIP BETWEEN REACTION RATE AND CHEMICAL EQUILIBRIUM

If a certain set of reactant molecules collide to produce products, these product molecules also will be in motion and also can collide. In the latter collision process, the product molecules can produce the original reactants. Thus, for any given reaction, a reverse reaction will take place unless something occurs that removes one or more of the product molecules as they are formed. We conclude from this that in a container from which neither reactants nor products can escape, both a forward and reverse reaction will take place.

Again, let us consider a general primary process in which two molecules collide to produce two different molecules in the ratio of $1:2$. The equation for the reaction is

$$2Y \rightarrow D + 2E$$

The rate of production of the products of this reaction, which we will refer to as the forward reaction, can be expressed by an equation of the form we developed for the $2A \rightarrow$ products case:

$$\text{rate}_f = k_f[Y]^2$$

in which k_f is the specific rate constant for the forward reaction.

Once the forward reaction has proceeded to produce some D and E molecules, these molecules can collide; the equation for the reverse reaction is

$$D + 2E \rightarrow 2Y$$

For this reverse reaction, the rate law is a composite of the expression developed for the $A + B \rightarrow$ products and the $2A \rightarrow$ products cases:

$$\text{rate}_r = k_r[D][E]^2$$

When the reactant Y is first introduced into the container, its concentration is high, so the forward reaction, $2Y \rightarrow D + 2E$ is rapid. However, as the forward reaction proceeds, the concentration of Y present in the container will diminish. This will cause a gradual decrease in the rate of the forward reaction. As Y is used up, more D and E are produced. The result will be that the rate of the reverse reaction will increase steadily from an initial value of zero (no D or E present).

Clearly, since the rate of the forward reaction steadily decreases and the rate of the reverse reaction steadily increases as the reaction

Will It React?
An Introduction
to Chemical
Equilibrium

166

progresses, at some time the rates of the forward and the reverse reactions must become equal. Then the Υ molecules will be forming D and E molecules just as fast as the D and E molecules are regenerating Υ molecules. Therefore, although the conversion of Υ to D and E and the reverse reaction of D and E recombining to form Υ are taking place continuously, the concentrations of Υ, E, and D will remain fixed. It is at this point that the condition of *chemical equilibrium* is attained. A sampling of a reacting system *at equilibrium* always will reveal that the concentrations of products and reactants are constant, even though both the forward and reverse reactions continue to take place.

We can analyze our hypothetical reaction system at equilibrium in a manner analogous to that done for the $2NO \rightarrow N_2 + O_2$ reaction given in the text. For the reaction $2\Upsilon \rightarrow D + 2E$

$$\text{rate}_f = k_f[\Upsilon]^2 \qquad \text{and} \qquad \text{rate}_r = k_r[D][E]^2$$

At equilibrium

$$\text{rate}_f = \text{rate}_r$$

therefore,

$$k_f[\Upsilon]^2 = k_r[D][E]^2$$

Solving for the ratio of the specific rate constant for the forward reaction to the specific rate constant for the reverse reaction, we obtain

$$\frac{k_f}{k_r} = K_{eq} = \frac{[D][E]^2}{[\Upsilon]^2}$$

K_{eq}, the ratio of the two specific rate constants, is the equilibrium constant for the reaction.

The equilibrium-constant expression for the $aA + bB \rightleftarrows cC + dD$ is given in the text (Equation 5–8):

$$K_{eq} = \frac{[C]^c[D]^d}{[A]^a[B]^b}$$

The development of this equilibrium-constant expression is based on equating the forward and reverse rates of reactions that represent primary processes. That is, the reactions are considered to take place by the collision of the molecules just as they are represented in the chemical equation. In this case, the equilibrium constant is equal to the ratio of the rate constant for the forward reaction to that for the reverse reaction.

One should not conclude that the general expression for the equilibrium constant implies that the forward reaction proceeds by the collisions of a molecules of A and b molecules of B, and that the reverse reaction proceeds by the collision of c molecules of C and d molecules of D. This equilibrium-constant expression is based on the chemical equation for the overall reaction and not that of a primary collision process. As mentioned previously, most reactions occur by a sequence of primary reaction steps. The rate law for each of these is as we formulated them from our simple collision model. That the equilibrium-constant expression can be derived from the overall stoichiometry of the reaction is because the contributions of the intermediate reactions cancel. We will illustrate this with a simple two-step mechanism.

Consider a hypothetical reaction that has the overall chemical stoichiometry represented by the equation

$$2A + B \rightleftarrows 2C + D$$

Suppose the following series of primary reactions represent the mechanism for this reaction:

$$2A \rightarrow A_2$$
$$A_2 + B \rightarrow 2C + D$$

Note that the sum of the two reaction steps $(2A + A_2 + B \rightarrow A_2 + 2C + D)$ is the same as the overall reaction $(2A + B \rightleftarrows 2C + D)$. The molecule A_2, which appears on both sides of the summation equation for the two-step mechanism and thus cancels, is called a *reaction intermediate*.

This section of *Chemical Principles* ends with some examples of specific chemical reactions and discusses how to formulate the equilibrium constant for them. This is a very straightforward procedure, since it merely involves direct substitution into the formula that specifies the conventions to be followed in writing the K_{eq} expression. Let us summarize the procedure for the general reaction $aA + bB \rightleftarrows cC + dD$, for which the equilibrium-constant expression is

$$K_{eq} = \frac{[C]^c[D]^d}{[A]^a[B]^b}$$

✳
IMPT.

(1) The balanced chemical equation for the reaction must be written before the equilibrium-constant expression can be formulated. The designation of what are the products and what are the reactants, and the values for the exponents are obtained from the balanced equation.

(2) The concentrations of the products are written in the numerator and the concentrations of the reactants in the denominator.

(3) The concentrations are expressed in moles per liter. One exception frequently followed is in the case of reactions in which gases are the only chemical species to be written in the K_{eq} expression. In such instances, the partial pressures of the gases are used instead of the molar concentrations. Of course, the partial pressure of a gas is directly proportional to its molar concentration.

(4) The molar concentrations of each of the reactant and product species are raised to an exponential power, which is the same as the coefficient that appears before the species in the balanced equation.

(5) After raising the molar concentrations to the appropriate powers, the values are multiplied in the equilibrium-constant expression; they are not added.

Examples 1 through 5 in *Chemical Principles* apply the preceding procedures.

5-3 USING EQUILIBRIUM CONSTANTS

To test the validity of the form chosen for the equilibrium constant and to support the theory that we have outlined in a qualitative way, one should resort to experimental verification. *Chemical Principles* illustrates how this can be done with data from a study of the gaseous H_2, I_2, and HI equilibrium system (Table 5–1). This experiment, and many others carried out on other equilibria, support the concept of the equilibrium constant as we have formulated it. Historically, the experimental data were obtained first, then the theory was developed to explain the data. This sequence of events is common to the so-called scientific method.

Once the K_{eq} for a reaction has been established, it is possible to determine the equilibrium concentrations of all substances, given either the amounts of reactants (Examples 9 and 11 in the text) or of products (Example 10). To work such problems, we recommend that you use a definite routine, which you should be able to apply to almost any equilibrium calculation with little modification. It is simple to overlook a fact or make a mistake in a substitution in equilibrium problems, but if you follow a routine as suggested below, your chances of making such mistakes will be minimized significantly.

✳ (1)   Write the balanced equation for the equilibrium involved.

(2)   Formulate the equilibrium constant expression, K_{eq}.

(3)   Using the balanced equation as a guide, construct a table listing the molar concentrations of each substance present at the beginning of the reaction and when equilibrium is attained. It is here that ingenuity is required because you must formulate these concentrations in terms of the data given and a single unknown. Remember, all concentrations in the equilibrium-constant expression are in moles per liter; therefore, consider everything in terms of moles per liter.

(4)   Substitute the values given in the table for the equilibrium concentrations in the K_{eq} expression, and solve the resulting equation.

Now we will apply our routine to an equilibrium reaction that is somewhat more complicated than those in the text. Let us calculate the equilibrium concentrations of all the substances present if 1.0×10^{-2} mole each of the gases NO and O_2 are placed in a 1-liter flask at $10°C$.

(1)   Write the balanced equation for the reaction:

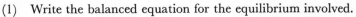

$$2NO(g) + O_2(g) \rightleftarrows 2NO_2(g) \tag{5-1}$$

(2)   Formulate the K_{eq} expression from the above equation:

$$K_{eq} = \frac{[NO_2]^2}{[NO]^2[O_2]} \tag{5-2}$$

(3) Construct a table listing the molar concentrations of each substance present at the beginning of the reaction and at equilibrium. The concentrations of the substances present at the beginning are obtained readily from the data in the problem: $[NO] = [O_2] = 1.0 \times 10^{-2}$ mole liter^{-1}, and $[NO_2] = 0.0$.

The calculation of the equilibrium concentrations is another matter. What we must do is attempt to express these in terms of a single unknown. That in itself is not too difficult. However, we also should keep in mind that we ultimately are going to substitute these equilibrium-concentration expressions into the equation for K_{eq} and solve for the unknown. It would be to our benefit to keep the solution to this equation as simple as possible.

Knowing this, let us first let x equal the equilibrium concentration of NO_2 in moles liter^{-1}. From the stoichiometry of the balanced equation (Equation 5–1) we see that for every mole of NO_2 formed, one mole of NO and 1/2 mole of O_2 must be consumed. The amount of NO and O_2 left at equilibrium will be the difference between what was present before the reaction began and what was consumed. If x is the molar concentration of NO_2 at equilibrium, then we must conclude that x moles per liter of $NO(g)$ and $1/2(x) = x/2$ moles per liter of $O_2(g)$ reacted in reaching equilibrium. It follows that $1.0 \times 10^{-2} - x$ is the molar concentration of NO left at equilibrium and $1.0 \times 10^{-2} - x/2$ is the molar concentration of O_2 left at equilibrium. Therefore, our table for Step (3) is

Concentrations in moles liter^{-1}:	[NO]	[O$_2$]	[NO$_2$]
At start of reaction:	1.0×10^{-2}	1.0×10^{-2}	0.00
At equilibrium:	$1.0 \times 10^{-2} - x$	$1.0 \times 10^{-2} - \dfrac{x}{2}$	x

(4) Substituting the equilibrium concentrations in the K_{eq} expression gives

$$K_{eq} = \frac{[NO_2]^2}{[NO]^2[O_2]} = \frac{x^2}{(0.010 - x)^2(0.010 - x/2)} = 1.1 \text{ (at } 10°C)$$

It remains for us to solve this equation for x. However, the denominator shows that the equation will be a cubic equation (x to the third power), which is not too easy to solve by any method other than successive approximations. The presence of the fraction $x/2$ in the one factor in the denominator can make the arithmetic a bit cumbersome, so it is worthwhile to see if the situation can be simplified by choosing some other value for the unknown.

Let us try letting y = the moles per liter of O_2 that reacts as the reaction proceeds to equilibrium. From the stoichiometry of the reaction, for every mole of O_2 that reacts 2 moles of NO must react and 2 moles of NO_2 are produced. Our table now becomes

Will It React?
An Introduction
to Chemical
Equilibrium

170

Concentrations in moles liter^{-1}: | [NO] | [O$_2$] | [NO$_2$]

At the start of the experiment: 0.010 0.010 0.0

At equilibrium: $0.010 - 2y$ $0.010 - y$ $2y$

Substitution of these equilibrium concentrations in the expression for K_{eq} gives

$$K_{eq} = \frac{[NO_2]^2}{[NO]^2[O_2]} = \frac{(2y)^2}{(0.010 - 2y)^2(0.010 - y)} = 1.1$$

To complete Step (4), you must solve this equation for y. If you multiply the terms in the denominator you will see that the equation is a cubic equation; frequently equations of higher order result in problems involving homogeneous equilibria. A method of successive approximations is required to solve these equations. As mentioned previously, problems of such complexity as to require you to use successive approximations are not likely to be encountered in this course, so we will not solve this problem here. We have included this problem to illustrate how even the more complex equilibrium problems can be set up following the simple rules that have been given for solving equilibrium problems in general. Also, we have demonstrated how, by a judicious choice of unknowns, one can arrive at an equation that is solved more easily.

You may wish to try to solve this problem using the procedures of successive approximation outlined on pages 27–28 in this Study Guide. The result is $y = 4.6 \times 10^{-4}M$, from which the concentrations of the species present at equilibrium can be computed:

$$[NO] = [O_2] = 0.010 - 0.00046 = \mathbf{0.010}$$

and

$$[NO_2] = 2y = 2(0.00046) = \mathbf{9.2 \times 10^{-4}}$$

Previously, we discussed how the equilibrium constant for the H$_2(g)$, I$_2(g)$, HI(g) system was determined by analysis of an equilibrium mixture for each of the species present. In practice, such a complete analysis often is very difficult to carry out without disturbing the equilibrium itself. Before continuing to the next section, let us consider the determination of the equilibrium constant for a system in which the only experimental data necessary are the initial concentration of reactants and the concentration of only one of the substances present after equilibrium is attained—in this case, one of the reactants. Observe how the four-step routine we have been using for equilibrium calculations is applicable to this K_{eq} calculation as well.

It is found that after mixing 1.0 mole of NO and 1.0 mole of O$_2$ in a 2-liter flask at 1 atm and 10°C, the concentration of O$_2$ remaining in the flask after equilibrium is reached is 0.4 mole liter^{-1}. Our

Using, Equilibrium Constants

problem is to use the above data to calculate the equilibrium constant K_{eq} for the gaseous NO, O_2, NO_2 reaction.

(1) First we write the equation representing the reaction:

$2NO + O_2 \rightleftarrows 2NO_2$ (all substances are gases)

(2) Using this equation, we write the equilibrium-constant expression:

$$K_{eq} = \frac{[NO_2]^2}{[NO]^2[O_2]}$$

(3) We now construct a table listing the concentration of all the substances before equilibrium was established and their concentration after equilibrium has been established.

Concentrations in moles liter^{-1}:	[NO]	[O$_2$]	[NO$_2$]
At the start of the experiment:	1.0 mole/ 2.0 liter $= 0.5$	1.0 mole/ 2.0 liter $= 0.5$	0.00
At equilibrium:	$0.5 - 2(0.10)$ $= 0.30$	0.40 (given in data)	$2(0.50 - 0.40)$ $= 0.20$

The concentrations of NO, O_2, and NO_2 remaining at equilibrium were determined from the fact that 0.40 mole liter^{-1} of O_2 was left at equilibrium. This means that the difference between the molar concentration of O_2 present at the start of the experiment and 0.40 is the molar concentration of O_2 that reacted on the way to reaching equilibrium (*i.e.*, $0.50 - 0.40 = 0.10$ mole liter^{-1}). From the stoichiometry given in the balanced chemical equation for the reaction, we see that for every mole of O_2 that reacts, 2 moles of NO react and 2 moles of NO_2 are produced. Therefore, the reaction of 0.10 mole liter^{-1} of O_2 would require the consumption of $2 \times 0.10 = 0.20$ mole liter^{-1} of NO, and $2 \times 0.10 = 0.20$ mole liter^{-1} of NO_2 would be produced when the reaction reached equilibrium. All that remains for us to determine is the NO left at equilibrium. We had 0.5 mole liter^{-1} at the start of the experiment and we just determined that 0.20 mole liter^{-1} reacts in reaching equilibrium. Therefore, the concentration of NO at equilibrium $= 0.50 - 0.20 = 0.30$ mole liter^{-1}.

Now we substitute the equilibrium values for [NO], [O_2], and [NO_2] in the K_{eq} expression:

$$K_{eq} = \frac{[NO_2]^2}{[NO]^2[O_2]} = \frac{(0.20)^2}{(0.30)^2(0.40)} = 1.1 \qquad \text{(at 10°C)}$$

Will It React?
An Introduction
to Chemical
Equilibrium

172

5–4 FACTORS AFFECTING EQUILIBRIUM:
LE CHATELIER'S PRINCIPLE

When a reaction attains equilibrium, both reactants and products are present such that the ratio of the products of their concentrations satisfies the equilibrium constant for that reaction at a particular temperature. This can be a problem for the chemist who desires to prepare a particular substance by a given chemical reaction, because the maximum amount of product he can expect to produce is governed by the magnitude of the equilibrium constant. If K_{eq} is small, the concentrations of the products at equilibrium will be small. The vast and very profitable chemical industry testifies to the fact that there are ways of circumventing these apparent limitations so that reactions other than those with high K_{eq}'s can be used to produce materials in large yields economically. The clue to how this can be done for a particular reaction can be ascertained by consideration of the fact that the equilibrium constant for a reaction is truly a constant or by applying Le Chatelier's principle. Let us look at both of these approaches to the problem.

Once again let us consider the K_{eq} for a general reaction

$$aA + bB \rightleftarrows cC + dD$$

$$K_{eq} = \frac{[C]^c[D]^d}{[A]^a[B]^b}$$

Suppose that we wish to produce product C in as large a yield as possible. Recognizing that K_{eq} is a constant, we see that there are two conditions under which we can reach equilibrium with a high concentration of C present: (1) the concentration of D is low, or (2) the concentrations of A or B or both are low.

If the concentration of D is low, then the numerator of the equilibrium-constant expression must decrease. However, since the value for K_{eq} must remain constant, the reacting system must adjust itself to compensate for any decrease in the concentration of D. It can do this by decreasing the concentrations of A and B, the reactants, and increasing the concentration of C, the product we have chosen as the one we wish to prepare in quantity. Since the ultimate amount of product we obtain is determined by the amount of starting material we use, decreasing the concentrations of the reactants will not be of any benefit to us in terms of producing large amounts of C. Therefore, the approach to use is to keep the concentration of D as low as possible. The most direct way to do this is to remove D as fast as it is generated. Several techniques that have been used for doing this are described in Section 5–4 in *Chemical Principles*.

APPLICATION OF LE CHATELIER'S PRINCIPLE

Factors
Affecting
Equilibrium:
Le Chatelier's
Principle

173

Le Chatelier's principle can be stated as follows: When a stress is applied to any system at equilibrium, the system will adjust itself spontaneously in such a way as to relieve the applied stress. We reason that if D is removed from the system $aA + bB \rightleftarrows cC + dD$ at equilibrium, then according to the Le Chatelier principle, the system will adjust itself to compensate for the removal of D. To do this, more

A and B must react to replace the D removed. In the process of producing additional D, more C will be generated. Therefore, the reaction can be driven to the right and more C produced by removing D. This was the conclusion we reached from the requirement that K_{eq} remain a constant.

Another way by which more C can be produced is deduced readily by applying Le Chatelier's principle. If one adds more A to the system, the system spontaneously adjusts itself to relieve "the stress" of the added A. It can do this if more B reacts with the additional A to form products C and D. A similar result would be obtained if additional B were added to the reacting mixture. Almost all chemical reactions are run with one of the reactants in excess to take advantage of the increased yield of product that will result as the equilibrium is shifted to the right, the direction for the production of products as the equation is written.

From Le Chatelier's principle we would predict that if we increase the pressure on a system at equilibrium, the system will act to relieve the applied pressure by decreasing in volume. Because the volume of a system containing gases will be determined by the volume of the gases, under an increase in pressure the equilibrium position will shift in favor of the reaction that produces the smallest amount (number of moles) of gas. If the total number of moles of gaseous products is equal to the total number of moles of gaseous reactants, the system cannot alter its volume by producing more products and reducing the number of moles of reactants, or vice versa. Therefore, a change in pressure will have no effect on an equilibrium system in which the number of moles of gaseous reactants and products are the same. Should the number of moles of gaseous reactants be larger than the number of moles of gaseous products, the equilibrium position would shift toward an increase in the number of moles of products at the expense of the reactants. In this way the system would achieve a smaller volume. Similarly, a decrease in pressure would cause the equilibrium position to shift in the direction of forming more reactants at the expense of the products.

Neither the reaction

$$H_2(g) + I_2(g) \rightleftarrows 2HI(g)$$

nor the reaction

$$N_2(g) + O_2(g) \rightleftarrows 2NO(g)$$

is affected by pressure, because in both reactions there are 2 moles of gas in the reactants and 2 moles of gas in the products.

However, in the reaction

$$N_2(g) + 3H_2(g) \rightleftarrows 2NH_3(g)$$

the production of $NH_3(g)$ is favored by an increase in pressure. Note that there are 1 mole $N_2(g) + 3$ mole $H_2(g) = 4$ moles of gas in the reactants and 2 moles $NH_3(g)$ in the products. An increase in

Will It React?
An Introduction
to Chemical
Equilibrium

174

pressure will result in the system shifting towards the production of more $NH_3(g)$ at the expense of the $N_2(g)$ and $H_2(g)$, because in this way the total volume of the system will decrease.

If we calculate the enthalpy change at 25°C for the preceding reaction as written, we find that it is an exothermic process:

$$\Delta H^0_{\text{reaction}} = \Sigma \Delta H^0_{\text{products}} - \Sigma \Delta H^0_{\text{reactants}}$$
$$= 2\Delta H^0_{NH_3} - (\Delta H^0_{N_2} + 3\Delta H^0_{H_2})$$
$$= 2(-11.04) - (0.00 - 0.00) = -22.08 \text{ kcal mole}^{-1}$$

Since the reaction produces heat, from Le Chatelier's principle we predict that removing heat will drive the reaction toward the right. Therefore, the best yields of NH_3 can be obtained by running this reaction at high pressures and low temperatures. In practice, this reaction, the Haber process, is run at high pressures and moderate temperatures; too low a temperature slows the rate of the reaction too much.

The $N_2(g) + O_2(g) \rightleftarrows 2NO(g)$ reaction, one of the principal smog-producing processes, has a very low K_{eq} (10^{-30}) at 25°C, but a much higher K_{eq} at the elevated temperatures of an automobile engine. One would interpret this to mean that the equilibrium position is shifted to the right, in favor of the production of more NO as the temperature is raised. Applying Le Chatelier's principle, we would predict the reaction to be endothermic. Using the ΔH^0 values in Appendix 2 in *Chemical Principles*, we see that the reaction is indeed endothermic as written and ΔH is positive:

$$\Delta H^0_{\text{reaction}} = 2\Delta H^0_{NO} - (\Delta H^0_{N_2} + \Delta H^0_{O_2})$$
$$= 2(21.600) - (0.00 - 0.00)$$
$$\Delta H^0_{\text{reaction}} = +43.200 \text{ kcal mole}^{-1}$$

5-5 EQUILIBRIA IN AQUEOUS SOLUTIONS: ACIDS AND BASES

Most of the chemistry with which we will be concerned in this course will take place in aqueous solutions. Therefore, an understanding of chemical equilibria in water solutions is fundamental to the study of chemistry.

Water itself is slightly dissociated into solvated protons, or hydronium ions, and hydroxide ions. Because water molecules are polar and have electron pairs that can be donated easily to empty orbitals on an ion to form a covalent bond, practically every ionic species in aqueous solution must have associated with it a number of water molecules. There is considerable doubt as to the exact number of water molecules associated with most ions, so rather than attempt to state the number explicitly, the symbol (aq) frequently is inserted after the symbol of the ion, or no special notation is used at all. In either case, since the ion is in aqueous solution, it is inferred that it is hydrated.

Equilibria in
Aqueous
Solutions:
Acids and
Bases

175

Because the hydrogen ion (proton) is very small and thus has an extremely high electrical charge density, it is hydrated in water. But for convenience we will write the equation for the dissociation of water simply as $H_2O \rightleftarrows H^+ + OH^-$. The equilibrium-constant expression for the dissociation of water is

$$K_{eq} = \frac{[H^+][OH^-]}{[H_2O]}$$

But because the water dissociates only slightly (10^{-7} mole liter^{-1} at 25°C), the concentration of undissociated water itself is essentially constant (55.5 moles liter^{-1}). Therefore, we can derive another expression that also will be constant by multiplying both sides by the factor 55.5 moles liter^{-1}. The result, K_w, is referred to as the ion-product constant and, like the equilibrium constant, is a true constant that varies only with the temperature. As demonstrated by the data in Table 5–2 in *Chemical Principles*, the value for K_w is about 1×10^{-14} at 25°C. At this temperature that one uses as a standard for most solution measurements, this number (1×10^{-14}) is a fundamental constant and should be memorized:

$$55.5 \times K_{eq} = [H^+][OH^-] = K_w = 1.0 \times 10^{-14}$$

When dealing with aqueous solutions we encounter for the first time equilibria in which the equilibrium-constant expressions are very small. Consequently the concentrations of some of the substances at equilibrium also are very small. When dealing with such small numbers it is convenient to utilize logarithms. A particularly useful logarithmic notation that has been devised to handle acid–base equilibria is the pH scale. The pH is defined as

$$pH = -\log [H^+]$$

Note that the logarithm chosen is to the base 10 and that the negative sign will result in positive values for the pH in all cases for which the molar concentration of hydrogen ions, $[H^+]$, is less than unity. The pH of pure water is 7, since the hydrogen ion concentration in pure water is $1 \times 10^{-7}M$.

$$pH = -\log [H^+] = -\log (1 \times 10^{-7}) = -(0.00 - 7.00) = 7.0$$

At this point it would be well if you review the sections on the use of logarithms and on finding logarithms on the slide rule in Part 1 of this Study Guide. You should be able to calculate the pH of a solution given its $[H^+]$ and to carry out the reverse computation, that is, to calculate the molar concentration of hydrogen ions in a solution, given the solution's pH.

Chemists frequently express small numbers as logarithms, using the notation for pH. Thus one can define pOH as $pOH = -\log [OH^-]$ and pK_{eq} as $pK_{eq} = -\log [K_{eq}]$, or pK_w as $pK_w = -\log [K_w]$. These expressions are used extensively, and it pays to note that because of the negative sign in the definition of pH, pOH, and so on, the larger the

Will It React?
An Introduction
to Chemical
Equilibrium

176

numerical value of the pH, pOH, or pK_{eq}, the lower is the value of $[H^+]$, $[OH^-]$, or K_{eq}.

Returning to the water equilibrium

$$H_2O \rightleftarrows H^+ + OH^-$$

for which

$$K_w = [H^+][OH^-] = 1 \times 10^{-14}$$

we can predict, using Le Chatelier's principle, that the OH^- and the H^+ concentrations will change when either acid (substances that donate protons) or bases (substances that accept protons) are added to water. Rearrangement of the K_w expression permits us to calculate the concentration of OH^- ions in a solution that has a concentration of H^+ ions that is either greater or less than the 1×10^{-7} molar found in neutral water:

$$[OH^-] = \frac{[K_w]}{[H^+]} = \frac{1 \times 10^{-14}}{[H^+]}$$

EXAMPLE.   Calculate the OH^- ion concentration in $0.010M$ HCl.

SOLUTION.   Since HCl is a strong acid, it is dissociated completely in aqueous solution, and the hydrogen ion concentration in $0.010M$ HCl is $0.010M$:

$$[OH^-] = \frac{1 \times 10^{-14}}{[H^+]} = \frac{1 \times 10^{-14}}{1.0 \times 10^{-2}} = 1 \times 10^{-12}$$

The pOH of this solution is

$$pOH = -\log [OH^-] = -\log (1 \times 10^{-12}) = 12$$

We can use the pH, pOH, and pK_w notation to simplify calculations similar to this example. Taking the logarithms of both sides of the relationship $[H^+][OH^-] = K_w$ and multiplying each by -1 gives

$$-\log [H^+] - \log [OH^-] = -\log K_w$$

or

$$pH + pOH = pK_w$$

EXAMPLE.   Calculate the pOH of a solution having a pH of 4.2.

SOLUTION.

$$pH + pOH = pK_w = 4.2 + pOH = 14$$
$$pOH = 14 - 4.2 = 9.8$$

Since $pH + pOH = 14$, in neutral water, where the H^+ and OH^- ion concentrations each equal $10^{-7}M$, the $pH = pOH = 7$. We

Equilibria in
Aqueous
Solutions:
Acids and
Bases

177

conclude that if a solution has a concentration of H^+ greater than $1 = 10^{-7}M$ the concentration of OH^- ions must be less; such solutions are acidic. However, a solution that has a H^+ ion concentration less than $1 \times 10^{-7}M$ must have an OH^- ion concentration that is greater than this; such solutions are basic. Recall that the larger the pH, the lower the H^+ ion concentration; therefore, a solution that has a pH less than 7 is acidic, whereas a solution that has a pH greater than 7 is basic.

STRONG AND WEAK ACIDS

The Brønsted–Lowry theory expands the concept of acids and bases to include solvent systems other than water, but does not alter useful concepts such as pH, pOH, and pK_w, which have been developed for aqueous systems. According to this theory, an acid is any substance that is capable of donating a proton (H^+) and bases are substances that have an electron pair available that can form a covalent bond with the H^+ ion. The main difference in this concept from the older one of Arrhenius is that any substance that has an electron pair available and forms a covalent bond with the H^+ ion qualifies as a base. Whereas the Arrhenius theory would classify LiOH, NaOH, and so on as bases, the Brønsted–Lowry theory would consider the OH^- ion in these substances as the base.

By this definition, an acid and base would display their properties by a chemical reaction that we can generalize in the following way. Let the acid be abbreviated HA and the base abbreviated B. When these two substances are brought together the following reaction must take place:

$$HA + B \rightleftarrows HB + A$$

That is, the acid must donate a proton and the base must accept it. The reverse reaction to the one written above also must take place to some extent and, as the double arrow in the equation indicates, an equilibrium will be established. If we concentrate on the reverse reaction,

$$HB + A \rightarrow HA + B$$

we see that HB now functions as an acid and donates a proton to A, which in turn functions as a base. That is, in functioning as an acid, the molecule HA produces base A. This base is merely the deprotonated form of the acid. Similarly, when base B acts as a base and accepts a proton, a potential proton donor, that is, another acid, HB, is produced. The acid and its deprotonated residue are referred to as a conjugate base of the acid HA, and B is the conjugate base of the acid HB. (See Section 4–3.)

The presence of a forward and a reverse reaction allows the estab-

Will It React?
An Introduction
to Chemical
Equilibrium

178

lishment of an equilibrium for which an equilibrium-constant expression can be written:

$$HA + B \rightleftarrows HB + A$$

$$K_{eq} = \frac{[HB][A]}{[HA][B]}$$

(Of course, HB, A, HA, and B may be charged species.) One can consider the acid–base reaction as a competition of the two bases A and B for the proton. The extent to which each base is successful in obtaining the proton will be reflected in the magnitude of K_{eq}. If A (the conjugate base of the acid HA) is a much weaker base than B, then B will obtain a greater share in the protons and the concentration of its conjugate acid, HB, will be the larger at equilibrium. This will result in a high value for K_{eq}, or a low pK_{eq}. Similarly, if A is a stronger base than B, it will tend to hold on to its proton and transfer few protons to B. As a result, the equilibrium concentration of HA will be higher, the K_{eq} will be lower, and the pK_{eq} will be higher. We can generalize these conclusions in the following way: (a) The weaker the conjugate base of an acid, the stronger the acid; and (b) When an acid reacts with a base, the weaker that base relative to the conjugate base of the acid, the greater will be the pK_{eq} for the reaction.

These statements can be clarified by looking at some specific examples taken from Table 5–4 in *Chemical Principles*. Let us attempt to evaluate the relative strength of acetic acid, hydrogen sulfate ion, and hydrochloric acid in aqueous solution. Consider acetic acid first.

When acetic acid is dissolved in water, a reaction takes place in which solvated protons and acetate ions are produced. Writing the solvated protons as H_3O^+ for simplicity, the equation for this reaction is

$$HC_2H_3O_2 + H_2O \rightleftarrows H_3O^+ + C_2H_3O_2^-$$

We observe that $HC_2H_3O_2$ is an acid since it donates protons to H_2O; consequently H_2O, although it is the solvent, is acting as a base. The $C_2H_3O_2^-$ ion is the conjugate base of $HC_2H_3O_2$ and H_3O^+, the hydronium ion, is the conjugate acid of the base, H_2O.

Formulating the equilibrium-constant expression for this reaction, we obtain

$$K_{eq} = \frac{[H_3O^+][C_2H_3O_2^-]}{[HC_2H_3O_2][H_2O]}$$

Equilibria in
Aqueous
Solutions:
Acids and
Bases

179

We will simplify this expression in a manner similar to the simplification used to derive K_w. In cases of acids that are considered to be weak, and acetic acid is in this category, the amount of water used in forming the hydronium ion is negligible compared to the large amount of water present as the solvent. Thus the concentration of water at equilibrium is constant at 55.5 molar within the limits of our measurements. By convention, both sides of the K_{eq} expression can be multiplied by

$[H_2O]$ to yield a product, $[H_2O] \cdot K_{eq}$, which is symbolized by K_a, the acid dissociation constant.

$$[H_2O]K_{eq} = K_a = \frac{[H_3O^+][C_2H_3O_2{}^-]}{[HC_2H_3O_2]}$$

$$= 1.76 \times 10^{-5} \quad \text{(at 25°C)}$$

The magnitude of K_a or pK_a will be a measure of the strength of acetic acid in water relative to the base H_2O:

$$pK_a = -\log K_a = -\log (1.76 \times 10^{-5}) = -(\log 1.76 + \log 10^{-5})$$

$$= -(0.246 - 5.00) = \textbf{4.75}$$

Hydrogen Sulfate Ion

$$HSO_4{}^- + H_2O \rightleftarrows H_3O^+ + SO_4{}^{2-}$$

($SO_4{}^{2-}$ is the conjugate base of the acid $HSO_4{}^-$ ion.)

$$K_a = \frac{[H_3O^+][SO_4{}^{2-}]}{[HSO_4{}^-]} = 1.20 \times 10^{-2}; pK_a = \textbf{1.92}$$

Hydrochloric Acid. This acid is a very strong acid and its conjugate base, Cl^- ion, is an extremely weak base, much weaker than H_2O. Consequently, in the presence of so many solvent water molecules, the concentration of HCl left undissociated in solution is virtually immeasurable. All the so-called strong acids have extremely weak conjugate bases and are effectively completely converted to H_3O^+ ions in aqueous solution. They are, in effect, equally strong and have the strength of the hydronium ion itself. By the same token, ionic bases such as the alkali metal hydroxides are completely ionized in water and virtually all exist as the OH^- and have the same base strength, namely, that of the OH^- ion. The property of a solvent to equalize the acidity or basicity of a series of compounds is called the *leveling effect*. If one uses a solvent that is less basic than water, such as anhydrous acetic acid or methanol, the difference in strengths of these acids becomes apparent. A more basic solvent such as liquid ammonia can differentiate between the strengths of various strong bases. In NH_3 solvent, the $NH_2{}^-$ ion is a stronger base than OH^- ion, for example.

It is interesting to interpret the dissociation of water itself in terms of the Brønsted–Lowry concept. The equation is

$$H_2O + H_2O \rightleftarrows H_3O^+ + OH^-$$

Water is acting both as an acid, with OH^- as its conjugate base, and donates a proton to another water molecule, which serves as a base. Substances which act both as acids and bases are said to be *amphoteric* or *amphiprotic*. Water is such a substance.

The magnitude of the K_a for the dissociation of a particular acid can be used as a measure of the strength of that acid. The greater the ability of an acid to donate protons to water, the larger will be the value of the K_a for the acid, the stronger will be the acid, and weaker will be its conjugate base.

The two general classifications of acids, strong and weak, are based on the degree to which the proton is donated to water, that is, the degree to which the acid is dissociated into hydronium ions and the acid's conjugate base. Substances such as $HClO_4$, HCl, HNO_3, and H_2SO_4 all have conjugate bases (ClO_4^-, Cl^-, NO_3^-, and HSO_4^- ions, respectively) that are much weaker bases than H_2O. Consequently, when these substances are placed in water, within the limits of measurement all the protons in these acids are transferred to the H_2O solvent molecules, and virtually no undissociated acid molecules remain at equilibrium. The K_a's for these reactions approximate infinity:

$$HA + H_2O \rightleftarrows H_3O^+ + A^-$$

$$K_a = \frac{[H_3O^+][A^-]}{[HA]} = \frac{[H_3O^+][A^-]}{0.00} = \infty$$

These acids, which are completely dissociated, are called strong acids.

Many acids have conjugate bases that are of a strength comparable to that of water, hence they do not dissociate completely. Rather, they reach equilibrium at a point where there is an appreciable concentration of the undissociated acid remaining. In other words, the H_2O molecules are unable to compete successfully for all of the protons held by an acid's conjugate base. These weak acids have definite values for K_a. Such acids are called weak acids. The values for their K_a's and pK_a's are given in Table 5–4 in *Chemical Principles*. The smaller the value of K_a, the dissociation constant, or the larger the pK_a of an acid, the weaker the acid. Thus acetic acid, CH_3CH_2COOH, with a $K_a = 1.76 \times 10^{-5}$ and a $pK_a = 4.75$, is a stronger acid than hydrocyanic acid, HCN, for which the $K_a = 4.93 \times 10^{-10}$ and the $pK_a = 9.31$.

STRONG AND WEAK BASES

The same procedure one uses to define the strength of an acid can be used to designate the strength of a base. However, there has been a tendency to retain the older Arrhenius terminology in reference to bases in aqueous solution, and the equilibrium considered as being representative of a base is one that demonstrates the dissociation into OH^- ions. A general formulation of this equilibrium and its base dissociation constant is

$$MOH \rightleftarrows M^+ + OH^-$$

$$K_b = \frac{[M^+][OH^-]}{[MOH]}$$

Equilibria in
Aqueous
Solutions:
Acids and
Bases

181

The strong bases such as the alkali metal hydroxides fit this dissociation:

$$NaOH \rightleftarrows Na^+ + OH^-$$

Like for strong acids, the dissociation constant, K_b, is infinity because the alkali metal hydroxides are dissociated completely in aqueous solution so there are effectively no NaOH "molecules" in solution at equilibrium:

$$K_b = \frac{[Na^+][OH^-]}{[NaOH]} = \frac{[Na^+][OH^-]}{0.00} = \infty$$

When ammonia is dissolved in water, NH_4^+ and OH^- ions are produced. Arrhenius fit this into his concept of a base by picturing these ions to be the result of the dissociation of ammonium hydroxide molecules, NH_4OH, formed by the reaction of NH_3 and water. He formulated the equilibrium in a solution of ammonia and water as

$$NH_4OH \rightleftarrows NH_4^+ + OH^-$$

and formulated the dissociation constant of this base, K_b, to follow the same convention as the K_a used for acids,

$$K_b = \frac{[NH_4^+][OH^-]}{[NH_4OH]}$$

If one considers bases to be substances that donate OH^- to aqueous solution, then the magnitude of K_b is a measure of the basicity of NH_4OH.

The main fault in this representation is that there is absolutely no evidence for the existence of the molecular species NH_4OH. Rather, what takes place when ammonia is dissolved in water is that NH_3 is a sufficiently strong Brønsted base to remove protons from some of the water molecules present. This process takes place to but a slight extent, but to the extent that it does take place, the products are NH_4^+ and OH^- ions. Along with solvent water molecules, the principal constituent in an equilibrium mixture of ammonia and water is NH_3 molecules. The true representation of the equilibrium and K_b is

$$NH_3 + H_2O \rightleftarrows NH_4^+ + OH^-$$

$$K_b = \frac{[NH_4^+][OH^-]}{[NH_3]}$$

Will It React?
An Introduction
to Chemical
Equilibrium

182

Note that the convention followed in other equilibria representations is followed here in that the concentration of water in these solutions is treated as a constant and incorporated with the equilibrium constant to give K_b.

We will find it necessary to determine the acidity or basicity of solutions of acids and bases. Generally, this acidity or basicity will be expressed in terms of the pH or pOH of the solution.

Before we begin to discuss these calculations, the terms millimole and millimole per milliliter should be defined, because the authors of *Chemical Principles* frequently use these quantities, rather than the more familiar mole and moles per liter or molarity. Their choice is for purposes of convenience in solving problems. In most laboratory situations, a few milliliters of solution are used, rather than volumes of liters or more. If one defines a millimole as 0.001 mole, than one milliliter of a 1.0M solution will contain one millimole of solute:

$$1.0 \text{ mole liter}^{-1} \times 0.001 \text{ liter} = 0.001 \text{ mole} = 1 \text{ millimole}$$

In other words, a solution that is x molar will contain x moles of solute per liter of solution or x millimoles of solute per milliliter of solution. The familiar expression,

$$\text{Molarity} \times \text{Liters of solution} = \text{Moles of solute},$$

also can be translated to read:

$$\text{Molarity} \times \text{Milliters of solution} = \text{Millimoles of solute}$$

Thus one may use milliliters as the volume unit without converting it to liters in solving problems if the quantities of reacting substances are expressed in millimoles instead of moles.

The calculation of the acidity or basicity of a solution of a strong acid or a strong base is a relatively straightforward calculation. These substances are completely dissociated, so the H^+ ion or the OH^- ion concentration can be determined directly from the concentration of acid or base used in the solutions. The relationships to remember in performing these calculations are:

$$pH = -\log [H^+] \qquad pOH = -\log [OH^-]$$
$$K_w = 1 \times 10^{-14} \qquad pH + pOH = 14.$$

EXAMPLE. What is the H^+ ion concentration and the pH of a 0.015M $HClO_4$ solution?

SOLUTION. Since perchloric acid is a strong acid and is dissociated completely, $HClO_4 \rightarrow H^+ + ClO_4^-$, 0.015$M$ $HClO_4$ will produce 0.015M H^+ ions. There is another source of H^+ ions in this solution, the dissociation of water. Recall that in pure water the concentration of H^+ is but $1 \times 10^{-7}M$. The addition of the H^+ ions from the perchloric acid will suppress the dissociation of the water, so we can expect the H^+ ions present in the acid solution from the dissociation of water to be even less than $1 \times 10^{-7}M$. Compared to the $0.015M$ H^+ delivered to the solution by the $HClO_4$ dissociation, the contribution from the dissociation of water is certainly negligible ($10^{-7}M$ compared to $0.015M$) and we need not consider it in our calculations. In summary,

$$[H^+] = \mathbf{0.015}$$
$$\begin{aligned} pH &= -\log [H^+] = -\log (1.5 \times 10^{-2}) \\ &= -(\log 1.5 + \log 10^{-2}) \\ &= -[0.18 + (-2)] = 2 - 0.18 = \mathbf{1.82} \end{aligned}$$

EXAMPLE. What is the H^+ ion concentration and the pH of a $6M$ HCl solution?

SOLUTION. Following the reasoning used in the preceding example, we conclude that the concentration of H^+ ions in a $6M$ solution of the strong monoprotic acid HCl will be $6M$. The contribution of the H^+ from the dissociation of water will be negligible. Therefore,

$$[H^+] = \mathbf{6}$$
$$pH = -\log [H^+] = -\log 6 = \mathbf{-0.78}$$

(*Note*: Here the pH is a negative number. However, there is no advantage in expressing such a high H^+ ion concentration in logarithms, and the pH terminology seldom is used when the concentrations are larger than $0.1M$. Consequently, one seldom sees acidities expressed in terms of negative pH values, but this does not prohibit one from calculating them if he so desires.)

EXAMPLE. What is the H^+ concentration and the pH of a $0.004M$ KOH solution? What is its pOH?

SOLUTION. KOH, a strong base, will dissociate completely into K^+ and OH^- ions: $KOH \rightarrow K^+ + OH^-$. From the stoichiometry of this dissociation, we see that the OH^- ion concentration of a $0.004M$ KOH solution will be $0.004M$. Again the small amount of OH^- present from the dissociation of water (less than $1 \times 10^{-7}M$) need not be considered. There are two ways we can approach this problem.

Approach A. From the water ion-product and the OH^- concentration, compute the H^+ ion concentration, and then proceed as in the preceding examples.

$$[OH^-] = 0.0040 = 4.0 \times 10^{-3}$$
$$[H^+][OH^-] = K_w = 1.0 \times 10^{-14}$$

Will It React?
An Introduction
to Chemical
Equilibrium

184

Substituting the OH^- ion concentration into the K_w expression gives

$$[H^+][OH^-] = [H^+](4.0 \times 10^{-3}) = 1.0 \times 10^{-14}$$

$$[H^+] = \frac{1.0 \times 10^{-14}}{4.0 \times 10^{-3}} = \mathbf{2.5 \times 10^{-12}}$$

$$\begin{aligned} pH &= -\log [H^+] = -\log (2.5 \times 10^{-12}) \\ &= -(\log 2.5 + \log 10^{-12}) \\ &= -(0.40 + (-12)) = 12.0 - 0.40 = \mathbf{11.6} \end{aligned}$$

Note that the pH is very high, as it should be for a strong base solution.

To calculate the pOH of this solution, we substitute in the relationship $pH + pOH = 14.0$:

$$11.6 + pOH = 14.0$$
$$pOH = 14.0 - 11.6 = \mathbf{2.4}$$

Approach B. Calculate the pOH first, then obtain the pH from the $pH + pOH = 14$ relationship.

$$\begin{aligned} [OH^-] &= 4.0 \times 10^{-3} \\ pOH &= -\log [OH^-] = -\log (4.0 \times 10^{-3}) \\ &= -(\log 4.0 + \log 10^{-3}) \\ pOH &= -[0.60 + (-3)] = 3.0 - 0.60 = \mathbf{2.4} \\ pH + pOH &= pH + 2.4 = 14.0 \\ pH &= 14.0 - 2.4 = 11.6 \\ pH &= -\log [H^+] = \mathbf{11.6} \\ \log [H^+] &= -11.6 \end{aligned}$$

$$[H^+] = 10^{-11.6} = 10^{-11} \times 10^{-0.6} = 10^{-11} \times \frac{1}{10^{0.6}}$$

$$[H^+] = 10^{-11} \times \frac{1}{4.0} = 0.25 \times 10^{-11} = \mathbf{2.5 \times 10^{-12}}$$

EXAMPLE. What will be the pH of the solution that results when 25.00 ml of $0.050M$ HNO_3 and 12.50 ml of $0.100M$ NaOH are mixed?

SOLUTION. When an acid and a base are mixed, they will neutralize one another. In this particular case, the reaction is

$$HNO_3 + NaOH \rightarrow NaNO_3 + H_2O$$

Since both HNO_3 and $NaOH$ are strong and completely dissociated in solution, the total ionic equation is $H^+ + NO_3^- + Na^+ + OH^- \rightarrow Na^+ + NO_3^- + H_2O$ and the net ionic equation is $H^+ + OH^- \rightarrow H_2O$. Thus we see that one mole of H^+ ions (1 mole of HNO_3) will react with exactly one mole of OH^- ions (1 mole of $NaOH$).

Determine the number of moles, n, of HNO_3 and $NaOH$ mixed.

HNO_3: 0.02500 liter $\times$ 0.050 mole liter^{-1}
$$= 1.25 \times 10^{-3} \text{ mole } HNO_3$$

$NaOH$: 0.01250 liter $\times$ 0.100 mole liter^{-1}
$$= 1.25 \times 10^{-3} \text{ mole } NaOH$$

There has been exactly enough HNO_3 mixed to neutralize all the $NaOH$ present. Therefore, the mixture will consist of pure water and Na^+ and NO_3^- ions. These ions will not alter the equilibrium between water and its ions, so one can expect the concentration of H^+ (and OH^-) to be the same as that present in equilibrium with pure water, namely, $1 \times 10^{-7}M$. The pH of the mixture will be **7.0**, a neutral solution.

EXAMPLE. What will be the pH of a solution that results when 50.0 ml of $0.125M$ HNO_3 and 25.0 ml of $0.0500M$ $NaOH$ are mixed?

SOLUTION. As in the preceding example, the net ionic equation for the neutralization is $H^+ + OH^- \rightarrow H_2O$, and the H^+ and OH^- ions react on a mole-to-mole basis. We determine the moles of H^+ and OH^-.

n_{H^+}: 0.0500 liter $\times$ 0.125 mole liter^{-1}
$$= 6.25 \times 10^{-3} \text{ mole } HNO_3$$
$$= 6.25 \times 10^{-3} \text{ mole } H^+$$

n_{OH^-}: 0.0250 liter $\times$ 0.0500 mole liter^{-1}
$$= 1.25 \times 10^{-3} \text{ mole } NaOH$$
$$= 1.25 \times 10^{-3} \text{ mole } OH^-$$

There is an excess of H^+ ions in the mixture, 1.25×10^{-3} mole will react with the 1.25×10^{-3} mole of OH^- ions present to produce water and $6.25 \times 10^{-3} - 1.25 \times 10^{-3} = 5.00 \times 10^{-3}$ mole of H^+ will remain in the solution after the reaction. Since the contribution of H^+ ions to the solution from the ionization of the water present will be negligible in comparison, the number of moles of H^+ in the solution will be 5.00×10^{-3}. To compute the pH, the molar concentration of H^+ is needed. The total volume of the reaction mixture is $0.0500 + 0.0250 = 0.0750$ liter.

Will It React?
An Introduction
to Chemical
Equilibrium

186

Therefore, the molar concentration of H^+ ion is

$$[H^+] = \frac{5.00 \times 10^{-3} \text{ mole}}{7.50 \times 10^{-2} \text{ liter}} = 0.667M$$

and

$$\begin{aligned}
pH &= -\log [H^+] = -\log (6.67 \times 10^{-1}) \\
&= -(\log 6.67 + \log 10^{-1}) \\
&= -[0.82 + (-1)] = 1.00 - 0.82 = \mathbf{0.18}
\end{aligned}$$

The reaction mixture will be quite acidic.

PREPARATION OF A SOLUTION HAVING A GIVEN pH

EXAMPLE.   How much $0.010M$ HCl must be added to 200 ml of water to give a solution having a pH of 2.5?

SOLUTION.   First we calculate the hydrogen ion concentration necessary to give a pH of 2.5. Since $pH = -\log [H^+] = 2.5$, this is a problem of determining the antilog of 2.5:

$$\begin{aligned}
-\log [H^+] &= 2.5 \\
\log [H^+] &= -2.5 \\
[H^+] &= 10^{-2.5} = 10^{-3} \times 10^{+0.5} \\
[H^+] &= 3.17 \times 10^{-3}
\end{aligned}$$

The total H^+ ions in the solution will come from the HCl we add and the dissociation of the water. The H^+ ion concentration present at equilibrium in pure water is but $1 \times 10^{-7}M$. The addition of HCl will depress the dissociation of water even more (Le Chatelier's principle). Therefore, we know that the contribution of H^+ ions to the solution from the dissociation of water will be less than $1 \times 10^{-7}M$ and certainly will be negligible compared to the H^+ added in the form of HCl to adjust the pH to 2.5. Therefore, we need only consider the amount of completely dissociated $0.010M$ HCl that must be added to 200 ml (0.200 liter) water to provide a solution with a concentration of H^+ equal to $3.17 \times 10^{-3}M$.

The volume of the solution will be 200 ml plus the volume of $0.010M$ HCl to be added (*i.e.*, 0.200 liter $+ V$); V is the volume in liters of $0.010M$ HCl to be added. Since essentially all the H^+ ion in the solution will be that added as HCl, the moles of H^+ in the solution will be equal to the liters of $0.010M$ HCl to be added times its molar concentration. Making these substitutions in the equation defining the molarity of the solution gives

$$M = \frac{\text{Moles of solute}}{\text{Liters of solution}} = 3.17 \times 10^{-3} = \frac{0.010 \times V}{0.200 + V}$$

Solution of this equation by first multiplying both sides by the quantity $(0.200 + V)$ and then collecting all terms in V on the left side gives

$$(3.17 \times 10^{-3})(0.200 + V) = 0.01 \times V$$
$$6.34 \times 10^{-4} + 3.17 \times 10^{-3}\, V = 0.01\, V$$
$$3.17 \times 10^{-3}\, V - 0.01\, V = -6.34 \times 10^{-4}$$
$$(0.0100 - 3.17 \times 10^{-3})V = 6.34 \times 10^{-4}$$
$$(10.0 \times 10^{-3} - 3.17 \times 10^{-3})V = 6.34 \times 10^{-4}$$
$$(6.8 \times 10^{-3})V = 6.34 \times 10^{-4}$$

$$V = \frac{6.34 \times 10^{-4}}{6.8 \times 10^{-3}} = 9.3 \times 10^{-2} = 0.093 \text{ liter}$$

$$V = 93 \text{ ml}$$

5–7 WEAK ACIDS AND BASES

As was mentioned in the discussion of strong and weak acids in Section 5–5, the strength of an acid depends to a large degree on the value of the K_a for the equilibrium

$$HA + H_2O \rightleftarrows H_3O^+ + A^-$$

or, more simply,

$$HA \rightleftarrows H^+ + A^-$$

for which

$$K_a = \frac{[H^+][A^-]}{[HA]}$$

Weak acids and weak bases are only partly dissociated. Therefore, when a solution is prepared by dissolving one mole of a weak acid or weak base, something less than one mole of H^+ ions or OH^- ions will be present in the solution. A certain amount of the acid or base will remain in the solution as undissociated molecules. The presence of this undissociated HA (or its counterpart MOH in the case of bases) results in a low value for the K_a (or K_b). The very low K_a and K_b values in Tables 5–4 and 5–5 in *Chemical Principles* testify that some acids and bases can be very weak indeed. The concentrations of undissociated acid or base can be very high and the concentrations of H^+ or OH^- can be very low in such solutions.

It is the presence of both the dissociated and the undissociated species in solutions of weak acids and weak bases that complicate their treatment. Comparatively, strong acids and strong bases represent simple systems to treat quantitatively.

The procedure to use in making calculations of the species present at equilibrium in systems involving weak acids or weak bases follows

Will It React?
An Introduction
to Chemical
Equilibrium

188

the same three basic steps used in Section 5–3 for treating equilibrium systems in general. These can be summarized as:

(1) Write the balanced equation for the equilibrium involved.
(2) Formulate the K_a or K_b expression.
(3) Using the balanced equation as a guide, and the data given, derive expressions for the equilibrium concentrations of each of the species in the K_a or K_b expression in terms of a single unknown. The solution of the resulting equation is a problem in algebra, which generally lends itself to simplification by approximation techniques.

It is in Step 3 that one encounters the most difficulty in dealing with weak-acid or weak-base systems. Among the information that one frequently has available for establishing the expressions for the equilibrium concentrations of all the species present in the K_a or K_b expression is the initial concentration of acid or base in the system. By this is meant the molar concentration of acid or base in the solution before dissociation begins and equilibrium has been reached. For example, a $0.1M$ HCN solution is prepared by dissolving 0.1 mole of HCN in a liter of solution. In the solution process the HCN will begin to react with water and undergo dissociation into hydrogen ions and cyanide anions. The concentration of HCN molecules will decrease until equilibrium is reached when the molar concentration of HCN in the solution reaches some constant equilibrium value that will be less than $0.1M$. The initial concentration of HCN in this solution, c_0, is said to be $0.1M$, whereas, the equilibrium molar concentration of HCN will be equal to 0.1 less the number of moles per liter of the HCN that reacts in the process of attaining equilibrium.

It may be possible to measure the molar concentration of one or more of the species present in the system at equilibrium. For example, a pH meter can be used to measure the hydrogen ion concentration in a solution at equilibrium directly. This information can be used to establish the concentration of other species present at equilibrium if the equilibrium constant is known, or in some cases, one can calculate the equilibrium constant itself. Since the net electrical charge in any solution must be zero, it follows that the total molar concentration of unit positive charges carried by all the cations present must equal the total molar concentration of unit negative charges carried by all the anions present. This relationship, referred to as the charge-balance equation, sometimes can be helpful in solving a problem.

Another useful aid towards developing the equations necessary for solving a particular equilibrium problem is the law of conservation of mass, which tells us that the total molar concentration of atoms present in a system before it reaches equilibrium must equal the total molar concentration of atoms afterwards. This relationship frequently can be expressed in terms of what is referred to as a mass balance and used in the computations.

Finally, we should make reference to the fact that since we are dealing with aqueous solutions, water always is present, and the hydrogen ions and hydroxide ions in the solution must be at equilibrium so that the water ion product, K_w, is satisfied. This fact is often very helpful and always should be kept in mind when you approach a problem involving aqueous systems at equilibrium.

Another point should also be mentioned before we proceed. You note in Tables 5–4 and 5–5 in *Chemical Principles* that the K_a values and K_b values of some of the acids and bases approach the value of K_w. This means that some acids and bases are nearly as weak as water itself. In such cases both the acid or base and the solvent water itself may contribute comparable amounts of H^+ or OH^- to the solution. We will not deal with such situations in this chapter, but one should keep this fact in mind. It can become a major factor when dealing with very dilute solutions of very weak acids or bases.

The best way to discuss the solution of equilibrium problems is to look at some typical examples and discuss their solutions in detail. In Section 5–7 of *Chemical Principles*, the solution to the problem of determining the pH and degree of dissociation of acetic acid is carried out in two examples. You should follow the reasoning used in these problems very closely. Note how the mass-balance and charge-balance relationships are used to establish expressions for the equilibrium concentrations of hydrogen ion, acetate ion, and undissociated acetic acid for substitution into the K_a expression for acetic acid. Note also that implicit in this solution is the assumption that the contribution of H^+ and OH^- ions to the equilibrium system from the dissociation of the solvent water need not be considered. That this is indeed true is evident from the fact that the results show that the concentration of H^+ ions in both examples is about $10^{-4} M$. The H^+ ion concentration in pure water is but $10^{-7} M$, and in these acid solutions the dissociation of water will be depressed by the hydrogen ions introduced from the acid. Therefore, the actual contribution of H^+ from the dissociation of water can be expected to be less than $10^{-7} M$, a quantity that is insignificant when compared to $10^{-4} M$.

A more direct approach may be taken to solving equilibrium problems such as these by making some initial assumptions. However, one should exercise care to check the validity of these assumptions as he proceeds. If it turns out that the assumptions are not justified, one can resort to the more rigorous procedure followed in the text. Let us illustrate this by doing one of the examples given in Section 5–7 of *Chemical Principles*.

Will It React?
An Introduction
to Chemical
Equilibrium

190

EXAMPLE. What is the pH of a solution of 0.0100 molar acetic acid?

SOLUTION. Using Ac^- to represent the acetate ion, CH_3COO^-, write the equation for the equilibrium involved:

$$HAc \rightleftarrows H^+ + Ac^- \tag{5-3}$$

Formulate the K_a expression for acetic acid, taking the numerical value from Table 5–4 in *Chemical Principles*:

$$K_a = \frac{[H^+][Ac^-]}{[HAc]} = 1.76 \times 10^{-5}$$

We observe that K_a is considerably larger than K_w ($K_w = 10^{-14}$) so we assume any H^+ ions in the solution at equilibrium due to the dissociation of water will be negligible in comparison to those furnished by the dissociated acetic acid. In other words, our first assumption is that effectively all the H^+ present in the solution at equilibrium will be those introduced by the dissociation of the HAc added in making the 0.0100M solution. From Equation 5–3 it is evident that every time an H^+ ion is introduced into the solution by the dissociation of an HAc molecule, an Ac^- anion also will be placed in the solution. Therefore, the equilibrium molar concentrations of H^+ and Ac^- will be the same. Equation 5–3 also shows that for each mole of H^+ ions and each mole of Ac^- ions introduced into the solution, one mole of HAc must dissociate. Therefore, the molar concentration of HAc left at the time equilibrium is achieved will be equal to the initial concentration of HAc, 0.0100M, less the number of moles per liter of H^+ ion (or of Ac^- ions) present at equilibrium.

To keep things well in mind, we should continue with Step 3 of the four-step routine we developed previously for solving equilibrium problems and write the conclusions we have just reached in the form of two tables, one listing the concentrations of the species involved in the K_a expression at the time the acid was added to the water to prepare the solution, and the other listing the equilibrium concentrations.

Initial	At equilibrium
$[H^+] = 0.000$	x
$[Ac^-] = 0.000$	x
$[HAc] = 0.0100$	$0.0100 - x$

Here we have let x represent the molar concentration of H^+ ions at equilibrium. Now we can proceed with Step 4 and substitute the expressions we have derived for the concentrations of the species present at equilibrium (all in terms of a single unknown quantity, x) in the K_a expression:

$$K_a = \frac{[H^+][Ac^-]}{[HAc]} = \frac{(x)(x)}{(0.0100 - x)} = \frac{x^2}{0.0100 - x}$$

$$= 1.76 \times 10^{-5}$$

To simplify the solution of this quadratic equation, let us make another assumption. We already have observed that K_a is quite small because acetic acid is a weak acid and dissociates only slightly. Therefore, the concentration of H^+ present at equilibrium will be small. Our assumption will be that x, the molar concentration of

H^+ at equilibrium, is insignificant when compared to 0.0100. Therefore, we can rewrite the K_a expression omitting the x subtracted from 0.0100 in the denominator. Thus

$$K_a = \frac{x^2}{0.0100} = 1.76 \times 10^{-5}$$

This equation is solved more readily than the original quadratic:

$$x^2 = (1.76 \times 10^{-5})(0.0100) = 1.76 \times 10^{-7}$$
$$x = [H^+] = (17.6 \times 10^{-8})^{1/2} = 4.20 \times 10^{-4}$$

We must confirm our assumptions before proceeding. One would expect the H^+ ions contributed by the dissociation of water to be less than $10^{-7}M$. Observing the rules for addition, one readily sees that 0.0000001 will not be a significant addition to 0.000411. Thus our first assumption was justified and the results would not be altered by including the dissociation of water as a source of H^+ ions. Our second assumption resulted in the use of 0.0100 in the denominator of the K_a expression instead of $0.0100 - x$. To test the validity of this assumption, we substitute the approximate value we obtained for x in the more exact form of the denominator. The result is

$$0.0100 - x = 0.0100 - 0.000411 = 0.0096$$

This is within 4% of 0.0100; that is, $[(0.0100 - 0.0096)/0.0100] \times 100 = 4\%$. We can feel confident that our approximate answer is within 5% of being correct, which generally is acceptable for this type of calculation.

Now that the H^+ ion concentration has been calculated, the pH can be determined:

$$\text{pH} = -\log [H^+] = -\log (4.20 \times 10^{-4})$$
$$= -(0.623 - 4) = \mathbf{3.38}$$

To calculate the degree of dissociation of acetic acid in this $0.0100M$ solution, we observe that 4.20×10^{-4} mole liter^{-1} of HAc dissociated to give the computed ion concentration; therefore, the percent of the HAc originally present in the solution that dissociated, that is, the degree of dissociation, is

$$\frac{4.20 \times 10^{-4}}{1.00 \times 10^{-2}} \times 100 = 4.20\%$$

Will It React?
An Introduction
to Chemical
Equilibrium

192

To support the use of the approximations further, note that the result for $[H^+]$ obtained in *Chemical Principles* by solving the more exact quadratic equation is $4.11 \times 10^{-4}M$. Our approximate result, $4.20 \times 10^{-4}M$, differs from this by only 2%. The exact solution yields a pH value of 3.39, compared to our approximated pH of 3.38. Of course, there are instances when the precision of the data given requires one to use the more exact methods of solutions. Also, there are instances in which the H^+ and OH^- ion concentrations are close to those available from the dissociation of the solvent water. This will be true when very dilute solutions of acids or bases that have very low K_a or K_b values are involved. These calculations are more complicated algebraically because more than a single unknown must be dealt with. Solutions to such complicated equilibrium systems are treated in Appendix 3 in *Chemical Principles*.

INDICATORS

An indicator is itself a weak acid and dissociates upon reaction with the solvent water to form hydronium ions and anions. The characteristic property of indicators is that the undissociated acid and the anion have pronounced but distinctly different colors. (It is also possible that only one species, the undissociated acid or the anion, may be colorless and the other colored. Such is the case with phenolphthalein, one of the more popular indicators used as an indicator for titrations of strong acids and weak bases.)

We may formulate the equilibrium for a typical weak-acid indicator as

$$HIn \rightleftarrows H^+ + In^-$$

and write the K_a for the dissociation

$$K_a = \frac{[H^+][In^-]}{[HIn]}$$

In this notation, HIn represents the undissociated indicator acid, which reacts with water to release the hydronium ions (abbreviated H^+) and anions, In^-. Because K_a is a constant at a given temperature for a particular indicator, the ratio of concentrations of HIn to In^- is dependent on the hydrogen ion concentration in the solution:

$$K_a \frac{[HIn]}{[In^-]} = [H^+]$$

Both HIn and In^- are present in a solution of an indicator, and if each has a different color, the overall color of the solution will depend on the color of each species, the relative amount of each species present, and the sensitivity of your eye to color changes.

Figure 5–3 shows the range of pH values in which different indicators can be observed to change from one color to the other. For example, bromthymol blue will appear to have the same yellow color at all pH values lower than about pH = 6. Above a pH of about 7.5 it will appear a characteristic blue. In the range of pH values from 6 to 7.5 the presence of both the yellow undissociated acid (HIn) and the blue anions of the compound (In^-) can be distinguished in the solution by the eye. Since yellow and blue combine to give green, for each pH

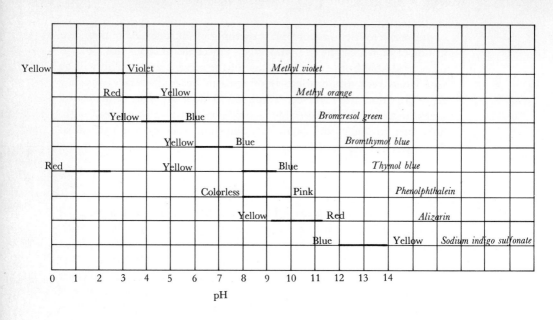

Figure 5–3. Some common acid–base indicators, with the pH ranges in which their color changes occur.

value within this range, there will be a different shade of green, ranging from an extreme yellow-green to an intense blue-green. In fact, one can use solutions of bromthymol blue in acids of known pH between 6 and 7.5 as so-called comparison standards. If an unknown solution has a pH between these limits, its pH can be determined by adding bromthymol blue and matching the observed shades with those of the comparison standards. Papers, such as litmus paper and pH paper, impregnated with different indicators can be used to determine the pH of unknown solutions by merely touching a drop of the solution to the paper and comparing the observed color change in the shades of color observed when solutions of known pH (standards) are placed on the paper. One should be aware that the solutions being tested must not have a color of their own, since this color may combine with the color of the indicator to give a totally different shade than is indicative of the pH.

In strong base–strong acid titrations, the pH at the equivalence point is exactly 7. However, within a few hundredths of a milliliter of the equivalence point the pH of the solution undergoes a change of several units. Suppose that we were to carry out the titration shown in Figure 5–4 by adding base to the acid, but first placing a few drops of bromthymol blue in the acid solution. At the beginning of the titration, the acid solution will show the bright yellow color characteristic of the undissociated bromthymol blue molecule. When enough base has been added to bring the pH to 6, one should begin to notice the appearance of a green shade for the first time. We see from the titration curve that the volume of base required to reach pH 6 is almost exactly the same as

Will It React?
An Introduction
to Chemical
Equilibrium

194

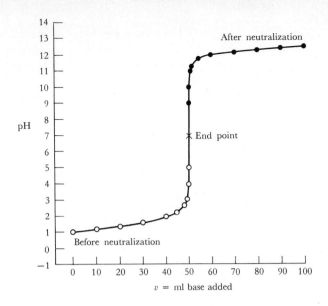

Figure 5–4. Titration curve for typical strong acid and base.

that required to reach pH 7, the pH corresponding to the equivalence point. In fact, with normal equipment, burettes capable of being read to within ± 0.01 ml, one would not be able to distinguish this volume from that at the equivalence point. If one continued to add base until the solution just appeared blue with no trace of green, corresponding to pH 7.5, the volume added would be essentially the same within the limits of measurement with the apparatus. The appearance of the color change that one uses to estimate the equivalence point in a titration is referred to as the end point of the titration.

Because of the steep rise of the titration curve over a rather wide range of pH values at the end point, it is not necessary to have an indicator that begins to change color at the pH corresponding to the equivalence point. Among those listed in Figure 5–3, bromthymol blue, which is in the process of undergoing an observed change from yellow to blue at pH 7, can be used to titrate any strong acid, such as HCl, with any strong base, such as KOH. However, thymol blue and phenolphthalein, which do not begin to show a detectable color until a pH of 8 is reached, serve just as well. If one titrates with thymol blue until a change from yellow to blue is observed, pH = 9.4, the end point will be coincident with the equivalence point within the limits of the experimental technique. The first appearance of a pink tinge in a phenolphthalein solution, which is colorless up to a pH of a bit less than 8, is observed easily and gives an excellent end point.

In the titrations of weak acids with strong bases, strong acids with weak bases, or weak acids with weak bases, the pH at the equivalence point generally is not 7, but some other value. For such titrations, one can calculate the titration curve, determine the pH range at the equivalence point, and select an indicator from tables similar to that in Figure 5–3 that will give an observable color change in the pH region desired.

5–8 WEAK ACIDS AND THEIR SALTS

In this section, we look at equilibrium systems involving water solutions of weak acids or weak bases to which are added salts that have an ion common to the weak acid or weak base. The salts we will deal with are ionic compounds. When these salts dissolve, they can be considered to be completely converted into ions. Therefore, if a salt such as sodium acetate is dissolved in a solution of acetic acid, one knows that the problem is one in which sodium ions and acetate ions are added to a system containing acetic acid molecules, hydrogen ions, acetate ions, and hydroxide ions in equilibrium.[2]

In examples such as this, one might expect that the added cations would react with any anions present and the added anions with any cations present. In this particular example, the only anions in the solution are acetate ions and hydroxide ions. Since both sodium acetate and sodium hydroxide are ionic compounds and strong electrolytes, there will be no reaction. However, when the hydrogen ions in the solution come in contact with the added acetate anions, the product formed is acetic acid, a weakly dissociated substance. The net effect is that some of the added acetate ions will remove hydrogen ions from the acetic acid equilibrium and produce more undissociated acetic acid molecules. This is merely a manifestation of Le Chatelier's principle. One can see this by considering the equilibrium relationship

$$HAc \rightleftarrows H^+ + Ac^-$$

If one adds NaAc to such a solution at equilibrium, one will be adding Ac^- ions to the system. Le Chatelier's principle predicts that this addition of a *common ion* will exert a stress on the equilibrium system that will be counteracted by a shift to the left. That is, some of the Ac^- ions in the solution will react with the H^+ ions present to produce additional HAc until equilibrium is again established.

We can apply an alternative explanation. For a solution of acetic acid at equilibrium at a constant temperature, the following must prevail

$$K_a = \frac{[H^+][Ac^-]}{[HAc]}$$

in which K_a is the acid-dissociation constant at the temperature involved. The value of K_a must remain constant even upon the addition of

[2] Some of the H^+ ions and all of the OH^- ions originate from the dissociation of the solvent H_2O.

Ac⁻ ions in the form of NaAc. The presence of added Ac⁻ ions will increase the [Ac⁻] factor in the numerator of the K_a expression. To maintain the constancy of K_a, the [H⁺] concentration must decrease and the [HAc] concentration must increase as a new equilibrium is established. This amounts to shifting the equilibrium position to the left. We will be concerned with systems of this type in the next two sections.

Let us begin by stating that nothing new is necessary to carry out these calculations. The procedures are identical to those we have used repeatedly in this chapter. In fact, you will find that the actual arithmetic and algebra involved in these calculations generally will be much simpler than was the case when gas-phase equilibria or equilibria involving only weak acid or weak bases were investigated.

> EXAMPLE. Calculate the H⁺ ion concentration and the pH of a $0.010M$ HAc solution that is made $0.10M$ in NaAc. K_a for HAc is 1.76×10^{-5}.

> SOLUTION. We will use the same routine as we have used throughout this unit: (1) Write the equilibrium equation. (2) Write the K_a expression. (3) Construct a table showing the initial and equilibrium concentrations of the species involved expressed in a single unknown. (4) Substitute in the K_a expression and solve.
>
> The reaction equation is
>
> $$HAc \rightleftarrows H^+ + Ac^-$$
>
> The K_a expression is
>
> $$K_a = \frac{[H^+][Ac^-]}{[HAc]}$$
>
> In constructing the table it is convenient to consider the initial state to be the solution in which the sodium acetate has been dissolved and the acetic acid has been added the instant before any reaction with water takes place and before the acid begins to dissociate.

Initial	At equilibrium
$[H^+] = 0.000$	x
$[Ac^-] = 0.10$	$x + 0.10$
$[HAc] = 0.010$	$0.010 - x$

In setting up the table, we neglect the contribution to the equilibrium H⁺ concentration due to the dissociation of the solvent water. Because the NaAc will dissociate completely into Na⁺ and Ac⁻ ions when it dissolves, the initial concentration of a solution made $0.10M$ in NaAc will be $0.10M$ in Na⁺ ions and $0.10M$ in Ac⁻ ions. If we let the equilibrium concentration of H⁺ ions be represented by x moles per liter, we see from the equation for the dissociation reaction that if x moles of H⁺ ions are formed per liter of solution, then x moles of Ac$^-$ also will form per liter of solution, due to the dissociation of the HAc molecules. Therefore, the equilibrium concentration of Ac$^-$ ions will be the sum of the $0.10M$ Ac$^-$ present initially from the dissolved NaAc and the xM Ac$^-$ ions formed from the dissociation of the HAc. The equilibrium concentration of undissociated HAc will be the initial concentration, $0.010M$, less the number of moles of HAc per liter that dissociate in forming x moles per liter of H$^+$ ions; that is, $0.010 - x$.

Substituting the equilibrium values in the K_a expression gives

$$K_a = \frac{[\text{H}^+][\text{Ac}^-]}{[\text{HAc}]} = \frac{(x)(x + 0.10)}{(0.010 - x)} = 1.76 \times 10^{-5}$$

This equation presents a somewhat formidable job to solve as it stands, so let us first make some assumptions to try to simplify it and then check to see if these assumptions are justified. To do this, we can reason that because of the small value of K_a, the concentration of H$^+$ will be small in a solution of pure HAc. In the solution we are considering here, additional Ac$^-$ ions have been added in the form of NaAc. Le Chatelier's principle tells us that the dissociation of the acetic acid will be suppressed so that even less HAc will dissociate (*i.e.*, x will be a very small number). Let us first assume that x will be so small as to be negligible compared to 0.010. If this is true, we can neglect the subtraction of x from 0.010 in the denominator of the K_a expression. Not only that; if x is negligible compared to 0.010, it most certainly is negligible when compared to 0.10. On this basis, the x added to 0.10 in the numerator of the K_a expression also can be neglected. Making these assumptions results in a very simple equation to be solved for x:

$$K_a = \frac{(x)(0.10)}{(0.010)} = 1.76 \times 10^{-5}$$

$$x = 1.76 \times 10^{-5} \left(\frac{0.010}{0.10}\right) = \mathbf{1.76 \times 10^{-6}\ M}$$

We can check to see if our assumption of the negligible contribution of c was indeed legitimate by substituting this value into the term in the denominator and observing that, indeed, the rules to be followed in adding and subtracting numbers show that the inclusion of x will not alter the expression from the approximate form we used:

$$0.010 - x = 0.010 - 0.00000176 = 0.010$$

and

$$x + 0.10 = 1.76 \times 10^{-6} + 0.10 = 0.00000176 + 0.10$$
$$= 0.10$$

Will It React?
An Introduction
to Chemical
Equilibrium

198

Before completing this problem, we should consider the initial assumption that was made concerning the contribution of H^+ ions to the solution from the dissociation of the solvent H_2O. In pure water, this contribution is about $10^{-7}M$. Our calculations give an H^+ concentration of the order of $10^{-6}M$, which is only about one order of magnitude from that found in pure water. In this acetic acid solution, the H^+ from the acetic acid will suppress the dissociation of water (Le Chatelier's principle again) so that the contribution of water to the H^+ ion concentration will be less than $10^{-7}M$. In this system, we probably are operating at the limit at which we can neglect the contribution of water to the hydrogen ion concentration in the solution. In this system, a relatively large amount of acetate ions was added to a very dilute acetic acid solution. The concentration of H^+ in $0.010M$ HAc is small to begin with (about $4.20 \times 10^{-4}M$). The large amount of Ac^- ion added in the form of NaAc served to reduce this hydrogen ion concentration even further by suppressing the HAc dissociation. In fact, the H^+ ion concentration was reduced to the point that it compared to that present in pure water within a factor of 10.

A more exact solution to problems such as this and others where the hydronium ion or hydroxide ion concentrations resulting from added weak acid or weak base compare with that due to water can be applied, but the algebra is a bit more complex. Such calculations require the use of the K_w expression and the formulation of equations expressing the charge balance and the mass balance, which can be solved simultaneously.

To return to our example, now that the $[H^+]$ has been calculated, the pH of the $0.010M$ HAc $+ 0.10M$ NaAc solution can be determined:

$$pH = -\log [H^+] = -\log (1.76 \times 10^{-6}) = -(0.246 - 6)$$
$$pH = 5.7$$

The degree to which the acetic acid dissociates in this solution is very low due to the suppression by the added Ac^- ions:

$$\% \text{ dissociation} = \frac{1.76 \times 10^{-6}}{1.0 \times 10^{-2}} \times 100 = 0.018\%$$

IMPT

BUFFERS

Weak Acids and their Salts

Solutions that contain relatively high concentrations of a weak acid and a salt of that weak acid, or a weak base and a salt of that weak base, are buffers. Such solutions have the property of resisting changes in pH when additional acid or base is added to them. The salts referred to are ionic compounds that are capable of furnishing the anion common to the anion in the weak acid or the cation common to the cation in the weak base. These systems, then, are identical to the equilibrium systems we just described.

Before we look at buffer systems quantitatively, let us review how they work, that is, how they go about resisting changes in pH when acids or bases are added to them. Consider a buffer consisting of a solution of a weak acid, HA, and a salt of that weak acid, NaA. The predominant species in such a buffer solution are HA molecules and A^- anions. If a strong base, MOH, is added to the solution, the acid HA present will react with the base to neutralize it to form water and the cation of the base ($HA + MOH \rightarrow H_2O + M^+ + A^-$). The pH of the solution will not change much, even though strong base is added. Should a strong acid be added to this buffer, the protons in the strong acid will react with the plentiful supply of A^- ions present in the solution to form the weakly dissociated HA molecules. (One might also say that the protons from the strong acid will react with A^-, the relatively strong conjugate base of the weak acid, HA.) Therefore, there will be little change in pH.

In a similar way, a buffer solution containing ammonia and an ammonium salt such as NH_4NO_3 will resist a drop in pH when a strong acid is added because the NH_3 will neutralize the acid ($H^+ + NH_3 \rightarrow NH_4^+$). This buffer will resist an increase in pH upon addition of a strong base because the NH_4^+ ions present will react with the OH^- of the strong base to form ammonia molecules ($OH^- + NH_4^+ \rightarrow NH_3 + H_2O$).

The presence of the acid or base and the common-ion salt in an aqueous solution will establish a particular pH for that solution. Let us examine the relationship between the pH of the solution and the concentrations and nature of the acid or base involved.

Consider first a weak acid and salt of a weak acid system. The equilibrium can be generalized by the equation

$$HA \rightarrow H^+ + A^-$$

$$K_a = \frac{[H^+][A^-]}{[HA]}$$

Let us rearrange the K_a expression by solving it for $[H^+]$:

$$[H^+] = K_a\left(\frac{[HA]}{[A^-]}\right)$$

Taking the logarithm of both sides, we write

$$\log [H^+] = \log K_a + \log\left(\frac{[HA]}{[A^-]}\right)$$

Dividing through by -1:

$$-\log [H^+] = -\log K_a + \log\left(\frac{[A^-]}{[HA]}\right)$$

or

$$pH = pK_a + \log\left(\frac{[A^-]}{[HA]}\right) \tag{5-4}$$

Will It React?
An Introduction
to Chemical
Equilibrium

200

This expression will let us select the weak acid and salt and relative concentrations of these to use to prepare a buffer solution that has a particular pH. The rule to follow is to select an acid with a pK_a near that desired for the buffer solution. Then make up a solution of that acid and an alkali metal salt of that acid's anion (these are generally water-soluble strong electrolytes) in the proper ratio of concentrations. For a basic buffer, a weak base must be used, and the relationship will be

$$pOH = pK_b + \log \frac{[M^+]}{[MOH]} \qquad (5\text{-}5)$$

in which M^+ is the cation of the weak base used.

It should be understood that the practical use of these expressions is related to the extent to which the weak acid or weak base used in the buffer is dissociated in the presence of the common-ion salt. A precise expression for the pH expression, for instance, should be (neglecting contributions of H^+ ions from solvent water)

$$pH = pK_a + \log \frac{[A^+] + [H^+]}{[HA] - [H^+]}$$

A similar modification with $[OH^-]$ occupying positions analogous to the $[H^+]$ exists for the pOH expression.

In most buffer systems, the concentrations of acid (or base) and the salt must be relatively high so that there is an ample supply available to react with any base or acid added to the solution. In a weak-acid buffer under these conditions, the hydrogen ion concentration is suppressed by the common ion of the salt to the extent that its equilibrium concentration, $[H^+]$, is negligible compared to the equilibrium concentration of the undissociated acid, $[HA]$, and the acid anion, $[A^-]$. In such situations, the simplified expression (Equation 5-4) will apply. A similar situation will exist in the case of basic buffers. Take note that in such cases a buffer made up of equal concentrations of weak acid and salt (weak base and salt in the case of a basic buffer) will have a pH numerically equal to the pK_a of an acid (or a pOH equal to the pK_b of a base in the case of a basic buffer). This can be seen by observing that in Equation 5-4, when the numerator and the denominator in the log ($[A^-]/[HA]$) are equal, this term reduces to log 1, which is zero, and $pH = pK_a$. A similar situation will exist for a basic buffer, where $pOH = pK_b$.

EXAMPLE. Prepare a buffer solution that has a pH of 2.70.

SOLUTION. A solution having a pH of 2.70 is acidic. Therefore, the buffer will be made of a solution of a weak acid and a salt of this weak acid. The relationship we will use is that given by Equation 5-4:

$$pH = pK_a + \log \frac{[A^-]}{[HA]}$$

which assumes that the $[H^+]$ ion concentration will be suppressed to the extent that its concentration is negligible compared to the equilibrium concentration of A^- and HA.

To find a suitable weak acid, we look at a table of pK_a values for acids (Table 5–4 in *Chemical Principles*). In the table, we see that bromoacetic acid has a pK_a of 2.69, very close to the desired pH. Let us propose that we make the buffer of a solution of bromoacetic acid, $CH_2BrCOOH$, and sodium bromoacetate, $Na^+CH_2BrCOO^-$. The equilibrium in this solution is

$$CH_2BrCOOH \rightleftarrows H^+ + CH_2BrCOO^-$$

and from the K_a expression,

$$pH = pK_a + \log\left(\frac{[CH_2BrCOO^-]}{[CH_2BrCOOH]}\right)$$

When the pH is 2.70,

$$2.70 = 2.69 + \log\left(\frac{[CH_2BrCOO^-]}{[CH_2BrCOOH]}\right)$$

$$\log\left(\frac{[CH_2BrCOO^-]}{[CH_2BrCOOH]}\right) = 2.70 - 2.69 = 0.01$$

Taking the antilogarithm of both sides gives

$$\left(\frac{[CH_2BrCOO^-]}{[CH_2BrCOOH]}\right) = 1.02 \tag{5-6}$$

The preceding tells us that the ratio of bromoacetate anions and bromoacetic acid we must maintain in the solution of pH = 2.70 is 1.02. To determine what concentrations of these substances we should use, two factors must be considered:

(1) To maintain the buffer action, the solutions must be relatively concentrated so that there will be ample acid and acid anions to react with reasonable amounts of any acid or base added to the solution.

(2) Since we have assumed that the concentration of H^+ ions will be negligible when writing Equation 5–6, we should select an acid concentration such that this is true. To determine what this concentration should be, we must determine the H^+ ion concentration in a solution that has a pH of 2.70:

Will It React?
An Introduction
to Chemical
Equilibrium

202

$$pH = 2.70 = -\log[H^+]$$
$$\log[H^+] = -2.70$$
$$[H^+] = 10^{-2.70} = 10^{-2} \times 10^{-0.70}$$

$$= 10^{-2} \times \frac{1}{10^{0.70}}$$

From the table of logarithms, the number whose logarithm is 0.70 is 5.02. Therefore,

$$[H^+] = 10^{-2} \times \frac{1}{5.02} = 10^{-2} \times 0.199 = 2.0 \times 10^{-3}$$

For convenience, let us use a concentration of $CH_2BrCOOH$ of $0.50M$, since 2.0×10^{-3} is negligible compared to 0.50; that is, $0.50 - 0.002 = 0.50$ to the correct number of significant figures.

From Equation 5–6, we can compute the amount of bromoacetate anions we must have present in the solution with the $0.50M$ bromoacetic acid:

$$[CH_2BrCOO^-] = (1.02)([CH_2BrCOOH]) = (1.02)(0.50)$$
$$= 0.51M$$

The results of our calculations show that a solution that is $0.50M$ in $CH_2BrCOOH$ and $0.51M$ in $NaCH_2BrCOO$ will have a pH of 2.70.

Now let us demonstrate how this solution will act as a buffer and resist changes in pH when acid and base are added to it.

EXAMPLE. Calculate the pH of 1 liter of a solution that contains $0.050M$ $CH_2BrCOOH$ and $0.051M$ $NaCH_2BrCOO$ when 0.0010 mole of HCl is added.

SOLUTION. Let us symbolize the acid $CH_2BrCOOH$ by HA and the salt, $CH_2BrCOONa$, by NaA for simplicity. The HCl will be dissociated completely into hydrogen ions and chloride ions. In the presence of the excess bromoacetate ions, the hydrogen ions will react to produce bromoacetic acid according to the equation

$$H^+ + A^- \rightarrow HA$$

The equation shows that one mole of H^+ will react with one mole of A^- to produce one mole of HA. Therefore, 0.0010 mole of HCl will react with 0.0010 mole of the bromoacetate ions and produce an additional 0.0010 mole of bromoacetic acid in the solution. All this takes place in 1 liter of solution. Therefore, the concentration of acid and acid anions after the reaction has occurred is

$$[A^-] = [A^- \text{ before HCl added}] - [A^- \text{ reacting with HCl}]$$
$$= 0.051 - 0.0010 = 0.050M$$

$$[HA] = [HA \text{ before HCl added}] + [HA \text{ produced by}$$
$$\text{reaction with HCl}]$$
$$= 0.050 + 0.0010 = 0.051$$

We see that the concentrations of bromoacetic acid and bromoacetate ions have not been altered very much by the addition of the $0.0010M$ HCl. We can calculate the pH of the resulting solution using Equation 5–4:

$$pH = pK_a + \log \frac{[A^-]}{[HA]} = 2.69 + \log\left(\frac{0.050}{0.051}\right)$$

$$= 2.69 + \log (9.8 \times 10^{-1})$$

$$= 2.69 + 0.99 - 1.00 = 2.69 - 0.01 = \mathbf{2.68}$$

To show that the $0.050M$ $CH_2BrCOOH/0.051M$ $NaCH_2BrCOO$ solution acted as a buffer and resisted a change in pH note that before the $0.0010M$ HCl was added, the pH of the solution was 2.70. After the addition of the $0.0010M$ HCl, the pH was 2.68, a change of but 0.02 units. Compare this to the addition of $0.0010M$ HCl to pure water, which has a pH of 7. The H^+ ion concentration in $0.0010M$ HCl is $0.0010M$ because HCl is a strong acid and is dissociated completely. The pH of the solution will be

$$pH = -\log [H^+] = -\log (1.0 \times 10^{-3}) = 3$$

Compared to a pH of 7, there is a pH change of 4 units when the HCl is added to pure water, a nonbuffered solution.

5–9 SALTS OF WEAK ACIDS AND STRONG BASES: HYDROLYSIS

Hydrolysis can be defined as a metathesis (or displacement) reaction in which one of the reactants is water. We can represent a hydrolysis reaction by a generalized molecular equation

$$MA + HOH \rightleftarrows MOH + HA \tag{5–7}$$

To write this equation ionically requires one to indicate as molecules those substances that are only weakly dissociated into ions, and as ions those substances that exist predominantly as such. Note that the products of the reaction are a Brønsted acid HA and a base (here represented as an hydroxide base MOH). The compound MA is called a salt because it can be considered as the product of the neutralization of a base, which furnishes the cation M^{n+}, and an acid, which furnishes the anion X^{n-}. In fact, the reverse of Reaction 5–7 is such a neutralization reaction.

Suppose that we write the complete ionic equation for hydrolysis in which the product MOH is a strong base (completely ionized). We will assume that the reaction occurs with the dissolved MA salt, and that all the salt that dissolves does so by dissociating into ions:

$$M^+ + A^- + HOH \rightleftarrows M^+ + OH^- + HA \tag{5–8}$$

In this case, the salt MA can be described as the salt of a strong base (MOH) and a weak acid (HA). The net ionic equation for this reaction, arrived at by canceling the *spectator ions* from both sides, involves only

Will It React?
An Introduction
to Chemical
Equilibrium

204

the anion of the salt of the base and the weak acid:

$$A^- + HOH \rightleftarrows OH^- + HA \qquad (5\text{--}9)$$

If MA had been the salt of a weak base and a strong acid, the reaction would give the molecular form of the base (here formulated as an hydroxide base) and the ions of the completely dissociated acid:

$$M^+ + A^- + HOH \rightleftarrows MOH + H^+ + A^- \qquad (5\text{--}10)$$

and the net ionic equation is

$$M^+ + HOH \rightleftarrows MOH + H^+ \qquad (5\text{--}11)$$

Note that the previous net ionic equations indicate what the result of hydrolysis of the two types of salts will be, as far as the final pH of the solution is concerned. In Equation 5–8, the reaction of a salt of a strong base and a weak acid, OH^- ions are produced. These OH^- ions will cause the solvent water equilibrium, $H_2O \rightleftarrows H^+ + OH^-$, to shift to the left and, to maintain the constancy of K_w, the H^+ concentration will be decreased to a value less than $1 \times 10^{-7}M$. The solution after hydrolysis will be basic and its pH will be greater than 7. As Equation 5–10 shows, the hydrolysis of a salt of a weak base and a strong acid will introduce additional H^+ ions into the solution, make it acidic, and lower the pH to a value less than 7.

The phenomenon of hydrolysis can be explained by the conjugate acid–base concept. Consider the hydrolysis of an anion A^-, as typified by Equation 5–9. In this reaction, the anion acts as a base competing with the OH^- ion in water for the proton. Very weakly basic anions such as ClO_4^-, MnO_4^-, ClO_3^-, NO_3^-, Br^-, Cl^-, and HSO_4^-, the conjugate bases of the so-called strong mineral acids listed at the top of table 5–4 in *Chemical Principles*, are so weak that they cannot remove any significant number of protons from water. Therefore, such anions do not hydrolyze.

Those anions that are fairly strong bases can compete with the OH^- ion for a share of the protons in water. In so doing they produce their conjugate acids, and hydrolysis occurs, as depicted in Equation 5–9. The more basic the anion A^-, that is, the smaller the K_a or the larger the pK_a for its conjugate acid, the greater will be its ability to remove protons from the water molecule and the greater will be the degree of hydrolysis.

The K_a and pK_a values for various acids are given in Table 5–4. Therefore, to write the net ionic equation for the hydrolysis of the salt of a strong base and a weak acid, you need only consider the anion that originates from the salt and locate in the table the anion in the column headed A^-. The formula for its conjugate acid is to the left of the column headed HA. A check of the K_a or the pK_a will tell you if hydrolysis can occur. Extremely large K_a's and very low pK_a's indicate the anion is too weak a base (its conjugate acid is very strong) to compete effectively with OH^- ions for the protons in water and to hydrolyze. Tabulated low K_a's and high pK_a's indicate hydrolysis will occur and the equation for the reaction can be formulated following the form given in Equation 5–9, substituting the appropriate symbol for the anion A^-.

Table 5–5 in *Chemical Principles* can be used in a similar fashion for formulating equations for the hydrolysis of the salts of strong acids and weak bases, as depicted in Equation 5–10. The alkali and alkaline earth metal hydroxides do not appear in the table. These metal hydroxides are very strong bases; they are soluble strong electrolytes and are completely dissociated into the metal cation and OH^- ions in solution. Therefore, these metal cations (Li^+, Na^+, K^+, Rb^+, Fr^+, Sr^{2+}, and Ba^{2+}) do not compete with the proton for OH^- ions in the water equilibrium and do not hydrolyze. The substances that are listed in Table 5–5 are weak bases. The cations of these weak bases are listed in the column headed BH^+; these cations will hydrolyze. A close inspection of the formula for these cations reveals that each is a protonated form of the parent base, which is listed to the left in the column headed B. The cation of the weak base that will hydrolyze is therefore a possible proton donor, an acid, and its product on hydrolysis will be the conjugate base. (This is analogous to the hydrolysis of the anion of a weak acid; this anion is a base and hydrolyzes to produce its conjugate acid.)

To take account of the proton present in the weak-base cation in writing the net ionic equation for the hydrolysis reaction, it will be necessary to formulate the H^+ ions as a hydrated species such as H_3O^+. Instead of writing the general equation as

$$M^+ + HOH \rightleftarrows MOH + H^+$$

we write it as

$$BH^+ + HOH \rightleftarrows B + H_3O^+$$

We have discussed the result of the hydrolysis of salts of strong bases and weak acids (which yield solutions that are basic, pH > 7) and salts of weak bases and strong acids (which yield solutions that are acidic, pH < 7). What about salts of strong bases and strong acids and salts of weak bases and weak acids? Both of these situations can be approached by formulating the equation for the hydrolysis reactions.

SALTS OF STRONG BASES AND STRONG ACIDS

We already have mentioned that the cations of strong bases and the anions of strong acids do not hydrolyze. Consequently, one would predict that the presence of these ions in aqueous solution will have no effect on the position of the water equilibrium, and the pH of the solution will not be altered from that of pure water.

To illustrate this with an equation, consider the salt $KClO_3$. K^+ is the cation of the strong hydroxide base KOH, and ClO_3^- is the anion of the strong acid, $HClO_3$ (see Table 5–4):

$$K^+ + ClO_3^- + HOH \rightleftarrows K^+ + OH^- + H^+ + ClO_3^-$$

Will It React?
An Introduction
to Chemical
Equilibrium

206

The net ionic equation shows that the system contains only spectator ions, and the pH (7.0) is determined by the dissociation of the pure solvent water:

$$HOH \rightleftharpoons H^+ + OH^-$$

SALTS OF WEAK ACIDS AND WEAK BASES

Now consider the strong electrolyte NH_4CN, a salt of a weak acid, HCN, and a weak base, NH_3. To write the equation for the hydrolysis of this salt, we need to recognize, with the help of Tables 5–4 and 5–5, that the NH_4^+ ion is the conjugate acid of the weak base, ammonia, and will hydrolyze to NH_3, and that the CN^- ion is the conjugate base of the weak hydrocyanic acid and will hydrolyze to HCN. The total ionic equation becomes

$$NH_4^+ + CN^- + HOH \rightleftharpoons NH_3 + HCN + HOH$$

and the net ionic equation is

$$NH_4^+ + CN^- \rightleftharpoons NH_3 + HCN$$

A pH change generally accompanies the dissolution of these weak acid–weak base salts. However, the pH is dependent on the nature of the relative strengths of the weak acid and weak base formed on hydrolysis. The pK_a, K_a, pK_b, and K_b values can be used to determine the result. If the conjugate base of the cation has a larger K_b or a smaller pK_b than the K_a or pK_a of the conjugate acid of the anion, the resulting solution will be basic and have a pH greater than 7. One might say that in such a case the base is a stronger base than the acid is an acid. Conversely, if the K_a of the conjugate acid of the anion is larger than the K_b of the conjugate base of the cation (or if the pK_a is lower than the pK_b) the solution will be acidic and have a pH less than 7.

Let's illustrate the preceding discussion by working a few problems. Basically, the procedure already has been described, because it is no different than that followed in working problems involving weak-acid or weak-base equilibria. Let us calculate the pH of the following solutions: $0.010M$ NaCN, $0.010M$ NH_4Cl, and $0.010M$ NH_4CN.

PROBLEM 1.   Calculate the pH of a $0.010M$ NaCN solution.

SOLUTION.   We write the equation for the hydrolysis reaction as involving the hydrolysis of the CN^- anion only because NaCN is the salt of a strong base (NaOH) and a weak acid (HCN):

$$CN^- + HOH \rightleftharpoons HCN + OH^-$$

The equilibrium constant for this reaction, K_{eq}, is formulated in the conventional way

$$K_{eq} = \frac{[HCN][OH^-]}{[CN^-][HOH]}$$

Generally, the concentration of dissolved salt in the solutions we deal with is almost negligible in comparison to the concentration of the solvent water present. Therefore, we can approximate the concentration of water in the K_{eq} expression by that of pure water. As was done in the development of the K_a and K_b expressions, we recognize that the concentration of water in pure water is a constant, and simplify the above expression by multiplying both sides of the equation by this value. The result of this multiplication will be K_{eq} [HOH], which also is a constant. This constant is referred to as K_b or K_h, the hydrolysis constant. We will base all our quantitative considerations of hydrolysis on the existence of K_h:

$$K_{eq}[\text{HOH}] = \frac{[\text{HCN}][\text{OH}^-][\text{HOH}]}{[\text{CN}^-][\text{HOH}]} = \frac{[\text{HCN}][\text{OH}^-]}{[\text{CN}^-]} = K_h$$

We compute the numerical value of K_h, using the data in Table 5–4:

$$K_h = \frac{[\text{HCN}][\text{OH}^-]}{[\text{CN}^-]} = \frac{K_w}{K_a \ (\text{for HCN})} = \frac{1.0 \times 10^{-14}}{4.9 \times 10^{-10}}$$

$$= 2.0 \times 10^{-5}$$

We set up our concentration table (moles liter^{-1}):

	Initial	At equilibrium
[HCN] =	0.00	x
[OH$^-$] =	1×10^{-7}	$x + (1 \times 10^{-7})$
[CN$^-$] =	0.010	$0.010 - x$

In setting up the table, we have indicated that at the instant 0.010 mole of CN$^-$ ion enters a liter of the solution and before any HCN can be produced by hydrolysis, the only OH$^-$ ions present will be those in pure water ($1 \times 10^{-7}M$). We have let x represent the moles per liter of HCN produced by the hydrolysis that are present in the solution at equilibrium. The stoichiometry of the hydrolysis reaction indicates that for every mole of HCN produced by the hydrolysis of the CN$^-$ ion, a like number of moles of OH$^-$ ions also will be produced (in this case x moles of OH$^-$ per liter). This will make the total equilibrium concentration of OH$^-$ ions equal to the sum of the x moles per liter produced by hydrolysis and the 1×10^{-7} moles per liter initially present.

Substituting the values for the concentration of the species present at equilibrium into the K_h expression gives

$$\frac{[\text{HCN}][\text{OH}^-]}{[\text{CN}^-]} = \frac{(x)[x + (1 \times 10^{-7})]}{(0.010 - x)} = 2.0 \times 10^{-5}$$

To simplify the arithmetic required to solve this equation, let us assume that the value of x, the concentration of HCN produced by hydrolysis, will be small enough compared to 0.010 that it can be neglected in the denominator. We also will assume that the number 1×10^{-7} will be insignificant compared to x and will use x in place of the quantity $[x + (1 \times 10^{-7})]$ in the numerator. Solving the simplified expression for x gives

$$\frac{(x)[x + (1 \times 10^{-7})]}{(0.010 - x)} = \frac{(x)(x)}{(0.010)} = 2.0 \times 10^{-5}$$

$$x^2 = 2.0 \times 10^{-7} = 20 \times 10^{-8}$$

$$x = 4.5 \times 10^{-4}$$

Checking our assumptions, we see that to the correct number of significant figures $(4.5 \times 10^{-4} + 1 \times 10^{-7}) = (4.5 \times 10^{-4} + 0.001 \times 10^{-4}) = 4.5 \times 10^{-4}$ and $(0.010 - 4.5 \times 10^{-4}) = (0.010 - 0.00045) = 0.010$. Our assumption proves to be valid so $[OH^-] = x + (1 \times 10^{-7}) = 4.5 \times 10^{-4} + (1 \times 10^{-7}) = 4.5 \times 10^{-4}$. To determine the pH, we first find the pOH:

$$pOH = -\log[OH^-] = -\log(4.5 \times 10^{-4})$$
$$= -(\log 4.5 + \log 10^{-4}) = -(0.65 - 4)$$
$$= 3.35$$

Since $pH + pOH = 14$,

$$pH = 14 - pOH = 14.00 - 3.35 = \mathbf{10.6}$$

We predict from the equation for the hydrolysis of the salt of a strong base and a weak acid that the resulting solution will be basic and have a pH greater than 7, as our calculation has shown. Such a comparison of predictions with calculated results always should be made as a partial check of your work.

PROBLEM 2. Calculate the equilibrium concentrations of all the species present in a $0.010M$ NH_4Cl solution, and compute the pH of the solution.

SOLUTION. NH_4Cl is a salt of the weak base NH_3 and the strong acid HCl. The NH_4^+ ion will be the only ion that hydrolyzes; the equation for the hydrolysis is

$$NH_4^+ + HOH \rightleftarrows NH_3 + H_3O^+$$

Formulation and evaluation of K_h (or K_a) for the reaction yields the expression

$$\frac{[NH_3][H_3O^+]}{[NH_4^+]} = K_h = \frac{K_w}{K_b \text{ (for } NH_3)} = \frac{1 \times 10^{-14}}{1.79 \times 10^{-5}}$$

$$= 5.6 \times 10^{-10}$$

We set up our table, letting y equal the equilibrium molar concentration of NH_3 produced by hydrolysis:

	Initial	At equilibrium
$[NH_3] =$	0.00	y
$[H_3O^+] =$	1×10^{-7}	$y + (1 \times 10^{-7})$
$[NH_4^+] =$	0.010	$0.010 - y$

The reasoning used to formulate the equilibrium concentrations parallels that used in the preceding problem. In producing y moles per liter of NH_3 by hydrolysis, y moles per liter of H_3O^+ also will be formed to add to the $1 \times 10^{-7}M$ H_3O^+ initially present from the dissociation of the solvent water, and y moles per liter of the original $0.010M$ NH_4^+ ion will be consumed, thereby leaving $(0.010 - y)M$ NH_4^+ ion present at equilibrium. Substitution in the K_h expression gives

$$\frac{[NH_3][H_3O^+]}{[NH_4^+]} = \frac{(y)[y + (1 \times 10^{-7})]}{(0.010 - y)} = 5.6 \times 10^{-10}$$

If we consider the results of the simplifications made in the preceding problem, we can make similar assumptions here with considerable confidence. The very small K_h indicates that 0.010 NH_4^+ ions hydrolyzes to a lesser extent than CN^- ion (K_h for $CN^- = 2.0 \times 10^{-5}$). In the preceding problem, x, the concentration of the substance produced by hydrolysis, proved to be insignificant relative to 0.010; therefore we should expect to find y to be negligible compared to 0.010 in this problem. Although we know y will be a small number, let us assume it is still sufficiently large to allow us to neglect the addition of 1×10^{-7} to y in the numerator.

Solution of the simplified K_h expression gives

$$\frac{(y)[y + (1 \times 10^{-7})]}{(0.010 - y)} \simeq \frac{(y)(y)}{(0.010)} = 5.6 \times 10^{-10}$$

$$y^2 = 5.6 \times 10^{-12}$$

$$y = 2.4 \times 10^{-6}$$

In checking our assumptions before proceeding we see that $0.010 - (2.4 \times 10^{-6}) = 0.010$, so the omission of y in the denominator was safe. However, the magnitude of y is of the same order as 1×10^{-7}; that is, $[y + (1 \times 10^{-7})] = (2.4 \times 10^{-6} + 0.1 \times 10^{-6})$. When we neglect y, this will introduce a relative error of about $(0.1/2.5) \times 100 = 4\%$ in the factor. Since we have agreed to consider approximations acceptable if they do not alter the results more than 5%, it would appear that neglecting 1×10^{-7} in the $[y + (1 \times 10^{-7})]$ term will lead to an acceptable answer.[3]

[3] If one retains the factor $[y + (1 \times 10^{-7})]$ in the numerator and solves the resulting quadratic equation for y, the result is $y = 2.3 \times 10^{-6}$. This compares to our approximate result, 2.4×10^{-6}, within 4.4%; we are just within the limits we have arbitrarily set as acceptable.

The concentrations of the following species present at equilibrium are:

$$[NH_3] = y = 2.4 \times 10^{-6}$$
$$[H_3O^+] = y + (1 \times 10^{-7}) \simeq 2.4 \times 10^{-6}$$
$$[NH_4^+] = 0.010 - y = 0.010 - (1 \times 10^{-7}) = 0.010$$
$$[Cl^-] = 0.010 \text{ (no change, since } Cl^- \text{ does not hydrolyze)}$$

The pH of the solution is

$$pH = -\log [H_3O^+] = -\log (2.4 \times 10^{-6})$$
$$= -(\log 2.4 + \log 10^{-6})$$
$$= -(0.38 - 6) = 5.62 = 5.6$$

This result indicates that the solution will be acidic. We would predict this result from the hydrolysis equation. The small amount of OH^- ions present in this solution can be caclulated from $[H_3O^+]$ and K_w:

$$K_w = [H_3O^+][OH^-] = 1 \times 10^{-14}$$
$$[OH^-] = \frac{1 \times 10^{-14}}{[H_3O^+]} = \frac{1 \times 10^{-14}}{2.4 \times 10^{-6}} = 4.2 \times 10^{-9}$$

PROBLEM 3.   Calculate the molar concentration of the species produced upon hydrolysis of $0.010 M$ NH_4CN. What is the pH of the resulting solution?

SOLUTION.   As we already have shown in this section, Tables 5–4 and 5–5 in *Chemical Principles* indicate that NH_4CN is the salt of the weak base NH_3 ($pK_b = 4.75$) and the weak acid HCN   ($pK_a = 9.31$). The equation for the hydrolysis is

$$NH_4^+ + CN^- \rightleftarrows NH_3 + HCN$$

Because the pK_b of NH_3 is lower than the pK_a of HCN, we conclude that NH_3 is a stronger base than HCN is an acid. Therefore, we predict that the resulting solution will be basic because of the hydrolysis.

We formulate the K_h expression and compute its numerical value, using the K_a for HCN and K_b for NH_3 obtained from Tables 5–4 and 5–5:

$$K_h = \frac{[NH_3][HCN]}{[NH_4^+][CN^-]} = \frac{K_w}{K_a(HCN) \cdot K_b(NH_3)}$$
$$= \frac{1.0 \times 10^{-14}}{(4.9 \times 10^{-10})(1.79 \times 10^{-5})} = 1.1$$

We set up the table letting x = the molar concentration of NH_3 at equilibrium. The stoichiometry of the hydrolysis tells us that if x moles of NH_3 are produced on hydrolysis, then x moles of HCN will be produced simultaneously and x moles of NH_4^+ and x moles of CN^- ions will be consumed. We note also that since NH_4CN is a strong electrolyte, a $0.010M$ NH_4CN solution will contain $0.010M$ NH_4^+ ions and $0.010M$ CN^- ions before hydrolysis begins.

	Initial	At equilibrium
$[NH_4^+]$ =	0.010	$0.010 - x$
$[CN^-]$ =	0.010	$0.010 - x$
$[NH_3]$ =	0.000	x
$[HCN]$ =	0.000	x

Substitution into the K_h expression gives

$$\frac{[NH_3][HCN]}{[NH_4^+][CN^-]} = \frac{(x)(x)}{(0.010 - x)(0.010 - x)} = 1.1$$

The value 1.1 for K_h is relatively high. This means that x is likely to be a large number and we may not be able to neglect it when compared to 0.010 in the two factors in the denominator. However, the simplified equation will be so easy to solve, let us make the assumption anyway to ascertain whether it is or is not valid. If x is negligible compared to 0.010, the solution to the simplified expression is

$$\frac{(x)(x)}{(0.010 - x)(0.010 - x)} \simeq \frac{x^2}{(0.010)(0.010)} \simeq 1.1$$

$$x^2 = 1.1. \times (0.010)^2 = 1.1 \times 10^{-4}$$

$$x = 1.05 \times 10^{-2} = 0.010$$

Obviously, we cannot neglect x in the denominator; $0.010M$ NH_4CN is almost completely hydrolyzed. We are forced to solve the complete equation:

$$\frac{(x)(x)}{(0.010 - x)(0.010 - x)} = 1.1$$

$$x^2 = (1.1)(0.010 - x)^2 = (1.1)(1.0 \times 10^{-4} - 0.020x + x^2)$$

$$x^2 = 1.1 \times 10^{-4} - 2.2 \times 10^{-2}x + 1.1x^2$$

$$1.1x^2 - x^2 - 0.022x + 1.1 \times 10^{-4} = 0$$

$$0.1x^2 - 0.022x + 1.1 \times 10^{-4} = 0$$

$$x^2 - 0.22x + 1.1 \times 10^{-3} = 0$$

$$x = \frac{-(-0.22) \pm \sqrt{(-0.22)^2 - 4(1.1 \times 10^{-3})}}{2}$$

$$x = \frac{0.22 \pm \sqrt{0.048 - 0.0044}}{2}$$

Will It React?
An Introduction
to Chemical
Equilibrium

212

$$x = \frac{0.22 \pm \sqrt{0.044}}{2} = \frac{0.22 \pm 0.21}{2}$$

$$x = \frac{0.43}{2} = 0.22 \qquad x = \frac{0.01}{2} = 0.005$$

Of these two answers for x, the value 0.22 cannot be an appropriate answer to this problem. Because only $0.010M$ NH_4^+ ions were present initially, no more than $0.010M$ NH_3 could possibly be formed (recall $x = [NH_3]$) and this would occur only upon complete hydrolysis. The solutions are $x = [NH_3] = [HCN] = \mathbf{0.005}$ and $[NH_4^+] = [CN^-] = 0.010 - x = 0.010 - 0.005 = \mathbf{0.005}$.

To calculate the pH of the solution, we should realize that a solution containing HCN must satisfy the equilibrium constant for HCN:

$$K_a = \frac{[H^+][CN^-]}{[HCN]} = 4.9 \times 10^{-10}$$

Substituting the concentrations we have just calculated for $[CN^-]$ and $[HCN]$, we can compute the hydronium ion concentration and the pH:

$$\frac{[H^+][0.005]}{[0.005]} = 4.9 \times 10^{-10}$$

$$[H^+] = \mathbf{4.9 \times 10^{-10}}$$
$$pH = -\log [H^+] = -\log (4.9 \times 10^{-10})$$
$$= -[\log 4.9 + \log 10^{-10}]$$
$$= -(0.69 - 10) = 9.31 = \mathbf{9.3}$$

As predicted, the solution is basic.

5–10 EQUILIBRIA WITH SLIGHTLY SOLUBLE SALTS

When a solid salt is placed in water some of it will dissolve. Frequently, salts are classified in a very qualitative way based on their relative solubilities at room temperature. Soluble, slightly soluble, and insoluble are terms used. Since every substance will dissolve in water to some extent, even if the solubility may be too small to measure, one might argue that a term such as "very slightly soluble" is more appropriate than insoluble; we will use both terms.

Some generalizations as to the solubilities of many of the simple salts of the more familiar metal ions are summarized in Table 5–1. It does not take much effort to memorize this table and you are encouraged to do so. Knowledge of the solubility of a compound can be useful to you as a chemistry student.

Table 5–1.   Summary of Solubilities of Ionic Compounds in Water

Water-soluble ionic compounds
Nearly all nitrates (NO_3^-), chlorates (ClO_3^-), and acetates ($C_2H_3O_2^-$)
Nearly all salts of Group IA elements (Li^+, Na^+, K^+)
Nearly all ammonium salts (NH_4^+)
Nearly all chlorides, bromides, and iodides except those of Cu^+, Ag^+, Tl^+, Pb^{2+}, and Hg_2^{2+}
Nearly all sulfates (SO_4^{2-}) except those of large dipositive ions, Ca^{2+}, Sr^{2+}, Ba^{2+}, and Pb^{2+}

Water-insoluble ionic compounds
Nearly all hydroxides (OH^-) except those of Group IA elements and heavy Group IIA elements such as Sr^{2+} and Ba^{2+}
Nearly all sulfides except those of cations with noble-gas structures (e.g., Na^+, Mg^{2+}, Al^{3+})
Nearly all carbonates (CO_3^{2-}), phosphates (PO_4^{3-}), and arsenates (AsO_4^{3-}) except those of Group IA elements

When a salt is added to water, it will dissolve until its solubility limit is reached. After this, the addition of more salt results in a two-phase system consisting of the saturated solution and the solid salt. Although it appears to the eye that the solid is not interacting, we know from experiments that a dynamic equilibrium exists in such a system. Solid salt is dissolving continuously into the saturated solution and the dissolved ions in the solution are precipitating as solid; both processes take place at the same rate.

In this section, we will do calculations involving the equilibria between slightly soluble salts and the ions in their saturated solutions. Such equilibria, like the equilibria we have discussed previously, can be described by a chemical equation and an equilibrium constant, K_{sp}, which is called the solubility-product constant.

DETERMINATION OF K_{sp} OF A SALT FROM SOLUBILITY DATA

EXAMPLE.   The concentration of a saturated solution of PbS at 25°C is found to be $8.5 \times 10^{-15}M$. What is the K_{sp} of PbS?

SOLUTION.   This problem is analogous to Example 26 in *Chemical Principles*; compare both solutions to reinforce your understanding. The equation for the reaction is

$$PbS(s) \rightleftarrows Pb^{2+} + S^{2-}$$

and the K_{sp} expression is

$$K_{sp} = [Pb^{2+}][S^{2-}]$$

Will It React?
An Introduction
to Chemical
Equilibrium

214

Now we must determine the equilibrium molar concentrations of Pb^{2+} and S^{2-} ions. The equation for the dissolution reaction shows that every time a mole of $PbS(s)$ dissolves it furnishes 1 mole of Pb^{2+} ions and 1 mole of S^{2-} ions. The data given in the problem states that 8.5×10^{-15} mole per liter of PbS is dissolved in the saturated solution. Therefore, we conclude that 8.5×10^{-15} mole of PbS dissolving in 1 liter of solution will furnish 8.5×10^{-15} mole per liter of Pb^{2+} ions and 8.5×10^{-15} mole per liter of S^{2-} ions. These are the equilibrium concentrations:

$$[Pb^{2+}] = 8.5 \times 10^{-15}$$

and

$$[S^{2-}] = 8.5 \times 10^{-15}$$

We substitute these values into the K_{sp} expression and solve for K_{sp}:

$$K_{sp} = [Pb^{2+}][S^{2-}] = (8.5 \times 10^{-15})(8.5 \times 10^{-15})$$
$$K_{sp} = 7.2 \times 10^{-29}$$

EXAMPLE. The solubility of Ag_3PO_4 is $0.000016M$; what is the K_{sp} of Ag_3PO_4?

SOLUTION. This problem is analogous to Example 27 in *Chemical Principles*; compare the two solutions. Write the equation for the equilibrium reaction:

$$Ag_3PO_4(s) \rightleftarrows 3Ag^+ + PO_4{}^{3-}$$

Write the K_{sp} expression:

$$K_{sp} = [Ag^+]^3[PO_4{}^{3-}]$$

Evaluate the equilibrium molar concentrations of Ag^+ and $PO_4{}^{3-}$. From the balanced equation we see that for every mole of Ag_3PO_4 that dissolves there will be 3 moles of Ag^+ and 1 mole of $PO_4{}^{3-}$ ions. The example states that a saturated solution contains 0.000016 mole of dissolved Ag_3PO_4 per liter. Therefore,

$$[Ag^+] = 3 \times \text{moles } Ag_3PO_4 \text{ dissolved per liter}$$
$$= 3 \times 0.000016 = 4.8 \times 10^{-5}M$$
$$[PO_4{}^{3-}] = 1 \times \text{moles } Ag_3PO_4 \text{ dissolved per liter}$$
$$= 1 \times 0.000016 = 1.6 \times 10^{-5}M$$

Substitute the values for the equilibrium concentrations into the K_{sp} expression:

$$K_{sp} = [Ag^+]^3[PO_4{}^{3-}] = (4.8 \times 10^{-5})^3(1.6 \times 10^{-5})$$
$$= 1.8 \times 10^{-18}$$

EXAMPLE. As a final example, calculate the K_{sp} for mercury(I) bromide, Hg_2Br_2. Mercury(I) exists as the dimeric cation Hg_2^{2+}. The literature states that 100 ml of a saturated Hg_2Br_2 solution contains 1.8×10^{-6} of Hg_2Br_2.

SOLUTION. We first must determine the solubility in moles of Hg_2Br_2 per liter if we are to calculate the K_{sp}. The formula weight of Hg_2Br_2 is 561.0 amu. The solubility in moles per liter will be

$$\frac{1.8 \times 10^{-6} \text{ g } Hg_2Br_2}{561 \text{ g } Hg_2Br_2 \text{ mole}^{-1}} \times \frac{1000 \text{ ml liter}^{-1}}{100 \text{ ml}}$$

$$= 3.2 \times 10^{-8} \text{ mole liter}^{-1}$$

We now can proceed as in the preceding two examples. Write the equation for the dissolution reaction:

$$Hg_2Br_2(s) \rightleftarrows Hg_2^{2+} + 2Br^-$$

Formulate the K_{sp} expression:

$$K_{sp} = [Hg_2^{2+}][Br^-]^2$$

Determine the equilibrium concentration of Hg_2^{2+} and Br^- ions. The stoichiometry of the dissolution reaction indicates that for each mole of Hg_2Br_2 present in the solution there will be 1 mole of Hg_2^{2+} ions and 2 moles of Br^- ions. We have determined that 3.2×10^{-8} mole of Hg_2Br_2 is present in 1 liter of the solution; therefore,

$$[Hg_2^{2+}] = 1 \times \text{moles } Hg_2Br_2 \text{ dissolved per liter}$$
$$= 1 \times 3.2 \times 10^{-8} = 3.2 \times 10^{-8} M$$
$$[Br^-] = 2 \times \text{moles } Hg_2Br_2 \text{ dissolved per liter}$$
$$= 2 \times 3.2 \times 10^{-8} = 6.4 \times 10^{-8} M$$

Substitute into the K_{sp} expression and solve:

$$K_{sp} = [Hg_2^{2+}][Br^-]^2 = (3.2 \times 10^{-8})(6.4 \times 10^{-8})^2$$
$$= 1.3 \times 10^{-22}$$

CALCULATE THE SOLUBILITY OF A SALT GIVEN ITS K_{sp}

Example 28 in *Chemical Principles* is a calculation of this type. For our first example we shall choose a problem that is similar; compare the two methods of calculation.

EXAMPLE. The K_{sp} of manganese carbonate, $MnCO_3$, is given as 8.8×10^{-11}. Calculate the solubility of $MnCO_3$ in moles per liter.

SOLUTION. Write the equation for the reaction:

$$MnCO_3(s) \rightleftarrows Mn^{2+} + CO_3^{2-}$$

Will It React?
An Introduction
to Chemical
Equilibrium

216

Formulate the K_{sp} expression:

$$K_{sp} = [\text{Mn}^{2+}][\text{CO}_3{}^{2-}] = 8.8 \times 10^{-11}$$

Up to now, our procedure has been exactly the same as for all the equilibrium calculations. Now we need to substitute into the K_{sp} expression a quantity that we can relate to the solubility of MnCO_3. To find this quantity we look at the stoichiometry expressed by the equation for the dissolution reaction. We see that for every mole of MnCO_3 that dissolves per liter we should find 1 mole of Mn^{2+} ions and 1 mole of $\text{CO}_3{}^{2-}$ ions in the liter of saturated solution. Therefore, the molar concentration of either the Mn^{2+} or the $\text{CO}_3{}^{2-}$ ions in the solution will be numerically equal to the moles of MnCO_3 that dissolve per liter of solution, that is, the molar solubility of MnCO_3.

Let x equal the equilibrium molar concentration of Mn^{2+}, since this will have the same numerical value as the molar solubility of MnCO_3. (We also could have let x be the molar equilibrium concentration of $\text{CO}_3{}^{2-}$ ions.) If $x = [\text{Mn}^{2+}]$, the stoichiometry of the dissolution reaction tells us that $x = [\text{CO}_3{}^{2-}]$ as well. We substitute these quantities into the K_{sp} expression and solve the resulting equation:

$$[\text{Mn}^{2+}][\text{CO}_3{}^{2-}] = (x)(x) = 8.8 \times 10^{-11}$$
$$x^2 = 8.8 \times 10^{-11} = 88 \times 10^{-12}$$
$$x = [\text{Mn}^{2+}] = 9.4 \times 10^{-6}$$

As the concentration of Mn^{2+} ion in the saturated solution is $9.4 \times 10^{-6} M$, we conclude that 9.4×10^{-6} mole of MnCO_3 must have dissolved. Therefore, the solubility of MnCO_3 is **9.4×10^{-6} mole liter^{-1}**.

EXAMPLE. Calculate the solubility in moles per liter of $\text{Ca}_3(\text{PO}_4)_2$. $K_{sp} = 1.3 \times 10^{-32}$.

SOLUTION. Write the equation for the dissolution reaction:

$$\text{Ca}_3(\text{PO}_4)_2(s) \rightleftarrows 3\text{Ca}^{2+} + 2\text{PO}_4{}^{3-}$$

Formulate the K_{sp} expression:

$$K_{sp} = [\text{Ca}^{2+}]^3[\text{PO}_4{}^{3-}]^2 = 1.3 \times 10^{-32}$$

The stoichiometry of the dissolution reaction indicates that when 1 mole of $\text{Ca}_3(\text{PO}_4)_2$ dissolves, 3 moles of Ca^{2+} ions and 2 moles of $\text{PO}_4{}^{3-}$ ions will be placed into solution. Therefore, it follows that the molar solubility of $\text{Ca}_3(\text{PO}_4)_2$ will be equal to $(1/3)[\text{Ca}^{2+}]$ or $(1/2)[\text{PO}_4{}^{3-}]$; the bracketed quantities represent the concentration of the ions in the saturated solution at equilibrium.

To calculate $[\text{Ca}^{2+}]$, let $[\text{Ca}^{2+}] = x$. From the stoichiometry of the dissolution reaction we see that the concentration of $\text{PO}_4{}^{3-}$ ion will be 2/3 that of the Ca^{2+} ion; therefore,

$$[PO_4{}^{3-}] = \frac{2}{3} x.$$

Substituting these values for $[Ca^{2+}]$ and $[PO_4{}^{3-}]$ into the K_{sp} expression and solving for x gives

$$[Ca^{2+}]^3[PO_4{}^{3-}]^2 = (x)^3\left(\frac{2}{3}x\right)^2 = 1.3 \times 10^{-32}$$

$$\frac{4}{9} x^5 = 1.3 \times 10^{-32}$$

$$x^5 = (1.3 \times 10^{-32})\frac{9}{4} = 2.9 \times 10^{-32}$$

$$x = (2900 \times 10^{-35})^{1/5}$$

$$x = 4.9 \times 10^{-7} = [Ca^{2+}]$$

$$\text{Solubility } Ca^{2+} = 1/3[Ca^{2+}] = \frac{4.9 \times 10^{-7}}{3}$$

$$= 1.6 \times 10^{-7}M$$

[*Note:* To obtain the fifth root of 2.9×10^{-32}, the number is rewritten to a power of 10 that is divisible by 5, 2900×10^{-35}, and the fifth root of 2900 obtained using logarithms.]

The preceding two problems are similar to the calculations required to obtain the solubility of Ag_2CO_3 in Example 29 in *Chemical Principles*. Example 29 also demonstrates that if one is to use the K_{sp} value to estimate the relative solubilities of two or more salts it is necessary that the K_{sp} expressions be of the same form. That is, the molar concentrations must be raised to the same exponents.

THE SOLUBILITY OF A SALT IN A SOLUTION
CONTAINING A KNOWN ADDED AMOUNT OF A COMMON ION

Le Chatelier's principle can be applied to equilibria involving slightly soluble salts in the same way as it can to other equilibria we have studied. Example 30 in *Chemical Principles* asks one to calculate the solubility of CaF_2 in (a) pure water, (b) in $0.10M$ $CaCl_2$, and (c) in $0.10M$ NaF. Let us elaborate on the calculation for Part (c).

Will It React?
An Introduction
to Chemical
Equilibrium

218

SOLUTION. The $0.10M$ NaF will introduce $0.10M$ F^- ions into the solution and will decrease the solubility of CaF_2. Since F^- ions are added from some source other than CaF_2, we must use the equilibrium concentration of Ca^{2+} ions to measure the solubility of CaF_2. From the dissolution equation, which we will write as the first step in solving this problem, we see that the molar solubility of CaF_2 will be numerically equal to the equilibrium molar Ca^{2+} ion concentration (one mole of CaF_2 furnishes 1 mole of Ca^{2+} when it dissolves).

The equation and K_{sp} expressions are

$$CaF_2(s) \rightleftarrows Ca^{2+} + 2F^-$$

$$K_{sp} = [Ca^{2+}][F^-]^2 = 3.9 \times 10^{-11}$$

The concentration table:

	Initial	At equilibrium
$[Ca^{2+}] =$	0.000	x
$[F^-] =$	0.010	$0.010 + 2x$

We must use the equilibrium Ca^{2+} ion concentration as a measure of the solubility. Therefore, we let x equal the molar concentration of Ca^{2+} at equilibrium. The molar equilibrium concentration of F^- will include the $0.10M$ F^- added initially as NaF plus the $2x$ moles per liter of F^- ions produced when the x moles of CaF_2 dissolves. Substituting the equilibrium quantities into the K_{sp} expression and neglecting $2x$ compared to 0.10 gives

$$[Ca^{2+}][F^-]^2 = (x)(0.10 + 2x)^2 = 3.9 \times 10^{-11}$$

$$(x)(0.10)^2 = 3.9 \times 10^{-11}$$

$$x = [Ca^{2+}] = \frac{3.9 \times 10^{-11}}{(0.10)^2} = 3.9 \times 10^{-9}$$

We confirm that our assumption that $2x$, here 7.8×10^{-9}, is negligible compared to 0.10 and accept the above result. The molar solubility of $CaF_2 = [Ca^{2+}] =$ **3.9×10^{-9} mole liter^{-1}**. This is much less than the solubility of CaF_2 in pure water (2.1×10^{-4} mole liter^{-1}), as we would predict from Le Chatelier's principle.

GIVEN THE INITIAL AMOUNTS OF TWO REAGENTS, DETERMINE IF A PRECIPITATE WILL FORM WHEN THEY ARE MIXED

This type of question has numerous variations, such as determining (a) if a precipitate will form, (b) if more than one precipitate can form, which one will form first, and (c) how much of one reagent can be added to another without causing a precipitate to form. The basic principle in all these variations is that if ions are present in a solution that can form a slightly soluble substance, they will do so *only* if their concentrations are such as to exceed the K_{sp} of the substance.

EXAMPLE. Suppose that 10.0 ml of a $0.0100M$ Na_2CrO_4 solution are added to 50.0 ml of $0.00100M$ $Pb(NO_3)_2$ solution. Will $PbCrO_4$ precipitate?

SOLUTION. To answer this question we must compute the molar concentration and substitute it in the K_{sp} expression for $PbCrO_4$. When the two solutions are mixed, the Pb^{2+} and CrO_4^{2-} ions will be in a total volume of solution equal to 10.0 ml + 50.0 ml, or 60.0 ml = 0.060 liter. The molar concentration of Pb^{2+} ions is

$$\frac{0.0500 \text{ liter} \times 0.00100 \text{ mole } Pb^{2+} \text{ liter}^{-1}}{0.060 \text{ liter}} = 8.3 \times 10^{-4}M$$

The molar concentration of CrO_4^{2-} ions is

$$\frac{0.0100 \text{ liter} \times 0.0100 \text{ mole } CrO_4^{2-} \text{ liter}^{-1}}{0.060 \text{ liter}} = 1.7 \times 10^{-3}M$$

Consulting Table 5–8 in *Chemical Principles*, we see that for $PbCrO_4$

$$PbCrO_4(s) \rightleftarrows Pb^{2+} + CrO_4^{2-}$$

$$K_{sp} = [Pb^{2+}][CrO_4^{2-}] = 2 \times 10^{-16}$$

Substitution of the Pb^{2+} and CrO_4^{2-} ion concentrations in the solution into the K_{sp} expression gives

$$[Pb^{2+}][CrO_4^{2-}] = (8.3 \times 10^{-4})(1.7 \times 10^{-3}) = 1.4 \times 10^{-6}$$

Since $1.4 \times 10^{-6} > 2 \times 10^{-16}$, the K_{sp} for $PbCrO_4$, **$PbCrO_4$ will precipitate.**

EXAMPLE. A solution is $0.020M$ in $AgNO_3$ and $0.010M$ in $Mg(NO_3)_2$. If solid $NaOH$ is added to this solution, which compound will precipitate first, $AgOH$ or $Mg(OH)_2$? From Table 5–8 we see that the K_{sp} for $AgOH$ is 2.0×10^{-8} and the K_{sp} for $Mg(OH)_2$ is 8.9×10^{-12}

SOLUTION. Formulate and write the K_{sp} expressions for both hydroxides:

$$AgOH(s) \rightleftarrows Ag^+ + OH^-$$

$$K_{sp}(AgOH) = [Ag^+][OH^-] = 2.0 \times 10^{-8}$$

$$Mg(OH)_2(s) \rightleftarrows Mg^{2+} + 2OH^-$$

$$K_{sp}(Mg(OH)_2) = [Mg^{2+}][OH^-]^2 = 8.9 \times 10^{-12}$$

For either $Mg(OH)_2$ or $AgOH$ to precipitate the respective K_{sp} must be exceeded.

We calculate the concentration of OH^- needed to precipitate each compound by substituting the metal-ion concentration in the solution into the K_{sp} expression and calculating the OH^- concentration. If the OH^- ion concentration exceeds this calculated value, the hydroxide will precipitate.

Will It React?
An Introduction
to Chemical
Equilibrium

220

For $Mg(OH)_2$ this value is

$$[Mg^{2+}][OH^-]^2 = (0.010)[OH^-]^2 = 8.9 \times 10^{-12}$$

$$[OH^-]^2 = \frac{8.9 \times 10^{-12}}{0.010} = 8.9 \times 10^{-10}$$

$$[OH^-] = 2.9 \times 10^{-5}M$$

For AgOH this value is

$$[Ag^+][OH^-] = (0.020)[OH^-] = 2.0 \times 10^{-8}$$

$$[OH^-] = \frac{2.0 \times 10^{-8}}{2.0 \times 10^{-2}} = 1.0 \times 10^{-6}M$$

It requires a lower concentration of $[OH^-]$ (more than $1.0 \times 10^{-6}M$) to exceed the K_{sp} of AgOH than is required to exceed the K_{sp} of $Mg(OH)_2$ (more than $2.9 \times 10^{-5}M$). Therefore, as solid NaOH is added the K_{sp} of AgOH will be exceeded first and **AgOH will precipitate first.**

Table 5–8 shows that there are a large number of sulfide salts and hydroxide salts that have very low K_{sp}'s. Separations of many cations can be facilitated by controlled precipitation of their sulfides or hydroxides. Two reagents are widely used to carry out such separations, aqueous ammonia and a saturated aqueous H_2S solution. One advantage offered by these reagents is that the concentration of the precipitating anion (OH^- in the case of ammonia solution and S^{2-} in the case of H_2S) can be controlled easily by adjusting the pH of the solutions. In the case of ammonia, the OH^- ions are furnished by the dissociation of a weak base:

$$NH_3 + HOH \rightleftarrows NH_4^+ + OH^-$$

By adding NH_4^+ ions in the form of a soluble ammonium salt, such as NH_4NO_3 or NH_4Cl, one can adjust the position of this equilibrium to maintain the OH^- ion concentration desired; what we do in fact is buffer the system.

Using H_2S is a bit more complex because its dissociation involves two steps, each of which has a different dissociation constant. These equilibria are discussed in detail in Example 31 in *Chemical Principles*. All we shall point out here is that the net result of the two H_2S equilibria can be combined in a single dissociation constant, K_{a12}, which is numerically equal to the product of the K_a's for each of the steps. (This is true for all polybasic acids, which dissociate in a series of steps.) Thus, for H_2S we can write an equation for the overall dissociation:

$$H_2S \rightleftarrows 2H^+ + S^{2-}$$

and formulate the dissociation constant:

$$K_{a12} = \frac{[H^+]^2[S^{2-}]}{[H_2S]} = 1.0 \times 10^{-19}$$

In practice, a solution saturated with H_2S is used as the precipitating agent. At room temperature the solubility of H_2S is such that the concentration of a saturated solution is $0.10M$. The concentration of H_2S molecules in this solution at equilibrium, the $[H_2S]$ term in the K_{a12} expression, will be 0.10 minus the number of moles per liter of H_2S that dissociate. The magnitude of K_{a12} tells us that the dissociation is extremely slight; in fact, the quantity of H_2S that dissociates is negligible compared to 0.10. Since $[H_2S]$ will be $0.10M$ for almost every situation at 25°C, one generally incorporates it into the K_{a12} value and works with an "H_2S ion-product constant" instead of K_{a12}:

$$[H^+]^2[S^{2-}] = (0.10)(1.0 \times 10^{-19}) = 1.0 \times 10^{-20}$$

It is easily seen from this relationship that the H^+ ion concentration necessary to adjust the $[S^{2-}]$ to a desired value can be computed. One word of caution: In the case of polybasic acid systems such as H_2S, an overall equilibrium equation and dissociation constant can be written and evaluated. However, don't be fooled by the stoichiometry of the equilibrium equation. For example, we write $H_2S \rightleftarrows 2H^+ + S^{2-}$ as the overall equilibrium in aqueous H_2S. But, as is clearly shown in Example 31 in *Chemical Principles*, this expression was arrived at by summing the equations for the two-step dissociation of the acid. In this procedure the HS^- ions, which actually are present in the equilibrium mixture, cancel out in the arithmetic. Although the overall equilibrium equation seems to indicate the ratio of H^+ to S^{2-} is 2 : 1, this is not true, because most of the sulfur is present as HS^- ions. The equilibrium concentration of S^{2-} ions is much less than half the H^+ ion concentration.

Our final problem illustrates how aqueous ammonia can be used to separate mixtures of ions.

EXAMPLE. In a common procedure followed in the qualitative analysis of minerals, a solution that may contain Cr^{3+} and Mg^{2+} ions is treated with a solution of ammonia buffered with NH_4NO_3. We see from Table 5–8 that both $Mg(OH)_2$ ($K_{sp} = 8.9 \times 10^{-12}$) and $Cr(OH)_3$ ($K_{sp} = 6.7 \times 10^{-31}$) are very slightly soluble compounds. Will both hydroxides precipitate from a solution that is $0.010M$ in both Mg^{2+} and Cr^{3+} ions and $0.10M$ in ammonia and $0.20M$ NH_4NO_3?

SOLUTION. To answer this we first must determine the concentration of OH^- ions required to precipitate the hydroxides of Mg^{2+} and Cr^{3+} from a solution. We can do this by substituting the values for the metal-ion concentrations into the respective K_{sp}'s. We then calculate the OH^- ion concentration in the buffered ammonia and compare this with that required for precipitation.

For $Mg(OH)_2(s) \rightleftarrows Mg^{2+} + 2OH^-$,

$$K_{sp} = [Mg^{2+}][OH^-]^2 = 8.9 \times 10^{-12}$$

Will It React?
An Introduction
to Chemical
Equilibrium

222

The minimum concentration of OH^- ions that can be present with $0.010M$ Mg^{2+} without precipitation of $Mg(OH)_2$ is

$$[Mg^{2+}][OH^-]^2 = (0.010)[OH^-]^2 = 8.9 \times 10^{-12}$$

$$[OH^-]^2 = \frac{8.9 \times 10^{-12}}{0.010} = 8.9 \times 10^{-10}$$

$$[OH^-] = 3.0 \times 10^{-5} \text{ mole per liter}$$

For $Cr(OH)_3(s) \rightleftarrows Cr^{3+} + 3OH^-$,

$$K_{sp} = [Cr^{3+}][OH^-]^3 = 6.7 \times 10^{-31}$$

The minimum concentration of OH^- ions that may be present with $0.010M$ Cr^{3+} ions without precipitation of $Cr(OH)_3$ is

$$[Cr^{3+}][OH^-]^3 = (0.010)[OH^-]^3 = 6.7 \times 10^{-31}$$

$$[OH^-]^3 = \frac{6.7 \times 10^{-31}}{0.010} = 6.7 \times 10^{-29}$$

$$= 67 \times 10^{-30}$$

$$[OH^-] = 4.1 \times 10^{-10} \text{ mole per liter}$$

The calculation of the $[OH^-]$ in a solution of $0.10M$ $NH_3(aq)$ and $0.20M$ NH_4NO_3 is similar to those described in Section 5–8 on buffers:

$$NH_3 + H_2O \rightleftarrows NH_4^+ + OH^-$$

$$[OH^-] = K_b \times \frac{[NH_3]}{[NH_4^+]} = 1.79 \times 10^{-5} \times \frac{[NH_3]}{[NH_4^+]}$$

Let $x = [OH^-]$ at equilibrium and neglect the OH^- ions present from the dissociation of H_2O; then

	Initial	At equilibrium
$[NH_4^+] =$	0.20	$0.20 + x$
$[OH^-] =$	0.00	x
$[NH_3] =$	0.10	$0.10 - x$

Substitution of the equilibrium values into the equation for $[OH^-]$, neglecting x compared to 0.10, gives

$$[OH^-] = x = 1.79 \times 10^{-5} \times \frac{(0.10 - x)}{(0.20 + x)}$$

$$= 1.79 \times 10^{-5} \times \frac{0.10}{0.20}$$

$$[OH^-] = 9.0 \times 10^{-6} \text{ mole liter}^{-1}$$

Since the OH^- ion concentration in the buffer solution (9.0 $\times$ $10^{-6}M$) is less than that needed to precipitate $Mg(OH)_2$ (3.0 $\times$ $10^{-5}M$) but more than that needed to precipitate $Cr(OH)_3$ (4.1 $\times$ $10^{-10}M$), only $Cr(OH)_3$ will precipitate from the solution.

To tell how efficient the separation is, we calculate the concentration of Cr^{3+} ions that can remain in equilibrium with the OH^- ions we have in the buffered solution:

$$[Cr^{3+}][OH^-]^3 = K_{sp} = 6.7 \times 10^{-31}$$

$$[Cr^{3+}](9.0 \times 10^{-6})^3 = 6.7 \times 10^{-31}$$

$$[Cr^{3+}] = \frac{6.7 \times 10^{-31}}{(9.0 \times 10^{-6})^3} = \frac{6.7 \times 10^{-31}}{7.30 \times 10^{-16}}$$

$$= 9.2 \times 10^{-16} \text{ mole liter}^{-1}$$

Only 9.2×10^{-16} mole per liter of Cr^{3+} can remain in this buffered solution. This means that of the original 0.010 mole per liter of Cr^{3+} ions present,

$$\frac{9.2 \times 10^{-16}}{0.010} \times 100 = 9.2 \times 10^{-12}\%$$

remain unprecipitated. This is certainly a negligible amount, so we say the separation is effectively 100% complete, and all the Cr^{3+} ions have been removed from the solution.

Example 30 in *Chemical Principles* is a variation of the preceding problem using H_2S as the separating reagent by adjusting the S^{2-} ion concentration by establishing the proper pH. Go over both these calculations carefully to be sure you firmly grasp the principle involved before you attempt the self-test for this chapter.

CHAPTER 6 CLASSIFICATION OF THE ELEMENTS AND PERIODIC PROPERTIES

When understood and used correctly, the periodic table is invaluable as a source of information. It provides a means of classifying, in an ordered way, much of the chemical behavior of the elements and their compounds encountered in textbooks or observed in the laboratory. In this regard, the table can serve as a study aid.

A periodic chart has been provided in the inside front cover of this study guide. When you read about a property of a substance, such as its valence, bond type, oxidation number, reactivity, or acidity, see if you can correlate this property with the periodic table. You will find that such information is recalled more readily as a part of a systematic trend followed by many substances than as an isolated fact. In this way, you can avoid much tedious memorization. Furthermore, the periodic table can help you to predict the chemical properties of an unfamiliar element or the products of a new reaction.

Chemical Principles discusses the historical development of classification schemes that culminated in our present form of the periodic table. Trends in atomic size, ionization energy, electron affinity, oxidation potentials, and a few chemical properties are covered. You will learn of other periodic properties as you continue your studies.

As you look closely at the periodic table, you will see that there are exceptions to the general trends in periodicity. The relative number of these exceptions is small, so the effectiveness of the table as a basis for predictions is not too impaired. Frequently, behavior that appears to be contrary to the trend has a logical explanation. In most instances, this explanation can be related to the position of the element in the table. Thus, what might otherwise be an unexpected characteristic can be understood later as expected behavior.

A complete understanding of the arrangement of the elements in the table must await information related to their electronic structures. This will be discussed in Chapter 9 of *Chemical Principles*.

6-1 EARLY CLASSIFICATION SCHEMES

The elements can be divided into three general categories: metals, nonmetals, and semimetals. The criteria used to define these categories are based both on physical appearance and chemical behavior.

METALS

Metals have a bright "metallic" luster. They are malleable and ductile and generally are conductors of heat and electric current. Many metals form positive ions. All metals show positive oxidation states in compounds and form positive ions in aqueous solution. The oxides of metals in which the oxidation number of the metal is $+1$, $+2$, or $+3$ are basic oxides.

NONMETALS

Nonmetals do not display a metallic luster and are not malleable or ductile. There is no single physical characteristic typical of all nonmetals. Some exist as gases, and some are powdery solids at room temperature. For example, carbon, a nonmetal, is either a hard, colorless crystal (diamond), a soft, slippery, black solid (graphite), or an amorphous black powder (lamp black). Bromine, another nonmetal, is a liquid at room temperature. Nitrogen, oxygen, chlorine, and fluorine are gases.

In all binary compounds of a metal and a nonmetal, the nonmetal is either a negative ion or it possesses a negative oxidation number. Nonmetal oxides are acidic oxides regardless of the oxidation number of the nonmetal. This property indicates a decided difference from the metals. For more information on acidic and basic oxides, see Section 6–5.

SEMIMETALS

The transition between metals and nonmetals is not an abrupt one. There are some elements that exhibit properties characteristic of both metals and nonmetals; these are the semimetals. The oxides of the

Classification
of the Elements
and Periodic
Properties

226

semimetals display both acidic and basic properties and are referred to as amphoteric oxides.

Of historical interest are the early attempts of Döbereiner and Newlands to classify the elements. Our present form of the periodic table is more directly related to the works of Mendelyeev, Meyer, and Moseley.

6-2 THE BASIS FOR PERIODIC CLASSIFICATION

Both Lothar Meyer and Dmitri Mendeleev developed similar periodic tables. Meyer based his table on the similarities in physical properties of the elements. Mendeleev used the similarities in chemical properties as the basis for locating the elements in his table. Both arranged the elements in order of increasing atomic weights. Mendeleev had complete confidence in his table. He predicted new elements, described their properties, and found errors in several atomic weights. He was so successful in this regard that history has given him credit as the father of the periodic table.

Moseley demonstrated that the basic difference in the elements is the atomic number. The atomic number is equal to the number of protons in the nucleus and to the number of electrons outside the nucleus of an atom. The modern periodic law was proposed by Moseley: The properties of elements are periodic functions of their atomic numbers. A revision of Mendeleev's periodic table placed the atoms in order of increasing atomic number instead of atomic weight. This removed the last major discrepancies in the table.

6-3 THE MODERN PERIODIC TABLE

Since the first work of Mendeleev, many versions of tables and schemes for classifying the elements have been proposed. We are concerned with only one version, the standard long form. This table is printed on the inside front cover. As described in Section 9–1 of *Chemical Principles*, this arrangement of elements is based on the electronic structure of atoms.

A chemical reaction is fundamentally the result of interactions between electrons in atoms. The physical properties of an element are a function of the bonding forces that exist between atoms in the solid, liquid, or gaseous state. These forces are closely dependent on the arrangement of the electrons in the component atoms. Hence, it is easy to understand that a table in which the atoms are arranged according to their electronic structures also should reflect similarities in their chemical and physical properties. (As you might suspect, there is some overlap between what is considered a chemical property and what is considered a physical property.)

In Chapters 8 and 9 of *Chemical Principles*, you will study the electronic structures of atoms. However, at this point we need only regard electrons as revolving in shells or orbits around the nucleus. Further, we can assume that electrons in the outermost or *valence* shell are the only ones involved in a chemical reaction.

In the periodic table, elements are arranged in rows, or periods, in order of increasing atomic number from left to right. There are seven of these periods. The first period contains only two elements, H and He. The second and third periods, called short periods, contain eight elements each. The fourth and fifth periods contain 18 elements. Finally, the sixth period has 32 elements and the seventh has the remaining 19. (The most recently discovered elements, atomic numbers 104 and 105, have not been named.)

To keep the proportions of the table such that it can be conveniently accommodated on a single page, 14 elements $_{57}$La to $_{70}$Yb (or $_{58}$Ce to $_{71}$Lu) are removed from the sixth period and are listed separately below the table. This row of 14 elements is referred to as the *lanthanide* or *rare earth* series of elements. Because their electronic structures are similar to the lanthanides, the 14 elements $_{89}$Ac to $_{102}$No (or $_{90}$Th to $_{103}$Lr), the *actinide* elements, are placed below the lanthanides. Both of these series also are referred to as the *inner transition elements*.

Excluding the lanthanides and actinides, there are 18 vertical columns or *groups* of elements. Eight of these groups are called long groups, or A groups. They are numbered from left to right, Group IA through Group VIIA. The eighth group, consisting of the elements He, Ne, Ar, Kr, Xe, and Rn, is referred to as the *noble gas* group. The elements in the A groups are called the *representative elements*. The remaining 10 groups of three elements each are referred to as the *transition metals*. The location of hydrogen is indefinite. It may be located at the top of either Group IA or Group VIIA, or at the top of both of these groups. It may even be shown in the center of the first period and not considered to be a member of any particular group of elements.

A diagonal stair-step line starting between $_4$Be and $_5$B is shown in many tables (see Figure 6–1). The elements on this line are typical semimetals. The line separates the metals on the left and the nonmetals on the right. The demarcation between metal, semimental, and nonmetal is not sharp. The elements become more nonmetallic in character from left to right along the periods.

REPRESENTATIVE ELEMENTS

In this chapter, we confine our discussion to the representative elements. The transition and inner transition elements are the subject of Section 9–4 and Chapter 11 in *Chemical Principles*. A few characteristic properties of each group of representative elements are listed in the following paragraphs.

Group IA. The alkali metals, Li, Na, K, Rb, Cs, and Fr, are soft, lustrous metals. They are extremely reactive. All the compounds of these elements are ionic and feature the metal atom as an ion with a single positive charge.

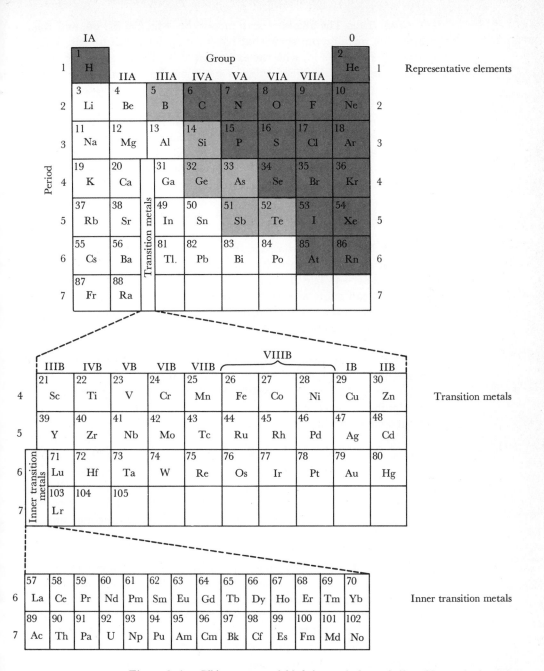

Figure 6–1. This compact, folded form of the periodic table emphasizes the natural division of elements into three categories: the extremely variable A-Group or representative elements, the more similar transition metals, and the quite similar inner transition metals. Of the representative elements, the elements on the left are metals, those on the right are nonmetals, and those elements along the dark stairlike line beginning between B *and* C *are the* semimetals *or* amphoteric elements.

Group IIA. The alkaline earth metals, Be, Mg, Ca, Sr, Ba, and Ra, are quite metallic but somewhat harder than the alkali metals. They are very reactive and, with the exception of Be, form many ionic compounds in which the metal exists as a $+2$ ion. Beryllium tends to form covalent compounds in which it has an *oxidation number* of $+2$.

Group IIIA. The boron group, B, Al, Ga, In, and Tl, shows both metallic and nonmetallic properties. The elements at the bottom of the group are the most metallic. (Note the proximity of the diagonal line denoting the semimetals.) Al_2O_3 is an amphoteric oxide. The common oxidation number for all the elements in the group is $+3$. Boron forms no ionic compounds, and AlF_3 is one of the few ionic compounds of Al. Ionic compounds are more common with Ga, In, and Tl.

Group IVA. The carbon group elements, C, Si, Ge, Sn, and Pb, manifest a combining capacity (valence) of four and a common oxidation state of $+4$. The elements C, Si, and Ge do not form ionic compounds. Lead exists as dipositive ions in compounds with some nonmetals, and it often has a $+2$ oxidation number. Silicon and germanium are typical semimetals.

Group VA. The nitrogen group, N, P, As, Sb, and Bi, varies from the nonmetals N and P at the top, to the metal Bi at the bottom. The elements As and Sb are semimetals. All elements in this group show a combining capacity of three, as indicated by the formulas for their hydrogen compounds: NH_3, PH_3, AsH_3, SbH_3, and BiH_3.

Group VIA. The chalcogen elements, O, S, Se, Te, and Po, are nonmetals, and Te and Po exhibit sufficient metallic character to be classed as semimetals. Oxygen has O^{2-} ions in many metal oxides. All of these elements have a combining capacity of two and oxidation numbers of -2. This is indicated by the formulas for their hydrogen compounds: H_2O, H_2S, H_2Se, H_2Te, and H_2Po.

Group VIIA. The halogen group, F, Cl, Br, I, and At, is comprised of nonmetals. With metals they form binary compounds in which the halogen has a -1 oxidation number. When they react with Group IA and IIA metals, they form ionic compounds in which the halogen atom is a negative ion. All the elements form extremely stable dimeric molecules at room temperature. The lighter members of the group, F_2 and Cl_2, are gases; Br_2 is a liquid, and I_2 and At_2 are solids.

Noble gases. The noble gases, He, Ne, Ar, Kr, Xe, and Rn, are inert. Only a few compounds are known, and these involve only the heavier members of the group in combination with active nonmetals such as fluorine and oxygen.

The chemical properties of the elements adjacent to one another in a period are quite different. The only exceptions to this statement are the 14 lanthanide elements and the 14 actinide elements. The adjacent members of these series have almost identical chemical properties. (What may be classed as a similarity between a few adjacent elements is that all elements with atomic numbers of 84 and larger are radioactive.)

6-4 TRENDS IN PHYSICAL PROPERTIES

Contrary to the order in which it is presented in *Chemical Principles*, we discuss the trends in atomic and ionic sizes first. Our reasoning is that trends in size can be predicted from first principles and that the trends in ionization energy and electron affinity can be related closely to differences in size.

THE SIZES OF ATOMS AND IONS

We determine the sizes of atoms and ions from diffraction measurements of crystals. X-ray diffraction is the principal technique for determining size. Electron and neutron diffraction measurements also are used. These measurements give the precise distances between the nuclei of the atoms. Furthermore, these measurements enable the determination of electron densities around various atoms in the crystal, and with this information we can identify different atoms.

In assigning a size to an atom, we consider it to be a sphere whose nucleus is at the center. Electrons occupy the region between the nucleus and the surface of the sphere. Three kinds of radii can be dis-

Figure 6–2. The relative radii of atoms and ions.

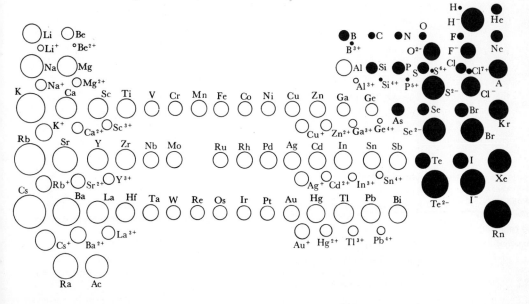

tinguished in these measurements: ionic, covalent, and van der Waals or nonbonding radii.

Ionic radii. Ionic radii are determined from measurements of the internuclear distances in ionic crystals. It is usually a simple matter to determine the cation-to-anion distances from such measurements because the cation and anion are in contact. The cation-to-anion distance will be equal to the sum of the cation radius and the anion radius. We will not go into detail about how to divide the cation-to-anion distance into a contribution from the cation and a contribution from the anion. We merely state that, from the interionic distances observed in several ionic compounds, it has been possible to assign ionic radii to each cation and anion. These are listed in Table 6–1. They are reasonably self-consistent. For example, the sum of the ionic radii (r) in Table 6–1 agrees closely with the interionic distances measured in

Table 6–1. Van der Waals, Ionic, and Covalent Radii for some Representative Elements

	H			He	Li	Be
van der Waals	1.2 Å			0.93	—	—
Ionic	2.08			(0.93)[a]	0.60	0.31
Covalent	0.37			—	1.35	0.90
	N	O	F	Ne	Na	Mg
van der Waals	1.5	1.4	1.25	1.12	—	—
Ionic	1.71	1.40	1.36	(1.12)	0.95	0.65
Covalent	0.70	0.66	0.64	—	1.54	1.30
	P	S	Cl	Ar	K	Ca
van der Waals	1.9	1.85	1.80	1.54	—	—
Ionic	2.12	1.84	1.81	(1.54)	1.33	0.99
Covalent	1.10	1.04	0.99	—	1.96	1.74
	As	Se	Br	Kr	Rb	Sr
van der Waals	2.0	2.00	1.95	1.69	—	—
Ionic	2.22	1.98	1.95	(1.69)	1.48	1.13
Covalent	1.21	1.17	1.14	—	2.11	1.92
	Sb	Te	I	Xe	Cs	Ba
van der Waals	2.2	2.20	2.15	1.90	—	—
Ionic	2.45	2.21	2.16	(1.90)	1.69	1.35
Covalent	1.41	1.37	1.33	—	2.25	1.98
Charge on the ion for ionic radii (H is +1)	−3	−2	−1	0	+1	+2

[a] Values in parentheses are repetitions of the van der Waals radii.

compounds. As an example, observe from the table that the ionic radii for Na^+ and Cl^- are $r_{Na^+} = 0.95$ Å and $r_{Cl^-} = 1.81$ Å. Also, $r_{Na^+} + r_{Cl^-} = 0.95 + 1.81 = 2.76$ Å. The Na^+-to-Cl^- distance measured in NaCl is 2.81 Å. Consider LiCl as a second example. The radius of the Li^+ ion is 0.60 Å. We calculate the Li^+-to-Cl^- distance as $r_{Li^+} + r_{Cl^-} = 0.60 + 1.81 = 2.41$ Å. The measured Li^+-to-Cl^- distance in LiCl is 2.41 Å.

Covalent radii and van der Waals radii. As we shall see, covalent bonds are formed by the sharing of pairs of electrons between two atoms. To share electrons, atoms must approach more closely than is necessary merely to touch each other. The more electron pairs shared between two atoms, the closer together the atoms must be.

Consider a solid of some homonuclear diatomic molecule such as Cl_2. The Cl_2 molecules are packed closely together in the solid so they are in contact. The two Cl atoms in each Cl_2 molecule are sharing electrons in a covalent bond. These bonded Cl atoms must come closer together to permit this. X-ray diffraction measurements on solid crystalline Cl_2 will give two short Cl-to-Cl distances. The shorter of the two corresponds to the distance between the nuclei of the two covalently bonded atoms. One half of this distance is called the covalent radius of chlorine. The other Cl-to-Cl distance is between the nuclei of two chlorine atoms on different Cl_2 molecules. Since these Cl atoms are assumed to be in contact in the crystal, one half of this distance is the radius of a nonbonded chlorine atom, or the van der Waals radius for chlorine. These van der Waals radii are taken as the atomic radii for nonmetals. Table 6–1 lists van der Waals and covalent radii for several atoms.

Atomic radii for metals are obtained by taking one half of the internuclear distance in metal crystals, as measured by x-ray diffraction. Although the metal crystal consists of a close packing of metal ions and not neutral atoms, this distance corresponds well with values estimated from the measured covalent radii in gaseous metal dimers.

The trend in atomic radii is shown in Figure 6–2. As you can see, the atomic radii decrease from left to right across a period; they increase from top to bottom in a group. This trend is explained by the fact that, when proceeding from left to right across a period, the number of protons in the nucleus and the number of electrons outside the nucleus increases. The protons and electrons have opposite charges and exert a force of attraction for each other that is equal to $(Ze_+)(Z'e_-)/r^2$, in which Z is the number of protons, Z' is the number of electrons, e_+ and e_- are the charge on a single proton and a single electron, respectively, and r is the distance separating the charges. This force of attraction pulls the electrons toward the nucleus and determines the radius of the atom. In proceeding from left to right across a period, the total number of positive charges in the nucleus and the total number of negative charges outside increase progressively. A change in atomic number of one unit corresponds to the addition of one proton and one electron.

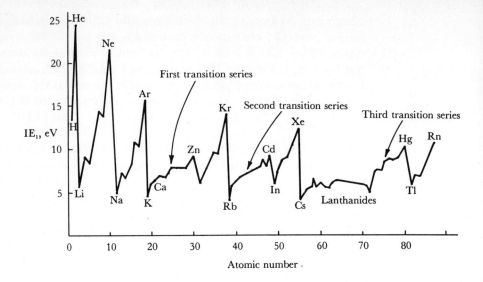

Figure 6-3. Variation of atomic ionization energy with atomic number. The energy scale is in electron volts. Note that maximum ionization energies in a given period occur with the noble gas elements and that the ionization energies of the transition elements all are similar.

As a result, the average force of attraction for each electron increases steadily; the electrons are drawn toward the nucleus, and the atomic radius decreases. A simple, approximate calculation will illustrate this phenomenon.

Consider the carbon atom. There are six protons in the nucleus and six electrons outside. Two of these electrons lie in a shell close to the nucleus; the other four electrons lie outside, in the valence shell. It is these valence electrons that determine the atom's radius. The two inner electrons will effectively cancel or shield the effect of two of the six protons in the nucleus on the valence electrons. Therefore, the four valence electrons will be under the influence of about $6 - 2 = 4$ of the protons in the nucleus. The total force of attraction will be

$$(4e_+)(4e_-)/r^2 = 16(e_+)(e_-)/r^2$$

The force of attraction per valence electron in carbon is

$$\tfrac{1}{4}(16e_+e_-/r^2) = 4e_+e_-/r^2$$

To form nitrogen (the element to the right of carbon in the second period) an additional proton must be added to the carbon nucleus and an additional electron must be added to the valence shell. The average force of attraction per valence electron in nitrogen will be

$$\tfrac{1}{5}(5e_+)(5e_-)/r^2 = \frac{25e_+e_-}{5r^2} = 5e_+e_-/r^2$$

Each nitrogen electron will be attracted toward the nucleus more than each carbon electron, so the atomic radius of nitrogen will be less than that of carbon.

Although the atomic radii decrease across a period of transition and inner transition elements, the relative decrease is not nearly so large as in a period consisting of representative elements. The reason for this is that the electrons are added to shells inside the valence shell in these atoms. We shall read more about this in Chapter 9 of *Chemical Principles*.

The reason why atomic radii increase from top to bottom in a group is that all atoms in a given group have the same number of electrons in their valence shell. (For the representative elements, this number corresponds to their Group A number. The alkali metals have one valence shell electron, the alkaline earths have two, the boron group elements have three, etc.) From top to bottom in a group, the distance of the valence shell from the nucleus increases. For example, the electron in the valence shell of sodium is much farther from the nucleus than is the electron in the valence shell of the element above it, Li. Because they are farther from the nucleus, the valence shell electrons are the most important in establishing the atomic radii. Consequently, since the distance from the nucleus to the valence shell increases downward in a group, the atomic radii increase from top to bottom.

When an atom forms a positive ion, one or more electrons are lost while the positive nuclear charge remains unchanged. This process increases the average force of attraction on each electron. The electrons are drawn closer to the nucleus, and the radius of the ion decreases. When an atom forms a negative ion, electrons are added to the atom while the positive nuclear charge remains constant. This situation decreases the average force of attraction on each electron. The mutual repulsion of the electrons carries them away from the nucleus, and the radius of the ion increases.

We find that the radius of a positive ion is always smaller than the neutral atom. Conversely, the radius of a negative ion is always larger than that of the neutral atom. Among the positive ions, the trends in size parallel those of their parent atoms. See Figure 6–2.

FIRST IONIZATION ENERGY

The first ionization energy is the energy required to remove one electron from a neutral gaseous atom and to produce a gaseous $+1$ cation:

$$M(g) \rightarrow M^+(g) + 1e^- \qquad \Delta H = \text{the ionization energy (IE)}$$

Since the removal of an electron is an endothermic process (energy is required), the ionization energy is a positive quantity.

The electron is bound to the atom by the positive attraction exerted by the nucleus. The farther the electron is from the nucleus, the less energy will be required to remove it. Therefore, we predict that trends in ionization energy should be opposite to those observed for the atomic radii: The larger the atomic radius, the smaller the ionization energy;

the smaller the atomic radius, the larger the ionization energy. That this is the general trend can be seen in Figure 6–3. The figure shows that the ionization energy decreases from top to bottom in a group and increases from left to right across a period.

Among the representative elements, there is a decrease in ionization energy across a period from a Group IIA to a Group IIIA element, and again from a Group VA to a Group VIA element. This is explained in Section 9–1 in *Chemical Principles*.

The first ionization energies of the noble gases are exceptionally large, which corresponds to their inertness. We can conclude that an arrangement of electrons like that of a noble gas is an exceedingly stable one.

SECOND AND HIGHER IONIZATION ENERGIES

The energy required to remove a second electron from a gaseous $+1$ ion to produce a gaseous $+2$ ion always will be much larger than the first ionization energy. The second electron must be taken from a positive ion, and additional energy must be supplied to overcome the whole unit of positive charge. To remove a third electron from a $+2$ ion to produce a $+3$ ion requires still more energy because the force of attraction of a full $+2$ charge must be overcome. The third ionization energy of an atom is indeed large.

Because of the large amount of energy required to produce positive ions, it may initially seem odd that there are any $+2$ or $+3$ ions at all. However, there are. All the Group IIA metals (except for beryllium) readily form $+2$ ionic salts. Although the number of ionic crystals containing tripositive ions is limited, the occurrence of $+1$, $+2$, and $+3$ ions in aqueous solution is quite common; in fact, a few ions with larger charges exist in solution.

The reason for this situation is that the ionization energy is not the only energy factor involved in the process of an atom's forming an ion in solution. We shall see in Chapter 15 of *Chemical Principles* that for a process to occur spontaneously, the change in Gibbs free energy, ΔG, must be negative. The Gibbs free energy takes into account any change in *enthalpy*, ΔH, that occurs during the reaction and also any energy associated with the order or disorder of the reaction system. This latter quantity is the change in *entropy*, ΔS. Recall that entropy was mentioned first in Section 2–6 of *Chemical Principles*, where it was stated that all real systems tend to proceed in the direction that leads to an increase in disorder or randomness. The relationship between these quantities is quite simple:

$$\Delta G = \Delta H - T\Delta S \qquad (6\text{–}1)$$

To repeat, any reaction will take place spontaneously if the free energy change, ΔG, is negative for the reaction. We can see from Equation 6–1 that there are three conditions leading to a negative ΔG.

(1) If ΔH is negative and the $T\Delta S$ term is positive, then ΔH (a negative quantity) minus $T\Delta S$ (a positive quantity) will give a negative value for ΔG. This corresponds to an exothermic reaction that leads to a more disordered state.

(2) If ΔH is negative and the $T\Delta S$ is negative but of small magnitude when subtracted from ΔH, then the ΔG value still may be negative. This corresponds to an exothermic reaction that leads to a more ordered state.

(3) If ΔH is positive but $T\Delta S$ is such a large positive value when it is subtracted from ΔH, the ΔG value is still negative. This corresponds to an endothermic reaction that proceeds to a highly disordered state. It describes a reaction at a very high temperature.

In many exothermic reactions, the entropy is increased and condition (1) pertains. In others, the change in entropy is so small that condition (2) is satisfied. Because of this, we often incorrectly infer that all exothermic processes will occur spontaneously.

The Gibbs free energy, like the enthalpy, is a state function. This means that, like ΔH values, ΔG values for a series of reactions can be added algebraically. The result will be a ΔG value for the process obtained by the same algebraic combination of equations for the series of reactions.

To return to the question, how can $+3$ and higher positively charged cations exist in aqueous solution if the second, third, and higher ionization energies are so large? The answer lies in the ΔG for the reaction

$$M(s) \rightarrow M^{n+}(aq) + ne^- \tag{6-2}$$

If ΔG for this reaction is negative, the reaction will proceed and the positive ions will form in the solution. Let us look at all the factors that might contribute to the ΔG for this reaction.

$$M(s) \rightarrow M(g) \qquad \Delta G_{sub} = \text{free energy of sublimation}$$

$$M(g) \rightarrow M^+(g) + 1e^- \qquad \text{IE}(1)$$
$$M^+(g) \rightarrow M^{2+}(g) + 1e^- \qquad \text{IE}(2)$$
$$M^{2+}(g) \rightarrow M^{3+}(g) + 1e^- \qquad \text{IE}(3)$$
$$\underline{M^{3+}(g) + xH_2O \rightarrow M^{3+}(aq)} \qquad \Delta G_{hyd} = \text{free energy of hydration}$$

$$M(s) + xH_2O \rightarrow M^{3+}(aq) + 3e^- \qquad \Delta G_{reax} = \Delta G_{sub} + \text{IE}(1) + \text{IE}(2) + \text{IE}(3) + \Delta G_{hyd}$$

In the preceding reactions, IE(1), IE(2), and IE(3) represent the first, second, and third ionization energies expressed as ΔG values for the process analogous to Equation 6–2.

The Gibbs free energy of sublimation, ΔG_{sub}, is generally positive It is an endothermic process that is spontaneous only at high temperatures. The ΔG equivalents of the first, second, and third ionization energies also are large positive values. The free energy change for the reaction is

$$\Delta G_{\text{reax}} = \Delta G_{\text{sub}} + \text{IE}(1) + \text{IE}(2) + \text{IE}(3) + \Delta G_{\text{hyd}}$$
$$= (\text{a high positive quantity}) + \Delta G_{\text{hyd}}$$

It is obvious that the last term, ΔG_{hyd}, the free energy of hydration, will be the determining factor if the metal is to form a positive ion with a $+3$ charge in solution. The free energy of hydration usually is negative. In water solutions containing highly charged ions it can have a very high negative value. Hence, even though the sublimation and ionization require large amounts of energy, the free energy change accompanying the hydration of the ion more than compensates for the requirement. The outcome is a negative ΔG for the formation of the ions in solution, and the reaction occurs spontaneously.

Hydration energies usually are large negative values because water is a polar molecule. The electron distribution in the molecule is such that there is a high concentration of electrons at one end and a relatively low accumulation of electrons at the other end. This situation gives rise to a charge distribution in the molecule; one end is more negatively charged than the other. When an object possesses two separated charges of opposite sign, it is a *dipole*. Because of the distribution of its electrons, the water molecule is a dipole.

The partial negatively charged end of the water molecule is attracted toward the positive ions in the solution. The larger and more concentrated the positive charge on the ion, the stronger will be this interaction. The water molecules will cluster around the metal ion with the negative end of the dipole directed toward the metal ion. The result is the formation of a hydrated ion, a new chemical species. The parenthetical term (aq) in equations indicates the formation of such hydrated ions. Strong covalent bonds occasionally are formed between the metal ion and the water molecules, and the salt that crystallizes from such solutions will contain the hydrated ion.

In the example in Section 6–4 of *Chemical Principles*, we see that, although the ΔG values for the sublimation and ionization of calcium are large and positive ($38 + 141 + 274 = 453$ kcal mole^{-1}), ΔG for the hydration of the Ca^{2+} ion and the reduction of H^+ ion to $H_2(g)$ in aqueous solution $[(-358 + (-230) = -588$ kcal mole$^{-1})]$ is sufficient to give a ΔG of -135 kcal mole^{-1} for the reaction

$$Ca(s) + 2H^+(aq) \rightarrow Ca^{2+}(aq) + H_2(g)$$

Therefore, metallic calcium will dissolve in a strong acid aqueous solution to form Ca^{2+} ions.

OXIDATION POTENTIALS

The oxidation potential is a quantity used to express the tendency for a metal or ion to be oxidized to a specified higher oxidation state in aqueous solution. It is related to the Gibbs free energy change per mole of electrons lost during the process, the free energy per equivalent, by the expression $\Delta G/n = -\mathcal{F}\mathcal{E}$, in which n = the number of moles of electrons lost per mole of substance oxidized, $\mathcal{F}$ is the faraday and $\mathcal{E}$ is the oxidation potential. From this expression, we can see that the more positive the value for the oxidation potential, the greater will be the tendency for the oxidation to occur.

We predict that as the ionization energy decreases, ΔG will become more negative and the oxidation potential will increase. Table 6–2

Table 6–2. Oxidation Potentials for the Production of Hydrated Cations from the Metal

Group IA	Group IIA
Li 3.02 V	Be 1.70 V
Na 2.14	Mg 2.34
K 2.92	Ca 2.87
Rb 2.99	Sr 2.89
Cs 3.02	Ba 2.90

lists the oxidation potentials for the alkali and alkaline earth metals. Note that, with one exception, the oxidation potentials increase from top to bottom in the groups. This follows the trend in increasing size and decreasing ionization energy.

The one exception is lithium, which has an exceptionally large oxidation potential. The reason is that the Li^+ ion is extremely small. Its single, positive charge is concentrated in a minute, almost pointlike, region of space. Therefore, this concentrated positive charge exerts an unusually strong attraction for water molecules. There is a large negative Gibbs free energy change for the hydration of the cation, and this more than compensates for lithium's large ionization energy. We will have occasion to see more apparent anomalous behavior because of extremes in atomic or ionic radii.

In Section 6–4 of *Chemical Principles*, the ΔG for the reaction

$$Ca(s) + 2H^+(aq) \rightarrow Ca^{2+}(aq) + H_2(g)$$

is -135 kcal mole^{-1}, or 5.85 eV ion^{-1}. The oxidation potential for calcium is the same value, 5.85 eV ion^{-1} or 2.98 V equiv^{-1}, if we neglect the error compounded by the uncertainties in the values used to obtain ΔG for the reaction. You need not feel concerned about how this conclusion was reached. It will become clear after you have studied Chapter 17 in *Chemical Principles*. The brief explanation included here is to accommodate those of you who wish more explanation at this time.

The $\Delta G = -135$ kcal mole^{-1} is the result of the free energy changes accompanying two reactions.

(1) The oxidation of $Ca(s)$ to Ca^{2+} ions in aqueous solution

$$Ca(s) \rightarrow Ca^{2+}(aq) + 2e^-$$

ΔG for this reaction, in electron volts, is the oxidation potential, $\mathcal{E}_{ox}$.

(2) The reduction of $H^+(aq)$ to $H_2(g)$

$$H^+(aq) + 2e^- \rightarrow H_2(g)$$

ΔG for this reaction measures the tendency for the $H^+(aq)$ ion to be reduced; let us call this the reduction potential, $\mathcal{E}_{red}$. The ΔG for the overall reaction is the sum of the ΔG values for the two half-reactions

$$\Delta G \text{ in eV} = \mathcal{E}_{ox} + \mathcal{E}_{red} = 5.85 \text{ eV ion}^{-1} \tag{6-3}$$

Since it is impossible to measure either $\mathcal{E}_{ox}$ or $\mathcal{E}_{red}$ separately, an arbitrary standard has been set by which comparisons are made. The situation is analogous to assigning enthalpies of zero to elements in their standard states to obtain enthalpies of formation from ΔH_{reax} measurements. The standard for oxidation potential comparisons is that $\mathcal{E}_{ox}$ for the oxidation of $H_2(g)$ at 1 atm to $1M$ $H^+(aq)$ at 25°C is assigned the oxidation potential of 0.000 V. Moreover, $\mathcal{E}_{red} = 0$ for the reduction of $1M$ $H^+(aq)$ to $H_2(g)$ at 1 atm and 25°C because the reduction reaction is the reverse of the oxidation reaction. Therefore, substitution of $\mathcal{E}_{red} = 0.000$ eV into Equation 6–3 gives $\mathcal{E}_{ox}$ for $Ca(s)$ to $Ca^{2+}(aq) = 5.85$ eV $- 0.00 = 5.85$ eV ion^{-1}, or 2.92 eV equiv^{-1}.

ELECTRON AFFINITIES

The electron affinity is the energy released when an electron adds to a gaseous atom to form the gaseous negative ion:

$$X(g) + 1e^- \rightarrow X^-(g)$$

We predict that trends in electron affinities will directly parallel the trends in atomic radii: The electron affinities for the elements will increase from left to right across periods and decrease from top to bottom in groups. The reasoning is as follows: The electron will add to the valence shell of the atom. The positive charge on the nucleus will help to attract the electron and to assist in holding it in the valence shell. The closer the valence shell is to the nucleus, the easier it will be for an electron to add to the atom, and the larger will be that atom's electron affinity.

Unfortunately, the experiment necessary to measure the electron affinity is extremely complex and difficult to execute. As a result, precise electron affinities are known for only a few elements. Therefore, it is difficult to make reliable generalizations about trends in electron affinities.

The electron affinities of some of the regular elements as they are arranged in the periodic table are given in Table 6–3; they also are presented in Figure 6–8 of *Chemical Principles*.

From Table 6–3, we can conclude the following.

(1) The predicted trend of increasing electron affinity with increase in size is generally true except for the top member of each group of nonmetals. Thus, the electron affinity of fluorine, the halogen with the smallest radius, is less than that of chlorine. After chlorine, the elec-

Table 6–3.   Electron Affinities of Some Gaseous Atoms in kcal mole⁻¹

| | | | H = 17.3 | | | | Noble |
IA	IIA	IIIA	IVA	VA	VIA	VIIA	Gases
Li	Be	B	C	N	O	F	
12.4	−13.8	4.6	28.8	−2.3	33.8	79.5	
Na	Mg	Al	Si	P	S	Cl	
17.0	−6.9	13.8	37.5	16.1	47.6	86.5	
		Ga	Ge	As	Se	Br	
		4.14	27.6	13.8	39.1	77.3	
		In			Te	I	
		4.6			50.6	70.4	

tron affinities decrease from top to bottom within the group. The reason for the apparent anomalous behavior of the top member of each group of nonmetals is not understood completely. It is attributed to the unavailability of low energy d orbitals in the second-period elements. (Orbitals are discussed in Section 9–1 of *Chemical Principles*.)

(2) The noble gases and Group IIA elements have no tendency to add electrons.

(3) The electron affinities of the halogens are high compared to the other elements.

6–5 TRENDS IN CHEMICAL PROPERTIES

The noble gas atoms are noticeably inert; hence we can make two assumptions that can account for many chemical properties: (1) The electronic configurations of the noble gases are most stable; (2) a preferred configuration for any atom is one similar to that of noble gas. (Two atoms or ions that have the same number of electrons are *isoelectronic*.)

To become isoelectronic with $_2$He, the atoms of $_3$Li, $_4$Be, and $_5$B must lose one, two, and three electrons, respectively. The atom $_6$C has four electrons and may become isoelectronic with $_2$He by losing four electrons and isoelectronic with $_{10}$Ne by gaining four electrons. To become isoelectronic with $_2$He, $_7$N can lose five electrons, or it can become isoelectronic with $_{10}$Ne by gaining three electrons. The energy required to gain three electrons is less than that required to lose five electrons, so the former process is favored. The most direct way for $_8$O and $_9$F to become isoelectronic with a noble gas is to add two and one electrons and achieve the electronic structure of $_{10}$Ne. Note that to become isoelectronic with a noble gas, an element must either lose n electrons or gain $(8 - n)$ electrons, where n is the element's A-group number.

When an atom with a small ionization energy reacts with an atom having a large electron affinity, electrons will be transferred. The atoms at the left of the periods have the largest sizes and the smallest ionization energies; these are the metals. The atoms having large electron affinities are on the right end of the periods; these are the nonmetals. When a metal and a nonmetal react, the metal will lose electrons to the nonmetal. The number of electrons that the metal loses will be the number necessary to become isoelectronic with the noble gas that precedes it in the periodic table. Similarly, the nonmetal will gain enough electrons to become isoelectronic with the noble gas that follows it. Thus, the metals in Group IA readily lose one electron to form cations bearing a single positive charge. The Group IIA elements (except for Be) easily lose two electrons to form dipositive cations. The halogens (Group VIIA) readily gain one electron and form anions with a single negative charge. Group VIA elements tend to gain two electrons to form anions of charge -2.

The energies required to lose and accept more than two electrons are quite large; so such things as hydration energies and the energies involved in arranging ions in a crystal lattice (the crystal lattice energy) become the factors that determine whether electrons are lost or gained and ions produced. The ionization energies of the metals in Groups IA and IIA (except for Be) are small enough, and the electron affinities of the nonmetals in Group VIIA, and O and S in Group VIA, are large enough that when these elements combine with one another they form ionic compounds. If a metal having a small ionization energy (Group IA elements and the larger Group IIA elements, for example) reacts with nitrogen, N^{3-} ions are formed. When these metals react with hydrogen, H^- ions form.

TYPES OF BONDS

As was discussed in Chapter 3 of *Chemical Principles*, the positive and negative ions in ionic compounds are held together by the electrostatic attraction caused by their opposite charges. This bonding force is called an *ionic bond*.

If the ionization energy of the metal is not small enough or the electron affinity of the nonmetal large enough to permit electron transfer, a covalent bond can form. In this type of bond, atoms achieve an electronic environment that is isoelectronic with the noble gases by sharing one or more pairs of electrons. Thus, two chlorine atoms, each with seven electrons, each can contribute one electron to a pair of electrons shared by both atoms. For example, each chlorine atom has 17 electrons. They contribute one electron each to the electron pair. This leaves each chlorine atom with 16 electrons plus the shared pair. Since this pair is shared between the two atoms, it can be counted as belonging to each atom. To be isoelectronic with argon, the nearest noble gas, each chlorine atom needs 18 electrons. The 16 electrons on one Cl plus the shared pair gives $16 + 2 = 18$ electrons, the necessary number. Similarly, the two electrons in the shared electron pair can be counted with the other Cl atom, so it, too, has 18 electrons and is isoelectronic with argon.

More than one electron pair can be shared in forming covalent bonds. Oxygen, with eight electrons, can become isoelectronic with $_{10}Ne$ by sharing two electrons with a second oxygen atom. Each oxygen contributes two electrons to be shared as two electron pairs. This leaves each oxygen atom with $8 - 2 = 6$ electrons plus the electrons in the two shared pairs, or $6 + 2$(2 electrons in each shared pair) $= 10$ electrons. Sharing of two electron pairs is called a *double covalent bond*. The sharing of three electron pairs, as is done by nitrogen in N_2, is called a *triple bond*.

The nonmetals exhibit a tendency for sharing electrons with other nonmetals. The number of shared electrons can be as many as $8 - n$, where n is the atom's group number. Elements in Group IVA share four electrons $(8 - 4)$, those in Group VA share three electrons $(8 - 5)$, and so forth.

Carbon shares electrons with itself more than any other element does. The diamond crystal is a 3-dimensional network of carbon atoms, all sharing four electrons in single covalent bonds with neighboring carbon atoms. The high melting point and hardness of diamond are due to the large amounts of energy needed to fracture these strong covalent bonds. In graphite, an allotropic form of carbon, three electrons on each carbon atom are shared with electrons in adjacent carbon atoms to form three strong covalent bonds. The result is a sheet or plane of covalently bonded carbon atoms. The unused electrons on the carbons are positioned above and below the sheets and are spread out, or delocalized, to give each carbon a partial double bond that holds the sheets together. This partial double bond is broken easily to permit the planes of carbon atoms to slide over one another; thus, graphite can be used as a lubricant.

The strong electrostatic forces that hold ions together in ionic crystals account for the high melting points and high heats of fusion characteristic of ionic compounds. In contrast, simple molecules, such as N_2, O_2, Cl_2, I_2, and so forth, have relatively low melting points. Although strong covalent bonds hold atoms together in individual molecules, there are no strong forces to hold molecular units together in a crystalline solid. In these cases, the physical state of the substance is often more a function of the mass of the molecular unit. For example, F_2 and Cl_2 exist as gases at room temperature. Fluorine, which has the lowest mass, boils at $-188°C$, whereas chlorine boils at $-34°C$. Bromine is a liquid, and iodine is a solid.

Another feature of covalent bonds is that they are directional in nature. This is in contrast to ionic bonds whose attractive forces extend from each ion uniformly in all directions.

COMBINING RATIOS WITH HYDROGEN

An H atom needs only one electron to become isoelectronic with helium. Since it has a rather small electron affinity, it is only able to receive the single electron from atoms that have extremely small ionization energies. The Group IA and IIA elements satisfy this requirement and form ionic metal hydrides in which hydrogen exists as H^- ions. The group number indicates the number of electrons that a metal must donate to form hydride ions. Therefore, the ratio of metal atoms combined with hydride ions is 1/1 in the alkali metal hydrides (e.g., NaH, CsH, and LiH) and 2/1 in the alkaline earth metal hydrides (e.g., CaH_2, MgH_2, and BeH_2). All metal hydrides will react with water to librate hydrogen gas and hydroxide ions:

$$MH_n + nH_2O \rightarrow M^{n+} + nOH^- + nH_2(g)$$

in which M represents any metal capable of forming an ionic metal hydride.

Only covalent bonding is possible between hydrogen and the remaining elements in the periodic table. Each hydrogen contributes one electron to the shared pair in the covalent bond. Therefore, the number of hydrogens bonding to a nonmetal is equal to the number of shared electron pairs $(8 - n)$, where n is the group number. Thus, HCl, HI, H_2O, H_2Se, NH_3, PH_3, CH_4, and SiH_4 are typical hydrogen compounds.

The covalent hydrogen compounds of the elements in Group VIIA and at the top of Group VIA act as Brønsted acids in aqueous solution and donate protons to water to form hydronium ions:

$$HX + H_2O \rightarrow H_3O^+ + X^-$$

Ammonia acts as a Brønsted base in water:

$$NH_3 + H_2O \rightarrow NH_4^+ + OH^-$$

The phenomenon of the hydrogen bridge is displayed in compounds of hydrogen with Be, B, and Al. Thus, trivalent aluminum and hydrogen form the dimer Al_2H_6 in which there are two hydrogen bridges:

COMBINATIONS WITH OXYGEN: THE BINARY OXIDES

The representative elements form oxides in which oxygen has its normal combining capacity of two, and the combining capacity of the metal or nonmetal is the same as its group number. For the elements in the second period, the formulas of the oxides are Li_2O, BeO, B_2O_3, CO_2 N_2O_5, and O_3. The small size of fluorine prevents the approach of many oxygen atoms; the formula for its oxide is OF_2. For elements in the third period, the formulas are Na_2O, MgO, Al_2O_3, SiO_2, P_2O_5, SO_3, and Cl_2O_7.

The metal oxides in which the metal atom has an oxidation number of $+3$ or less form basic oxides. Basic oxides react with water to form basic solutions by the release of OH^- ions:

$$K_2O + H_2O \rightarrow 2K^+ + 2OH^-$$
$$CaO(s) + H_2O \rightarrow Ca^{2+} + 2OH^-$$

The nonmetal oxides are acidic oxides. Acidic oxides react with water to form acidic solutions by the release of H_3O^+ ions:

$$N_2O_5 + 3H_2O \rightarrow 2H_3O^+ + 2NO_3^-$$
$$CO_2 + 3H_2O \rightarrow 2H_3O^+ + CO_3^{2-}$$

Semimetal oxides, or amphoteric oxides, react with both acids and bases:

$$Al_2O_3(s) + 3H_3O^+ \rightarrow 2Al^{3+} + 6OH^-$$
$$Al_2O_3(s) + 2OH^- + 3H_2O \rightarrow 2Al(OH)_4^-$$

The concept of acidic and basic oxides can be used with advantage to explain and predict many reactions. It becomes more valuable when one is familiar with the use of oxidation numbers. We shall return to this in connection with the discussion of oxidation numbers in Section 7–1.

CHAPTER 7 OXIDATION, COORDINATION, AND COVALENCE

Chemical bonding and molecular structure lie at the heart of the study of chemistry. The authors of *Chemical Principles* have been introducing you to this subject, a bit at a time, since the first chapter. Many of these bits and pieces will fit together in a more unified picture in Chapter 10. By then you should be familiar with many of the principles that underlie the more successful concepts, or models, we have of the chemical bond. Two of these concepts that are related directly to bonding appear for the first time in this chapter: *coordination number* and *isomerism*. Covalent and ionic bonds have been described in Chapters 3 and 6; in Chapter 10, it is shown that both types of bonds can exist in the same compound. The distinction between valence and oxidation number is also emphasized in this chapter, and rules for assigning oxidation number also is emphasized in this chapter, and rules for assigning can be applied to identify oxidation and reduction reactions and to balance the equations.

In addition, we have included in this chapter of the study guide some examples of how the concept of acidic and basic oxides can be helpful in understanding and predicting certain chemical reactions.

Ionic bonding was discussed at length in Chapter 3 of *Chemical Principles;* covalent bonding, the sharing of electrons, was introduced in Section 6–5. These are the two principal types of chemical bonds.

We have described many ions consisting of single atoms. There are also many complex ions; these are charged groups of more than one atom that pass unchanged through many chemical reactions. The entire group of atoms carries either a positive or negative charge. The groups form ionic compounds in which the complex ion occupies a point in the crystal lattice surrounded by ions of opposite charge. The SO_4^{2-} ion is a complex ion. The compound sodium sulfate, Na_2SO_4, is an ionic compound. Molten Na_2SO_4 conducts an electric current, and the solid dissolves in water to give two Na^+ ions and one SO_4^{2-} ion per formula unit. The Na^+ and SO_4^{2-} ions occupy points in the crystal lattice.

Another example of a complex ion is the blue cation observed in solutions of copper salts. This ion is a complex cation that has the formula $[Cu(H_2O)_4]^{2+}$. The blue, ionic compound $[Cu(H_2O)_4]Cl_2$ is an electrolyte, and $[Cu(H_2O)_4]^{2+}$ cations and Cl^- anions are located at the points in the crystal lattice.

These are examples of compounds that have both ionic and covalent bonds. Covalent bonds hold the S and four O atoms together in the SO_4^{2-} ion, and ionic bonds hold the Na^+ ions and the SO_4^{2-} ions together in crystalline Na_2SO_4. Similarly, in crystalline $[Cu(H_2O)_4]Cl_2$, the H_2O molecules are bonded to the Cu^{2+} ions by covalent bonds and form the complex cation $[Cu(H_2O)_4]^{2+}$. These complex cations form ionic bonds with the Cl^- ions in the crystal. As these examples illustrate, covalent bonds can be formed between neutral atoms, neutral atoms and ions, and ions and neutral molecules.

You should become familiar with the following common complex ions and their charges:

SO_4^{2-}	sulfate ion	$C_2H_3O_2^-$ or $CH_3CO_2^-$	acetate ion
SO_3^{2-}	sulfite ion	CO_3^{2-}	carbonate ion
NO_3^-	nitrate ion	PO_4^{3-}	phosphate ion
NO_2^-	nitrite ion	$C_2O_4^{2-}$	oxalate ion
CN^-	cyanide ion	NH_4^+	ammonium ion

ISOMERISM

It is possible for the same atoms to bond together in different ways. When this occurs, isomers are formed. Isomers are compounds that have the same number and kind of atoms but different chemical and physical properties. For example, two compounds exist that have the molecular formula C_2H_6O. One of them is ethyl alcohol (a colorless liquid that has a boiling point of 78.5°C, is soluble in water, and reacts with metallic sodium to produce H_2 gas). The other compound is dimethyl ether (a colorless liquid with a boiling point of -23.65°C, is insoluble in water, and does not react with metallic sodium). All the

Types of
Chemical
Bonding

247

atoms in both compounds are covalently bonded. However, they differ in the relative arrangement of the atoms. The two carbon atoms are bonded together, and the oxygen is bonded to a hydrogen and one of the carbon atoms in ethyl alcohol. If we use lines to represent a shared pair of electrons in a covalent bond, the arrangement of the atoms in ethyl alcohol is

$$
\begin{array}{ccc}
& H & H \\
& | & | \\
H- & C- & C-O-H \\
& | & | \\
& H & H
\end{array}
$$

In dimethyl ether, the oxygen is bonded to both carbon atoms:

$$
\begin{array}{ccc}
H & & H \\
| & & | \\
H-C- & O- & C-H \\
| & & | \\
H & & H
\end{array}
$$

This type of isomerism is referred to as *structural isomerism*.

An interesting type of compound capable of showing a different kind of isomerism is $[Co(NH_3)_5SO_4]^+Br^-$. As the charge indicates, there is an ionic bond between the Br^- ion and the $[Co(NH_3)_5SO_4]^+$ cation. The bonds between all the atoms in the complex cation are covalent. We have pointed out that the SO_4 group is an ion that has a -2 charge; NH_3 is the neutral ammonia molecule. The single positive charge on the complex ion indicates that the cobalt in the complex ion must be a Co^{3+} ion. (The three positive charges from the Co^{3+} and the two negative charges from the SO_4^{2-} combine to give the net single positive charge observed on the $[Co(NH_3)_5SO_4]^+$ complex cation.) The two ions and five neutral molecules must be covalently bonded together in some way.

The compound $[Co(NH_3)_5Br]^{2+}SO_4^{2-}$ also exists. Here there is a Br^- ion and five NH_3 molecules covalently bonded to the Co^{3+} ion in the complex cation. The complex cation is bonded to the SO_4^{2-} ion by an ionic bond. There are the same number and kinds of atoms in both $[Co(NH_3)_5SO_4]Br$ and $[Co(NH_3)_5Br]SO_4$. They are isomers that differ only in the formula of the cation and anion they produce. These are called *ionization isomers*.

Many of the terms used in chemistry were introduced early by chemists in connection with a property or phenomenon that was not completely understood at the time. As more information was obtained, it has been necessary to modify the definition of some of these terms to make them more relevant with respect to the new knowledge. The terminology used in describing chemical bonding has been especially prone to change through the years. In Section 1–9 we discussed how the terms "combining capacity" and "valence" have been revised to their present meaning. Oxidation numbers were introduced in Section 3–2. You might find it helpful to reread this material at this time.

Chemical Principles follows the historical development of chemistry in

Oxidation,
Coordination,
and
Covalence

considerable detail. As a result, a term may be introduced as it was defined originally and then this definition is later revised or modified to correspond to its present meaning. It is the purpose of this study guide to emphasize those concepts and principles of chemistry that are necessary to understand the science and to be able to proceed further in more advanced studies. Knowledge of the historical development of a term is of secondary importance to the understanding of its use now. Therefore, unless circumstances dictate otherwise, our emphasis will be placed on the modern usage of a term or interpretation of a concept.

OXIDATION NUMBERS

Oxidation numbers are merely numbers that are derived by following certain rules for counting electrons associated with atoms in molecules. The oxidation number of an element is the charge that the element *would* have if its electrons were counted according to the rules given in Section 7–2. Oxidation numbers can be integers, zero, or fractions. Although oxidation numbers may be positive or negative, they do not necessarily represent real electrical charges.

COVALENCE

The term "valence" means combining capacity or the number of chemical bonds. As mentioned in Section 1–9, there are two types of bonds: covalent bonds and electrovalent or ionic bonds. The covalence of an element is the number of covalent bonds it forms. An element's electrovalence is the number of ionic bonds it forms.

ELECTROVALENCE

Electrovalence is expressed as the number of units of positive or negative charge possessed by an ion in an ionic compound. Ionic compounds are formed principally by the reaction of metals in Groups IA and IIA in the periodic table with the nonmetals in Groups VIA and VIIA. The electrovalence shown by metals is positive and corresponds to their group number. The nonmetals exhibit negative electrovalences equal to their group number minus 8. Thus, Cl, Br, and F (Group VIIA elements) have an electrovalence of $7 - 8 = -1$; O and S, Group VIA elements, have electrovalences of $6 - 8 = -2$. The electrovalences of sodium and chlorine in NaCl are Na $= +1$ and Cl $= -1$. In CaF_2, the electrovalence of calcium is $+2$, and the electrovalence of fluorine is -1.

The electrovalences of complex ions such as those listed in Section 7–1 are the same as the charges on the ion. Thus, the electrovalences of the Na^+ ions and CO_3^{2-} ions in the ionic compound Na_2CO_3 are $+1$ and -2, respectively.

All the elements except the metals in Groups IA and IIA form bonds that are principally covalent. However, the number of covalent bonds can vary. As mentioned in Section 1–9, the combining capacity of an element can be the same as one of the several covalent states shown by the element. The most common covalence shown by the nonmetals in Groups IVA and VIIA is $8 - n$, but covalences of n and $n - 2$ are also possible (n is the group number). Thus, carbon in Group IVA has a covalence of $8 - 4 = 4$ in its compounds.

$$
\begin{array}{cccc}
\text{H} & \text{H}\ \ \text{H} & & \\
| & |\ \ \ | & & \\
\text{H—C—H} & \text{H—C—C—H} & \text{H—C}{=}\text{C—H} & \text{H—C}{\equiv}\text{C—H} \\
| & |\ \ \ | & |\ \ \ | & \\
\text{H} & \text{H}\ \ \text{H} & \text{H}\ \ \text{H} & \\
\text{methane} & \text{ethane} & \text{ethylene} & \text{acetylene}
\end{array}
$$

In the preceding formulas, each line represents a shared electron pair and is counted as one covalent bond.

Sulfur in Group VIA shows a covalence of $8 - 6 = 2$ in the following compounds:

$$\text{H—S—H} \qquad\qquad \text{S}{=}\text{C}{=}\text{S}$$

hydrogen sulfide, H_2S carbon disulfide, CS_2

Sulfur has a covalence of 4 ($n - 2 = 6 - 2 = 4$) in H_2SO_3 and 6 ($n = 6$) in H_2SO_4. Note that the oxygen (also in Group VIA) has a covalence of 2 ($8 - n = 8 - 6 = 2$) in both of these compounds

$$
\begin{array}{cc}
 & \text{O} \\
 & \| \\
\text{H—O—S—O—H} & \text{H—O—S—O—H} \\
\| & \| \\
\text{O} & \text{O} \\
\text{sulfurous acid, } H_2SO_3 & \text{sulfuric acid, } H_2SO_4
\end{array}
$$

COORDINATION NUMBER

The term "coordination number" was used first in reference to a particular type of covalent bond called the coordinate covalent bond or donor–acceptor bond. This type of bond is discussed in Chapter 10 in *Chemical Principles*. It refers to a covalent bond in which both the electrons in the shared pair are provided by one atom, the donor atom. The covalent bonds between the ammonia molecules and the transition metal ions in complex ions such as $[Co(NH_3)_6]^{3+}$ are of this type. The NH_3 molecules provide both electrons in the electron pair that constitutes the covalent bond holding NH_3 to the metal ion. Similarly, certain anions, such as Cl^-, F^-, and NO_3^-, can donate a pair of electrons to form a coordinate covalent bond with a transition metal ion. For example, in the $[Co(NH_3)_5Cl]^{2+}$ ion, five NH_3 molecules and one Cl^- ion each donate an electron pair to form six coordinate covalent bonds with a Co^{3+} ion. We say that the NH_3 molecule and Cl^- ion are coordinated to the Co^{3+} ion. The nomenclature used to describe such compounds refers to the donor groups (the NH_3 molecules and Cl^- ions in the preceding example) as ligands, and the metal ion as the central atom or ion. The compounds formed by such complex ions are called coordination compounds.

The number of ligands coordinated to the central ion is referred to as the coordination number of the ion. Thus, the coordination number of the Co^{3+} ion in $[Co(NH_3)_5Cl]^{2+}$ complex cation is six (five NH_3 molecules plus one Cl^- ion are coordinated). The coordination number of the Pt^{2+} ion in $[Pt(NH_3)_4]^{2+}$ is four (four NH_3 molecules are coordinated to the Pt^{2+} ion).

We now use the term "coordination number" in a more general way to refer to the number of nearest neighbors to a given atom or ion. These nearest neighbors can be covalently bonded as the ligands are in a transition metal complex, or they can be the atoms or ions nearest to a particular atom or ion in a crystal. Thus, the six Cl^- ions that are equidistant and closest to a Na^+ ion in a crystal of NaCl give the Na^+ a coordination number of six. Since lines joining the six nearest-neighbor Cl^- ions outline an octahedron, the Cl^- ions are octahedrally arranged around the Na^+ ion.

Figure 7–1 shows the octahedral coordination of the six NH_3 molecules in $[Co(NH_3)_6]^{3+}$ ion. The figure also shows that the nitrogen atoms in this complex ion have a coordination number of four. Three H atoms and a Co^{3+} ion are the four nearest neighbors to a N atom; they are grouped in a tetrahedral arrangement around a N atom.

The compound $[Co(NH_3)_6]Cl_3$ has three types of bonds. There are six coordinate covalent (donor–acceptor) bonds between the nitrogen atoms and the Co^{3+} ion. The three hydrogen atoms in each NH_3 molecule are covalently bonded to the nitrogen atom, with each atom contributing one electron to the electron pair in each bond. The three Cl^- ions are bonded to the $[Co(NH_3)_6]^{3+}$ complex cation by ionic bonds. Freezing point measurements of aqueous solutions of this compound show that the limiting mole number, i, is four, which indicates that 1 mole of the compound dissociates to give 4 moles of ions

$$[Co(NH_3)_6Cl_3] \rightarrow [Co(NH_3)_6]^{3+} + 3Cl^-$$

7–2 OXIDATION NUMBERS

Two rules are followed in assigning oxidation numbers:

(1) The electrons in bonds between like atoms are distributed equally between the two atoms.
(2) The electrons in bonds between unlike atoms are counted as belonging to the more electronegative of the two atoms.

(Electronegativities are discussed in Section 9–2 of *Chemical Principles*. The electronegativities of elements increase from left to right across the

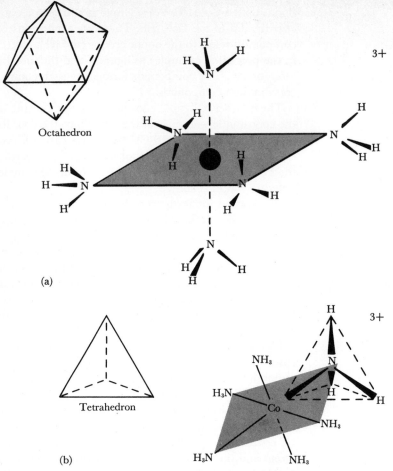

3+

3+

(a)

(b)

Figure 7–1. The structure of the complex ion, $Co(NH_3)_6^{3+}$. (a) The six NH$_3$ molecules form an octahedral complex around the Co^{3+} ion, with the groups at the six vertices of an octahedron. (b) Each nitrogen atom is tetrahedrally coordinated, with the Co^{3+} ion and the three H atoms at the four vertices of a tetrahedron.

periods and from the bottom to top in the groups in the periodic table. Hence, of two bonded atoms, the one that has the greater electronegativity lies above or to the right of the other in the periodic table.)

As examples of assigning oxidation numbers, consider the elements in H_2, N_2, H_2O, and H_2O_2. To count the electrons, we write the electron dot formulas for the compounds. We need only consider the valence shell electrons in computing the oxidation numbers. For H_2 we write

H:H

In H_2, both atoms are alike. Apply Rule 1 and distribute the electrons in the bond equally between the two H atoms:

H⦙∶⦙H

Distributing the electrons in this way gives each H atom one electron in its valence shell; this is the number of electrons in the valence shell of a neutral H atom. Thus, this assignment of the electrons would result in each atom having a charge of zero; therefore, the oxidation number of the H atoms in H_2 is 0.

The N_2 molecule contains a triple covalent bond. Three electron pairs (six electrons) are shared between the two atoms. Following Rule 1, we count three of the bonding electrons as belonging to one N atom and the other three electrons as belonging to the other (shown by the dashed line):

$$: \underline{N} : \vdots \overline{N} :$$

Each N atom has $2 + 3 = 5$ electrons in its valence shell. This is the number of valence shell electrons in the neutral nitrogen atom; thus, no charge results from this electron assignment. The oxidation number of nitrogen in N_2 is 0.

In H_2O, the two H atoms are bonded to the oxygen by single bonds

$$H : \overset{\cdot\cdot}{\underset{\cdot\cdot}{O}} :$$
$$H$$

As the O and H are different atoms, we apply Rule 2. Oxygen has a greater electronegativity than H; thus, both electrons in the H—O bond are counted as belonging to the oxygen atom:

$$\overline{H} : \underset{\cdot\cdot}{\overset{\cdot\cdot}{O}} :$$
$$\overline{H}$$

(The electronegativity of H (2.1) is almost the same as $_5B$ (2.0). Therefore, H should be considered to be to the left of O in the periodic table when assigning oxidation numbers.)

The counting of electrons in H_2O as we just did results in H atoms with no electrons in their valence shells. A neutral H atom has one valence electron; removal of this electron would give the atom a $+1$ charge. Therefore, the oxidation number of H in H_2O is $+1$. The O atom will have eight electrons in its valence shell, two more than the six valence electrons found in the neutral oxygen atom. Hence, the oxidation number of the oxygen in H_2O is -2.

In hydrogen peroxide, H_2O_2, the two oxygen atoms are bonded together:

$$: \overset{\cdot\cdot}{O} : \overset{\cdot\cdot}{O} :$$
$$\underset{\cdot\cdot}{H} \quad \underset{\cdot\cdot}{H}$$

This situation is found in all compounds that are classified as peroxides. We use Rule 1 to assign the electrons in the O—O bond, and Rule 2 is used to assign the electrons in the O—H bonds.

$$: \overset{-}{\overset{\cdot\cdot}{O}}\overset{\cdot\cdot}{\vdots}\overset{\cdot\cdot}{O} :$$

$$\overset{-}{H}\,\vdots\,\overset{-}{H}$$

This assigns no electrons to the valence shell of the H atoms; thus, as we found in H_2O, the oxidation number of the H atoms in H_2O_2 is $+1$. Each O atom is assigned seven electrons in its valence shell; this is one more valence electron than the six found in a neutral oxygen atom. Therefore, the oxidation number of the O atoms in H_2O_2 is -1.

The structure of the molecule N_4S_4 (mentioned in Section 7–2 of *Chemical Principles*) may be represented as

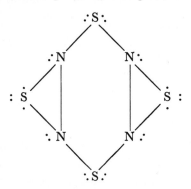

The electronegativity of N is larger (3.0) than that of S (2.5). We assign both of the electrons in the N—S bonds to N and divide the two N—N electrons equally between the two N atoms. Each S has four valence electrons, two less than in the valence shell of the neutral atom. Thus, the oxidation number of S is $+2$ in S_4N_4. Each N atom has seven valence electrons, two more than in the valence shell of a neutral nitrogen atom. Therefore, the oxidation number of N is -2.

The two rules for the assignment of oxidation numbers lead to several corollaries. If we use these corollaries (the eight "rules" given in Section 7–2 of *Chemical Principles*) we can assign oxidation numbers to the elements in many compounds without knowledge of the structure or bonding in the molecule.

(1) The oxidation number of a free element is zero. This is true if the element exists as free atoms or as molecules. Thus, Na, Fe, S_8, N_2, H_2, and P_4 all have oxidation numbers of zero.

(2) The oxidation number of an ion is the same as the charge on the ion. Thus, the oxidation numbers of Na^+ ion, Ca^{2+} ion, and Al^{3+} ion are $+1$, $+2$, and $+3$, respectively.

(3) In all compounds, the oxidation number of any Group IA element (Li, Na, K, Rb, Cs, Fr) is $+1$, and the oxidation number of any Group IIA element (Be, Mg, Ca, Sr, Ba, Ra) is $+2$.

(4) The oxidation number of hydrogen is $+1$ in all its compounds except the hydrides of Groups IA, IIA, and IIIA elements. In these metal hydrides (NaH, LiH, CaH_2, AlH_3, etc.) the oxidation number of H is -1.

(5) The oxidation number of oxygen in all its compounds is -2. Exceptions to this are the peroxides in which the oxidation number of O is -1, and in OF_2 in which the oxidation number is $+2$. (F is the only element with an electronegativity greater than oxygen).

(6) The sum of the oxidation numbers of the atoms in a neutral molecule is zero.

(7) The sum of the oxidation numbers in a complex ion is equal to the charge on the ion.

Without the above corollaries, it would be quite cumbersome to use oxidation numbers, and they would lose much of their value. To construct Lewis electron-dot formulas and to count electrons as we did in the previous examples would require us to have prior knowledge of the molecule's structure. In addition, such a procedure is much too time consuming to be practical. It is the corollaries that make it practical to employ oxidation numbers.

We generally can assign oxidation numbers to all but one of the elements in a molecule or complex ion by using the first five corollaries and then finding the oxidation number of the remaining atom by application of Corollary 6 or 7. Therefore, you should memorize the seven corollaries.

> EXAMPLE. Calculate the oxidation numbers for the elements in $CaCO_3$.

> SOLUTION. Calcium, a Group IIA element, has an oxidation number of $+2$ (Corollary 3). Oxygen has an oxidation number of -2 (Corollary 5). The oxidation number of the carbon can be computed from Corollary 6. Because $CaCO_3$ is neutral,

$$(\text{ox no. Ca}) + (\text{ox no. C}) + 3(\text{ox no. O}) = 0$$
$$+2 \quad + \quad \text{ox no. C} + 3\,(-2) \quad = 0$$
$$\text{ox no. C} = +6 - 2 \quad = +4$$

For convenience, the oxidation numbers of the elements are sometimes written above the elements in the formula. Thus,

$$\overset{+2}{\text{Ca}}\,\overset{+4}{\text{C}}\,\overset{-2}{\text{O}_3}$$

In oxidation numbers, the plus and minus signs are written before the number. This is to prevent confusion with actual units of electrical charge. The plus and minus signs are written after the number, such as $1+, 1-$, or $2+$ to denote ions with one positive, one negative, or two positive charges, respectively. $CaCO_3$ is an ionic compound, and the solid consists of Ca^{2+} ions and CO_3^{2-} ions at points in the crystal lattice.

In agreement with Corollary 7, the $+2$ oxidation number assigned to calcium corresponds to its $2+$ ionic charge.

EXAMPLE. Calculate the oxidation numbers for the elements in $S_4O_6{}^{2-}$ ion.

SOLUTION. Corollary 5 tells us that the oxidation number for O is -2. (The $S_4O_6{}^{2-}$ ion is not a peroxide.) The oxidation number for the sulfur atom follows from Corollary 7. Set the sum of the oxidation numbers equal to the charge on the ion.

$$4(\text{ox no. S}) + 6(\text{ox no. O}) = -2$$
$$4(\text{ox no. S}) + 6(-2) = -2$$
$$4(\text{ox no. S}) = 12 - 2 = +10$$
$$\text{ox no. S} = +\tfrac{10}{4} = +2\tfrac{1}{2}$$

$$\overset{+2\frac{1}{2}\ -2}{S_2\ O_6{}^{2-}}$$

EXAMPLE. Compute the oxidation numbers for the elements in peroxodisulfuric acid, $H_2S_2O_8$.

SOLUTION. Corollary 4 states that the oxidation number of the H atom is $+1$. The prefix "peroxo" indicates that the compound is a peroxide and contains at least one oxygen-to-oxygen bond. From Corollary 5, we know the oxidation number of O in peroxides is -1. To determine the oxidation number of the sulfur, we set the sum of the oxidation numbers equal to zero because $H_2S_2O_8$ is a neutral molecule.

$$2(\text{ox no. H}) + 2(\text{ox no. S}) + 8(\text{ox no. O}) = 0$$
$$2(+1) + 2(\text{ox no. S}) + 8(-1) = 0$$
$$\text{ox no. S} = (8 - 2)/2 = \tfrac{6}{2} = +3$$

EXAMPLE. Calculate the oxidation numbers of the elements in sucrose, $C_{12}H_{22}O_{11}$.

SOLUTION. The oxidation numbers of H and O are $+1$ and -2, according to Corollaries 4 and 5. To obtain the oxidation number for carbon, set the sum of the oxidation numbers equal to zero since sucrose is a neutral molecule.

$$12(\text{ox no. C}) + 22(\text{ox no. H}) + 11(\text{ox no. O}) = 0$$
$$12(\text{ox no. C}) + 22(+1) + 11(-2) = 0$$
$$12(\text{ox no. C}) = 22 - 22 = 0$$
$$\text{ox no. C} = 0$$

Before leaving this discussion of oxidation numbers, we should point out a contradiction in the last two examples in the rules for assigning oxidation numbers and the assignments made by using the corollaries. In a strict sense, in $H_2S_2O_8$ there are two different oxidation numbers for the oxygen atoms. That this is true can be seen by drawing the Lewis electron-dot formulas and counting electrons according to established rules.

$$H : \ddot{O} : \quad \begin{array}{c} : \ddot{O} : \\ S \\ : \ddot{O} : \end{array} \quad : \ddot{O} \dot{+} \ddot{O} : \quad \begin{array}{c} : \ddot{O} : \\ S \\ : \ddot{O} : \end{array} \quad : \ddot{O} : H$$

Because oxygen is the most electronegative element in the compound (further to the right of H and above S in the periodic table), the electrons in the H—O and S—O bonds are assigned to the O atom. The O—O electron pair in the peroxide link is divided equally between the two "like" O atoms. The oxidation numbers of the H and S atoms are +1 and +6, respectively. The six O atoms not involved in the peroxide link are assigned eight electrons and an oxidation number of −2; the two peroxide oxygen atoms are assigned seven electrons and an oxidation number of −1. The average oxidation number of the O atoms is $\frac{1}{8}[6(-2) + 2(-1)] = -\frac{14}{8} = -1\frac{3}{4}$.

In the same way, the oxidation numbers of the elements in $C_{12}H_{22}O_{11}$ are eleven O atoms, each −2; twenty-two H atoms, each +1; eight C atoms, each zero; two C atoms, each +1; and two C atoms, each −1. The average oxidation number of the C atoms is

$$\frac{2(+1) + 2(-1) + 8(0)}{12} = \frac{0}{12} = 0$$

You may rightly question why the two preceding examples were worked by using the corollaries without regard to structure when the oxidation numbers of the oxygen and carbon atoms are different.

For $H_2S_2O_8$, the S^{+3} and O^{-1} are not the S^{+6} and $O^{-1\frac{3}{4}}$ that one would obtain by using the rules and averaging the two oxidation numbers for the O atoms. For sucrose, although the C atoms have different oxidation numbers if the rules are followed, the average value does correspond to that obtained by using the corollaries without regard to structure. The effect of the corollaries is to distribute the electrons differently. (In $H_2S_2O_8$, some of the electrons from the $-1\frac{3}{4}$ oxygen atoms have been assigned to the sulfur atoms, thereby reducing the oxidation number of S from +6 to +3 and increasing the oxidation number of the oxygens to −1.) Although using the corollaries may give oxidation numbers that do not agree with those obtained by using the two rules, it is much simpler to use them than it is to draw the formulas and count the electrons. Remember that the oxidation numbers are merely numbers that have no physical significance, and the rules chosen for the assignment of the numbers are rather arbitrary. The values obtained by using the corollaries will be satisfactory for balancing equations and identifying oxidation and reduction processes; consequently, we customarily obtain the oxidation numbers by the more expedient application of the corollaries if it is possible to do so.

7-3 OXIDATION-REDUCTION REACTIONS

Reactions in which elements undergo a change in oxidation number (oxidation state) are classified as oxidation and reduction reactions. When the oxidation number of an element has been increased in a reaction we say that oxidation has occurred, and the substance containing the element has been oxidized. When an element's oxidation state is decreased, we say that reduction has occurred and the substance containing that element has been reduced. The substance that has undergone the oxidation is the reducing agent. Conversely, the substance that has undergone the reduction is the oxidizing agent. In any redox reaction, the total increase in oxidation number experienced by the reducing agent is equal to the total decrease in oxidation number experienced by the oxidizing agent.

There are two mechanisms by which redox can take place: electron transfer and atom transfer.

ELECTRON TRANSFER

By convention, the oxidation number of an ion is equal to the charge on the ion. Therefore, when positive ions accept electrons from the cathode during electrolysis, the positive charge on the ion (its oxidation number) decreases and reduction occurs. Similarly, when an ion deposits electrons on the anode, the charge on the ion becomes more positive and oxidation occurs. This is consistent with the definition given in Section 3-1: Oxidation, the loss of electrons, is the process that occurs at the anode; reduction, the gain of electrons, is the process that occurs at the cathode during electrolysis. In a reaction such as the electrolysis of fused NaCl,

$$Na^+ + 1e^- \rightarrow Na(s) \quad \text{at the cathode}$$
$$2Cl^- \rightarrow Cl_2(g) + 2e^- \quad \text{at the anode}$$

it is obvious that the increase in oxidation number experienced by chlorine (it increases from -1 in Cl^- ion to 0 in Cl_2) and the decrease in oxidation number experienced by the sodium ion (it decreases from $+1$ in Na^+ ion to 0 in Na) is accomplished by electron transfer. The very nature of the process by which electric current is carried through solutions during electrolysis requires that electron transfer occur.

When water is electrolyzed, H_2 gas is produced at the cathode. This is a reduction process because when $H_2O \rightarrow H_2(g)$, the oxidation number of the hydrogen is decreased from a $+1$ in H_2O to 0 in $H_2(g)$. It appears to be logical to assume that this change in oxidation state of the hydrogen is due to an electron transfer from the cathode to the water:

$$2e^- + 2H_2O \rightarrow H_2(g) + 2OH^-$$

When elemental sodium is placed in water, the Na is oxidized to Na^+ ions and the water is reduced to $H_2(g)$. The similarity of these products to those produced in the electrolysis of Na^+ ions (in fused NaCl) and H_2O suggests that this redox reaction results from the transfer of electrons from Na to the H_2O molecules. There is no proof that such an electron transfer occurs, however, and we must not rule out other possible mechanisms. The stoichiometry observed for the reaction is that shown in the equation

$$2Na(s) + H_2O \rightarrow 2Na^+ + 2OH^- + H_2(g)$$

Suppose we pretend that electron transfer was indeed the mechanism for this reaction and then write equations for this reaction as if the reduction occurred at a cathode and the oxidation occurred at an anode in an electrolysis cell:

$$2Na(s) \rightarrow Na^+ + 2e^-$$
$$\underline{2e^- + 2H_2O \rightarrow 2OH^- + H_2(g)}$$
$$2Na(s) + 2H_2O \rightarrow Na^+ + 2OH^- + H_2(g)$$

Note that the number of electrons lost during the oxidation of $Na(s)$ to Na^+ ion has been made the same as the number gained in the reduction of the H_2O. This situation is required for the current to flow through the cell during electrolysis. We see that when this stipulation is made and the two hypothetical electrode reactions (sometimes called half-reactions) are added, the result is the balanced chemical equation for the observed reaction. This procedure is the basis for one of the ion–electron methods of balancing equations described in Section 7–4.

ATOM TRANSFER

We know now that some oxidation–reduction reactions occur in which electrons are not transferred between atoms. Instead, atoms are re-combined in such a way that elements in the products have oxidation numbers that differ from those they had in the reactants. In Section 7–3 of *Chemical Principles*, the reaction

$$ClO_3^- + 3SO_3^{2-} \rightarrow Cl^- + 3SO_4^{2-}$$

is cited as an example of redox by atom transfer. The O atoms on the ClO_3^- ion are transferred directly to the SO_3^{2-}. The result is Cl^- and SO_4^{2-} ions. The oxidation number of chlorine in ClO_3^- is $+5$, and in Cl^- ion it is -1. The chlorine has decreased in oxidation number; it has been reduced. Similarly, sulfur in the SO_3^{2-} ion has been oxidized from the $+4$ oxidation state to the $+6$ oxidation state it had in SO_4^{2-} ion.

It is generally quite difficult to determine if a redox reaction occurs by electron transfer or by atom transfer. Consequently, the mechanism of only a few of the vast number of redox reactions are known with any degree of certainty.

The stoichiometry of redox reactions is often complex, and it is difficult to balance the equations correctly. For this reason, many procedures have been worked out to aid in this operation. You should be acquainted with some of these. Two methods will be given here. Slight modifications in each of the methods are required to balance equations written in the molecular form or net ionic form.

The rules for balancing equations, like the rules for assigning oxidation numbers, do not necessarily have any real physical significance. They merely describe a routine that, if followed, will help you to attain your objective—a balanced equation. Equations can be written either in the molecular form or in the net ionic form.

OXIDATION-NUMBER METHOD

Using both this method and the method of half-reactions, we will pretend that the changes in oxidation number occur because of electron transfer. When we do this, we do not imply that electron transfer *is* the mechanism. In fact, electron transfer may not bear any resemblance to the mechanism at all. Just as the plus and minus oxidation numbers are a formalism and do not represent actual electrical charges, so is our pretension that the change in oxidation number is due to electron transfer. Our justification for considering the reaction in this way is that it provides a simple means of attaining our objective, a balanced redox equation.

RULES FOR BALANCING MOLECULAR EQUATIONS BY THE OXIDATION-NUMBER METHOD

To demonstrate the application of these rules, the balancing of the following reaction will be used as an example:

$$As_2S_5 + HNO_3 \rightarrow H_3AsO_4 + H_2SO_4 + H_2O + NO_2$$

Using the corollaries given in Section 7–3, assign oxidation numbers to all the atoms to identify those that have changed oxidation numbers. H and O are $+1$ and -2 in all compounds. Because S is more electronegative than As, the electrons in any covalent bond between these two elements will be counted with the S atom. S can accommodate two electrons in its valence shell. Therefore, the oxidation number of S is -2, and the As must be $+5$ as As_2S_5. In H_3AsO_4, the oxidation number of the As is $+5$ also; therefore, the As has not been oxidized or reduced. The S in H_2SO_4 is $+6$. The N in HNO_3 is $+5$, and in NO_2 it is $+4$. The atoms that change oxidation number are S (it changes from -2 to $+6$) and N (it changes from $+5$ to $+4$).

If these changes in oxidation number have been the result of an electron transfer, then for one S atom to become a $\overset{-2}{S}$ atom, eight elec-

$$\overset{+5}{\text{trons must be lost. For one N atom to be reduced to a N atom, one}}\overset{+4}{}$$

trons must be lost. For one $\overset{+5}{\text{N}}$ atom to be reduced to a $\overset{+4}{\text{N}}$ atom, one electron must be gained.

We compute the number of electrons gained or lost per formula unit (fu) of oxidizing agent and reducing agent in the following way: Each formula unit of As_2S_5 contains five $\overset{-2}{\text{S}}$ atoms. One $\overset{-2}{\text{S}}$ atom loses eight electrons when it is oxidized to $\overset{+6}{\text{S}}$. Hence, there must be a loss of $5 \times 8 = 40$ electrons per formula unit of As_2S_5.

There is one $\overset{+5}{\text{N}}$ atom in a formula unit of HNO_3. One $\overset{+5}{\text{N}}$ atom gains one electron when it is reduced to $\overset{+4}{\text{N}}$. Therefore, one electron is gained per formula unit of HNO_3:

$$\overset{-2}{As_2S_5} \quad + \quad \overset{+5}{HNO_3} \rightarrow \overset{+6}{H_3AsO_4} + \overset{+6}{H_2SO_4} + H_2O + \overset{+4}{NO_2}$$
$$-8e^-/\text{S atom} \quad +1e^-/\text{N atom}$$
$$5(-8) = -40e^-/\text{fu} \quad +1e^-/\text{fu}$$

The total electrons lost in oxidation must equal the electrons gained in reduction. The loss of 40 electrons by one formula unit of As_2S_5 would require the presence of 40 formula units of HNO_3, each accepting one electron. Thus, the coefficients in front of the reactants ($1As_2S_5 + 40HNO_3$) are established.

The oxidized and reduced atoms are balanced by placing the appropriate coefficients in front of those products that contain these elements.

$$\overset{-2}{As_2S_5} \quad + \quad \overset{+5}{40HNO_3} \quad \rightarrow \overset{+6}{H_3AsO_4} + 5H_2SO_4 + H_2O + \overset{+4}{40NO_2}$$
$$-8e^-/\text{S atom} \quad +1e^-/\text{N atom}$$
$$-40e^-/\text{fu} \quad 40(+1e^-/\text{fu})$$

To complete the balancing of the remaining atoms that have not been oxidized or reduced is relatively simple. One cannot alter those coefficients in front of the molecules that have undergone redox; to do so would change the balance in the number of electrons gained and lost. To complete the balancing of this equation, a coefficient of 2 is placed in front of the H_3AsO_4 to balance the two As atoms in As_2S_5. Balancing the 40 H atoms is accomplished by placing a coefficient of 12 in front of the H_2O. That the equation is now completely balanced can be confirmed by totaling the O atoms; there are 120 on each side.

$$As_2S_5 \quad + \quad 40HNO_3 \rightarrow 2H_3AsO_4 + 5H_2SO_4 + 12H_2O + 40NO_2$$
$$-8e^-/\text{S atom} \quad +1e^-/\text{N atom}$$
$$-40e^-/\text{fu} \quad +40e^-/\text{fu}$$

Balancing Oxidation– Reduction Equations

The rules for balancing molecular redox equations by the change in oxidation-number method are summarized as follows:

(1) Compute the oxidation number of those atoms that change their oxidation number.

(2) Determine the number of electrons to be transferred per atom to cause the change in oxidation number.

(3) Determine the number of electrons to be transferred per formula unit.

(4) Make the electron gain equal the electron loss by writing appropriate coefficients in front of the oxidizing agent and the reducing agent.

(5) Insert appropriate coefficients to balance the oxidized and reduced atoms in the products.

(6) Balance the remaining atoms by inspection.

BALANCING NET IONIC EQUATIONS BY THE OXIDATION-NUMBER METHOD

To illustrate this method, the net ionic equation for the oxidation of Fe^{2+} ions by $Cr_2O_7^{2-}$ ions in acid solution will be balanced.

$$Fe^{2+} + Cr_2O_7^{2-} \rightarrow Fe^{3+} + Cr^{3+}$$

The H^+ ion and H_2O, which are present in aqueous acid solutions, need not be included in the equation now, but may be introduced later if needed to balance the equation.

As in balancing molecular equations, we determine the oxidation numbers of the elements that change and decide on the number of electrons that must be transferred per formula unit to account for the change.

Do not confuse ionic charge with oxidation number. The oxidation numbers of the Fe^{2+}, Fe^{3+}, and Cr^{3+} ions are the same as their ionic charges: $+2$, $+3$, and $+3$, respectively. The oxidation numbers of the Cr and O atoms in the $Cr_2O_7^{2-}$ ion are $+6$ and -2, respectively.

$$\overset{+2}{Fe^{2+}} \quad + \quad \overset{+6}{Cr_2O_7^{2-}} \rightarrow \overset{+3}{Fe^{3+}} + \overset{+3}{Cr^{3+}}$$

$-1e^-$/Fe atom $\qquad +3e^-$/Cr atom

$-1e^-$/fu $\qquad\qquad 2(+3e^-)$/fu

The electron gain is set equal to the electron loss by introducing the proper coefficients before the oxidizing agent ($Cr_2O_7^{2-}$) and the reducing agent (Fe^{2+}). The oxidizing and reduced atoms in the products are then balanced:

$$6Fe^{2+} \quad + \quad \overset{+6}{Cr_2O_7^{2-}} \rightarrow 6Fe^{3+} + 2Cr^{3+}$$

$-1e^-$/Fe atom $\qquad +3e^-$/Cr atom

$6(-1e^-)$/fu $\qquad 1(+6e^-)$/fu

In ionic equations, a net *ionic charge* balance must be maintained. That is, the sum of the ionic charges on the left of the equation must equal the sum of the ionic charges on the right. As this reaction is performed in acid solution, add sufficient H^+ ions to balance the ionic charge. To determine the number of H^+ ions needed, the net ionic charge is computed. (Again, use care; do not confuse oxidation numbers with ionic charges.) The total ionic charge of the reactants is the sum of the charges on 6 Fe^{2+} ions and on the $Cr_2O_7^{2-}$ ion: $6(2+) + 1(2-)$ $= (12+) + (2-) = 10+$.

The total ionic charge of the products is the sum of the charges on 6 Fe^{3+} ions and 2 Cr^{3+} ions: $6(3+) + 2(3+) = 24+$. Fourteen H^+ ions are added to the reactants to make the ionic charge equal $24+$ on each side of the equation.

$$\overset{+6}{6Fe^{2+}} \quad + \quad Cr_2O_7^{2-} \quad + 14H^+ \rightarrow 6Fe^{3+} + 2Cr^{3+}$$
$$-1e^-/Fe\ atom \quad +3e^-/Cr\ atom$$
$$6(-1e^-)/fu \quad\quad 1(+6e^-)/fu$$

Seven H_2O molecules are added to the products to balance the O atoms. This process introduces 14 H atoms in the products, which compliment the 14 H atoms in the reactants, and the equation is balanced.

$$\overset{+6}{6Fe^{2+}} \quad + \quad Cr_2O_7^{2-} \quad + 14H^+ \rightarrow 6Fe^{3+} + 2Cr^{3+}$$
$$-1e^-/Fe\ atom \quad +3e^-/Cr\ atom \quad\quad\quad\quad + 7H_2O$$
$$6(-1e^-)/fu \quad\quad 1(+6e^-)/fu$$

When a reaction is performed in basic solution, one uses OH^- ions to obtain the charge balance instead of H^+ ions.

The rules for balancing ionic redox equations by the change in oxidation number method can be summarized as follows:

(1) Assign oxidation numbers to the atoms that change.

(2) Determine the number of electrons to be transferred per atom to account for the change in oxidation number.

(3) Determine the number of electrons to be transferred per formula unit.

(4) Make the electron gain equal the electron loss by writing appropriate coefficients for the oxidizing agent and the reducing agent.

(5) Write coefficients to balance the oxidized and reduced atoms in the products.

(6) Balance the net ionic charge by adding H^+ as required if the reaction is done in acid solution, or OH^- if the reaction occurs in basic solution.

(7) Add H_2O when necessary to balance the oxygen atoms.

ION-ELECTRON (HALF-REACTION) METHOD

With this method, we pretend that the oxidation and reduction reactions are occurring separately. The separate oxidation and reduction reactions (often called half-reactions) are balanced and then combined to give the equation for the complete reaction. The reaction must be written as an ionic equation. It is not necessary to employ oxidation numbers to use this method.

To balance an equation by the ion–electron method, the only information needed is the ionic forms of the oxidizing agent and the reducing agent, their reduced and oxidized products, and whether the reaction is performed in acidic or basic solution.

As an example, consider the reaction between Mn^{2+} ions and $S_2O_8^{2-}$ ions in aqueous acid solution to form solid MnO_2 and SO_4^{2-} ions:

$$Mn^{2+} + S_2O_8^{2-} \rightarrow MnO_2(s) + SO_4^{2-}$$

The reaction is divided into two half-reactions, one involving the sulfur and the other involving the manganese:

$$S_2O_8^{2-} \rightarrow SO_4^{2-} \tag{1}$$
$$Mn^{2+} \rightarrow MnO_2(s) \tag{2}$$

The two half-reactions are balanced separately and then combined. Starting with Half-Reaction 1, first balance all the atoms except H and O. Two SO_4^{2-} are needed to balance the S atoms in one $S_2O_8^{2-}$:

$$S_2O_8^{2-} \rightarrow 2SO_4^{2-}$$

Note that the O atoms are balanced. Electrons are added to the left side of the equation to balance the ionic charges:

$$2e^- + S_2O_8^{2-} \rightarrow 2SO_4^{2-} \tag{3}$$

This half-reaction is balanced.

Half-Reaction 2 is balanced with a similiar routine. The Mn atoms, the atoms other than O and H, are already balanced.

$$Mn^{2+} \rightarrow MnO_2(s)$$

To remove the deficiency in O atoms, two molecules of H_2O are added to the left side of the equation

$$2H_2O + Mn^{2+} \rightarrow MnO_2(s)$$

The H atoms are not balanced. As this reaction is performed in acid solution, H^+ may be added. Four H^+ ions are added to the right side of the equation to balance the H atoms:

$$2H_2O + Mn^{2+} \rightarrow MnO_2(s) + 4H^+$$

The total ionic charge on the left is $+2$ (one Mn^{2+} ion), whereas the total ionic charge on the right of the equation is $+4$ (four H^+ ions). To balance the ionic charges, $2e^-$ are added to the right side of the equation:

$$2H_2O + Mn^{2+} \rightarrow MnO_2(s) + 4H^+ + 2e^- \tag{4}$$

Note that the balanced Half-Reaction 3 shows a gain of two electrons whereas two electrons are lost in Half-Reaction 4. The gain and loss of electrons are equal (a criterion to be satisfied in any redox reaction), so Half-Reactions 3 and 4 can be combined to obtain the complete balanced equation for the reaction:

$$2e^- + S_2O_8^{2-} \rightarrow 2SO_4^{2-}$$
$$2H_2O + Mn^{2+} \rightarrow MnO_2(s) + 4H^+ + 2e^-$$

$$\overline{S_2O_8^{2-} + 2H_2O + Mn^{2+} \rightarrow 2SO_4^{2-} + MnO_2(s) + 4H^+}$$

Since like things can be canceled from both sides of any equation, the $2e^-$ are not shown.

Note that the atoms and ionic charges balance in the final equation. Any balanced equation must demonstrate this conservation of mass and conservation of charge. Also, although oxidation numbers have not been mentioned, the gain of $2e^-$ shown in Half-Reaction 3 is what we would conclude is necessary to account for the oxidation number change by electron transfer (two S atoms, each with a $+7$ oxidation state in $S_2O_8^{2-}$ ion, accept $2e^-$ to form two SO_4^{2-} ions, each with the S atom in an oxidation state of $+6$). Similarly, for each Mn^{2+} ion to change oxidation state to Mn^{4+} in MnO_2 requires the loss of $2e^-$ per Mn^{2+} ion.

To balance molecular equations by the ion–electron method, first the reaction must be written as a net ionic equation. The net ionic equation is balanced, using the method shown, and then the ions are recombined and written as molecules.

When reactions are performed in basic solutions, the appearance of H^+ ions in the balanced equation is ruled out. To balance such equations, pretend that the reaction is performed in acid; then balance the half-reactions by following the procedure just described. After the two half-reactions have been combined, add sufficient OH^- ions and H_2O to remove all the H^+ ions written in the equation. We shall illustrate this with an example, but first we shall summarize the rules so you can learn the sequence of the operations.

RULES FOR BALANCING REDOX EQUATIONS BY THE ION–ELECTRON METHOD
The reaction must be written as a net ionic equation.

(1) Separate the reaction into two half-reactions.
(2) Balance each of the separate half-reactions in the following way:
    (a) Balance all atoms except H and O.
    (b) Balance O atoms by adding H_2O when needed.
    (c) Balance H atoms by adding H^+ ions when needed.
    (d) Balance ionic charges by adding electrons when needed.
(3) Multiply each half-reaction by an appropriate factor to make the electron gain equal the electron loss; then add the half-reactions.
(4) Subtract any duplication from the left and right sides of the combined equations.
(5) If the reaction is performed in basic solution, add to both sides of the equation sufficient OH^- ions to neutralize all the H^+, and again subtract like numbers of H_2O molecules so H_2O remains on only one side of the equation.

EXAMPLE. Balance the following equation by using the ion–electron method.

$$MnCl_2 + NaOH + Br_2 \rightarrow MnO_2(s) + NaCl + NaBr + H_2O$$

SOLUTION. Write the equation as an ionic equation.

$$Mn^{2+} + 2Cl^- + Na^+ + OH^- + Br_2 \rightarrow MnO_2(s) + Na^+$$
$$+ Cl^- + Br^- + H_2O$$

Omit common ions and arrive at the net ionic equation.

$$Mn^{2+} + OH^- + Br_2 \rightarrow MnO_2(s) + Br^- + H_2O$$

(1) Divide into two half-reactions.

$$Mn^{2+} \rightarrow MnO_2(s) \tag{1}$$
$$Br_2 \rightarrow Br^- \tag{2}$$

The OH^- and H_2O do not undergo redox and will be introduced when needed in balancing the equation.

(2) Balance Half-Reaction 1.

$$Mn^{2+} \rightarrow MnO_2(s)$$

(a) Balance all atoms except H and O; the Mn atoms are balanced as written.

(b) Balance O atoms by adding H_2O.

$$2H_2O + Mn^{2+} \rightarrow MnO_2(s)$$

(c) Balance H atoms by adding H^+ ions.

$$2H_2O + Mn^{2+} \rightarrow MnO_2(s) + 4H^+$$

(d) Balance ionic charge by adding electrons.

$$2H_2O + Mn^{2+} \rightarrow MnO_2(s) + 4H^+ + 2e^-$$

Balance Half-Reaction 2.

$$Br_2 \rightarrow Br^-$$

(a) Balance all atoms except H and O.

$$Br_2 \rightarrow 2Br^-$$

(b) and (c) Since there are no O atoms or H atoms in the equation, these steps can be omitted.

(d) Balance ionic charge by adding electrons.

$$Br_2 + 2e^- \rightarrow 2Br^-$$

(3) Make the electron gain equal to the electron loss in the balanced half-reactions (they are the same as written) and add.

$$2H_2O + Mn^{2+} \rightarrow MnO_2(s) + 4H^+ + 2e^-$$
$$Br_2 + 2e^- \rightarrow 2Br^-$$

_____

$$2H_2O + Mn^{2+} + Br_2 + 2e^- \rightarrow MnO_2(s) + 2Br^- + 4H^+ + 2e^-$$

(4) Subtract duplicates from right and left sides. (Subtract $2e^-$ from each side of the equation.)

$$2H_2O + Mn^{2+} + Br_2 \rightarrow MnO_2(s) + 2Br^- + 4H^+$$

(5) The reaction is performed in basic solution.

Add enough OH⁻ ions to both sides of the equation to neutralize the H⁺ ions. There are 4 H⁺ on the right; we add 4 OH⁻ to each side.

$$4OH^- + 2H_2O + Mn^{2+} + Br_2 \rightarrow MnO_2(s) + 2Br^- \\ + 4H^+ + 4OH^-$$

The 4 OH⁻ will neutralize the 4 H⁺ appearing in the products to form 4 H_2O.

$$4OH^- + 2H_2O + Mn^{2+} + Br_2 \rightarrow MnO_2(s) + 2Br^- + 4H_2O$$

Cancelation of duplicates from each side of the equation (here $2H_2O$) yields the balanced net ionic equation.

$$4OH^- + Mn^{2+} + Br_2 \rightarrow MnO_2(s) + 2Br^- + 2H_2O$$

Recombining in the molecular form and using the same coefficients, we obtain

$$MnCl_2 + 4NaOH + Br_2 \rightarrow MnO_2(s) + 2NaBr \\ + 2NaCl + 2H_2O$$

Let us look at some other examples.

EXAMPLE. Balance the reaction $Br_2 \rightarrow BrO_3^- + Br^-$ by the ion–electron method and by the oxidation number method. The reaction takes place in basic solution.

SOLUTION A. Balance by the ion–electron method.
(1) The half-reactions are

$$Br_2 \rightarrow BrO_3^-$$
$$Br_2 \rightarrow Br^-$$

(2) Balance the separate half-reactions.
   (a) For $Br_2 \rightarrow BrO_3^-$, balance atoms other than O and H.

$$Br_2 \rightarrow 2BrO_3^-$$

   (b) Balance O atoms by adding H_2O.

$$Br_2 + 6H_2O \rightarrow 2BrO_3^-$$

   (c) Balance H atoms by adding H⁺.

$$Br_2 + 6H_2O \rightarrow 2BrO_3^- + 12H^+$$

   (d) Balance charge by adding electrons.

$$Br_2 + 6H_2O \rightarrow 2BrO_3^- + 12H^+ + 10e^-$$

   (a) For the half-reaction $Br_2 \rightarrow Br^-$, balance atoms other than O and H.

$$Br_2 \rightarrow 2Br^-$$

(b) and (c) Balance O and H; these are balanced as the equation now stands.

(d) Balance the charge by adding electrons.

$$2e^- + Br_2 \rightarrow 2Br^-$$

(3) Multiply the balanced half-reactions by appropriate coefficients to make the electron gain equal the electron loss; then add.

$$Br_2 + 6H_2O \rightarrow 2BrO_3^- + 12H^+ + 10e^-$$
$$5(2e^- + Br_2 \rightarrow 2Br^-)$$
$$\overline{Br_2 + 6H_2O + 10e^- + 5Br_2 \rightarrow 2BrO_3^- + 12H^+ + 10Br^- + 10e^-}$$

(4) Cancel duplications from both sides of the equation (here $10e^-$).

$$Br_2 + 6H_2O + 5Br_2 \rightarrow 2BrO_3^- + 12H^+ + 10Br^-$$

(5) This reaction is performed in base, so add sufficient OH^- ions to each side to neutralize the H^+ ions. Twelve OH^- ions will react with the twelve H^+ ions in the products to form twelve H_2O; therefore, add twelve OH^- ions to both sides of the equation.

$$Br_2 + 6H_2O + 5Br_2 + 12OH^- \rightarrow 2BrO_3^- + 10Br^-$$
$$+ 12H^+ + 12OH^-$$

The twelve H^+ ions and twelve OH^- ions in the products will form twelve H_2O:

$$Br_2 + 6H_2O + 5Br_2 + 12OH^- \rightarrow 2BrO_3^- + 10Br^- + 12H_2O$$

Canceling duplicates from both sides (here six H_2O), we get the balanced net ionic equation.

$$6Br_2 + 12OH^- \rightarrow 2BrO_3^- + 10Br^- + 6H_2O$$

SOLUTION B. Balance the reaction $Br_2 \rightarrow \overset{+5}{Br}O_3^- + Br^-$ by using the oxidation number method.

(1) Assign oxidation numbers to those elements that change. These are written above the elements.

$$\overset{0}{Br_2} \rightarrow \overset{+5}{Br}O_3^- + \overset{-1}{Br}^-$$

(2) and (3) Decide on the number of electrons per atom (and then per formula unit) required to make this change. This reaction is an example of a disproportionation reaction; that is, an element in an intermediate oxidation state is both oxidized and reduced in a single reaction. The Br_2 is oxidized to BrO_3^- and reduced to Br^-. To simplify bookkeeping, write Br_2 twice for balancing purposes and then combine the results so Br_2 is written only once in the final balanced equation.

$$\overset{0}{Br_2} \quad + \quad \overset{0}{Br_2} \quad \rightarrow \overset{+5}{Br}O_3^- + \overset{-1}{Br}^-$$

$$0 \rightarrow +5 \qquad 0 \rightarrow -1$$
$$-5e^-/Br \text{ atom} \quad +1e^-/Br \text{ atom}$$
$$-10e^-/fu \qquad +2e^-/fu$$

(4) Make the electron gain equal the electron loss. One formula unit of Br_2 will transfer ten electrons per formula unit to five formula units of Br_2, which gains two electrons per formula unit.

$$\overset{0}{Br_2} \quad + \quad \overset{0}{5Br_2} \quad \rightarrow \overset{+5}{Br}O_3^- + \overset{-1}{Br}^-$$

$$0 \rightarrow +5 \qquad 0 \rightarrow -1$$
$$-5e^-/Br \text{ atom} \quad +1e^-/Br \text{ atom}$$
$$-10e^-/fu \qquad +2e^-/fu$$
$$5(+2e^-)/fu$$

(5) Balance the oxidized and reduced atoms to agree with these coefficients.

$$\overset{0}{Br_2} \quad + \quad \overset{0}{5Br_2} \quad \rightarrow \overset{+5}{2Br}O_3^- + \overset{-1}{10Br}^-$$

$$0 \rightarrow +5 \qquad 0 \rightarrow -1$$
$$-5e^-/Br \text{ atom} \quad +1e^-/Br \text{ atom}$$
$$-10e^-/fu \qquad +2e^-/fu$$
$$5(+2e^-)/fu$$

Writing the Br_2 a single time gives

$$6Br_2 \rightarrow 2BrO_3^- + 10Br^-$$

These coefficients can be simplified by dividing each by 2; that is,

$$\tfrac{1}{2}(6Br_2 \rightarrow 2BrO_3^- + 10Br^-) = 3Br_2 \rightarrow BrO_3^- + 5Br^-$$

This does not change the electron gain–electron loss balance or the atom balance. Had we treated the Br_2 as a single entry at the beginning rather than writing it twice, the simplest whole number coefficients would have been obtained. However, most beginning students find it easier to separate a substance that undergoes disproportionation and treat it as two separate substances, one the oxidizing agent and the other the reducing agent. Therefore, we have used this technique. The division to simplify the coefficients can be done at this step in the balancing process, or the large numbers can be retained until the final equation has been derived and the division of all the coefficients carried out for this equation.

(6) As this reaction is performed in basic solution, the net ionic charge is balanced by adding OH^- ions.

$$6OH^- + 3Br_2 \rightarrow BrO_3^- + 5Br^-$$

(7) The O atoms are balanced by adding H_2O molecules.

$$6OH^- + 3Br_2 \rightarrow BrO_3^- + 5Br^- + 3H_2O$$

A check for conservation of mass and charge shows that the equation is balanced.

One question remains to be answered: How do we decide on the method we should use to balance a given equation? The choice is usually merely a matter of personal preference. However, sometimes your choice may be governed by your knowledge of the substances involved. To use the oxidation-number method, you must be able to decide on an oxidation number for all the elements that are involved in the redox reaction. To use the ion–electron method, you must be able to identify those substances that exist in solution primarily as ions and then formulate these ions correctly. Your ability to do one or the other of these with confidence can lead you to favor one method over the other. Therefore, it is the wise student who becomes equally adept at balancing equations with both methods.

This next example illustrates a way that one might choose the most appropriate method to use in balancing an equation.

EXAMPLE. Balance the following redox equation:

$$K_3Fe(CN)_6 + KMnO_4 + H_2SO_4 \rightarrow Fe_2(SO_4)_3 + K_2SO_4$$
$$+ CO_2(g) + HNO_3 + MnSO_4 + H_2O$$

SOLUTION. Rapid examination shows that all the oxidation numbers can be computed readily except those for the Fe, C, and N atoms in $K_3Fe(CN)_6$. You might recall the formula for hydrocyanic acid (prussic acid), $H:C:::N:$, or you might recall from the list in Section 7–1 that the charge on the cyanide ion CN^- (its oxidation number) is -1. If you do, then you can assign oxidation numbers of $+2$ to the C, -3 to the N, and -1 to the CN group as a whole. Knowledge of the formula for the ionic compound KCN would permit you to obtain the same information. Knowledge of the CN group's oxidation number (-1) permits you to assign the $+2$ oxidation number to the Fe atom in $K_4Fe(CN)_6$. Now you can use the oxidation-number method to balance the equation.

Let us suppose that you were unable to decide on the oxidation numbers for all the atoms in the reaction; then what? The alternative is to use the ion–electron procedure. To do this, the net ionic equation must be written. Many of the compounds involved in the reaction are potassium salts. Potassium occurs in Group IA in the periodic table. All but one or two compounds of Group IA elements are ionic, so one should be safe in assuming that all the potassium compounds in the reaction are ionic salts and dissociate to form K^+ ions in aqueous solution. H_2SO_4 and HNO_3 are strong acids and completely dissociate to form H^+ and SO_4^{2-} and NO_3^- ions in aqueous solution. $CO_2(g)$ is a covalent compound, and most of it escapes the solution as a gas. Since no indication is given for the $Fe_2(SO_4)_3$ precipitating, we can conclude that it is in solution.

As you learned in Chapter 2 of *Chemical Principles*, most soluble salts dissolve in the form of ions. The required ionic equation can now be written. Even though some of the assumptions [such as the dissolved $Fe_2(SO_4)_3$ ionizing] may prove to be incorrect, we can at least continue with the hope that a correctly balanced equation can be obtained.

$$3K^+ + Fe(CN)_6{}^{3-} + K^+ + MnO_4{}^- + 2H^+ + SO_4{}^{2-}$$
$$\rightarrow 2Fe^{3+} + SO_4{}^{2-} + 2K^+ + SO_4{}^{2-} + CO_2(g)$$
$$+ H^+ + NO_3{}^- + Mn^{2+} + SO_4{}^{2-} + H_2O$$

The net ionic equation is

$$Fe(CN)_6{}^{3-} + MnO_4{}^- \rightarrow Fe^{3+} + CO_2(g) + NO_3{}^- + Mn^{2+}$$

The half-reactions are

$$Fe(CN)_6{}^{3-} \rightarrow Fe^{3+} + CO_2(g) + NO_3{}^-$$
$$MnO_4{}^- \rightarrow Mn^{2+}$$

Following the rules, we balance each half-reaction, make the electron gain equal to the electron loss, and add. The first half-reaction is a bit different from the others we have seen in this study guide. To show that the procedure followed in previous examples is applicable to this reaction, we will carry out the balancing of this half-reaction in detail. You should have no trouble following the procedure for balancing the $MnO_4{}^-$–Mn^{2+} half-reaction. For the half-reaction

$$Fe(CN)_6{}^{3-} \rightarrow Fe^{3+} + CO_2(g) + NO_3{}^-$$

(a) Balance atoms other than H and O.

$$Fe(CN)_6{}^{3-} \rightarrow Fe^{3+} + 6CO_2(g) + 6NO_3{}^-$$

(b) Balance O atoms by adding H_2O.

$$30H_2O + Fe(CN)_6{}^{3-} \rightarrow Fe^{3+} + 6CO_2(g) + 6NO_3{}^-$$

(c) Balance H atoms by adding H^+ ions.

$$30H_2O + Fe(CN)_6{}^{3-} \rightarrow Fe^{3+} + 6CO_2(g) + 6NO_3{}^- + 60H^+$$

(d) Balance ionic charges by adding electrons.

$$30H_2O + Fe(CN)_6{}^{3-} \rightarrow Fe^{3+} + 6CO_2(g) + 6NO_3{}^-$$
$$+ 60H^+ + 60e^-$$

Balance the second half-reaction and multiply by 12 to make the electrons lost equal the electrons gained; then add.

$$30H_2O + Fe(CN)_6{}^{3-} \rightarrow Fe^{3+} + 6CO_2(g) + 6NO_3{}^-$$
$$+ 60H^+ + 60e^-$$
$$\underline{12(5e^- + 8H^+ + MnO_4{}^- \rightarrow Mn^{2+} + 4H_2O)}$$
$$60e^- + 30H_2O + 96H^+ + Fe(CN)_6{}^{3-} + 12MnO_4{}^- \rightarrow Fe^{3+}$$
$$+ 6CO_2(g) + 6NO_3{}^- + 60H^+ + 60e^- + 12Mn^{2+} + 48H_2O$$

Subtracting duplicate electrons, H_2O, and H^+ ions from both sides of the equation, we get

$$36H^+ + Fe(CN)_6{}^{3-} + 12MnO_4{}^- \rightarrow Fe^{3+} + 6CO_2(g)$$
$$+ 6NO_3{}^- + 12Mn^{2+} + 18H_2O$$

Since this reaction is carried out in acid, no further changes in the equation are necessary. Recombining the ions, but retaining the coefficients in the balanced net ionic equation, we write the balanced molecular equation for the reaction:

$$K_3Fe(CN)_6 + 12KMnO_4 + 21H_2SO_4 \rightarrow \tfrac{1}{2}Fe_2(SO_4)_3 + 6CO_2(g)$$
$$+ 7\tfrac{1}{2}K_2SO_4 + 6HNO_3 + 12MnSO_4 + 18H_2O$$

To remove the fractions, multiply all the coefficients by 2:

$$2K_3Fe(CN)_6 + 24KMnO_4 + 42H_2SO_4 \rightarrow Fe_2(SO_4)_3 + 12CO_2(g)$$
$$+ 15K_2SO_4 + 12HNO_3 + 24MnSO_4 + 36H_2O$$

7-5 REDOX TITRATIONS

In Section 4–4 of this book and *Chemical Principles*, the equivalent weight concept was discussed and applied to chemical reactions involving acids and bases. Recall that the equivalent weight of an acid or base was defined as that weight of the acid or base capable of transferring or receiving 1 mole of protons. Since the protons lost by an acid must react with a base in a chemical reaction, it was shown that the same number of gram equivalent weights (referred to as the number of equivalents, or equiv) of acid and base always react with one another. The usefulness of this concept is that it permits us to carry out stoichiometry calculations involving acids and bases without balancing the chemical equation to determine the mole ratios of reactants and products. To realize this advantage in dealing with reactions in solution, a concentration unit, the normality, N, was defined, where N gives the number of equivalents of solute in 1 liter of solution.

A situation exists in oxidation and reduction reactions that is similar to the one in reactions involving acids and bases. Just as the number of protons lost by an acid must equal the number of protons gained by the base in an acid–base reaction, so must the number of units of oxidation number lost by a reducing agent equal the number of units gained in oxidation number by the oxidizing agent in a redox reaction. If we define the equivalent weight of a substance that participates in a redox reaction as the weight that produces 1 mole of oxidation number change, then the same relationships that were applied in stoichiometry calculations involving acids and bases will hold for redox reactions. These relations are described for acids and bases in Section 4–4. We repeat them here.

$$\text{no. of equiv of A} = \text{equiv A} = N_A \times \text{liters}_A$$

$$\text{no. of equiv of A} = \text{equiv A} = \frac{\text{grams A}}{\text{g equiv wt of A}}$$

$$N_A = \frac{\text{equiv A}}{\text{liters of solution}} = \frac{(\text{grams A})(\text{g equiv wt A})^{-1}}{\text{liters of solution}}$$

At the equivalence point in any redox reaction, equiv A = equiv B. A and B are the oxidizing or reducing agents that participate in the reaction, and N is the normality of the oxidizing or reducing agent.

The gram equivalent weight of a substance will be that weight which produces 1 mole of oxidation number change. In balancing redox equations, we have pretended that a change in oxidation number is brought about by a transfer of electrons. Although this may or may not be true in a particular reaction, we found this assumption useful in balancing the equations. It is generally useful in establishing the equivalent weight of a substance. For example, consider the oxidation and reduction reaction

$$\overset{+6}{\text{Cr}_2\text{O}_7^{2-}} + \overset{+2}{\text{Fe}^{2+}} \to \overset{+3}{\text{Cr}^{3+}} + \overset{+3}{\text{Fe}^{3+}}$$

$+3e^-/\text{Cr atom} \qquad -1e^-/\text{Fe atom}$
$+6e^-/\text{fu} \qquad\quad -1e^-/\text{fu}$

The oxidation number of Cr changes from a $+6$ in $\text{Cr}_2\text{O}_7^{2-}$ ion to a $+3$ in Cr^{3+} ion, a change of three units in the oxidation number of one Cr atom. There are two Cr atoms in each $\text{Cr}_2\text{O}_7^{2-}$ formula unit. Therefore, each $\text{Cr}_2\text{O}_7^{2-}$ ion is sufficient to produce a change in oxidation number of six units. One mole of $\text{Cr}_2\text{O}_7^{2-}$ ions (216 g) will produce 6 moles of oxidation number change. The equivalent weight of $\text{Cr}_2\text{O}_7^{2-}$ ion—that weight capable of producing 1 mole of oxidation number change—will be $\frac{1}{6}(216) = 36$ g. (We will symbolize this as $\text{Cr}_2\text{O}_7^{2-}/6$, where the formula stands for the gram formula weight of the substance.) Note that the gram equivalent weight of the $\text{Cr}_2\text{O}_7^{2-}$ ion is the same as its gram formula weight divided by the number of electrons lost per formula unit if the change in oxidation number is assumed to be caused by a loss of electrons. A good operational definition for the gram equivalent weight of any substance involved in an oxidation or reduction is given by the expression

$$\text{g equiv wt} = \frac{\text{g formula wt}}{\text{no. of electrons lost or gained per formula unit}}$$

Had we balanced this equation by the ion–electron method, the $\text{Cr}_2\text{O}_7^{2-}-\text{Cr}^{3+}$ half-reaction would have been

$$6e^- + 14\text{H}^+ + \text{Cr}_2\text{O}_7^{2-} \to 2\text{Cr}^{3+} + 7\text{H}_2\text{O}$$

The number of electrons per mole required to balance the half-reaction will be equal to the number of electrons lost or gained per formula unit.

EXAMPLE. Calculate the gram equivalent weight of those oxidizing and reducing agents used in the examples in Section 7–4.

SOLUTION. The gram equivalent weights will be determined by dividing the gram formula weight of the substance by n, where n is the number of electrons lost or gained per formula unit, or the number of electrons per molecule required to balance the half-reaction involving that substance. We need only refer back to the examples to obtain these values for n.

In the reaction of As_2S_5 and HNO_3, the products of the oxidation and reduction are H_2SO_4 and NO_2. For the -2 S in As_2S_5 to be oxidized to a $+6$ S in H_2SO_4 there must be a loss of $8e^-$ per S atom or a loss of $5 \times 8e^-$ per As_2S_5 formula unit.

$$\text{g equiv wt of } As_2S_5 = \frac{As_2S_5}{n} = \frac{As_2S_5}{40}$$

$$= \frac{310}{40} = 7.75 \text{ g equiv}^{-1}$$

(The g formula weight of As_2S_5 is 310 g.)

For the $+5$ in HNO_3 to be reduced to the $+4$ oxidation state in NO_2, there must be a gain of $1e^-$ per N atom or a gain of $1e^-$ per HNO_3 formula unit.

$$\text{g equiv wt of } HNO_3 = \frac{HNO_3}{1} = 63 \text{ g equiv}^{-1}$$

(The g formula weight of HNO_3 is 63 g.)

In the reaction $Fe^{2+} + Cr_2O_7^{2-} \rightarrow Fe^{3+} + Cr^{3+}$, for the Fe to undergo a change in oxidation number from $+2$ to $+3$ would require a loss of $1e^-$ per Fe atom or a loss of $1e^-$ per Fe^{2+} formula unit. For the $+6$ Cr in $Cr_2O_7^{2-}$ ion to be reduced to the $+3$ state in Cr^{3+} ion requires a gain of $3e^-$ per Cr atom or a gain of $2 \times 3 = 6e^-$ per $Cr_2O_7^{2-}$ formula unit.

$$\text{equiv wt of } Fe^{2+} \text{ ion} = \frac{Fe}{1} = 55.85 \text{ g equiv}^{-1}$$

(The g atomic wt of Fe is 55.85 g.)

$$\text{g equiv wt of } Cr_2O_7^{2-} \text{ ion} = \frac{Cr_2O_7^{2-}}{6}$$

$$= \frac{216}{6} = 36.0 \text{ g equiv}^{-1}$$

(The g formula wt of $Cr_2O_7^{2-}$ is 216 g.)

In the reaction $MnCl_2 + Br_2 \rightarrow MnO_2 + NaBr$, the Mn is oxidized from a $+2$ state in $MnCl_2$ to a $+4$ state in MnO_2. This requires a loss of $2e^-$ per $MnCl_2$ formula unit. The Br_2 is reduced from a 0 oxidation state to a -1 oxidation state in KBr; this represents a gain of $1e^-$ per Br atom or a gain of $2e^-$ per Br_2 formula unit.

$$\text{g equiv wt of } MnCl_2 = \frac{MnCl_2}{2} = \frac{126}{2} = 63.0 \text{ g equiv}^{-1}$$

$$\text{g equiv wt of } Br_2 = \frac{Br_2}{2} = \frac{160}{2} = 80.0 \text{ g equiv}^{-1}$$

(The g formula wts of $MnCl_2$ and Br_2 are 126 and 160, respectively.)

The remaining equivalent weights will be calculated by using the balanced half-reactions to determine the value for n.

The half-reactions involved in the reaction of Mn^{2+} and $S_2O_8^{2-}$ ions to produce $MnO_2(s)$ and SO_4^{2-} in acid solution are

$$S_2O_8^{2-} + 2e^- \rightarrow 2SO_4^{2-}$$
$$Mn^{2+} + 2H_2O \rightarrow MnO_2(s) + 4H^+ + 2e^-$$

$$\text{g equiv wt of } S_2O_8^{2-} = \frac{S_2O_8^{2-}}{2} = \frac{160}{2} = \textbf{80 g equiv}^{-1}$$

$$\text{g equiv wt of } Mn^{2+} = \frac{Mn^{2+}}{2} = \frac{55}{2} = \textbf{27.5 g equiv}^{-1}$$

(The formula weights of $S_2O_8^{2-}$ ion and Mn^{2+} ion are 160 and 55, respectively.)

The half-reactions involved in the reaction of $MnCl_2$ and Br_2 to produce $MnO_2(s)$ and $NaBr$ in basic solution are

$$Mn^{2+} + 2H_2O \rightarrow MnO_2(s) + 4H^+ + 2e^-$$
$$Br_2 + 2e^- \rightarrow 2Br^-$$

$$\text{g equiv wt of } MnCl_2 = \frac{MnCl_2}{2} = \frac{126}{2} = \textbf{63.0 g equiv}^{-1}$$

$$\text{g equiv wt of } Br_2 = \frac{Br_2}{2} = \frac{160}{2} = \textbf{80.0 g equiv}^{-1}$$

(Gram formula weights: $MnCl_2 = 126$, $Br_2 = 160$.)

The half-reactions involved in the disproportionation of Br_2 in basic solution to yield BrO_3^- and Br^- ions are

$$Br_2 + 6H_2O \rightarrow 2BrO_3^- + 12H^+ + 10e^-$$
$$Br_2 + 2e^- \rightarrow 2Br^-$$

Since Br_2 serves as both an oxidizing and reducing agent in the disproportionation, it has two equivalent weights. Br_2 is an oxidizing agent in this reaction by oxidizing some of the Br_2 present to BrO_3^- ions. In so doing, this Br_2 is reduced to Br^- ions. Some of the remaining Br_2 acts as a reducing agent, reducing Br_2 to Br^- ions; this Br_2 is oxidized to BrO_3^- ions in the process. The g equiv wt of Br_2 as an oxidizing agent is

$$\frac{Br_2}{2} = \frac{160}{2} = \textbf{80.0 g equiv}^{-1}$$

The g equiv wt of Br_2 as a reducing agent is

$$\frac{Br_2}{10} = \frac{160}{10} = \textbf{16.0 g equiv}^{-1}$$

[*Note:* In performing stoichiometry calculations we must remember that Br_2 serves as both the oxidizing and reducing agent. For example, it will require 2 equiv of Br_2 to produce 1 equiv of BrO_3^- ions; 1 equiv of Br_2 will oxidize 1 equiv of Br_2 to give 1 equiv of BrO_3^- (and 1 equiv of Br^-).]

The half-reactions for the reaction of $K_3Fe(CN)_6$ and $KMnO_4$ in acid solution to give $Fe(SO_4)_3$, $CO_2(g)$, HNO_3, and $MnSO_4$ are

$$Fe(CN)_6{}^{3-} + 30H_2O \rightarrow Fe^{3+} + 6CO_2(g) + 6NO_3{}^-$$
$$+ 60H^+ + 60e^-$$

$$MnO_4{}^- + 8H^+ + 5e^- \rightarrow Mn^{2+} + 4H_2O$$

$$\text{g equiv wt of } K_3Fe(CN)_6 = \frac{K_3Fe(CN)_6}{60}$$

$$= \frac{251}{60} = \textbf{4.2 g equiv}^{-1}$$

$$\text{g equiv wt of } KMnO_4 = \frac{KMnO_4}{5} = \frac{158}{5} = \textbf{31.6 g equiv}^{-1}$$

In Section 4–4, the relationship between the molar (M) and normal (N) concentration of an acid or base was shown to be $N = xM$, where x is the number of moles of protons accepted per mole of base or donated per mole of acid. Similarly, we can relate the normality and molarity of solutions of oxidizing and reducing agents to the expression $N = nM$, where n is the number of electrons transferred per formula unit.

The equivalent weight of a substance depends on the reaction in which it participates. Consequently, the equivalent weight and the normality concepts are useful only when the reaction is known.

EXAMPLE.   Sulfuric acid is a very versatile chemical reagent. Not only is it a strong diprotic acid, but it is a strong oxidizing agent as well. Depending on the reducing agent present and the reaction conditions, it may form a variety of products. The following is a list of the reactions of various substances with $18M$ H_2SO_4. Indicate the gram equivalent weight and the normal concentration of the H_2SO_4 in each solution.

(A) $H_2SO_4 + OH^- \rightarrow HSO_4{}^- + H_2O$
(B) $H_2SO_4 + 2OH^- \rightarrow SO_4{}^{2-} + 2H_2O$
(C) $H_2SO_4 + Cu \rightarrow SO_2 + Cu^{2+}$
(D) $H_2SO_4 + Zn \rightarrow H_2S + Zn^{2+}$

SOLUTION.   Reactions A and B are acid–base reactions. In A, H_2SO_4 acts as a monoprotic acid and donates 1 mole of protons per mole of H_2SO_4. Its equivalent weight is

$$\frac{H_2SO_4}{1} = \frac{98}{1} = \textbf{98 g equiv}^{-1}$$
$$N_{H_2SO_4} = xM = (1)(18) = 18N$$

In Reaction B, H_2SO_4 acts as a diprotic acid and donates 2 moles of protons per mole of acid. The equivalent weight of H_2SO_4 is

$$\frac{H_2SO_4}{2} = \frac{98}{2} = \textbf{49 g equiv}^{-1}$$
$$N_{H_2SO_4} = xM = (2)(18) = 36N$$

(C) $\overset{+6}{H_2SO_4} + Cu \rightarrow \overset{+4}{SO_2} + Cu^{2+}$

$+2e^-/atom$

$+2e^-/fu$

$$\text{equiv wt of } H_2SO_4 = \frac{H_2SO_4}{2} = \frac{98}{2} = 49 \text{ g equiv}^{-1}$$

$$\mathcal{N}_{H_2SO_4} = nM = (2)(18) = 36\mathcal{N}$$

(D) $\overset{+6}{H_2SO_4} + Zn \rightarrow \overset{-2}{H_2S} + Zn^{2+}$

$-8e^-/atom$

$-8e^-/fu$

$$\text{equiv wt of } H_2SO_4 = \frac{H_2SO_4}{8} = \frac{98}{8} = 12.2 \text{ g equiv}^{-1}$$

$$\mathcal{N}_{H_2SO_4} = nM = (8)(18) = 144\mathcal{N}$$

We can see from this example why it is a poor policy to express the concentration of reagents for general laboratory use in normality units. Normality is useful as a means of expressing concentration only in working problems.

As the balancing of equations for oxidation and reduction reactions is somewhat tedious, the equivalent weight concept is useful in performing stoichiometry calculations. This is true especially for computations related to redox titrations. At the end point of a redox titration, the equivalents of oxidant equal the equivalents of reductant.

In Section 7–5 of *Chemical Principles*, the milliequivalent (meq) is used in the calculations; there are 1000 meq in 1 equiv, or 0.001 equiv = 1 meq. There is no particular advantage in using this unit. All it does is to eliminate the need for converting the milliliters read on a burette to liters when using the relationship (liters$_A$) ($\mathcal{N}_A$) = (liters$_B$) ($\mathcal{N}_B$). As 1 ml = 10^{-3} liter, the product of (ml$_A$) ($\mathcal{N}_A$) will give a number 1000 times greater than the number of equivalents—the number of milliequivalents. Since meq$_A$ = meq$_B$, it follows that ml$_A\mathcal{N}_A$ = ml$_B\mathcal{N}_B$. When weights are involved, it becomes necessary to divide by 1000 when using milliequivalents (1 meq wt = equiv wt/1000), and there is no advantage gained in using meq units for these calculations. If the unit confuses you, do not use it; base all your calculations on equivalents as you have been doing.

The examples of titration calculations at the end of Section 7–5 in *Chemical Principles* are worked by using the equivalent weight concept. Balanced chemical equations are given for the reactions in the examples. This does not mean that it is necessary to balance the equations to do the problems. If the balanced equation is available, the calculations can be obtained easily by using the mole ratios, and there is no real advantage in using equivalent weights.

Redox
Titrations

277

EXAMPLE. A 35.50-ml portion of a solution containing I_2 is titrated with a solution of $0.100M$ $Na_2S_2O_3$, and 28.75 ml of the $Na_2S_2O_3$

solution are required to reach the end point. What is the molar concentration of the I_2 solution? The reaction is $I_2 + S_2O_3^{2-} \rightarrow I^- + S_4O_6^{2-}$. (Note that this equation is not balanced.)

SOLUTION. Determine the number of electrons transferred per formula unit from the unbalanced equation.

$$I_2 \qquad + \qquad S_2O_3^{2-} \qquad \rightarrow \quad I^- + S_4O_6^{2-}$$
$$0 \rightarrow -1 \qquad\qquad +2 \rightarrow +\tfrac{5}{2}$$
$$+1e^-/\text{I atom} \qquad -\tfrac{1}{2}e^-/\text{S atom}$$
$$+2e^-/\text{fu} \qquad 2(-\tfrac{1}{2}) = -1e^-/\text{fu}$$

Because there is 1 electron lost per formula unit of $S_2O_3^{2-}$, and there is 1 formula unit of $S_2O_3^{2-}$ in $Na_2S_2O_3$, the normality of the $0.100M$ $Na_2S_2O_3$ is

$$\mathcal{N}_{Na_2S_2O_3} = nM = (1)(0.100) = 0.100\mathcal{N}$$
$$\text{equiv } Na_2S_2O_3 = \text{equiv } I_2$$
$$V_{Na_2S_2O_3} \times \mathcal{N}_{Na_2S_2O_3} = V_{I_2} \times \mathcal{N}_{I_2}$$
$$(0.02875)(0.100) = (0.0355)(\mathcal{N}_{I_2})$$
$$\mathcal{N}_{I_2} = \frac{(0.02875)(0.100)}{(0.0355)} = 0.0810\mathcal{N}$$

Since there are two electrons gained per formula unit of I_2,

$$M_{I_2} = \frac{\mathcal{N}_{I_2}}{n} = \frac{0.0810}{2} = \mathbf{0.0405}M$$

To calculate the normality of the I_2 solution using milliequivalents, we do the following:

$$\text{meq}_{Na_2S_2O_3} = \text{meq}_{I_2}$$
$$\text{ml}_{Na_2S_2O_3} \times \mathcal{N}_{Na_2S_2O_3} = \text{ml}_{I_2} \times \mathcal{N}_{I_2}$$
$$(28.75)(0.100) = (35.5)(\mathcal{N}_{I_2})$$
$$\mathcal{N}_{I_2} = \frac{(28.75)(0.100)}{(35.5)} = 0.0810$$

EXAMPLE. Determine the concentration of a $KMnO_4$ solution. To do this, 0.2800 g of $Na_2C_2O_4$ are weighed, dissolved in dilute H_2SO_4, and titrated with the $KMnO_4$ solution. It takes 35.48 ml of the $KMnO_4$ solution to reach the end point. In the titration reaction, the $C_2O_4^{2-}$ ions from the $Na_2C_2O_4$ are oxidized to $CO_2(g)$ and the MnO_4^- ions in the $KMnO_4$ are reduced to Mn^{2+} ions. What is the normality of the $KMnO_4$ in this case? The molarity?

SOLUTION.

$$\overset{+3\ 2-}{C_2O_4} \rightarrow \overset{+4}{CO_2}(g)$$
$$-1e^-/\text{C atom}$$
$$-2(1)e^-/\text{fu}$$

Two electrons are lost per formula unit of $C_2O_4^{2-}$. There is one formula unit of $C_2O_4^{2-}$ in 1 mole of $Na_2C_2O_4$. Therefore, the equivalent weight of $Na_2C_2O_4$ in this reaction is

$$\frac{Na_2C_2O_4}{2} = \frac{134}{2} = 67.0 \text{ g equiv}^{-1}$$

$$\text{equiv } Na_2C_2O_4 = \text{equiv } KMnO_4$$

$$\frac{\text{g } Na_2C_2O_4}{\text{g } Na_2C_2O_4 \text{ equiv}^{-1}} = V_{KMnO_4} \times N_{KMnO_4}$$

$$\frac{0.2800 \text{ g } Na_2C_2O_4}{67.0 \text{ g } Na_2C_2O_4 \text{ equiv}^{-1}} = 0.3548 \, V_{KMnO_4} \times N_{KMnO_4}$$

$$N_{KMnO_4} = \frac{0.2800 \text{ equiv}}{(67.0)(0.3548) \text{ liters}} = \mathbf{0.118}N$$

$$\overset{+7}{Mn}O_4^- \to \overset{+2}{Mn}^{2+}$$

$$+5e^-/\text{Mn atom}$$

$$+5e^-/\text{fu}$$

$$M_{KMnO_4} = \frac{N_{KMnO_4}}{n} = \frac{0.118}{5} = \mathbf{0.0236}M$$

7–6 COVALENCY

Most of the topics discussed in this section of *Chemical Principles* have been covered in Section 7–1 of the study guide. However, there are a few additional items that should be mentioned here.

The fact that two elements can share one, two, or three pairs of electrons has been mentioned in Section 6–5. The compounds

$$\begin{array}{c} \text{H} \quad \text{H} \\ | \quad | \\ \text{H—C—C—H} \\ | \quad | \\ \text{H} \quad \text{H} \\ \text{ethane} \end{array} \qquad \begin{array}{c} \text{H} \quad \text{H} \\ | \quad | \\ \text{H—C=C—H} \\ \\ \text{ethylene} \end{array} \qquad \begin{array}{c} \text{H—C} \equiv \text{C—H} \\ \\ \text{acetylene} \end{array}$$

are examples of similar compounds that have single, double, and triple C—C bonds. Carbon monoxide, $:C:::O:$, and carbon dioxide, $:O::C::O:$, are common examples of triple and double C—O bonds. In Section 7–1, we saw that SO_2 and CS_2 contain double covalent bonds. Even as simple a compound as gaseous nitrogen, N_2, has a triple N—N bond, $:N:::N:$. (A line or two dots represent a pair of electrons.)

In addition to the structural isomers described in Section 7–1, *Chemical Principles* mentions another slightly different type of isomerism, stereoisomerism. Both structural isomers and stereoisomers are molecules that differ in the arrangement of their atoms. The distinction between these two classes of isomers is that the arrangements of the atoms in the structural isomers are such that different kinds of atoms are bonded together. (Compare the C—O—C bond in dimethyl ether to the C—O—H bond in ethyl alcohol, the two structural isomers shown

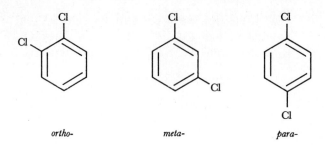

ortho-   meta-   para-

Figure 7–2. The three possible stereoisomers of dichlorobenzene: ortho-*dichlorobenzene,* meta-*dichlorobenzene, and* para-*dichlorobenzene. Each apex of the hexagonal rings represents a C atom; one H atom (not shown) is bonded to each C that is not bonded to Cl.*

in Section 7–1.) Stereoisomers have the same bonds between the same pairs of atoms; they differ only in the spatial arrangement of the bonds. For example, the three compounds *ortho*-dichlorobenzene, *meta*-dichlorobenzene, and *para*-dichlorobenzene, shown in Figure 7–2, are stereoisomers. There are the same number of C—C, C—H, and C—Cl bonds in the three compounds, but in the three stereoisomers the C—Cl and C—H bonds are arranged differently. The *cis-trans* isomerism discussed in Section 12–4 is a type of stereoisomerism.

7–7 COORDINATION NUMBER

This topic has been discussed in Section 7–1 of the study guide.

7–8 REACTIONS INVOLVING ACIDIC AND BASIC OXIDES

In Section 6–5, acidic oxides are defined as those oxides that react with water to produce H_3O^+ ions, and basic oxides are defined as those oxides that react with water to produce OH^- ions. It was stated that metal oxides are basic oxides and nonmetal oxides are acidic oxides.

A typical basic oxide is CaO (commonly referred to as quicklime). Its reaction with water can be represented by the equation

$$CaO(s) + H_2O \rightarrow Ca^{2+} + 2OH^-$$

The Ca^{2+} and OH^- ions are those to be expected from the dissociation of the hydroxide base, calcium hydroxide, $Ca(OH)_2$. In fact, the mixture of quicklime and water not only contains residual solid CaO and a solution of Ca^{2+} and OH^- ions, but some solid $Ca(OH)_2$ (slaked lime) is also present. Since the dissolution of $Ca(OH)_2$ in water produces Ca^{2+} and two OH^- ions in a 1/2 mole ratio we can consider this reaction as if the $CaO(s)$ and the H_2O first react to form $Ca(OH)_2$, followed by its dissociation into Ca^{2+} and OH^- ions:

$$CaO(s) + H_2O \rightarrow [Ca(OH)_2] \rightarrow Ca^{2+} + 2OH^-$$

Oxidation,
Coordination,
and
Covalence

280

Note also that the elements in the $Ca(OH)_2$ are those in $1CaO + 1H_2O$, that is, one Ca atom, two H atoms, and two O atoms. In other words, the base, which may be thought of as a possible intermediate in the reaction, can be determined by the addition of the elements of water to the oxide and rearranging the atoms to formulate the hydroxide. One might say that the metal oxide is the anhydride of the hydroxide base. Note also that this is not a redox reaction; the oxidation number of the metal remains the same.

EXAMPLE.   Formulate the reaction of Na_2O with H_2O.

SOLUTION.   Reason as follows: Na_2O is a metal oxide. (Na is in Group IA of the periodic table.) Adding H_2O to Na_2O gives

$$Na_2O + H_2O \rightarrow [Na_2OH_2O]$$

Formulating the hypothetical compound in the brackets as an hydroxide base gives $Na_2(OH)_2$. Reducing the subscripts to the smallest whole number ratio yields NaOH as a possible hydroxide base intermediate. NaOH dissociates to give $Na^+ + OH^-$ ions in a 1/1 ratio. Therefore, the equation for the reaction of Na_2O with water is

$$Na_2O(s) + H_2O \rightarrow 2Na^+ + 2OH^-$$

The same procedure can be followed when dealing with nonmetal oxides. These oxides can be considered as anhydrides of acids that have the nonmetal atom in the same oxidation state as it is in the oxide.

In almost all acids that contain oxygen atoms (the so-called oxyacids), the acidic hydrogen atoms are bonded to oxygen atoms. (An acidic hydrogen atom is an H atom in an acid that reacts with water, thereby forming an hydronium ion.) Like NaOH, KOH, and so forth, the oxyacids are hydroxides. The difference in the two types of hydroxides is that, when they react with water, the basic hydroxides dissociate as cations and OH^- ions, whereas the acidic hydroxides dissociate so that the H atom in the OH group forms a H_3O^+ ion with water and the O remains with the nonmetal in the anion. Metal hydroxides in which the oxidation state of the metal atom is $+4$ or greater tend to act as acids.

EXAMPLE.   Write the equation for the reaction of SO_3 with H_2O.

SOLUTION.   Sulfur, in Group VIA in the periodic table, is a nonmetal; therefore, SO_3 is an acidic oxide. Add H_2O to the SO_3 and formulate the acid:

$$SO_3 + H_2O = [H_2OSO_3] = SO_2(OH)_2 = H_2SO_4$$

The acid is H_2SO_4, which dissociates completely to $2H^+ + SO_4{}^{2-}$. Therefore, the reaction of SO_3 and water produces H^+ and $SO_4{}^{2-}$ in a 2/1 ratio:

$$SO_3 + H_2O \rightarrow 2H^+ + SO_4^{2-}$$

Since H^+ ions are solvated in aqueous solution and are written more properly as hydronium ions, H_3O^+, the equation is better written

$$SO_3 + 3H_2O \rightarrow 2H_3O^+ + SO_4^{2-}$$

Many oxides react with aqueous solutions of acids or bases, and anhydrous oxides may react with one another when heated. We can predict the products of many of these reactions. Consider the products of the reaction between aqueous NaOH (a hydroxide base) and SO_3 (an acidic oxide). Formulate the expected products for the reaction in aqueous solution. The SO_3 is the anhydride of H_2SO_4. When aqueous solutions of NaOH and H_2SO_4 are combined, the products are the salt, Na_2SO_4, and water. Therefore, when the acidic oxide SO_3 is placed in an aqueous solution of NaOH, it can be presumed to react first with the water to form the acid, H_2SO_4; then the acid reacts with the NaOH to form the salt and water. The predicted reaction, which has been confirmed by experiment, is

$$2NaOH + SO_3 \rightarrow Na_2SO_4 + H_2O$$

EXAMPLE. Write balanced equations for the following reactions:

(A) $ZnO(s) + HNO_3(aq)$
(B) $BaO(s) + SO_3(g)$
(C) $CaO(s) + CO_2(g)$

SOLUTION.
(a) ZnO is a basic oxide (Zn is in Group IIB in the periodic table.) Formulate its hydroxide base by adding water:

$$ZnO + H_2O = [ZnOH_2O] = Zn(OH)_2$$

In aqueous solution, $Zn(OH)_2 + 2HNO_3 \rightarrow Zn(NO_3)_2 + 2H_2O$. Therefore,

$$ZnO(s) + HNO_3(aq) \rightarrow Zn(NO_3)_2 + H_2O$$

(b) BaO is a basic oxide. (Ba is in Group IIA in the periodic table.) Formulate its hydroxide base by adding water:

$$BaO + H_2O = [BaOH_2O] = Ba(OH)_2$$

SO_3 is an acidic oxide. (S is in Group VIA in the periodic table.) Formulate its acid by adding water:

$$SO_3 + H_2O = [SO_3H_2O] = H_2SO_4$$

In aqueous solution,

$$Ba(OH)_2 + H_2SO_4 \rightarrow BaSO_4 + 2H_2O$$

In the absence of H atoms there would be no H_2O formed; therefore, the predicted reaction of the oxides is

$$BaO + SO_3 \rightarrow BaSO_4$$

(c) CaO is a basic oxide. (Ca is in Group IIA in the periodic table.) Formulate its hydroxide base by adding H_2O:

$$CaO + H_2O = [CaOH_2O] = Ca(OH)_2$$

CO_2 is an acidic oxide. (Carbon is in Group IVA in the periodic table.) Formulate its acid by adding H_2O:

$$CO_2 + H_2O = [CO_2H_2O] = H_2CO_3$$

In aqueous solution,

$$Ca(OH)_2 + H_2CO_3 \rightarrow CaCO_3 + 2H_2O$$

In the absence of H atoms, there would be no water formed; therefore, the predicted reaction of the oxides is

$$CaO(s) + CO_2(g) \rightarrow CaCO_3(s)$$

APPENDIXES

APPENDIX 1 LOGARITHMS

	0	1	2	3	4	5	6	7	8	9
10	0000	0043	0086	0128	0170	0212	0253	0294	0334	0374
11	0414	0453	0492	0531	0569	0607	0645	0682	0719	0755
12	0792	0828	0864	0899	0934	0969	1004	1038	1072	1106
13	1139	1173	1206	1239	1271	1303	1335	1367	1399	1430
14	1461	1492	1523	1553	1584	1614	1644	1673	1703	1732
15	1761	1790	1818	1847	1875	1903	1931	1959	1987	2014
16	2041	2068	2095	2122	2148	2175	2201	2227	2253	2279
17	2304	2330	2355	2380	2405	2430	2455	2480	2504	2529
18	2553	2577	2601	2625	2648	2672	2695	2718	2742	2765
19	2788	2810	2833	2856	2878	2900	2923	2945	2967	2989
20	3010	3032	3054	3075	3096	3118	3139	3160	3181	3201
21	3222	3243	3263	3284	3304	3324	3345	3365	3385	3404
22	3424	3444	3464	3483	3502	3522	3541	3560	3579	3598
23	3617	3636	3655	3674	3692	3711	3729	3747	3766	3784
24	3802	3820	3838	3856	3874	3892	3909	3927	3945	3962
25	3979	3997	4014	4031	4048	4065	4082	4099	4116	4133
26	4150	4166	4183	4200	4216	4232	4249	4265	4281	4298
27	4314	4330	4346	4362	4378	4393	4409	4425	4440	4456
28	4472	4487	4502	4518	4533	4548	4564	4579	4594	4609
29	4624	4639	4654	4669	4683	4698	4713	4728	4742	4757
30	4771	4786	4800	4814	4829	4843	4857	4871	4886	4900
31	4914	4928	4942	4955	4969	4983	4997	5011	5024	5038
32	5051	5065	5079	5092	5105	5119	5132	5145	5159	5172
33	5185	5198	5211	5224	5237	5250	5263	5276	5289	5302
34	5315	5328	5340	5353	5366	5378	5391	5403	5416	5428
35	5441	5453	5465	5478	5490	5502	5514	5527	5539	5551
36	5563	5575	5587	5599	5611	5623	5635	5647	5658	5670
37	5682	5694	5705	5717	5729	5740	5752	5763	5775	5786
38	5798	5809	5821	5832	5843	5855	5866	5877	5888	5899
39	5911	5922	5933	5944	5955	5966	5977	5988	5999	6010
40	6021	6031	6042	6053	6064	6075	6085	6096	6107	6117
41	6128	6138	6149	6160	6170	6180	6191	6201	6212	6222
42	6232	6243	6253	6263	6274	6284	6294	6304	6314	6325
43	6335	6345	6355	6365	6375	6385	6395	6405	6415	6425
44	6435	6444	6454	6464	6474	6484	6493	6503	6513	6522
45	6532	6542	6551	6561	6571	6580	6590	6599	6609	6618
46	6628	6637	6646	6656	6665	6675	6684	6693	6702	6712
47	6721	6730	6739	6749	6758	6767	6776	6785	6794	6803
48	6812	6821	6830	6839	6848	6857	6866	6875	6884	6893
49	6902	6911	6920	6928	6937	6946	6955	6964	6972	6981
50	6990	6998	7007	7016	7024	7033	7042	7050	7059	7067
51	7076	7084	7093	7101	7110	7118	7126	7135	7143	7152
52	7160	7168	7177	7185	7193	7202	7210	7218	7226	7235
53	7243	7251	7259	7267	7275	7284	7292	7300	7308	7316
54	7324	7332	7340	7348	7356	7364	7372	7380	7388	7396

	0	1	2	3	4	5	6	7	8	9
55	7404	7412	7419	7427	7435	7443	7451	7459	7466	7474
56	7482	7490	7497	7505	7513	7520	7528	7536	7543	7551
57	7559	7566	7574	7582	7589	7597	7604	7612	7619	7627
58	7634	7642	7649	7657	7664	7672	7679	7686	7694	7701
59	7709	7716	7723	7731	7738	7745	7752	7760	7767	7774
60	7782	7789	7796	7803	7810	7818	7825	7832	7839	7846
61	7853	7860	7868	7875	7882	7889	7896	7903	7910	7917
62	7924	7931	7938	7945	7952	7959	7966	7973	7980	7987
63	7993	8000	8007	8014	8021	8028	8035	8041	8048	8055
64	8062	8069	8075	8082	8089	8096	8102	8109	8116	8122
65	8129	8136	8142	8149	8156	8162	8169	8176	8182	8189
66	8195	8202	8209	8215	8222	8228	8235	8241	8248	8254
67	8261	8267	8274	8280	8287	8293	8299	8306	8312	8319
68	8325	8331	8338	8344	8351	8357	8363	8370	8376	8382
69	8388	8395	8401	8407	8414	8420	8426	8432	8439	8445
70	8451	8457	8463	8470	8476	8482	8488	8494	8500	8506
71	8513	8519	8525	8531	8537	8543	8549	8555	8561	8567
72	8573	8579	8585	8591	8597	8603	8609	8615	8621	8627
73	8633	8639	8645	8651	8657	8663	8669	8675	8681	8686
74	8692	8698	8704	8710	8716	8722	8727	8733	8739	8745
75	8751	8756	8762	8768	8774	8779	8785	8791	8797	8802
76	8808	8814	8820	8825	8831	8837	8842	8848	8854	8859
77	8865	8871	8876	8882	8887	8893	8899	8904	8910	8915
78	8921	8927	8932	8938	8943	8949	8954	8960	8965	8971
79	8976	8982	8987	8993	8998	9004	9009	9015	9020	9025
80	9031	9036	9042	9047	9053	9058	9063	9069	9074	9079
81	9085	9090	9096	9101	9106	9112	9117	9122	9128	9133
82	9138	9143	9149	9154	9159	9165	9170	9175	9180	9186
83	9191	9196	9201	9206	9212	9217	9222	9227	9232	9238
84	9243	9248	9253	9258	9263	9269	9274	9279	9284	9289
85	9294	9299	9304	9309	9315	9320	9325	9330	9335	9340
86	9345	9350	9355	9360	9365	9370	9375	9380	9385	9390
87	9395	9400	9405	9410	9415	9420	9425	9430	9435	9440
88	9445	9450	9455	9460	9465	9469	9474	9479	9484	9489
89	9494	9499	9504	9509	9513	9518	9523	9528	9533	9538
90	9542	9547	9552	9557	9562	9566	9571	9576	9581	9586
91	9590	9595	9600	9605	9609	9614	9619	9624	9628	9633
92	9638	9643	9647	9652	9657	9661	9666	9671	9675	9680
93	9685	9689	9694	9699	9703	9708	9713	9717	9722	9727
94	9731	9736	9741	9745	9750	9754	9759	9763	9768	9773
95	9777	9782	9786	9791	9795	9800	9805	9809	9814	9818
96	9823	9827	9832	9836	9841	9845	9850	9854	9859	9863
97	9868	9872	9877	9881	9886	9890	9894	9899	9903	9908
98	9912	9917	9921	9926	9930	9934	9939	9943	9948	9952
99	9956	9961	9965	9969	9974	9978	9983	9987	9991	9996

APPENDIX 2   THE GRAPH AND THE EQUATION
FOR A STRAIGHT LINE

Consider the simple equation $y = x$. To plot
this equation, assign a value to x, substitute this value of x into the equation, and
solve for y. (Since $y = x$, both values are the
same.) Then count x units along the abscissa
of the graph paper and y units along the
ordinate and place a point. (The x and y
values that locate the point are called its
coordinates.) This process is repeated for other
values of x, the corresponding values for y
are obtained, and the series of points are
plotted. The graph is completed by drawing
a line through the points. However, with a
little reflection, you can see that it is possible
to draw the line directly without calculating
the points.

Refer to Figure A–1. Any point x and its
corresponding y coordinate will lie at one
corner of a rectangle that has vertical sides
of a length equal to y units and horizontal
sides of a length equal to x units. In Figure
A–1, the dotted lines and the axes indicate
a series of rectangles, each determined by
the different x and y coordinates that lie on
the curve $y = x$. Note that the curve itself
lies along the diagonal of the rectangle.

Now we return to the equation $y = x$
and suppose that we have not yet plotted it
point by point. Since both x and y are equal
in this equation, the following observations

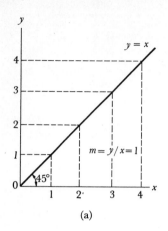
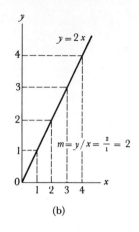
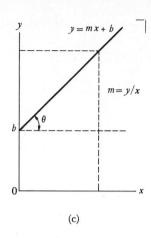

(a) (b) (c)

*Figure A–1. Graphs of the linear equation y = mx + b. (a) m = 1, b = 0.
(b) m = 2, b = 0. (c) m = y/x, b = b.*

can be made. If we were to plot this equation, the rectangles determined by the x and y coordinates obtained from this equation would be squares; that is, the sides of the rectangles formed from the axes and the coordinates are equal. The curve will be the straight line that is the diagonal of the square. Since simple geometry shows that the diagonal of a square bisects the angles, the angle at which the curve will intersect the x axis (one of the sides of the square) will be 45°. This angle determines the inclination or *slope* of the line.

The slope of a hill indicates how much higher (the y direction on the graph) one travels while proceeding forward (the x direction on the graph). The slope is measured by comparing the height obtained (y) relative to the horizontal distance traveled (x). Since $y = x$, the slope of this curve is $1: y/x = 1$. If the angle that the curve makes with the x axis is greater than 45° [Figure A–1(b)], the slope of the curve is steeper, and $y/x > 1$.

Consider the equation $y = 2x$. For every value of x, the corresponding value for y will be twice as large. The points will generate rectangles with their heights (y) larger than their bases (x). The curve that we would obtain by plotting this equation will again be the diagonal of these rectangles. The slope is $y/x = 2$. For the equation $y = 0.5x$, rectangles having heights one half the length of their bases will result, and the curve will be a straight line having a slope $y/x = 0.5$. In general, the plot of any equation having the form $y = mx$, in which m is constant, will give a straight line that has a slope equal to m. Since, when $x = 0, y = mx = m(0) = 0$, the line will pass through the origin of the graph. Therefore, when we recognize an equation in this form, we can draw its graph merely by constructing a straight line that has a slope of m and passes through the origin. (If you have had any trigonometry, you should recognize that m is the tangent of the angle that the straight line makes with the x axis.)

**The Graph
and the
Equation
for a
Straight Line**

Better yet, it is necessary only to substitute a single value for x into the equation and to compute y to determine one point on the line. This point and the origin are the only two points needed to construct the straight line representing the equation. Thus, we see that the plot of the equation $y = mx$ can be obtained rapidly without plotting the point-by-point solutions to the equation.

What if the plot of an equation is a straight line that does not pass through the origin but intersects the y axis at some point b, as is shown in Figure A–1(c)? This means that when $x = 0$, y will have the value b. This value for y is called the y intercept. Such an equation will have the general form $y = mx + b$, where, as before, m is the slope. It is relatively easy to draw the line for an equation of this form by using the point b units up on the y axis as the first point for the line. To determine the second point needed to draw the line, you can use a protractor to measure the angle, θ, that will give a slope m [Figure A–1(c)]. (The angle θ is an angle that has a tangent equal to m). Another method to determine the second point is to calculate a point from the equation and then draw the straight line from b on the y axis through the second point.

A scientist wishes to interpret his experimental data in terms of a statement or law that describes the behavior of the system under study. The most convenient way to do this is to write the statement in the form of a mathematical expression. Examples of such expressions are Boyle's law, $PV = k$; Charles' law, $V = kT$; and the ideal gas law, $PV = nRT$. When all that is available are experimental data, often it is not easy to see the relationships that can exist between the numbers. One approach to this problem that is frequently taken by scientists is to plot the experimental data in different forms. For example, Boyle plotted P versus V, V versus $1/P$, log V versus log P, and so on in hopes that the shape of the curve would be such that he could recognize the mathematical equation that represented the curve.

One generally seeks a linear representation of data. There are two reasons for this. First, the equation for a straight line is very simple, as we have shown. Second, experimental data are not obtained without some degree of error, and it is much easier to recognize that a plot of irregular data shows a linear trend than it is to ascertain the nature of the trend if it is nonlinear.

Boyle obtained a straight line when he plotted P on the ordinate (the y axis) and $1/V$ on the abscissa (the x axis). When the line is extrapolated, it passes through the origin. As we have shown, the equation for such a line is $y = mx$. Substituting $1/V$ for x and P for y gives $P = m(1/V)$, in which m, the slope, depends on the amount of gas used and the temperature of the measurements. From such a plot, Boyle could evaluate m (reported as k, a constant) by measuring the slope of the line on the graph. The resulting expression, now known as Boyle's law, generally is rearranged to read $PV = k$ (n and T remain constant).

The Graph
and the
Equation
for a
Straight Line

291

APPENDIX 3 EXPRESSING VECTORS IN TERMS OF THEIR COMPONENTS

EXPRESSING A VECTOR IN TWO DIMENSIONS IN TERMS OF ITS COMPONENTS

From the theorem of Pythagoras, $\bar{\mathbf{c}}^2 = \bar{x}^2 + \bar{y}^2$, in which $\bar{x}$ and $\bar{y}$ are the components of the vector $\bar{\mathbf{c}}$ in the x and y directions, respectively [see Figure A–2(a)].

EXPRESSING A VECTOR IN THREE DIMENSIONS IN TERMS OF ITS COMPONENTS

Consider the vector $\bar{\mathbf{c}}$ lying in the three-dimensional Cartesian coordinate system with axes x, y, and z [Figure A–2(b)]. The components $\bar{x}$, $\bar{y}$, and $\bar{z}$ are obtained by dropping perpendiculars from the tip of the vector to the x, y, and z axes. In the xy

Figure A–2

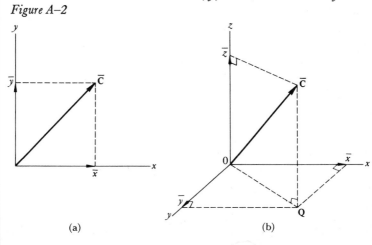

(a)　　　　　　　　　　　　(b)

plane, note that $\overline{OQ}$ is the hypotenuse of a right triangle having sides equal to x and y. Therefore,

$$\overline{OQ}^2 = \bar{x}^2 + \bar{y}^2$$

The line dropped from the tip of the vector $\bar{c}$, perpendicular to the xy plane, will be of a length equal to $\bar{z}$.

$\overline{OQ}$ is also a side of a right triangle that has $\bar{z}$ as a side and $\bar{c}$ as the hypotenuse.

$$\bar{c}^2 = \overline{OQ}^2 + \bar{z}^2 = \bar{x}^2 + \bar{y}^2 + \bar{z}^2$$

APPENDIX 4 SELF-EVALUATION QUIZZES

The true–false questions in this appendix should assist you in evaluating your understanding of some of the more important concepts discussed in *Chemical Principles*. Most of these concepts have received elaboration in this study guide. The questions are grouped together according to the chapters in *Chemical Principles* to which they apply. After you have studied a chapter thoroughly and have read the study guide to enforce your understanding of the material, you should answer the self-evaluation questions related to that chapter.

The answers to the questions in these self-evaluation quizzes are given in Appendix 5. If you do not answer a question correctly, your grasp of the principles related to the question is somewhat uncertain. Return to *Chemical Principles* and the study guide to see where you have gone astray. You may even find it wise to resort to additional assistance such as Lassila's *Programed Reviews of Chemical Principles*.

CHAPTER 1

1 The atomic number indicates the number of electrons associated with a neutral atom.

2 The isotope of tin, which has a mass of 118 amu, contains 68 neutrons in its nucleus.

3   The mass of the proton can be determined by taking half the difference between the atomic mass of the He atom and the atomic masses of two electrons and two neutrons.

4   Suppose that the hypothetical element "isone" consists of only two isotopes. In naturally occurring isone, 25% by weight is the isotope with a mass of 44 amu and 75% is the isotope of mass 40 amu. The atomic weight of isone will be 41 amu.

5   The same number of atoms of helium are in 4.0 g He as there are atoms of oxygen in 16 g of O_2.

6   The molecular weight of $C_6H_4(CO_2H)_2$ is 121 amu.

7   There are 18 atoms of hydrogen in 1 mole of CH_3Cl.

8   In forming C_8H_{16}, 0.5 g of hydrogen reacts with 3 g of carbon.

9   When the chemical equation

$$C_6H_5OH + O_2 \rightarrow CO_2 + H_2O$$

is properly balanced, the sum of the coefficients will be 17.

10 There are 3×10^{23} atoms of oxygen in 82 g of H_2SO_3.

11 Thirty-five and one half grams of chlorine and 25 g of arsenic are combined with 1 g of hydrogen in the compounds hydrogen chloride and arsine, respectively. In arsenic(III) chloride, the ratio by weight of arsenic combined with chlorine is 25 to 35.5. This is an example of Richter's law of equivalent proportions.

12 The balanced chemical reaction for the formation of PCl_3 gas from phosphorus vapors and chlorine gas is

$$P_4(g) + 6Cl_2(g) \rightarrow 4PCl_3(g)$$

Four liters of P_4 vapor will react with 6 liters of Cl_2 gas.

13 At 0°C and 1 atm pressure, the density of nitrogen gas (N_2) is 1.25 g liter^{-1}. Avogadro has shown that the gram molecular weight of a gas is proportional to its density. At 0°C and 1 atm, the proportionality constant is 11.2 liter mole^{-1}.

14 An oxide of sulfur is 50% by weight sulfur and 50% by weight oxygen. Its simplest formula is SO.

15 The simplest formula for a compound is CH_2Cl. From measurements of its density as a gas, its molecular weight is approximately 100. The molecular formula for this compound is $C_3H_6Cl_3$.

16 The approximate atomic weight of a metal that has a specific heat of 0.02 cal g^{-1}°C^{-1} is 60.

17 Specific heat measurements indicate that the approximate atomic weight of the metal Q is 50. Analysis of an oxide of the metal

shows that 1.5 g of Q are combined with 1.00 g of O. The simplest formula for this oxide is Q_2O.

18 The combining capacity of phosphorus (P) in PH_3 is 3. The combining weight of P is 10.3.

19 To determine the molecular formula for a compound, both the elemental composition by weight and the molecular weight are required.

20 Cannizzaro's determination of accurate atomic weights required application of Avogadro's hypothesis about gas densities.

CHAPTER 2

1 The volume occupied by 0.5 mole of oxygen (O_2) will be the same as the volume occupied by 1 mole of helium (He) at the same temperature and pressure.

2 A gas that exerts a pressure sufficient to support a column of mercury 1 mm high has a pressure of 1 torr.

3 Two 1-liter glass bulbs are separated by a valve. One bulb contains air at 0.5 atm pressure; the other bulb contains a vacuum. The valve connecting the bulbs is opened and air is allowed to fill both bulbs. The pressure exerted by the air, now in both bulbs, measures 1 atm.

4 A given quantity of gas is heated from 20°C to 40°C at a constant pressure. The gas will expand to twice its original volume.

5 At 1 atm and 27°C, 2.00 g of a gas occupy 12 liters. The volume occupied by this amount of gas at 227°C and 4 atm pressure can be calculated from the expression

$$V = (12) \times \left(\frac{1}{4}\right) \times \left(\frac{500}{300}\right)$$

6 Three grams of a gas occupy 7.60 liters at 8.20 mm pressure and 27°C. The gas has a molecular weight of 30.

In answering Questions 7 through 10, consider two flasks (A and B) of equal volume. Flask A contains nitrogen, and flask B contains the same weight of oxygen. Both gases are at the same temperature.

7 Each flask contains the same number of molecules of gas.

8 The average kinetic energy of the nitrogen molecules in flask A will be the same as the average kinetic energy of the oxygen molecules in flask B.

9 The average speed of the nitrogen molecules in flask A is greater than the average speed of the oxygen molecules in flask B.

10 The pressure of the nitrogen in flask A is larger than the pressure of the oxygen in flask B.

11 A thermometer has been likened to a speedometer for molecules because it measures the temperature of a gas, and the temperature of a gas is a measure of the average velocity of its molecules.

12 A molecule's "mean free path" means the distance a molecule travels between two successive collisions.

13 A container holds 2 moles of nitrogen and 3 moles of helium. The pressure exerted by the two gases is 1 atm. The pressure exerted by the nitrogen in the container is $\frac{2}{3}$ atm.

14 Five liters of oxygen are collected by the displacement of water from an inverted bottle such as the one in Figure 2-13 in *Chemical Principles*. The water level in the bottle is adjusted to be the same as the water level outside the bottle. The barometric pressure is 760 torr. The pressure exerted by the oxygen collected in the bottle is 760 torr.

15 The density of a gas at standard conditions is 1.5 g liter^{-1}. The molecular weight of the gas is 33.6.

16 A real gas will have a pressure that is equal to or less than that of the same amount of an ideal gas at the same temperature.

17 In the van der Waals equation of state for a real gas, a term is added to the volume to account for the volume occupied by the gas molecules.

18 Ideal gas behavior is more likely to be observed for gases at high pressures and high temperatures than for gases at low pressures and high temperatures.

19 The compressibility factor, PV/RT, is unity for 1 mole of an ideal gas.

20 Consider two containers of equal volume containing gases at the same temperature. Each container is connected to a manometer. One container registers a pressure of 2 atm; the other container registers a pressure of 4 atm. When the gas in the first container is forced into the second container, the pressure in the second container will rise to 6 atm.

21 The equilibrium vapor pressure of a gas is independent of the amount of gas and the size of the container.

CHAPTER 3

1 Five grams of a metal are deposited in 5 min when a current of 5 A (A is the accepted symbol for amperes) is passed through a

solution containing the metal ion. Ten grams of the metal can be deposited in the same length of time if the current is doubled.

2 One faraday is the quantity of electricity carried by a current of 9.65 A in 10^4 min.

3 In the electrolysis of molten NaBr, the reaction that takes place at the cathode in the electrolysis cell is

$$2Br^- \rightarrow Br_2(l) + 2e^-$$

4 In an electrolysis cell, cations migrate to the cathode and are reduced; anions migrate to the anode and are oxidized.

5 Oxidation is a process in which charged ions give up electrons, and reduction is a process in which charged ions accept electrons.

6 In the electrolysis of a metal salt solution, 3 $\mathcal{F}$ of electricity are required to deposit 60 g of the metal. The combining weight of the metal is 30 g.

7 A current of 482 A will transfer 1.2×10^{23} electrons in 100 sec.

8 Carbon has an oxidation number of $+1$ in sucrose, $C_{12}H_{22}O_{11}$.

9 The heat evolved when 1 mole of NaOH neutralizes 1 mole of HCl is 13,600 cal. Because the same reaction, $H^+ + OH^- \rightarrow H_2O$, is involved, the heat evolved when 1 mole of NaOH reacts with H_3PO_4 is also 13,600 cal.

10 The freezing point of a solution containing 0.5 mole of a non-electroyte dissolved in 1 kg of benzene is 78.80°C. The freezing point of pure benzene is 80.1°C. We expect a solution containing 1.0 mole of the nonelectrolyte in 0.5 kg of benzene to be 74.9°C.

11 Because the mole number of the salt $K_3Fe(CN)_6$ is 4, a possible ionization for this salt is

$$K_3Fe(CN)_6 \rightarrow 3K^+ + Fe(CN)_6^{3-}$$

12 The weak electrolyte H_2A dissociates according to the equation $H_2A \rightarrow 2H^+ + A^-$. The i number for this compound is given by the expression $(C_o + C_i)/C_o$, in which C_o is the original concentration of H_2A before dissociation occurs, and C_i is the concentration of H^+ formed by the dissociation of H_2A.

13 The percent dissociation for the weak electrolyte H_2A, in Question 12, is given by the expression

$$\text{Percent dissociation} = \frac{100(i-1)}{2}$$

14 Gas-discharge tubes were used to characterize electrons, protons, and neutrons.

15 When the three isotopes of neon, ^{20}Ne, ^{21}Ne, and ^{22}Ne, are ionized and passed through the magnetic field in a mass spectrograph,

the positive $^{20}Ne^+$ ions will be deflected more than the positive $^{22}Ne^+$ ions.

16 Ions occur in two types of solids: metals and salts.

17 The hexagonal close packed (hcp), face-centered cubic (fcc), and body-centered cubic (bcc) arrangements of equal-sized spheres represent closest packing.

18 NaCl can be thought of as a close packed arrangement of Cl^- ions with Na^+ ions occupying all the octahedral holes.

19 There are five atoms in a body-centered cubic unit cell.

20 One need only measure the distance between a cation and anion in a crystal to be able to calculate Avogadro's number.

CHAPTER 4

1 The empirical formula of a compound may give the number of each kind of atom in a molecule of a substance.

2 There are 5 atoms in 1 mole of $POCl_3$.

3 The molecular formula A_3B_2C indicates there there are 3 moles of A atoms, 2 moles of B atoms, and 1 mole of C atoms in 1 mole of A_3B_2C.

4 The atomic weights of the hypothetical elements M and A are 20 and 10, respectively. When M combines with A to form a certain compound, 0.4 g of M reacts with 0.6 g of A. The empirical formula for this compound is M_2A_3.

5 An amount of 11.2 g of a gas that has an empirical formula CH_2 occupies 8.20 liters at 1 atm and 500°K. The molecular formula for this gas is C_3H_6.

6 $MnO_4^- + 7H_2O_2 + 6H^+ \rightarrow Mn^{2+} + 4O_2 + 10H_2O$ is a balanced chemical equation.

Consider the following reaction in answering Questions 7 through 10:

$$PH_3(g) + 4N_2O(g) \rightarrow H_3PO_4(l) + 4N_2(g)$$

7 An amount of 0.20 mole of H_3PO_4 can be produced from the reaction of 6.8 g of PH_3.

8 To produce 0.20 mole of H_3PO_4, 35 g of N_2O are needed.

9 When 0.5 mole of PH_3 reacts with N_2O, 11.2 liters of N_2 gas (measured at STP) will be produced.

10 A vessel contains 8.2 liters of PH_3 at 1 atm and 500°K. Sufficient N_2O is introduced into the vessel to react with all the PH_3 present. About 20 g of H_3PO_4 are produced.

In Questions 11, 12, and 13 use as atomic weights A = 10, B = 20, and C = 30.

11   If we start with 6×10^{23} atoms of A and 10 g of B, $\frac{3}{2}$ moles of C atoms are required to form the compound A_2BC_3.

12   When 1 mole of A, 10 g of B, and 3 g of C react, $\frac{1}{2}$ mole of A_2BC_3 is formed.

13   When 5.0 g of A, 10 g of B, and 15 g of C react, 65 g of A_2BC_3 are formed.

14   $4NH_3 + 7O_2 \rightarrow 4NO_2 + 6H_2O$. When 1.7 g of NH_3 and 3.2 g of O_2 are mixed under conditions such that the preceding reaction takes place, 4.6 g of NO_2 will form.

15   The molar and molal concentrations of very dilute solutions are similar.

16   A solution containing 4.9 g of H_2SO_4 in 250 ml is $0.2M$.

17   A solution containing 430 g of acetic acid (CH_3CO_2H) per liter is $7.16m$.

18   To make 20 ml of a $2M$ HCl solution, we must add 6.7 ml of $6M$ HCl to 13.4 ml of H_2O. Assume that no volume change occurs upon mixing.

19   A $0.1M$ solution of H_3AsO_4 is $0.3N$.

20   In a titration with $2N$ H_2SO_4, 25.0 ml of the acid are required to neutralize 30.00 ml of a NaOH solution. The NaOH solution is $1.67M$.

21   A 7.4-g sample of $Ca(OH)_2$ (formula weight = 74) is completely neutralized by 100 ml of $2.0M$ HCl.

22   From the enthalpies for the reactions

$$CaO(s) + CO_2(g) \rightarrow CaCO_3(s) \qquad \Delta H^0 = -38 \text{ kcal mole}^{-1}$$

and

$$CaO(s) + H_2O(l) \rightarrow Ca(OH)_2(s) \qquad \Delta H^0 = -16 \text{ kcal mole}^{-1}$$

one can calculate that the standard enthalpy change associated with the reaction

$$Ca(OH)_2(s) + CO_2(g) \rightarrow CaCO_3(s) + H_2O(l)$$

is -22 kcal mole^{-1}.

23   Knowledge of the standard enthalpies of formation for $CO_2(g)$ (-94 kcal mole^{-1}), $H_2O(l)$ (-68 kcal mole^{-1}), and hexane, $C_6H_{14}(l)$ (-40 kcal mole^{-1}) permits us to calculate that the heat of combustion of hexane is 1000 kcal mole^{-1}.

Unless it is stated otherwise, one should assume temperatures are 25°C and solutions are aqueous solutions, in evaluating these quiz items.

1   One may synthesize $HCl(g)$ by the following light-catalyzed reaction:

$$H_2(g) + Cl_2(g) \rightleftarrows 2HCl(g)$$

The rate of formation of $HCl(g)$ in this reaction must be given by the equation

$$Rate = k[H_2][Cl_2]$$

in which k is the rate constant.

2   For the combustion of ethane,

$$C_2H_6(g) + \tfrac{7}{2}O_2(g) \rightleftarrows 2CO_2(g) + 3H_2O(g)$$

$$K_{eq} = \frac{[CO_2]^2[H_2O]^3}{[C_2H_6][O_2]^{3.5}}$$

3   For the synthesis of $NH_3(g)$ from $N_2(g)$ and $H_2(g)$ at 25°C,

$$N_2(g) + 3H_2(g) \rightleftarrows 2NH_3(g)$$
$$K_{eq} = 4.0 \times 10^8 \text{ mole}^{-2} \text{ liter}^2$$

If a gaseous mixture consisting of 2 moles of N_2, 1 mole of H_2, and 2 moles of NH_3 is allowed to attain equilibrium in a 1-liter flask at 25°C, one would expect to find less than 2 moles of NH_3 in the container.

4   K_{eq} for the formation of $NO(g)$ from $N_2(g)$ and $O_2(g)$ at 25°C is only 10^{-30}. The reaction is

$$N_2(g) + O_2(g) \rightleftarrows 2NO(g)$$

If 1 mole of $N_2(g)$ and 1 mole of $O_2(g)$ are placed in a 1-liter container at 25°C, we can expect to find only about 1×10^{-15} mole of $NO(g)$ present when the system has set long enough to attain equilibrium.

5   Consider the Deacon process for producing chlorine gas:

$$O_2(g) + 4HCl(g) \rightleftarrows 2H_2O(g) + 2Cl_2(g)$$

To increase the yield of $Cl_2(g)$ one might carry out this reaction at low pressures.

6   The yield of $Cl_2(g)$ from the Deacon process (see quiz question 5) can be increased by condensing the $H_2O(g)$ present in the mixture and removing it from the system as liquid water.

7 The Deacon process for the production of chlorine gas is an exo-thermic reaction (see quiz question 5). Increased amounts of $Cl_2(g)$ can be obtained from this reaction if it is carried out at low temperatures.

8 The equilibrium constant for the reaction of $H_2(g)$ with $Cl_2(g)$ to produce $HCl(g)$ has the same value at 25°C as it has at 200°C.

9 The equilibrium constant for the reaction of $H_2(g)$ with $Cl_2(g)$ to produce $HCl(g)$ has the same value at 1 atm total pressure as it has at 2 atm.

10 A catalyst is used in the Haber process for the production of $NH_3(g)$ and $H_2(g)$ to increase the rate of reaction and to increase the amount of NH_3 present in equilibrium with N_2 and H_2.

11 The pH of a $0.01M$ HCl solution is 2.

12 The pH of a $0.001M$ NaOH solution is 4.

13 Pure water is more acidic than a solution that has a pH of 8.0.

14 The OH^- ion concentration in a buffer solution that has a pH of 3.0 is $1.0 \times 10^{-11}M$.

15 Using the information in Table 5–5, one should formulate the K_b expression for aniline, $C_6H_5NH_2$, as

$$K_b = \frac{[C_6H_5NH_3{}^+][OH^-]}{[C_6H_5NH_3OH]}$$

(C_6H_5 may be represented structurally by ⬡·.)

16 The pK_a for acetic acid ($HC_2H_3O_2$) is 4.75. The pK_a for the $NH_4{}^+$ cation is 9.25. $NH_4{}^+$ is a stronger acid than acetic acid.

17 The pK_a of HCN is 9.31 and the pK_a of the bisulfite ion, $HSO_3{}^-$, is 6.91. One can conclude that the CN^- ion is a stronger base than the sulfite ion, $SO_3{}^{2-}$.

18 When 5.0 ml of a $0.01M$ HCl solution is added to 5.0 ml of a $0.02M$ NaOH solution, the resulting solution will have a pH of 8.

19 According to Figures 5–5 and 5–7 in *Chemical Principles*, brom-thymol blue is an acceptable indicator for the titration of a strong acid with a strong base.

20 The pH of a $0.01M$ HCN solution lies between 5 and 6. K_a for HCN $= 4.9 \times 10^{-10}$.

21 The molar hydrogen ion concentration in a solution that contains 1.0 mole of HF and 1.0 mole of NaF in one liter is about the same as the dissociation constant of HF.

22 The base B is only about 0.01% dissociated in a $0.1M$ solution. The dissociation reaction can be represented by the equation

$$B + H_2O \rightleftarrows BH^+ + OH^-$$

K_b for the base is about 10^{-4}, and its pK_b is 4.

23 One wishes to prepare a buffer solution capable of maintaining a pH of *about* 2. A solution of H_3PO_4 and NaH_2PO_4 is a possible choice. Use Table 5–4 to evaluate this question.

24 Using Table 5–4 as a guide, one would predict the following:

> $0.1M$ NaCl has a pH less than 7.
> $0.1M$ $NaNO_2$ has a pH greater than 7.
> $0.1M$ NH_4ClO_3 has a pH less than 7.
> $0.1M$ $(NH_4)_2SO_4$ has a pH less than 7.

25 The hydrolysis constant for the hydrolysis of $NaNO_2$ is about 2×10^{-11}. Consult Table 5–4.

26 The solubility of a salt MX_2 is 1×10^{-3} mole per liter. The K_{sp} of $MX_2 = 1 \times 10^{-9}$.

27 The solubility of Hg_2CrO_4 is 1×10^{-3} mole per liter. K_{sp} $Hg_2CrO_4 = 2 \times 10^{-9}$.

28 The sulfide ion concentration in a saturated solution of H_2S that is buffered at a pH of 1.0 is $1 \times 10^{-18}M$. The "ion product" for $H_2S = 1.0 \times 10^{-20}$.

29 If H_2S gas is bubbled through a solution containing 0.01 mole of Hg^{2+} ions and 0.01 mole of Cu^{2+} ions per liter, black CuS will precipitate first.

$$K_{sp} \text{ HgS} = 1.6 \times 10^{-54}, \qquad K_{sp} \text{ CuS} = 8 \times 10^{-37}$$

30 If 10.0 ml of a $1 \times 10^{-3}M$ $AgNO_3$ solution are added to 10.0 ml of a $2 \times 10^{-3}M$ Na_3PO_4 solution, Ag_3PO_4 will precipitate. K_{sp} $Ag_3PO_4 = 1.8 \times 10^{-18}$.

31 If a $0.10M$ ammonia solution is made $1.0M$ in NH_4Cl, one can add 0.010 mole of $MgCl_2$ to 1 liter of the resulting solution without precipitating $Mg(OH)_2$. K_a for aqueous $NH_3 = 1.8 \times 10^{-5}$ and K_{sp} for $Mg(OH)_2 = 8.9 \times 10^{-12}$.

32 Sodium hydroxide is added slowly to a solution that is $0.1M$ in Fe^{3+} ions and $0.1M$ in Ba^{2+} ions. The rust-colored $Fe(OH)_3$ precipitates before the white $Ba(OH)_2$. By stopping the addition of NaOH at the first sign of the appearance of the white $Ba(OH)_2$, one can precipitate essentially all the Fe^{3+} ions present in the solution. K_{sp} $Fe(OH)_3 = 6 \times 10^{-38}$ and K_{sp} $Ba(OH)_2 = 5.0 \times 10^{-3}$.

1   John Newlands and Dmitri Mendeleev are credited as being the founders of the modern periodic table.

2   X rays are generated when electrons drop into vacant shells near the nucleus of excited atoms. The energy of the emitted x ray is dependent on the nuclear charge.

3   Moseley's work proved that the charge on the nucleus (the atomic number, not the atomic weight) is the essential property in explaining chemical behavior.

4   The Group VIA elements O, S, Se, and Te are referred to as the halogens.

5   The alkali and alkaline earth elements are found in Groups IA and IIA, respectively.

6   The actinides and the lanthanides are members of a group of metals classified as inner transition elements.

7   In general, metals have comparatively high ionization energies.

8   For any given element, the first ionization energy is always less than the second ionization energy.

9   The oxidation potential and ionization energy for the production of sodium ions are the same.

10   The first ionization energy for lithium (Li) is greater than the first ionization energy for potassium (K).

11   The electron affinity of chlorine (Cl) is greater than that of sulfur (S).

12   X-ray diffraction measurements of Cl_2 crystals show two different Cl—Cl distances, 1.98 Å and 3.60 Å. The longer distance is the sum of the covalent radii of the two Cl atoms; the shorter distance is the sum of the two van der Waals radii.

13   The phosphide ion (P^{3-}) is isoelectronic with neon (Ne).

14   A characteristic difference between covalent and ionic bonds is that covalent bonds are directional in character, whereas ionic bonds are nondirectional.

15   Most nonmetals form small molecules that employ multiple covalent bonds.

16   Alkali and alkaline earth metal hydrides have crystal structures in which there is extensive hydrogen bridging.

17   Ionic hydrides react with water to form OH^- ions and basic solutions. In contrast, the covalent compounds of hydrogen and halogen atoms are acidic.

18 Strontium oxide is an acidic oxide. Its reaction with water can be described by

$$SrO + H_2O \rightarrow 2H^+ + SrO_2{}^{2-}$$

19 $NaBrO_3$ is known. This can be regarded as evidence of the acidic properties of Br_2O_5.

20 At room temperature, CO_2 is a gas and SiO_2 is a hard crystalline solid. This difference is because carbon readily forms double bonds with oxygen atoms, but silicon can form only single bonds.

CHAPTER 7

1 The covalence of the sulfur in H_2SO_4 is 6.

$$\begin{array}{c} O \\ \parallel \\ H-O-S-O-H \\ \parallel \\ O \end{array}$$

2 In the complex ion $[Co(NH_3)_6]^{3+}$, the coordination number and the covalence of the cobalt(III) ion is the same.

3 The maximum oxidation state shown by a nonmetal in Group VA is +5.

4 Minus 4 is a possible oxidation state for a Group IVA element.

5 The maximum positive oxidation state shown by a transition metal is the one corresponding to its group number.

6 A common oxidation state for the lanthanide and actinide elements is +2.

7 Electron-deficient compounds generally are good reducing agents.

8 An element in one of its high oxidation states is a potential oxidizing agent.

9 A substance must undergo a change in oxidation number to be oxidized.

10 To change oxidation numbers, an element must either lose or accept electrons.

11 In balancing oxidation and reduction reactions by the oxidation-number method or the ion–electron method, we assume that oxidation and reduction involve electron transfer from the substance being oxidized to the substance being reduced.

12 Sulfur has fractional oxidation numbers in the following ions: $S_6O_6{}^{2-}$, $S_4O_6{}^{2-}$, and $S_2O_3{}^{2-}$.

Consider the reaction $V_2O_5 + KI + HCl \rightarrow V_2O_4 + KCl + I_2 + H_2O$ in answering Questions 13 through 19.

13 In balancing the equation by the oxidation-number method, we assume that each V_2O_5 formula unit loses two electrons.

14 Chlorine has been oxidized in this reaction.

15 Iodine is the reducing agent in this reaction.

16 In balancing this reaction by the ion–electron method, the balanced half-reaction that specifies I^- forming I_2 can be added directly to the balanced $V_2O_5 \rightarrow V_2O_4$ half-reaction.

17 The molecular weight of V_2O_5 is 182. Its equivalent weight is 91.

18 A $1.0M$ solution of KI is $0.50N$.

19 A 0.455-g sample of V_2O_5 will react with 5.0 ml of $1.0N$ KI.

20 The fact that there are two isomers of $Pt(NH_3)_2Cl_2$ and only one isomer of H_2CCl_2 indicates that the four covalent bonds to the Pt are in a square planar orientation, whereas the four covalent bonds to the C are in a tetrahedral orientation.

21 The fact that all three of the N—O bond distances are the same in the NO_3^- ion, and that there is no difference in the chemical reactivity of the three oxygen atoms, can be explained by resonance theory.

APPENDIX 5 ANSWERS TO THE SELF-EVALUATION QUIZZES

CHAPTER 1

1   True. Strictly speaking, the atomic number is the number of protons in the nucleus. However, in a neutral atom the number of extranuclear electrons is the same as the number of protons (unit positive charges) in the nucleus.

2   True.

3   False. When protons and neutrons combine to form a nucleus, some of their mass is converted to energy. This energy is the binding energy that holds the nucleus together. This means that the mass of the proton (and neutron) in the nucleus will be less than the mass of a free proton.

4   True. $0.25(44) + 0.75(40) = 11 + 30 = 41$ amu.

5   True. 1 g-atom of each.

6   False. Did you forget to double the CO_2H unit in the parentheses?
$6C + 4H + 2C + 4O + 2H$
$= 72 + 4 + 24 + 64 + 2 = 166$ amu.

7   False. There are three *atoms* of H in one molecule of CH_3Cl. In 1 mole of CH_3Cl there are 6×10^{23} molecules; therefore, there are $3(6 \times 10^{23}) = 1.8 \times 10^{24}$ atoms of H in 1 mole of CH_3Cl.

8   True. 3 g C = (3 g C)/(12 g g-atom^{-1}) = ¼ g-atom C. (16 g-atom H)/(8 g-atom H) = 2 g-atoms H per g atom C are required to produce C_8H_{16}. Therefore, ¼ g-atom C requires

$$2 \frac{\text{g-atoms H}}{\text{g-atom C}} \times \frac{1}{4} \text{ g-atom C} = \frac{1}{2} \text{ g-atom H}$$

½ g-atom H × 1.0 g H g-atom^{-1} = 0.5 g H

9   True. $C_6H_5OH + 7O_2 \rightarrow 6CO_2 + 3H_2O$
    1 + 7 + 6 + 3 = 17

10   False. In 82 g H_2SO_3 there is 82 g H_2SO_3/(82 g mole^{-1}) = 1 mole H_2SO_3. There are 3 atoms of O per molecule of H_2SO_3. There are 6.0 × 10²³ molecules of H_2SO_3 in 1 mole. Therefore, there are 3 × 6 × 10²³ = 1.8 × 10²⁴ atoms of O in 1 mole of H_2SO_3.

11   True.

12   False. The balanced equation shows that 1 mole of P_4 requires 6 moles of Cl_2. As Avogadro's law states, at the same temperature and pressure, equal volumes of all gases contain the same number of molecules. Therefore, six times as many moles of Cl_2 will be required as the number of moles of P_4 contained in 4 liters. This number of moles of Cl_2 will be in 6 × 4 = 24 liters of Cl_2 at the same temperature and pressure.

13   False. $M = kD$, in which M = molecular weight, D = the density, and k = the proportionality constant. $k = M/D$ = (28 g mole^{-1} N_2)/(1.25 g liter^{-1}) = 22.4 liters mole^{-1}. Did you use the gram atomic weight of nitrogen (14 g) instead of the gram molecular weight of nitrogen (N_2 = 28 g mole^{-1})?

14   False. If we assume 100.0 g of the oxide, then 50.0 g S, or (50.0 g S)/(32 g g-atom^{-1}) = 1.56 g-atom S, are combined with 50.0 g O, or (50 g O)/(16 g g-atom^{-1}) = 3.12 g-atom O. (1.56 g-atom S)/(3.12 g-atom O) = (1 g-atom S)/(2 g-atom O). The simplest formula is SO_2.

15   False. The simplest formula weight of CH_2Cl = 1 × 12.0 + 2 × 1.0 + 1 × 35.5 = 49.5. (100)/(49.5) ≈ 2. Therefore, the molecular formula is twice the simplest formula, or $C_2H_4Cl_2$.

16   False. The law of DuLong and Petit states that (atomic wt) × (specific heat) = 6. Therefore, atomic wt = 6/0.02 = 300.

17   False. If 1.5 g Q are combined with 1.00 g O, there will be 1.5 × 16 = 24 g Q combined with 16 g (1 g-atom) of oxygen. This is about (24 g Q)/(50 g Q g-atom^{-1}) = 0.5 g-atom Q. The simplest formula for the oxide is $Q_{0.5}O$, or QO_2.

18   True. 30.9/3 = 10.3

19   True.

20   True.

CHAPTER 2

1 False. Avogadro's law states that, at a given temperature and pressure, the number of molecules of any gas in a specified volume will be the same. Or stating this in another way, at the same temperature and pressure, equal volumes of gases contain the same number of molecules. The volume occupied by 0.5 mole of oxygen $(0.5 \times 6.0 \times 10^{23}$ O_2 molecules) will be one half that occupied by 1 mole of helium $(6.0 \times 10^{23}$ He atoms) at the same temperature and pressure.

2 True.

3 False. In filling the second bulb, the volume occupied by the gas will be doubled (from 1 liter to 2 liters); the pressure of the gas should *decrease* proportionally (as stated by Boyle's law):

$$[P = 1 \text{ liter}/2 \text{ liters} \times (0.5 \text{ atm}) = 0.25 \text{ atm}]$$

4 False. The centigrade temperature is doubled $[(40°C/20°C) = 2/1]$, but Charles' law states that the change in volume of the gas will be proportional to the change in its *absolute* temperature. Conversion of 20°C and 40°C to absolute temperature results in 293°K and 313°K, respectively. The ratio of the absolute temperatures is not 2/1. The volume of the gas will be increased by a factor of $(313°K/293°K) = 1.07$.

5 True.

6 False. $PV = nRT = (g/M)RT$

$$M = \frac{gRT}{PV} = \frac{(3.00\text{g})(0.082 \text{ liter atm mole}^{-1}°K^{-1})(300°K)}{[8.20 \text{ mm} \times (1/760) \text{ atm mm}^{-1}](7.60 \text{ liter})}$$

$$M = \frac{(3.00)(8.2 \times 10^{-2})(3 \times 10^2)(7.60 \times 10^2)}{(8.20)(7.60)}$$

$$= 9.00 \times 10^2 \text{ g mole}^{-1}$$

7 False. The molecular weight of N_2 (28) is less than that of O_2 (32). Therefore, 1 g of N_2 will contain more molecules (1/28 mole N_2) than 1 g of O_2 (1/32 mole O_2). Since both flasks contain the same weight of gas, there will be more N_2 molecules in flask A than there are molecules of O_2 in flask B.

8 True. $E_k = 3/2 \, RT$

9 True. Because both flasks are at the same temperature, the average kinetic energies of the molecules are the same: $\frac{1}{2}m_{N_2}v_{N_2}^2 = \frac{1}{2}m_{O_2}v_{O_2}^2$. Since the masses of the two gases are directly proportional to their molecular weights we can write

$$\frac{v_{N_2}^2}{v_{O_2}^2} = \frac{m_{O_2}}{m_{N_2}} = \frac{32}{28} = 1.14$$

Then $v_{N_2} = (1.14)^{1/2}v_{O_2} = 1.07 \, v_{O_2}$.

10 True. Because the volume and the temperature are the same in both flasks, the pressure will be proportional to the number of moles of gas in each flask.

11 True.

12 True.

13 False. Dalton's law of partial pressures states that the partial pressure of one gas in a mixture of gases is equal to its mole fraction times the total pressure. The mole fraction of nitrogen in the container is $X_{N_2} = 2/(2 + 3) = 2/5$. The partial pressure of the nitrogen is $(2/5)(1 \text{ atm}) = 2/5$ atm.

14 False. Both O_2 and water vapor are in the bottle; therefore, the total pressure, 760 torr, represents the sum of the partial pressure of the O_2 and the partial pressure of the water vapor:

$$p_{O_2} = 760 - p_{H_2O}$$

15 True. $1.5 \text{ g liter}^{-1} \times 22.4 \text{ liter mole}^{-1} = 33.6 \text{ g mole}^{-1}$

16 True.

17 False. The ideal gas law is formulated with the assumption that the volume occupied by the gas molecules is negligible. This is not the case. Therefore, the actual volume of a real gas will be larger than the one calculated for an ideal gas by the volume actually occupied by the molecules. In the van der Waals equation of state, the "ideal" gas volume is obtained by *subtracting* a term (b for 1 mole of a gas) that is a measure of the actual volume occupied by the molecules.

18 False. Ideal gas behavior is more likely when the attractions between the molecules are minimized. This situation is more possible when the molecules are farther apart and their kinetic energy is greater, a situation favored by low pressures and high temperatures.

19 True. $PV = nRT$ or $\dfrac{PV}{RT} = n = 1$

20 True.

21 True.

CHAPTER 3

1 True.

2 False. $1 \mathcal{F} = 96{,}500$ coulombs, where 1 coulomb is the quantity of electricity carried by a current of 1 A in 1 sec. $10^4 \text{ min} = 10^4 \text{ min} \times 60 \text{ sec min}^{-1} = 6 \times 10^5$ sec. In 10^4 min a current of 9.65 A will carry $9.65 \text{ A} \times 6 \times 10^5 \text{ sec} = 5.79 \times 10^6$ coulombs, or $(5.79 \times 10^6 \text{ coulombs})/(9.65 \times 10^4 \text{ coulombs } \mathcal{F}^{-1}) = 60.0 \mathcal{F}$.

3   False. The cathode of an electrolysis cell is the electrode at which electrons enter. Since this situation places a negative charge on the cathode, positive ions will migrate to the cathode and accept these electrons; Br^- is a negative ion and will migrate to the positive electrode, the anode. The reaction is one in which electrons are given up, not accepted.

4   True. In fact, the cathode is best defined as the electrode at which reduction occurs and the anode as the electrode at which oxidation occurs.

5   True.

6   False. The combining weight of an element, often called the "equivalent weight of the element," is the weight in grams deposited in electrolysis by 1 $\mathfrak{F}$ of electricity. Here, the combining weight of the metal is 60 g/3 $\mathfrak{F}$ = 20 g/$\mathfrak{F}$, or 20.

7   False. 482 A $\times 10^2$ sec = 4.82×10^4 coulombs. $(4.82 \times 10^4$ coulombs$)/(9.65 \times 10^4$ coulombs $\mathfrak{F}^{-1}) = 0.500$ $\mathfrak{F}$. There are 6.02×10^{23} electrons in a faraday of electricity. Therefore, 0.500 $\mathfrak{F} \times 6.02 \times 10^{23}$ electrons $\mathfrak{F}^{-1} = 3.01 \times 10^{23}$ electrons are transferred.

8   False. The oxidation number of hydrogen is $+1$, and the oxidation number of oxygen is -2. The algebraic sum of the oxidation numbers of 22 H atoms, 11 O atoms, and 12 C atoms must equal zero because $C_{12}H_{22}O_{11}$ is a neutral compound. From these data we see that the oxidation number of carbon in this compound must be zero: $12(0) + 22(1) + 11(-2) = 0 + 22 - 22 = 0$.

9   True.

10   True. A 0.5-mole sample of solute in 1 kg of benzene gives a $0.5m$ solution. $\Delta T_f = k_f m$. ΔT_f = the freezing point lowering for the $0.5m$ solution = $80.1 - 78.8 = 1.3°C$; therefore, $k_f = (T_f/m) = (1.3/0.5) = 2.6°C$ molal^{-1}. A solution containing 1.0 mole of solute in 0.5 kg of benzene is (1.0 mole)/(0.5 kg benzene) = $2.0m$. Its freezing point lowering $\Delta T_f = k_f m = 2.6°C$ $m^{-1} \times 2.0m = 5.2°C$. The freezing point of the solution will be $80.1 - 5.2 = 74.9°C$.

11   True. Three K^+ and one $Fe(CN)_6{}^{3-}$ make $3 + 1 = 4$ ions per molecule. For such a dissociation, i should be 4.

12   True. We see from the dissociation equation that the concentration of A^- will be one half that of H^+. Every mole of H_2A that dissociates releases 1 mole of A^-. Therefore, if C_i is the concentration of H^+, $C_i/2$ is the concentration of A^-, and $C_o - C_i/2$ is the concentration of H_2A remaining after the dissociation. The total concentration of particles (H^+, A^-, and H_2A) is $C_i + C_i/2 + C_o - C_i/2 = C_i + C_o$. If none of the H_2A dissociated, the con-

centration of solute is C_o. $i =$ (total concentration of solute particles)/(concentration of solute if none dissociates) $= (C_i + C_o)/C_o$.

13 True. The degree of dissociation

$$\alpha = \frac{\text{conc. of dissociated solute ions}}{\text{conc. of ions if all solute is dissociated}}$$

In Question 12, the concentration of dissociated solute ions, H^+ and A^-, was $C_i + C_i/2$. If completely dissociated, C_o H_2A, would give $2C_o$ H^+ and C_o A^-, or $3C_o$ ions.

$$\alpha = \frac{C_i + C_i/2}{3C_o} = \frac{(2C_i + C_i)/2}{3C_o} = \frac{3C_i}{6C_o} = \frac{C_i}{2C_o}$$

In Question 12, it was shown that $i = (C_i + C_o)/C_o$, or $C_o i - C_o = C_i$. Substitution of this value for C_i into the expression for α gives

$$\alpha = \frac{C_o i - C_o}{2C_o} = \frac{C_o(i - 1)}{2C_o} = \frac{(i - 1)}{2}$$

The degree of dissociation is the fraction of the solute that dissociates. This fraction times 100 is the percent dissociation; therefore, percent dissociation $= 100\,\alpha = [100(i - 1)/2]$.

14 False. Electrons and protons (canal rays) were identified in gas-discharge tubes. Neutrons, since they are electrically neutral, are not observed in discharge tube experiments.

15 True. The deflection is greater when there is a larger ratio of charge to mass.

16 True.

17 False. The hexagonal close packed and face-centered cubic (also called the cubic close packed) arrangements are true close packed structures since they make the most efficient use of the available space. Seventy-four percent of the available space is occupied by spheres in these arrangements. A body-centered cubic packing is not a close packed structure since only 68% of the available volume is occupied by spheres in this arrangement.

18 True. The unit cell of NaCl consists of a Na^+ ion in the center of eight Cl^- ions that occupy the corners of an octahedron. The coordination number of the Na^+ is 6, as it would be if it were in an octahedral hole. The one Na^+ to one Cl^- stoichiometry is satisfied in such an arrangement because there are the same number of octahedral holes as there are atoms in a close packed structure.

19 False. There are only two atoms. The eight atoms at the corners of the cube are shared equally by the eight adjacent unit cells. Therefore, there is only one eighth of an atom at each corner of a given unit cell, or $8 \times \frac{1}{8} = 1$ atom total within the unit cell.

The one "corner atom" plus the atom in the body center constitute a total of two atoms in the unit cell.

20 False. The density of the crystal also must be known if we are to
determine the volume occupied by a mole of the ions.

CHAPTER 4

1 True. The molecular formula = n(empirical formula), where
n is sometimes 1, but more often n is some other whole number.

2 False. There are Avogadro's number (6.02×10^{23}) of atoms in
1 mole of atoms and the same number of molecules in 1 mole of
molecules, formula units in 1 mole of formula units, and so forth.
1 mole of $POCl_3$ is 6.02×10^{23} $POCl_3$ molecules. Each molecule
contains five atoms: one P atom plus one O atom plus three Cl
atoms equals five atoms; therefore, 1 mole of $POCl_3$ contains
$5 \times 6.02 \times 10^{23} = 3.01 \times 10^{24}$ atoms.

3 True.

4 False.

$$(0.4 \text{ g M})/(20 \text{ g M mole}^{-1}) = 0.02 \text{ mole M}$$

$$(0.6 \text{ g A})/(10 \text{ g A mole}^{-1}) = 0.06 \text{ mole A}$$

$$M_{0.02}A_{0.06} = M_{0.02/0.02}A_{0.06/0.02} = MA_3$$

5 False.

$$n = \frac{PV}{RT} = \frac{(1 \text{ atm})(8.20 \text{ liter})}{(0.082 \text{ liter atm mole}^{-1}°K^{-1})(500°K)} = \frac{1}{5}$$

$11.2 \text{ g} = \frac{1}{5}$ mole; therefore, $(11.2 \text{ g})/(\frac{1}{5} \text{ mole}) = 56.0 \text{ g mole}^{-1}$.
The empirical formula weight of $CH_2 = 1(C) + 2(H) = 12 +
2 = 14.$ $56.0/14 = 4.$ The molecular formula of the gas is
$4(CH_2) = C_4H_8$.

6 False. The number of atoms balance, but the total ionic charge
on the left is $+5$ ($MnO_4^- + 6H^+ = +5$), and the total ionic
charge on the right is only $+2$ (Mn^{2+}).

7 True. $(6.8 \text{ g PH}_3)/(35 \text{ g PH}_3 \text{ mole}^{-1}) = 0.20 \text{ mole PH}_3$. From the
stoichiometry of the reaction, 0.20 mole PH_3 will produce 0.20
mole H_3PO_4.

8 True.

$$0.2 \text{ mole } H_3PO_4 \times \frac{4 \text{ moles } N_2O}{1 \text{ mole } H_3PO_4} \times \frac{44 \text{ g } N_2O}{\text{mole } N_2O} = 35 \text{ g } N_2O$$

9 False.

$$0.5 \text{ mole } PH_3 \times \frac{4 \text{ moles } N_2}{1 \text{ mole } PH_3} \times \frac{22.4 \text{ liters } N_2}{\text{mole } N_2} = 44.8 \text{ liters } N_2$$

10 True.

$$n_{PH_3} = \frac{PV}{RT} = \frac{(1 \text{ atm})(8.2 \text{ liters})}{(0.082 \text{ liter atm mole}^{-1}\text{K}^{-1})(500°\text{K})} = \frac{1}{5} \text{ mole}$$

$$\frac{1}{5} \text{ mole PH}_3 \times \frac{1 \text{ mole H}_3\text{PO}_4}{\text{mole PH}_3} \times 98 \text{ g H}_3\text{PO}_4 \text{ mole}^{-1} = 19.6$$

$$= 20 \text{ g H}_3\text{PO}_4$$

11 True. Change all quantities to moles.

$$\frac{6 \times 10^{23} \text{ atoms A}}{6 \times 10^{23} \text{ atoms mole}^{-1}} = 1 \text{ mole A}$$

$$\frac{10 \text{ g B}}{20 \text{ g mole}^{-1}} = \frac{1}{2} \text{ mole B}$$

$$\frac{3}{2} \text{ mole C} = \frac{3}{2} \text{ mole C}$$

In A_2BC_3, the ratio of moles A to moles B to moles C is 2/1/3, which equals 1/½/3/2.

12 False. Change all quantities to moles.

$$1 \text{ mole A}$$

$$\frac{10 \text{ g B}}{20 \text{ g mole}^{-1}} = \frac{1}{2} \text{ mole B}$$

$$\frac{3 \text{ g C}}{30 \text{ g mole}^{-1}} = \frac{1}{10} \text{ mole C}$$

To form ½ mole of A_2BC_3, 1 mole A, ½ mole B, and 3/2 mole of C are needed. There is not enough C present in the mixture to form ½ mole of A_2BC_3.

13 False. Change all quantities to moles.

$$\frac{5.0 \text{ g A}}{10 \text{ g mole}^{-1}} = 0.5 \text{ mole A}$$

$$\frac{10 \text{ g B}}{20 \text{ g mole}^{-1}} = 0.5 \text{ mole B}$$

$$\frac{15 \text{ g C}}{30 \text{ g mole}^{-1}} = 0.5 \text{ mole C}$$

Determine those substances in excess. To react with 0.5 mole A, 0.5 mole A $\times$ (1 mole B/2 moles A) = 0.25 mole B is required. An amount of 0.5 mole B is in excess. To react with 0.5 mole A, 0.5 mole A $\times$ (3 moles C/2 moles A) = 0.75 mole C is required. An amount of 0.5 mole C is insufficient to react with the A and B

present; C is the limiting reagent, and 22 g A_2BC_3 are formed:

$$0.5 \text{ mole C} \times \frac{1 \text{ mole A}_2\text{BC}_3}{3 \text{ moles C}} = 0.17 \text{ mole A}_2\text{BC}_3$$

$$0.17 \text{ mole A}_2\text{BC}_3 \times 130 \text{ g A}_2\text{BC}_3 \text{ mole}^{-1} = 22 \text{ g A}_2\text{BC}_3$$

14 False. $(1.7 \text{ g NH}_3)/(17 \text{ g NH}_3 \text{ mole}^{-1}) = 0.10$ mole NH_3 will require 0.10 mole NH_3 × (7 moles O_2/4 moles NH_3) = 0.175 mole O_2. However, only $(3.2 \text{ g O}_2)/(32 \text{ g O}_2 \text{ mole}^{-1}) = 0.10$ mole O_2 is present; O_2 is the limiting reagent. 0.10 mole O_2 × (4 moles NH_3/7 moles O_2) = 0.057 mole NH_3 will react. This will produce

$$0.057 \text{ mole NH}_3 \times \frac{4 \text{ moles NO}_2}{4 \text{ moles NH}_3} \times 46 \text{ g NO}_2 \text{ mole}^{-1} = 2.6 \text{ g NO}_2$$

15 True.

16 True.

$$\frac{(4.9 \text{ g H}_2\text{SO}_4)/(98 \text{ g H}_2\text{SO}_4 \text{ mole}^{-1})}{(250 \text{ ml})/(1000 \text{ ml liter}^{-1})} = 0.20 \text{ mole liter}^{-1} = 0.20M$$

17 False. It is $7.16M$. To determine the *molal* concentration of this solution, its density must be known. For example, the density is 1.05 g ml^{-1}. Therefore, 1 liter will weigh 1000 ml × 1.05 g ml^{-1} = 1050 g. Of this amount, 430 g are acetic acid and $1050 - 430 = 620$ g are water. The molality, m, is

$$m = \frac{\text{moles CH}_3\text{CO}_2\text{H}}{\text{kg H}_2\text{O}} = \frac{(430 \text{ g})/(60 \text{ g mole}^{-1})}{(620 \text{ g})/(1000 \text{ g kg}^{-1})} = 11.5 \text{ m}$$

18 True.

$$X \text{ ml} \times 6M = 20 \text{ ml} \times 2M$$
$$X = (20 \times 2)/6 = 6.7 \text{ ml}$$

19 True, provided that the acid is used in a reaction in which it is completely neutralized, that is, all three protons are transferred.

20 True.

$$N_{\text{H}_2\text{SO}_4} \times V_{\text{H}_2\text{SO}_4} = N_{\text{NaOH}} \times V_{\text{NaOH}}$$

$$N_{\text{NaOH}} = \frac{(2.00)(25.0)}{(30.00)} = 1.67N$$

As 1 mole of NaOH accepts 1 mole of protons, $N_{\text{NaOH}} = M_{\text{NaOH}} = 1.67M$.

21 True.

$$\frac{7.4 \text{ g Ca(OH)}_2}{(74/2)\text{g Ca(OH)}_2 \text{ equiv}^{-1}} = 0.20 \text{ equiv Ca(OH)}_2$$

$2.0M$ HCl is $2.0N$.

$N_{\text{HCl}} \times$ liters HCl = equiv HCl = 2.0 × 0.100 = 0.20 equiv
0.20 equiv Ca(OH)$_2$ = equiv HCl = 0.20 equiv

22 True.

23 True.

$$2C_6H_{14}(l) + 19O_2(g) \rightarrow 12CO_2(g) + 14H_2O(l)$$
$$\Delta H_{comb} = 12\Delta H_f^0[CO_2(g)] + 14\Delta H_f^0[H_2O] - 2\Delta H_f^0[C_6H_{14}(l)]$$
$$= 12(-94) + 14(-68) - 2(-40)$$
$$= -1130 - 950 + 80 = -2000 \text{ kcal for 2 moles}$$
$$C_6H_{14}$$

or

$$\Delta H_{comb} = -1000 \text{ kcal mole}^{-1}$$

CHAPTER 5

1   False. The overall equation for a chemical reaction does not tell us anything about the mechanism for the reaction. The rate of a reaction is dependent on the mechanism. Only if the mechanism for the production of HCl molecules did indeed involve the direct collision of an H_2 molecule with a Cl_2 molecule would the rate law for the forward reaction be the one indicated.

2   True. However, the preferred form of a K_{eq} expression is one in which only whole-number exponents are employed. It would be more acceptable to write the equation

$$2C_2H_6(g) + 7O_2(g) \rightleftarrows 4CO_2(g) + 6H_2O(g)$$

and write

$$K_{eq} = \frac{[CO_2]^4[H_2O]^6}{[C_2H_6]^2[O_2]^7}$$

3   False. For this reaction at equilibrium

$$K_{eq} = \frac{[NH_3]^2}{[N_2][H_2]^3} = 4.0 \times 10^8$$

Substituting the initial concentrations into the K_{eq} expression, we obtain a number, Q, the reaction quotient, which is less than K_{eq}:

$$Q = \frac{(2)^2}{(2)(1)} = 2 < 4 \times 10^8$$

To reach the K_{eq} value, more NH_3 will be formed at the expense of N_2 and H_2 until those concentrations that will satisfy the equilibrium constant are attained. (The reaction quotient, Q, is discussed in *Chemical Principles*, page 162.)

4   True. Let x = molar concentration of NO at equilibrium. The equation shows that 1 mole of N_2 and O_2 react to form 2 moles NO; therefore, $x/2$ mole N_2 and O_2 react to form x moles of NO.

	Initial	At equilibrium
[NO]	0.00	x
[N_2]	1	$1 - \dfrac{x}{2}$
[O_2]	1	$1 - \dfrac{x}{2}$

$$K_{eq} = \frac{[NO]^2}{[N_2][O_2]} = \frac{(x)^2}{(1 - x/2)(1 - x/2)} = \frac{x^2}{(1)(1)} = 10^{-30}$$

$$x = [NO] = 10^{-15}$$

($x/2$ is negligible compared to 1.)

5　False. Le Chatelier's principle predicts the equilibrium will shift in favor of the reaction producing the *largest* number of moles of gas when the pressure on the system is *decreased*:

5 moles of gas → 4 moles of gas

The equilibrium would shift to the left in favor of reactants at the expense of the products, Cl_2 and H_2O.

6　True. Le Chatelier's principle predicts that removal of a product from an equilibrium system will result in the equilibrium shifting to the product side. This will increase the amount of $Cl_2(g)$ produced.

7　True. Le Chatelier's principle predicts that when the temperature on an equilibrium system is lowered (heat is removed) the system will shift to generate more heat. For an exothermic reaction this shift will favor the production of products. $Cl_2(g)$ is a product in the Deacon process.

8　False. Equilibrium constants vary with temperature.

9　True. Equilibrium constants are independent of the total pressure on the equilibrium system.

10　False. The catalyst has no effect on the equilibrium constant, so it cannot change the relative amounts of products and reactants present at equilibrium. The catalyst is added to increase the reaction rate and shorten the time necessary for the system to reach equilibrium.

11　True. $pH = -\log [H^+] = -\log (1 \times 10^{-2}) = 2$

12　False. The OH^- ion concentration in $0.001M$ NaOH is $0.001M$. Therefore,

$$[H^+] = \frac{1 \times 10^{-14}}{0.001} = 1 \times 10^{-11}$$

$$pH = -\log [H^+] = -\log (1 \times 10^{-11}) = 11$$

13　True. The pH of pure water is 7, which corresponds to $[H^+] = 1 \times 10^{-7}$; $pH = 8$ corresponds to $[H^+] = 1 \times 10^{-8}$.

14　True. $pH = 3.0$ corresponds to $[H^+] = 1 \times 10^{-3}$. $[H^+][OH^-] = 1 \times 10^{-14}$.

$$[OH^-] = \frac{1 \times 10^{-14}}{[H^+]} = \frac{1 \times 10^{-14}}{1 \times 10^{-3}}$$

$$[OH^-] = 1 \times 10^{-11}$$

15 False. Just as the molecular species in aqueous ammonia is NH_3 and not NH_4OH, one would expect, and the table indicates, that the molecular species in aqueous aniline is $C_6H_5NH_2$.

$$C_6H_5NH_2 + HOH \rightleftarrows C_6H_5NH_3^+ + OH^-$$

$$K_b = \frac{[C_6H_5NH_3^+][OH^-]}{[C_6H_5NH_2]}$$

16 False. $pK_a = -\log K_a$; therefore, the larger the pK_a, the smaller is the K_a. A small K_a indicates that the ability of the acid to donate protons to water is low (*i.e.*, the acid is weak). Consequently, the larger a pK_a, the weaker the acid.

17 True. HCN has the higher pK_a so it is the weaker acid. Its conjugate base, CN^- ion, must have a greater affinity for protons and, therefore, be a stronger base than SO_3^{2-}, the conjugate base of the stronger acid, HSO_3^-.

18 False. $HCl + NaOH \rightarrow NaCl + H_2O$.

$$\frac{5.0 \text{ ml}}{1000 \text{ ml liter}^{-1}} \times 0.01 \text{ mole liter}^{-1} = 5.0 \times 10^{-5} \text{ mole HCl}$$

$$\frac{5.0 \text{ ml}}{1000 \text{ ml liter}^{-1}} \times 0.02 \text{ mole liter}^{-1} = 10 \times 10^{-5} \text{ mole NaOH}$$

The NaOH is in excess.

$$10 \times 10^{-5} \text{ mole} - 5.0 \times 10^{-5} \text{ mole} = 5 \times 10^{-5} \text{ mole NaOH}$$

is left after the reaction is complete. Neglecting OH^- ions from H_2O, there will be 5×10^{-5} mole OH^- in $5.0 + 5.0 = 10.0$ ml of solution after the reaction.

$$[OH^-] = \frac{5 \times 10^{-5} M}{0.0100 \text{ liter}} = 5 \times 10^{-3} M$$

$$[H^+] = \frac{1 \times 10^{-14}}{[OH^-]} = \frac{1 \times 10^{-14}}{5 \times 10^{-3}} = 2 \times 10^{-12}$$

$$pH = -\log [H^+] = -\log (2 \times 10^{-12}) = -(0.3 - 12)$$
$$= 12$$

19 True. Any indicator that changes color over the pH range 3 to 11 should be acceptable.

20 True. Letting $x = [H^+]$ at equilibrium, neglecting the H^+ ions from the dissociation of water, and assuming x is negligible compared to 0.1, we can write:

	Initial	At equilibrium
$[H^+]$	0	x
$[CN^-]$	0	x
$[HCN]$	0.10	$0.10 - x$

$$\frac{[\text{H}^+][\text{CN}^-]}{[\text{HCN}]} = \frac{(x)(x)}{(0.10) - x} = 4.9 \times 10^{-10}$$

$$x^2 = 4.9 \times 10^{-11} = 49 \times 10^{-12}$$

$$x = [\text{H}^+] = 7 \times 10^{-6}$$

$$\text{pH} = -\log[\text{H}^+] = -\log(7 \times 10^{-6})$$

$$= -(0.8 - 6) = 5.2$$

21 True. $K_a = \dfrac{[\text{H}^+][\text{F}^-]}{[\text{HF}]}$

$$[\text{H}^+] = K_a \frac{[\text{HF}]}{[\text{F}^-]} = K_a \frac{(1.0 - x)}{(1.0 - x)}$$

in which x = the moles per liter of H^+ ion present from the dissociation of HF. This value will be negligible compared to 1.0 so

$$[\text{H}^+] = K_a \frac{(1.0)}{(1.0)} = K_a$$

22 False. If 0.01% of the base dissociates, then $0.1 \times 0.0001 = 1 \times 10^{-5}$ mole of B dissociates per liter. This will give 1×10^{-5} mole per liter of BH^+ and 1×10^{-5} mole per liter of OH^-; $0.1 - 1 \times 10^{-5} = 0.1$ mole per liter of B will remain at equilibrium.

$$K_b = \frac{[\text{BH}^+][\text{OH}^-]}{[\text{B}]} = \frac{(1 \times 10^{-5})(1 \times 10^{-5})}{(1 \times 10^{-1})} = 1 \times 10^{-9}$$

$$pK_b = -\log K_b = -\log(1 \times 10^{-9}) = 9$$

23 True. $\text{pH} = pK_a + \log[\text{HA}]/[\text{A}^-]$. If we choose an acid having a pH close to 2 and a salt of its conjugate base, we can control the pH of the buffer by adjusting the ratio of acid to salt concentration, $[\text{HA}]/[\text{A}^-]$. The pK_a of H_3PO_4 is 2.12; its conjugate base, the H_2PO_4^- ion, can be obtained from NaH_2PO_4.

24 False. NaCl (salt of a strong base and a strong acid) pH = 7; NaNO_2 (salt of strong base and weak acid, HNO_2) pH > 7; NH_4ClO_3 (salt of weak base, NH_3, and strong acid, HClO_3) pH < 7; $(\text{NH}_4)_2\text{SO}_4$ (salt of weak base, NH_3, and weak acid, HSO_4^- ion) pH < 7 because $pK_a \ \text{HSO}_4^- = 1.92 < pK_b \ \text{NH}_3 = 4.75$. Therefore, the last three statements are true.

25 True.

$$K_h = \frac{[\text{HNO}_2][\text{OH}^-]}{[\text{NO}_2^-]} = \frac{K_w}{K_a \ \text{HNO}_2} = \frac{1 \times 10^{-14}}{4.6 \times 10^{-4}}$$

$$= 2.2 \times 10^{-11}$$

26 False. $MX_2(s) \rightleftarrows M^{2+} + 2X^-$. If solubility is 1×10^{-3} mole per liter, then

$$[M^{2+}] = 1 \times 10^{-3} \quad \text{and} \quad [X^-] = 2(1 \times 10^{-3})$$
$$= 2 \times 10^{-3}$$
$$K_{sp} = [M^{2+}][X^-]^2 = (1 \times 10^{-3})(2 \times 10^{-3})^2$$
$$= 4 \times 10^{-9}$$

27 False. $Hg_2CrO_4(s) \rightleftarrows Hg_2^{2+} + CrO_4^{2-}$. If 1×10^{-3} mole per liter Hg_2CrO_4 dissolves,

$$[Hg_2^{2+}] = 1 \times 10^{-3} \quad \text{and} \quad [CrO_4^{2-}] = 1 \times 10^{-3}$$
$$K_{sp} = [Hg_2^{2+}][CrO_4^{2-}] = (1 \times 10^{-3})(1 \times 10^{-3})$$
$$= 1 \times 10^{-6}$$

28 True. $pH = - \log [H^+] = 1$.

$$\log [H^+] = -1; \quad \text{therefore } [H^+] = 1 \times 10^{-1}$$
$$[H^+]^2[S^{2-}] = 1.0 \times 10^{-20}$$
$$(1 \times 10^{-1})^2[S^{2-}] = 1.0 \times 10^{-20}$$
$$[S^{2-}] = \frac{1.0 \times 10^{-20}}{1 \times 10^{-2}} = 1 \times 10^{-18}$$

29 False. The salt requiring the smallest concentration to attain its K_{sp} will precipitate first.

$$[Hg^{2+}][S^{2-}] = 1.6 \times 10^{-54}$$
$$[0.01][S^{2-}] = 1.6 \times 10^{-54}$$
$$[S^{2-}] = \frac{1.6 \times 10^{-54}}{0.01} = 1.6 \times 10^{-52}$$

$$[Cu^{2+}][S^{2-}] = 8 \times 10^{-37}$$
$$[0.01][S^{2-}] = 8 \times 10^{-37}$$
$$[S^{2-}] = \frac{8 \times 10^{-37}}{0.01} = 8 \times 10^{-35}$$

HgS, which requires the S^{2-} ion concentration to exceed only $1.6 \times 10^{-52}M$, will precipitate first.

30 True. After equal volumes of the two solutions are mixed, the concentrations of salt in the resulting solution will be one-half their original concentrations. Therefore, in the resulting solution $[Ag^+] = 0.5 \times 10^{-3}$ and $[PO_4^{3-}] = 1 \times 10^{-3}$.

$$K_{sp} = [Ag^+]^3[PO_4^{3-}] = 1.8 \times 10^{-18}$$
$$(0.5 \times 10^{-3})^3(1 \times 10^{-3}) = 1.25 \times 10^{-13} > K_{sp}$$

Therefore, Ag_3PO_4 will precipitate.

31 True. $\dfrac{[NH_4{}^+][OH^-]}{[NH_3]} = 1.8 \times 10^{-5}$

	Initial	At equilibrium
$[NH_4{}^+]$	1.0	$x + 1.0$
$[OH^-]$	0.00	x
$[NH_3]$	0.10	$0.10 - x$

Neglecting the $[OH^-]$ from H_2O, letting $x = [OH^-]$ formed at equilibrium by the dissociation of NH_3, and neglecting x compared to 0.10 gives the following acceptable solution for $[OH^-]$.

$$\frac{[NH_4{}^+][OH^-]}{[NH_3]} = \frac{(x + 1.0)(x)}{(0.10 - x)} = \frac{(1.0)x}{0.10} = 1.8 \times 10^{-5}$$

$$x = [OH^-] = 1.8 \times 10^{-6}$$

$$K_{sp}\ Mg(OH)_2 = [Mg^{2+}][OH^-]^2 = 8.9 \times 10^{-12}$$

In this solution,

$$[Mg^{2+}][OH^-]^2 = (0.010)(1.8 \times 10^{-6})^2 = 3.2 \times 10^{-14}$$

This number is less than the K_{sp}, so $Mg(OH)_2$ will not precipitate.

32 True. $[Fe^{3+}][OH^-]^3 = 6 \times 10^{-38}$

$$(0.1)[OH^-]^3 = 6 \times 10^{-38}$$

$$[OH^-]^3 = \frac{6 \times 10^{-38}}{0.1} = 0.6 \times 10^{-36}$$

$[OH^-] \simeq 10^{-12}M$ required to precipitate $Fe(OH)_3$. $Ba(OH)_2$ will not precipitate until

$$[Ba^{2+}][OH^-]^2 = 5.0 \times 10^{-3}$$

$$(0.1)[OH^-]^2 = 5.0 \times 10^{-3}$$

$$[OH^-]^2 = \frac{5.0 \times 10^{-3}}{1.0 \times 10^{-1}} = 5.0 \times 10^{-2}$$

$$[OH^-] = 2.2 \times 10^{-1} = 0.22M$$

Obviously, $Fe(OH)_3$ will precipitate first. When $[OH^-]$ finally reaches $0.22M$ and $Ba(OH)_2$ begins to precipitate, the Fe^{3+} ions left in solution will be

$$[Fe^{3+}][OH^-]^3 = [Fe^{3+}][2.2 \times 10^{-1}]^3 = 6 \times 10^{-38}$$

$$[Fe^{3+}] = \frac{6 \times 10^{-38}}{(2.2 \times 10^{-1})^3} = 6 \times 10^{-36} \text{ mole per liter}$$

This is a negligible amount so the precipitation of the $0.1M$ Fe^{3+} ions is virtually complete.

1   False. Mendeleev and Lothar Meyer are considered to be the codiscoverers of the modern periodic table. Although Meyer based his classification on the periodicity in the physical properties of the elements, he published essentially the same table of the elements as Mendeleev's. Newlands based his classification on the similarities in every eighth element when the elements were arranged according to their atomic weights.

2   True.

3   True.

4   False. The Group VIIA elements, F, Cl, Br, I, and At, are halogens. The Group VIA elements are called the chalcogens.

5   True.

6   True.

7   False. Ionization energies measure the energy required to remove electrons from gaseous atoms to form gaseous cations. A property characteristic of metals is the ease with which they loose electrons, that is, their low ionization energies.

8   True.

9   False. The oxidation potential measures the energy required to oxidize sodium metal to the ion in aqueous solution:

$$Na(s) \rightarrow Na^+(aq) + 1e^-$$

The oxidation potential will differ from the ionization energy by the energy required to vaporize solid sodium metal and the energy released when the Na^+ ions react with water and form the hydrated ions that exist in aqueous solution.

$$Na(s) \xrightarrow[\text{energy}]{\text{vaporization}} Na(g) \xrightarrow[\text{energy}]{\text{ionization}} Na^+(g) + 1e^-$$
$$\xrightarrow[\text{energy}]{\text{hydration}} Na^+(aq)$$

10   True.

11   True.

12   False. One half the Cl—Cl distance between two bonded Cl atoms (the covalent radius) will be shorter than one half the distance between the Cl atoms on two adjacent Cl_2 molecules that are in contact. This latter distance is the van der Waals radius.

13 False. Neutral P atoms have 15 electrons. P^{3-} ions will have $15 + 3 = 18$ electrons. $_{18}Ar$, which also has 18 electrons, is isoelectronic with P^{3-}.

14 True.

15 True.

16 False. Cations and H^- anions exist in the crystal lattices of these compounds in a manner analogous to the Na^+ and Cl^- ions in the sodium chloride crystal. Divalent hydrogens, or bridged hydrogens, are characteristic of covalent compounds such as BeH_2, MgH_2, AlH_3, and the hydrides of boron.

17 True.

18 False. Groups IA and IIA elements (Sr is in Group IIA) form basic oxides.

$$SrO + H_2O \rightarrow Sr^{2+} + 2OH^-$$

19 True. A nonmetal oxide, Br_2O_5, would be expected to be acidic. Its reaction with water would lead to the presence of hydronium ions and bromate ions:

$$Br_2O_5 + H_2O \rightarrow 2H^+ + 2BrO_3^-$$

Formulating the aqueous solution as an acid, $HBrO_3$, would account for the formation of the salt $NaBrO_3$ when such an acid is neutralized by NaOH:

$$HBrO_3 + NaOH \rightarrow NaBrO_3 + H_2O$$

20 True.

CHAPTER 7

1 True. There are six covalent bonds to the sulfur atom.

2 True. They are both six.

3 True.

4 True.

5 True. There are a few exceptions, especially among the Group VIII elements.

6 False. A $+2$ oxidation state is known only for a few of these elements. Their common oxidation state is $+3$.

7 False. Electron-deficient compounds are generally good oxidizing agents because they tend to accept electrons from other sub-

stances. Therefore, these compounds are generally poor reducing agents.

8   True. This is especially true if the element has a lower oxidation state that is quite stable. In such cases, a weak reducing agent will suffice to reduce the element to this lower oxidation state. In the process, the reducing agent will be oxidized readily.

9   True. The oxidation number must change to a more positive (less negative) value.

10   False. Although most oxidation–reduction reactions involve an electron transfer, in some reactions the change in oxidation number is achieved by means of an atom-transfer process.

11   True.

12   False. The oxidation numbers are $+10/6 = +1\frac{2}{3}$ in $S_6O_6^{2-}$, $+10/4 = +2.5$ in $S_4O_6^{2-}$, but $+2$ in $S_2O_3^{2-}$.

13   False. The oxidation states of V are $+5$ in V_2O_5 and $+4$ in V_2O_4. To be reduced from $+5$ to $+4$, each atom of V($+5$) gains one electron. One formula unit of V_2O_5 contains two V($+5$) atoms and will *gain* two electrons.

14   False. The oxidation state of the chlorine in HCl and KCl is -1. The chlorine does not change its oxidation number; consequently, it has not been oxidized or reduced.

15   False. The word "iodine" is not specific enough. The iodine atom (actually the I^- ion in the ionic compound KI) is oxidized from the -1 oxidation state in KI to the 0 oxidation state in I_2. KI (or I^- ions), the substance which contains the oxidized element, is the reducing agent.

16   True. The two-electron loss in the I^-/I_2 half-reaction equals the two-electron gain in the V_2O_5/V_2O_4 half-reaction.

17   True. Two electrons are gained per formula unit of V_2O_5. Therefore, the equivalent weight $= (V_2O_5/2) = (182/2) = 91$.

18   False. The reaction

$$\overset{-1}{KI} \underset{-1e^-}{\longrightarrow} \overset{0}{I_2}$$

corresponds to the loss of one electron per formula unit of KI, and the equivalent weight of KI $=$ KI/1. $1.0M$ KI contains 1 mole of KI per liter or 1 gram equivalent weight of KI per liter. $1.0M$ KI $= 1.0N$ KI.

19   True.

$$\text{equiv KI} = \text{equiv V}_2\text{O}_5$$
$$1.0N \times \text{volume KI} = (0.455 \text{ g V}_2\text{O}_5)/(91 \text{ g V}_2\text{O}_5 \text{ equiv}^{-1})$$
$$= 0.0050 \text{ equiv V}_2\text{O}_5$$
$$\text{volume KI} = 0.0050/1.0 = 0.0050 \text{ liter} = 5.0 \text{ ml}$$

20 True. All the positions in a tetrahedron are equivalent. There are two possible ways to arrange the two pairs of atoms in a square planar orientation: cis and trans.

21 True. The NO_3^- ion can be described as having a structure that is intermediate between the following three resonance forms. Such a hybrid structure should have equivalent oxygen atoms and N—O bond lengths of a size half way between a single N—O covalent bond and a double N=O covalent bond.

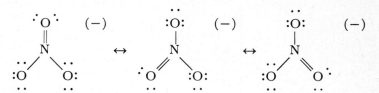

$10^3 = 1000$

$10^2 = 100$

$10^1 = 10$

$10^0 = 1$

$10^{-1} = \frac{1}{10}$